Climate Change and Aviation

Climate Change and Aviation

Issues, Challenges and Solutions

Edited by Stefan Gössling and Paul Upham

publishing for a sustainable future

London • Sterling, VA

First published by Earthscan in the UK and USA in 2009

Copyright © Stefan Gössling and Paul Upham, 2009

ISBN: 978-1-84407-619-2 HB
        978-1-84407-620-8 PB

Typeset by MapSet Ltd, Gateshead, UK
Cover design by Susanne Harris

For a full list of publications please contact:

Earthscan
Dunstan House
14a St Cross St
London, EC1N 8XA, UK
Tel: +44 (0)20 7841 1930
Fax: +44 (0)20 7242 1474
Email: earthinfo@earthscan.co.uk
Web: www.earthscan.co.uk

22883 Quicksilver Drive, Sterling, VA 20166-2012, USA

Earthscan publishes in association with the International Institute for
Environment and Development

A catalogue record for this book is available from the British Library

Library of Congress Cataloging-in-Publication Data

Climate change and aviation : issues, challenges and solutions / edited by
Stefan Gössling and Paul Upham.
    p. cm.
  Includes bibliographical references and index.
  ISBN 978-1-84407-619-2 (hbk.) – ISBN 978-1-84407-620-8 (pbk.) 1.
Aeronautics–Environmental aspects. 2. Climatic changes–Economic aspects. I.
Gössling, Stefan. II. Upham, Paul, 1966–
  HE9776.C525 2009
  363.738'74–dc22

                                                            2008040313

At Earthscan we strive to minimize our
environmental impacts and carbon footprint
through reducing waste, recycling and offsetting
our CO_2 emissions, including those created
through publication of this book.
For more details of our environmental policy,
see www.earthscan.co.uk.

This book was printed in the UK by MPG Books Ltd,
an ISO 1400 accredited company. The paper used is
FSC certified and the inks are vegetable-based.

Mixed Sources
Product group from well-managed
forests and other controlled sources
www.fsc.org Cert no. SA-COC-1565
© 1996 Forest Stewardship Council
FSC

Contents

Part I Aviation and Atmosphere

Part II Drivers and Trends

Part III Socio-economics and Politics

Part IV Mitigation

List of Figures and Tables

Figures

Tables

List of Contributors

Dr Kevin Anderson is an engineer by training, with experience in the petrochemical industry. He is a professor who leads the Tyndall Centre's energy research programme and works on themes of carbon reduction instruments and construction of demand for aviation.

Philip Boucher is currently undertaking a PhD with the Tyndall Centre for Climate Change Research and the University of Manchester. His work, funded by Supergen's Bioenergy Consortium, explores how conflicting biofuel narratives have developed in the public communications of various institutions, particularly industry, the press and movements for social/environmental justice.

Dr Alice Bows trained as an astrophysicist, then took a PhD in climate modelling at Imperial College, London. She joined the Tyndall Centre in 2003 as an interdisciplinary researcher to investigate conflicts between the climate change and aviation policies and to develop energy system scenarios. Alice leads the University of Manchester's Aerospace Research Institute's (UMARI) environment theme.

John Broderick is a doctoral researcher with the Tyndall Centre for Climate Change Research at Manchester Business School. His work on emissions trading in the aviation industry is funded by the UK Energy Research Centre (UKERC).

Dr Jean-Paul Ceron is a social scientist who has been working for three decades on environmental issues, first within CIRED, a team which specializes in climate change issues and now at CRIDEAU (University of Limoges). The relationship between tourism and climate change is now his main field of interest. He has been a lead author within the Fourth Assessment Report of the IPCC, dealing there mainly with tourism.

Dr Ben Daley is a researcher with the Centre for Air Transport and the Environment at Manchester Metropolitan University. A geographer and environmental historian by training, he is currently working on issues covering air transport, climate change and environmental change more generally. He also lectures in sustainable development and environmental management.

Dr Nigel Dennis is a senior research fellow in the Transport Studies Group at the University of Westminster. Airline economics and operations have been Nigel's major area of research interest. He has carried out studies for organizations including BAA, the new Berlin-Brandenburg Airport, British Airways, Ryanair, DHL and the European Commission. Nigel is also leader of the University's extensive range of annual aviation seminars and short courses.

Ghislain Dubois is an associate professor at the University of Versailles Saint-Quentin-en-Yvelines. He is also the managing director of Tourism Environment Consultants, and has worked for UNESCO, UNEP, the Mediterranean Action Plan and UNWTO. He has been a contributing author for the Fourth Assessment Report of the IPCC (WGII).

Dr David Timothy Duval is an associate professor in the School of Business at the University of Otago. He holds expertise in the areas of aviation management, economics and international regulatory environments and has published in the areas of aeropolitics, the economics of international aviation emissions and the relationship between regulation and competition in international civil aviation.

Anthony Footitt has been an environmental consultant since 1995. Working principally in the fields of risk, economics, regulation and policy development and appraisal, he has worked on more than 70 projects for a range of government departments, agencies and European and international institutions across a diversity of environmental and human health issues. Currently he is Senior Research Consultant at the Tyndall Centre, leading the Centre's capabilities in respect of targeted studies and consultancies on specific issues relating to both climate change adaptation and mitigation.

Dr Stefan Gössling holds a PhD in human ecology from Lund University, Sweden. He is research coordinator at the Centre for Geotourism and Sustainable Development, Western Norway Research Institute, and Professor at the Service Management Programme, Lund University, Sweden. He has been a contributing author to the IPCC's Fourth Assessment Report and has recently contributed to *Climate Change and Tourism: Responding to Global Challenges* (UNWTO-UNEP-WMO, 2008).

Dr Alexander de Haan has studied aerospace engineering at Delft University of Technology as well as social and organizational psychology at the University of Leiden, both in the Netherlands. He currently holds the position of Assistant Professor at Delft University of Technology, and teaches policy analysis.

Dr Michael C. Hall is a professor in the Department of Management, University of Canterbury, New Zealand and Docent in the Department of Geography, University of Oulu, Finland. Co-editor of *Current Issues in Tourism* he has published widely in the fields of tourism, environmental history and gastronomy, including research on social marketing, climate change and sustainable consumption.

Dr David S. Lee is Professor of Atmospheric Science and Director of the Centre for Aviation, Transport and the Environment, a research group of 22 staff at Manchester Metropolitan University, and is a visiting research fellow of the Atmospheric Oceanic and Planetary Physics Department of the University of Oxford. David is active in major science research programmes investigating transportation effects on climate and is also the World Meteorological Organization's Rapporteur on Aviation and the Environment. He is also active in providing technical advice to the policy community, including the UK Department for Transport, DEFRA and BERR, the UK Climate Change Committee and the European Commission. He represents the UK in various technical working groups within the International Civil Aviation Organization's Committee on Aviation Environmental Protection.

Dr Cherie Lu gained her PhD in air transport management at Cranfield University. She has worked for consultancy companies, universities and international aviation organizations in the United Kingdom, the Netherlands and Taiwan. Dr Lu is author of a number of publications on the economic and environmental aspects of the air transport industry.

Dr Sarah Mander is Deputy Leader of Tyndall's Energy Programme. A chemical engineer by training, she worked in industry before joining the Tyndall Centre in 2000 to study for a PhD; her current research focuses on the construction of demand for aviation. Sarah is also member of the UK Carbon Capture and Storage Consortium, working on public perceptions of carbon capture and storage.

Dr Cordula Neiberger is an associate professor at Philipps University in Marburg, Germany and has done research in the fields of economic and transport geography. She is the author of several publications on the globalization of logistics providers as well as the organization and spatial patterns of the air freight sector.

Dr Jan Henrik Nilsson is a senior lecturer in economic geography at the Department of Service Management, Lund University, Sweden. He has researched and published in the areas of transport geography, destination marketing and urban historical geography. Most of his empirical work is connected to the development process in the Baltic Sea area.

Paul Peeters studies the relations between tourism transport and the environment, with a focus on climate change. Since 2002 he has been an associate professor at the Center for Sustainable Tourism and Transport, NHTV University for Applied Science, Breda, the Netherlands.

Holly Preston is a researcher at the Centre for Air Transport and the Environment (CATE) at Manchester Metropolitan University, with interests in international climate regimes, climate policy and sustainability. At CATE, Holly is currently working on a variety of projects investigating aviation environmental impacts, including studies of carbon offsetting, climate policy options and aviation noise.

Dr Sally Randles is a research fellow attached to the Manchester Institute of Innovation Research and Tyndall-Manchester at the University of Manchester. With colleagues at the Tyndall Centre she has been researching aviation via a production–consumption systems framework. Sally's work is theoretically informed by economic sociology and political economy, using entry points such as Karl Polanyi's notion of economy as instituted process; practice theory and complex systems thinking.

Julia Tomei is a research associate at King's College London in the Environment, Politics and Development (EPD) group within the Department of Geography. A biologist by training, and previously of the Policy Studies Institute, Julia is currently working on future demand for hydrogen, and bio-energy and biofuels policy.

Dr Paul Upham is a research fellow at Tyndall Centre Manchester and the Manchester Institute of Innovation Research, University of Manchester, with research interests in public and stakeholder perceptions of low-carbon energy systems and aviation climate change policy. Current projects include bioenergy and biofuels policy and carbon labelling controversies.

Dr Victoria Williams has recently completed a research fellowship in the Centre for Transport Studies, Imperial College London, working mainly on aviation and climate change. Recent research has addressed contrail avoidance strategies, the vulnerability of UK air transport to climate change and environmental decision support for both pilots and airspace planners.

Preface

Aviation has only recently received the attention of politicians and the broader public in industrialized countries as a sector relevant to climate change, despite the fact that research has addressed its special role in the chemistry and physics of the atmosphere for at least 30 years. The delay may be explained by the understanding of aviation as an exclusive means of transport contributing only to a minor share of global emissions of greenhouse gases. Indeed, compared to the automobile, which has seen a rapid, though still ongoing, expansion in user numbers for more than half a century, aviation has only just entered its boom and bust cycle. This has more recently been fostered by the rise of low-fare airlines, offering cheap mass mobility, as well as the emergence of new markets in previously less airborne societies, such as India and China.

With an emerging understanding of the problematic interference of aviation with the climate system, political solutions have been sought to address the sector's environmental performance. The European Union will be the first region in the world to include aviation in its Emissions Trading Scheme (EU ETS). By 2012, all airlines departing from or landing in Europe will have to comply with the EU's emission reduction plans, even though aviation has been treated favourably, with considerably lower reduction demands than those faced by other sectors. These plans coincide with the development of oil prices, which peaked in mid-2008 at around US$145 per barrel, even though it is unclear at the time of writing whether this was a warning signal for coming increasingly high prices for jet fuel, or a short-term high caused by hedging at resource exchanges, which will be followed by more moderate oil prices.

For many years, aviation research has primarily focused on chemistry and physics. It was not before the mid-1990s that it came to be understood that the economic and sociocultural dimensions deserve attention as well. Indeed, one may argue that the study of the drivers of the rapid expansion of aviation is now as important as the study of the sector's interference with the climate system. Likewise, research into the technical and social options for mitigation has grown in importance. This book attempts to examine all these issues, and thus in many ways updates Earthscan's first book on aviation and sustainability – *Towards Sustainable Aviation* (TSA). Here, though, we go wider and deeper on the climate change connection, omitting the noise, health and community issues explored in TSA, and covering issues wider than those related to tourism alone. Rather, our aim here is to provide an account of aviation drivers and climate impacts from several perspectives. Inevitably there is some overlap between some of the chapters, but this has the advantage of emphasizing that there is no one way of characterizing and understanding the problem, nor of resolving the problem. While it is clear that a substantial rise in the cost of air travel would (and perhaps will) mitigate its adverse impacts, it is far less clear how a political mandate for this can be brought about (other than waiting for evidence of the adverse impacts of climate change to become undeniable). In the meantime, the least that we need to do to respond to the situation of ongoing aviation growth and climate impact is to understand it as thoroughly as possible.

Many people have contributed with their time, energy and expertise to this book. In particular, Stefan wishes to thank Robert Bockermann, Dietrich Brockhagen, Jean-Paul Ceron, Hervé Corvellec, Ghislain Dubois, David Duval, Michael C. Hall, Jan Henrik Nilsson, Paul Peeters, Daniel Scott and David Weaver for sharing their expert knowledge on various issues; Erik Köpberg for his enthusiasm in last-minute reference checking; Nadine Heck for her immensely appreciated work in formatting the book; Mathias Gößling for his brilliant, inspiring and paradigm-shifting ideas; as well as Meike and Linnea Rinsche for their support and love, and their patience with a scientist lifestyle. Paul wishes to thank colleagues at Tyndall Centre Manchester for their wide-ranging knowledge and good humour, and of course family and friends for their support. We also wish to thank our commissioning editor Michael Fell as well as Alison Kuznets and the Earthscan team for their support of this project.

Stefan Gössling and Paul Upham
Sogndal and Manchester, July 2008

List of Acronyms and Abbreviations

ACI	Airports Council International
ACARE	Advisory Council for Aeronautics Research in Europe
AGWP	absolute global warming potential
AIC	aircraft-induced cirrus
ANCAT	Abatement of Nuisance Caused by Air Transport
ANS	autonomic nervous system
AOGCM	Atmosphere-Ocean General Circulation Model
APD	air passenger duty
APT	air passenger transport
ASHRAE	American Society of Heating, Refrigerating and Air-conditioning Engineers
ASK	available seat kilometre
ATAG	Air Transport Action Group
ATC	air traffic control
ATFM	air traffic (flow) management
ATK	available tonne kilometre
ATM	air traffic management
atm	atmospheres
ATS	air traffic system
AvGas	aviation gasoline
AWP	Aviation White Paper
BAA	British Airports Authority
BERR	UK Government Department for Business, Enterprise and Regulatory Reform
BSI	British Standards Institution
BWB	blended wing body
CAA	UK Civil Aviation Authority
CAEP	Committee on Aviation and Environmental Protection (of ICAO)
CASK	cost per available seat kilometre
CATE	Centre for Air Transport and the Environment
CBA	cost–benefit analysis

CCC	cirrus cloud cover
CCM	climate chemistry model
CCX	Chicago Climate Exchange
CDA	continuous descent approach
CDM	Clean Development Mechanism (Kyoto Protocol mechanism)
CER	Certified Emissions Reduction
CFCs	chlorofluorocarbons
CFD	computational fluid dynamics
CFMU	Central Flow Management Unit (European Airspace)
CH_4	methane
CIRED	Centre International de Recherche sur l'Environnement et le Développement
CLEAN	Component vaLidator for Environmentally friendly Aero eNgine
CNEL	community noise equivalent level
CNS	communications, navigation and surveillance
CO	carbon monoxide
CO_2	carbon dioxide
CRIDEAU	Centre de Recherche Interdisciplinaires en Droit de l'Environnement, de l'Aménagement et de l'Urbanisme
CTM	chemical transport model
dB(A)	decibel noise unit, weighted with an 'A' filter to account for human hearing characteristics
DEFRA	UK Department for Environment, Food and Rural Affairs
DETR	UK Department of Environment, Transport and the Regions (now DEFRA)
DLR	Deutsches Zentrum für Luft- und Raumfahrt
Dp/Foo	ICAO regulatory parameter for gaseous emissions, expressed as the mass of pollutant emitted during the landing/take-off (LTO) cycle divided by the rated thrust (maximum take-off power) of the engine
DTLR	UK Department for Transport, Local Government and the Regions
DVT	deep vein thrombosis
EAN	European article number
EATMP	European Air Traffic Management Programme
EC	European Commission
ECAC	European Civil Aviation Conference (standing)
ECHAM4	the fourth-generation atmospheric general circulation model
ECHR	European Court of Human Rights
ECMWF	European Centre for Medium-Range Weather Forecasts
EDI	electronic data interchange
EEA	European Environment Agency, *also* European Economic Area
EI	emission index, *also* energy intensity
EIT	economies in transition

EMIC	Earth system model of intermediate complexity
ENSO	El Niño Southern Oscillation
ETS	emissions trading scheme
EU	European Union
EU ETS	European Union Emissions Trading Scheme
EWF	emissions weighting factor
FAA	Federal Aviation Administration
FESG	Forecasting and Economic Analysis Sub-Group of CAEP
FFP	frequent flyer programme
FT	Fischer-Tropsch
FTK	freight ton kilometres
FUA	flexible use of airspace
GCM	global climate model
GDP	gross domestic product
GDS	global distribution system
GHG	greenhouse gas
GTP	global temperature change potential
GWP	global warming potential
HC	hydrocarbon
HEPA	high efficiency particle arresting (filter)
HIRS	high resolution infrared radiometer sounder
HPA	hypothalamic-pituitary-adrenal
HPM	hedonic price method
HS	high speed
HSCT	high speed civil transport
HSR	high speed rail
IATA	International Air Transport Association
ICAO	International Civil Aviation Organization
ICSA	International Coalition for Sustainable Aviation
IEA	International Energy Agency
IN	ice nuclei
IPCC	Intergovernmental Panel on Climate Change
ISCCP	International Satellite Cloud Climatology Project
IWC	ice water content
JI	Joint Implementation (Kyoto Protocol mechanism)
JIT	just in time freight operations
LCA	life-cycle analysis
LCC	low-cost carrier
LDF	local development frameworks
Leq	equivalent sound level (long-term average noise exposure)
LH_2	liquid hydrogen
LLGHG	long-lived greenhouse gas
$Lmax$	Maximum (A-weighted) sound level
LTO	landing/take-off
MAGLEV	Magnetic Levitation transport system

NAFC	North Atlantic flight corridor
NAFTA	North American Free Trade Area
NAO	North Atlantic Oscillation
NASA	National Aeronautics and Space Administration
NGO	non-governmental organization
NMVOC	non-methane volatile organic compounds
NO_x	nitrogen oxides (the sum of $NO+NO_2$)
NO_y	reactive nitrogen
O/D	origin/destination
O_3	ozone
OAG	Offical Airline Guide
OBO	oil-bulk-ore carrier
OECD	Organisation for Economic Co-operation and Development
OEW	operating empty weight
OPR	overall pressure ratio
OPYC3	ocean general circulation model
PAH	polyaromatic hydrocarbons
PM_{10}	particulate matter with a mass median aerodynamic diameter of less than 10 micrometres
ppmv	parts per million by volume
ppt	parts per trillion
PSC	polar stratospheric cloud
PSZ	public safety zone
QBO	quasi-biennial oscillation
R&D	research and development
RAIN	Reduction of Airframe and Installation Noise
RASK	revenue earned per available seat kilometre
RCEP	UK Royal Commission on Environmental Pollution
RESOUND	Reduction of Engine Source Noise through Understanding & Novel Design
RF	radiative forcing
RFI	radiative forcing index
RFID	radio frequency identification
RNAV	Area Navigation
RPK	revenue passenger kilometre
RSS	regional spatial strategy
RTK	revenue tonne-kilometre
RVSM	reduced vertical separation minimum
SAD	surface aerosol density
SARS	severe acute respiratory syndrome
SASS	Subsonic Assessment Program (of NASA)
SBAC	Society of British Aerospace Companies
SBSTA	Subsidiary Body on Scientific and Technological Advice (UNFCCC)
SES	Single European Sky

SO$_2$	sulphur dioxide
SRES	IPCC Special Report on Emission Scenarios
SST	supersonic transport (aircraft)
SRA	strategic research agenda
TEN	trans-European transport network
TERM	transport and environment reporting mechanism
TET	turbine entry temperature
TMA	terminal area (in air traffic management)
UBP	Umweltbelastungspunkte, i.e. environmental impact points, a Swiss life-cycle analysis metric for aggregated environmental impact
UHC	unburned hydrocarbons
UKERC	UK Energy Research Centre
UMARI	University of Manchester's Aerospace Research Institute
UNEP	United Nations Environment Programme
UNESCO	United Nations Educational, Scientific and Cultural Organization
UNFCCC	United Nations Framework Convention on Climate Change
UNWTO	United Nations World Tourism Organization
USEPA	US Environmental Protection Agency
UTLS	upper troposphere and lower stratosphere
UV	ultraviolet radiation
VAT	Value Added Tax
VER	Verified, or Voluntary, Emissions Reduction
VFR	visiting friends and relatives
VOC	volatile organic compound
WHO	World Health Organization
WMO	World Meteorological Organization

1
Introduction: Aviation and Climate Change in Context

Stefan Gössling and Paul Upham

The age of aviation

Looking back in time, the history of aviation covers more than 220 years, at least if the brothers Montgolfier's hot-air balloon is considered as the first functioning flying machine (see Grant, 2007). The balloon made its first manned flight in 1783, even though the brothers Montgolfier preferred not to be on board themselves. There then followed 120 years of various attempts to build manoeuvrable flight machines, until the Wright brothers achieved powered aeroplane flight in 1903. Within two and a half decades of the event, Charles Lindberg embarked on the first transatlantic flight (in 1927), and the speed of the development of aircraft accelerated: in the mid-1930s, Douglas DC-3s came into service, the first all-metal aircraft, which could carry 21 passengers. Another 15 years later, jet aircraft went into regular service with the de Havilland Comet and, somewhat later, the Boeing 707 and Douglas DC-8, commencing the age of mass passenger transportation (Grant, 2007).

As with individual motorized transportation more generally, the use of aircraft has developed at an accelerating speed reflected in transport statistics. For instance, the United Nations World Tourism Organization (UNWTO, 2008a) reports that the number of international tourist arrivals – comprising both leisure and business travellers using all means of transport – was 25 million in 1950, increasing to about 900 million in 2007. Annual growth in international tourist arrivals is now more than twice the total number of international arrivals up to 1950, that is more than 50 million per year. While the share of international tourists arriving by air in 1950 is unknown, though it can be assumed to be low, it is now more than 40 per cent. In the near future, tourism is believed to expand rapidly: UNWTO (2008b) estimates that international tourist arrivals will double to 1.6 billion in the period 2005–2020, that is in less than 15 years. An increasing share of these will arrive by air (UNWTO-UNEP-WMO, 2008).

Transport statistics more generally reveal the same developments and trends. Even though global statistics are difficult to obtain, those available for example for the United States show how rapidly aviation gained importance: revenue passenger ton-miles increased from about 3.2 billion to 84.1 billion in the period 1954–2007, and in 2007, US flights alone carried 663 million passengers (Bureau of Transportation Statistics, 2008). In the same year, 831 million passengers were carried worldwide on international air trips and 1249 million on domestic trips (IATA, 2008a).[1] US flights thus account for almost one third of global passenger transport. In the context of this book, it may also be interesting to look at the distribution of premium class (first class and business class) versus economy class travellers. Statistics provided by the Internationa Air Transport Association (IATA, 2008a) show that in 2007, there were 73.4 million domestic and 69.8 million international premium class passengers travellers, compared to 1.2 billion domestic and 760.7 million international travellers, representing a ratio of 1:16 (domestic) and 1:11 (international) of premium to economy class passengers. This is of importance as premium class travellers can be assumed to consume roughly twice as much space as business class travellers, thus substantially increasing fuel use.

While the number of air travellers has increased, the number of aircraft manufacturers has declined, with two major players (Airbus in Europe and Boeing in the United States) as well as three smaller manufacturers (Bombardier in Canada, Embraer in Brazil and Tupolev in Russia) dominating the markets for civil aircraft. China will soon re-enter the ranks of aircraft manufacturing countries, primarily to cater to its own domestic market, which is anticipated to develop its current fleet of about 1000 aircraft to 3400 by 2026, according to the news magazine *Time* (2007). China's demand will thus add considerably to the global demand for civil commercial aircraft. Boeing presumes that 29,400 aircraft will be delivered worldwide in the period 2008–2027, despite a challenging economic situation: 'Air transport is in a highly dynamic period. Challenges include a slowing world economy, high oil prices, and in some markets, slowing traffic growth' (Boeing, 2008, p1). By 2027, 35,800 aircraft are anticipated to be in service, representing growth of 88 per cent from 19,000 aircraft in 2007. Passenger numbers will grow by 4.0 per cent per year and distances travelled at 5.0 per cent per year (measured in revenue passenger kilometres, RPKs) over the coming 20 years; while air cargo (measured in revenue tonne kilometres, RTKs) will grow by 5.8 per cent, a development fuelled in particular by the fastest growing economies, that is the Asia-Pacific region (Boeing, 2008). Note that Airbus (2007) projects even higher growth rates, with an annual 4.9 per cent increase in passenger numbers up to 2026, but an identical estimate for air cargo growth (5.8 per cent per year).

It becomes clear from these figures that aviation has seen considerable growth in the past 50 years. It also seems evident that emissions from aviation will grow even more rapidly in the near future, though at a slower pace than transport volumes. For instance, Boeing (2008) suggests that aeroplanes will carry about 40 per cent more traffic in 2027 (measured RPK) than the average aircraft today.

Aviation and climate change

As the Intergovernmental Panel on Climate Change (IPCC, 2007) has stressed in its synthesis report, warming of the climate system is now 'unequivocal' (IPCC, 2007, p30). Temperature increases are widespread over the globe, with 11 of the 12 years in the period 1995–2006 ranking among the warmest since the beginning of the recording of global surface temperatures in 1850. In the past 100 years, temperatures are assumed to have increased by 0.74°C on global average. The change of the climate system already has a wide range of consequences for biological and socio-economic systems, all of which are antic-ipated to become significantly more relevant for humanity in the medium- to long-term future (Stern, 2006, see also Schneider, 2008). For instance, global and regional impacts of even a 2°C rise include the destruction of the vast majority of current coral reefs, 3 billion people experiencing water stress and changes in global cereal production that could expose as many as 220 million more people to the risk of hunger (Warren, 2006). At a global average of +3°C temperature increase, few ecosystems would be able to adapt and, for example, there would be much larger losses in global cereal production than predicted at 2°C, potentially exposing a further 400 million people to hunger (Warren, 2006). Note that the range of projections by the IPCC (2007, p8) includes a far greater range of temperature changes (Table 1.1). According to scenarios B1 to A1FI, temperature changes in the period 2090–2099, relative to 1980–1999, will vary between 1.8 and 4.0°C. Concomitant sea-level rise will be in between 18 and 59cm, not considering future rapid changes in ice flow. The latter is an important omission and serves to reminds one that the IPCC is always conserv-ative in its statements. It would be wise to keep in mind the admonition of Hansen et al (2008):

> If humanity wishes to preserve a planet similar to that on which civilization developed and to which life on Earth is adapted, paleoclimate evidence and ongoing climate change suggest that CO_2 will need to be reduced from its current 385ppm to at most 350ppm... If the present overshoot of this target CO_2 is not brief, there is a possibility of seeding irreversible catastrophic effects.

Table 1.1 shows the increase and distribution of emissions of greenhouse gases (GHGs) from various sources. As shown, emissions have vastly increased since

Table 1.1 *Projected global average surface warming and sea-level rise at the end of the 21st century*

Case	Temperature change (°C at 2090–2099 relative to 1980–1999)[a,c]		Sea-level rise (m at 2090–2099 relative to 1980–1999)
	Best estimate	Likely range	Model-based range excluding future rapid dynamical changes in ice flow
Constant year 2000 concentrations[b]	0.6	0.3–0.9	Not available
B1 scenario	1.8	1.1–2.9	0.18 – 0.38
A1T scenario	2.4	1.4–3.8	0.20 – 0.45
B2 scenario	2.4	1.4–3.8	0.20 – 0.43
A1B scenario	2.8	1.7–4.4	0.21 – 0.48
A2 scenario	3.4	2.0–5.4	0.23 – 0.51
A1FI scenario	4.0	2.4–6.4	0.26 – 0.59

Notes: a Temperatures are assessed best estimates and likely uncertainty ranges from a hierarchy of models of varying complexity as well as observational constraints.
b Year 2000 constant composition is derived from atmosphere–ocean general circulation models (AOGCMs) only.
c Temperature changes are expressed as the difference from the period 1980–1999. To express the change relative to the period 1850–1899, add 0.5°C.
Source: IPCC, 2007

1970, from less than $29GtCO_2$-eq to $49GtCO_2$-eq in 2004. Out of these, emissions from burning fossil fuels account for 56.6 per cent (Figure 1.1(b)). More than 17 per cent are caused by deforestation, the remainder largely being attributable to emissions of methane (CH_4) and nitrous oxide (N_2O). Finally, if looked at by sector, transport seems to account for only a minor share of global emissions of greenhouse gases, that is slightly more than 13 per cent (Figure 1.1(c)). It has thus often been argued that the transport sector is responsible for only a small share of emissions, and aviation for an even smaller one within the transport sector, that is typically about 2 per cent of global anthropogenic emissions of CO_2. IATA (2008c) reports that in 2004, aviation's emissions of CO_2 were 705 million tonnes, including commercial, military and general aviation. Statistically, this represents 2.54 per cent of global emissions of CO_2 from fossil fuel use (56.6 per cent of $49GtCO_2$-eq in 2004). IATA (2008c) also states that if other greenhouse gases are included, aviation accounts for 3 per cent of the total humanmade contribution to climate change (see also Chapter 2, this volume).

While a contribution of 3 per cent to global anthropogenic greenhouse gas emissions may still seem negligible, the percentage should be considered with regard to (i) growth rates in the aviation sector, (ii) the reduction in greenhouse gas emissions demanded by the IPCC (2007; see also Parry et al, 2008), as well as the fact that (iii) aviation is still an activity largely confined to industrialized countries with high per capita emissions levels. For instance, aviation contributes to a considerably larger share of emissions in industrialized

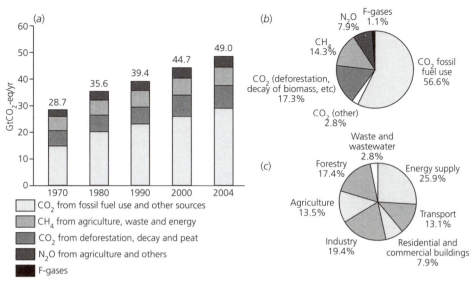

Note: Forestry includes deforestation.
Source: IPCC, 2007

Figure 1.1 *(a) Global annual emissions of anthropogenic GHGs from 1970 to 2004 (b) Share of different anthropogenic GHGs in total emissions in 2004 in terms of carbon dioxide equivalents (CO_2-eq) (c) Share of different sectors in total anthropogenic GHG emissions in 2004 in terms of CO_2-eq*

countries (e.g. Gössling and Hall, 2008), and it is estimated that only 2–3 per cent of the global population participate in international air travel on an annual basis (Peeters et al, 2006). Furthermore, emissions should be seen in the light of their relative importance: there is no other human activity pushing individual emission levels as fast and as high as air travel. For instance, a return trip from Europe to Thailand, currently a popular holiday destination for Swedes, will typically cause emissions of about $2tCO_2$ per traveller, that is about half the global average per capita emissions of $4tCO_2$. Given the fact that average emissions of $4tCO_2$ per capita per year need to be considered too high (see IPCC, 2007), it seems evident that air travel has a huge potential to contribute to unsustainable development.

The IPCC (2007) has made it very clear that substantial emissions reductions are necessary in the near future and some climate scientists (see Hansen et al, 2008) are increasingly referring to the need for steep reductions. For instance, Parry et al (2008) argue that stabilization of atmospheric GHGs should be at 400–470ppm CO_2-eq, for which global emissions need to peak in 2015 and decline by 3 per cent per year in the following period, with the authors pointing out that 'Limiting impacts to acceptable levels by mid-century and beyond would require an 80 per cent cut in global emissions by 2050'

Table 1.2 Characteristics, stabilization scenarios and resulting long-term equilibrium global average temperature

Category	CO$_2$ concentration at stabilization (2005 = 379ppm)[b] ppm	CO$_2$-equivalent concentration at stabilization including GHGs and aerosols (2005 = 375ppm)[b] ppm	Peaking year for CO$_2$ emissions[a,c] Year	Change in global CO$_2$ emissions in 2050 (percentage of 2000 emissions)[a,c] Per cent	Global average temperature increase above pre-industrial at equilibrium using best estimate climate sensitivity[d,e] °C	Global average sea-level rise above pre-industrial at equilibrium from thermal expansion only[f] metres	Number of assessed scenarios
I	350–400	445–490	2000–2015	–85 to –50	2.0–2.4	0.4–1.4	6
II	400–440	490–535	2000–2020	–60 to –30	2.4–2.8	0.5–1.7	18
III	440–485	535–590	2010–2030	–30 to +5	2.8–3.2	0.6–1.9	21
IV	485–570	590–710	2020–2060	+10 to +60	3.2–4.0	0.6–2.4	118
V	570–660	710–855	2050–2080	+25 to +85	4.0–4.9	0.8–2.9	9
VI	660–790	855–1130	2060–2090	+90 to +140	4.9–6.1	1.0–3.7	5

Notes: a The emission reductions to meet a particular stabilization level reported in the mitigation studies assessed here might be underestimated due to missing carbon cycle feedbacks.

b Atmospheric CO$_2$ concentrations were 379ppm in 2005. The best estimate of total CO$_2$-eq concentration in 2005 for all long-lived GHGs is about 455ppm, while the corresponding value including the net effect of all anthropogenic forcing agents is 375ppm CO$_2$-eq.

c Ranges correspond to the 15th to 85th percentile of the post-TAR (IPCC *Third Assessment Report*) scenario distribution. CO$_2$ emissions are shown so multi-gas scenarios can be compared with CO$_2$-only scenarios.

d The best estimate of climate sensitivity is 3°C.

e Note that the global average temperature at equilibrium is different from expected global average temperature at the time of stabilization of GHG concentrations due to the inertia of the climate system. For the majority of scenarios assessed, stabilization of GHG concentrations occurs between 2100 and 2150.

f Equilibrium sea-level rise is for the contribution from ocean thermal expansion only and does not reach equilibrium for at least many centuries. These values have been estimated using relatively simple climate models (one low-resolution AOGCM and several EMICs based on the best estimate of 3°C climate sensitivity) and do not include contributions from melting ice sheets, glaciers and ice caps. Long-term thermal expansion is projected to result in 0.2 to 0.6m per degree Celsius of global average warming above pre-industrial. (AOGCM refers to atmosphere–ocean general circulation model and EMICs to Earth system models of intermediate complexity.)

Source: IPCC, 2007

(Parry et al, 2008, p69). Note that this goes beyond emissions reduction goals in even the most ambitious industrialized countries. Table 1.2 illustrates this for a range of greenhouse gas stabilization scenarios, indicating that only the most stringent ones are likely to lead to an average global warming not exceeding 2°C by 2100, that is the European Union's policy goal, or what is considered to avoid dangerous interference with the climate system.

In this context it is interesting to note that although the European Commission has proposed that the EU pursues – within the framework of international negotiations – the objective of a 30 per cent reduction in greenhouse gas emissions by developed countries by 2020 (compared to 1990 levels), it also sees an expanded role for the Clean Development Mechanism (CDM) in this process (EC, 2008, p11). Rather than deal with the substantial domestic political difficulties of taking responsibility for emissions – difficulties compounded through years of ignoring the problem – there is thus a growing likelihood that Commissioners will opt to make significant use of the CDM. This will enable the EU to simultaneously retain a relatively stringent climate target, while also maintaining industrial and political support for that climate policy. In other words, with the current weak level of support for meaningful action to reduce carbon emissions (rhetoric and good intentions aside), trade-out from EU ETS will be critical to the economic, commercial and hence political acceptability of the proposed Directive to bring aviation into EU ETS (see further discussion below). As long as China and India do not agree on emissions caps (though emissions reductions in the US under its next president can be anticipated), as the CDM remains an open system, it will allow for both the generation of emissions reductions (accounted for in Kyoto Annex I countries) *and* overall emissions growth (taking place in non-Annex I countries).

The key question this begs is whether extensive use of Joint Implementation (JI; which allows one 'developed' country to earn emissions credits via investment in another developed country) and the CDM will undermine a genuine global transition to a low-carbon future. This could happen in two main ways (Upham et al, 2008). First, unless trade-out is accompanied by strong and mandatory fuel efficiency and renewable/low-carbon energy targets, the pressure for a shift within the EU to low-carbon supply, more efficient technologies and behavioural changes will be limited. EU ETS will be weakened by a low-carbon price, through an influx of external carbon credits. Second, even assuming that most CDM/JI projects are of high environmental and social quality, there will be economic multiplier effects in the host countries that reduce, and may even eliminate, the direct equivalence with EU emissions. That is to say, investments overseas will hopefully raise standards of living. Yet this will also stimulate demand for consumer goods and Western lifestyles and it is likely that these will be fuelled in part by carbon-based energy sources. Development benefits could be real but climate policy benefits less than expected, or even negative, that is the volume of CO_2 offset could be wholly negated, or worse, through economic multiplier effects, even if there is improvement relative to baseline within a single project. Many questions regarding emissions trading schemes arise from these observations, one key question being whether it will be possible to reduce greenhouse gas emissions at a considerable speed on a global scale, while energy use will in all likelihood vastly increase over the next decades. Aviation, as an economic sector showing rapid growth in a world of contracting emissions scenarios, certainly deserves special attention.

One aspect to look at may be attitudes in the aviation industry towards environmental issues. The industry presents itself frequently as an environmental champion (e.g. Airbus, 2007; Boeing, 2008; IATA, 2008c; ICAO, 2008b), but much of this may be rhetoric (Gössling and Peeters, 2007). Recent claims put forward by IATA (2008c) include for instance that fuel efficiency has improved by 20 per cent over the past 10 years, but it remains unclear on which comparison this figure is based. In the past, such comparisons have usually focused on the performance of the worst and best aircraft in the market (see Gössling and Peeters, 2007), while a realistic assumption for efficiency gain may be annual savings in the order of 1–1.5 per cent (UNWTO-UNEP-WMO, 2008), that is far less than anticipated by the industry. Likewise, the claim that aircraft have become 75 per cent more fuel efficient over the past 40 years may be true, but as Peeters and Middel (2007) have so eloquently shown, going back 50 years in time, that is including earlier and more efficient piston engines, results may not be equally impressive. More important yet, most of the efficiency gains in aviation history were achieved in the early periods of aircraft development. Efficiency gains by new aircraft are likely to be comparably lower, while it will take considerably longer to develop new aeroplanes.

Overall, the argument could be made that aircraft manufacturers and airlines create and maintain an elaborate discourse on pro-environmental action, usually forgetting to point out that absolute emissions from the sector are constantly increasing. In this context, IATA's (2008c) 'zero carbon future' is an interesting example of a discourse lacking substantiation: IATA does not provide a single reference that would illustrate how this can plausibly be achieved. IATA even goes as far as to suggest that 'a solar-powered aircraft is being built' (IATA, 2008c, p1), with the obvious goal to create the idea that commercial aircraft may be driven by the sun in the near future. It does not take much of an understanding of physics to calculate that the amount of energy needed to lift significant payload at commercial speed both day and night vastly exceeds the amount of energy that can be generated through the sun. Helios, the National Aeronautics and Space Administration's (NASA's) flying wing, for instance, was an ultralight structure travelling at a speed of 32kph (Grant, 2007). It may be that IATA's 'zero carbon future' is referring to the use of voluntary emissions offset projects and the CDM, but as we have explained above, while these may provide positive development benefits (depending on the quality of the specific projects), they should not be relied upon to compensate for actual emissions (see also Chapter 15, this volume).

With regard to policy making, aviation organizations, and in particular the International Civil Aviation Organization (ICAO), have also been counterproductive in contributing to emissions reductions. While national (domestic) emissions from aviation are covered under the Kyoto Protocol in Annex I countries, emissions from international aviation do not fall under the Kyoto Protocol targets, and were in fact neither considered nor discussed in post-Kyoto emissions reduction negotiations at COP-13 in Bali, Indonesia in December 2007. Instead, Article 2 of the Kyoto Protocol states that the responsibility for limiting and reducing emissions from international aviation in Annex I nations is the responsibility of ICAO (ICAO, 1997). However, ICAO has a history of negotiations without result (see T&E, 2007). In 2004, the ICAO annual assembly dismissed the idea of establishing a global emissions trading scheme (ETS) for aviation, but endorsed the inclusion of aviation in existing national/regional ETS as a more cost-effective measure than fuel taxes. However, in October 2007 the annual assembly of ICAO decided against requiring airlines to limit GHG emissions through participation in the European ETS, effectively rejecting their earlier decision (Environment News Service, 2007; for a more comprehensive discussion see also T&E, 2007). ICAO has thus been accused of effectively preventing action towards emissions reductions in the aviation sector over more than a decade (T&E, 2007), and from current debates it is not evident that much progress will be made in the near future to identify a suitable system for emissions reductions (see ICAO, 2008c). In looking beyond the rhetoric of pro-environmental action, it seems clear that most achievements in reducing specific (not absolute) emissions in the aviation sector have been made because of economic bottom lines, that is in situations where the cutting of costs has coincided with reductions in fuel use and emissions.

Given the combination of a rapidly closing window of opportunity for avoiding the worst impacts of climate change, attitudes within the aviation industry that are trenchantly pro-growth, and demand that shows little sign of satiation, not least because of the development of social middle classes in India and China, it is difficult to see how the sector will achieve absolute reductions in greenhouse gas emissions. Yet, somehow, a new consensus needs to be forged, involving the aviation industry, its customers and its stakeholders: that a low-growth and low-carbon industry is necessary. This is surely not impossible, but it will involve firmer decision making by governments and a greater awareness of the potential for sociotechnical systems to become locked in to development paths that involve highly mobile societies. In recent years, air travel has become embedded deeply in many people's understanding of mobility as a self-evident transport choice. Likewise, many of the goods consumed in industrialized countries are now imported by air, including flowers, electronics and clothes. While the urgency of fast delivery of such goods could be questioned with a view to the consequences of climate change, these developments are currently not questioned by either politicians or the broader public. Once again, discourses created by the aviation industry may play a vital role in the perception of aviation as a sector crucial to society. For instance, under the heading 'Speed = value', Boeing (2008, p5) presents its perspective on the importance of freight transport:

> *Air transport sustains many developing world economies by making it possible to ship perishable products such as fresh flowers, fruit, and live animals to distant markets. Reliable, regularly scheduled air freight flights make pharmaceuticals, life-saving blood and tissue products, and emergency equipment available and affordable. Prompt delivery actually adds to the value of a variety of products, including fashion items and leading-edge consumer electronics.*

Likewise, the sociocultural importance of aviation has changed immensely in recent years, and various newspapers have reported on the consequences of increasing oil prices for air travellers. For instance, *Die Zeit*, a large German weekly newspaper, asks under the headline 'The end of low fare airlines?': 'As energy is becoming more expensive, a dream is coming to an end: to reach any destination for little money. What will millions of short break holidaymakers and commuters do now?' (*Die Zeit*, 10 July 2008). The growth of low-cost carriers in less than 10 years in Europe (though over a longer period in the US) and associated sociocultural changes are a telling example of the speed at which societies can evolve towards highly mobile, energy-intensive lifestyles – and the difficulties associated with reversing such patterns. For instance, had it not been oil price developments driving recent (December 2007–July 2008) increases in air fares rather than taxes, the level of public opposition against rising air fares might have been different. In the current situation, pleas for government intervention have almost entirely been made by airlines and airline organizations, not consumer groups. Interestedly, calls against hedging, one of the most prevalent reasons for high oil prices, were made predominantly in the US, where airlines asked consumers to sign calls for government action. Apparently, the wish for free market capitalism is situational.

Overall, this raises the question of the instruments that could steer aviation towards greater environmental sustainability. For as long as mitigation looks unlikely to come from individual actions taken, that is a reduction in the number of flights made as well as the overall distances covered by air, economic instruments become ever more important. Two issues of relevance in this context will be discussed in more detail in the following section, that is trading schemes as well as increasing oil prices (for a more general discussion of economic measures, see Peeters et al, 2006; UNWTO-UNEP-WMO, 2008).

Turbulent times ahead: Emission trading and oil prices

Two recent developments have substantially affected aviation or are antici-pated to do so in the future, at least if one is to follow the rhetoric of statements released by airlines and airline organizations. The first are plans to include aviation in emissions trading schemes, particularly the EU ETS, the second is the unexpected steep rise in fuel prices experienced in the period December 2007–July 2008.

The European Union (EU) is currently the only economic region in the world with a regulatory system to reduce emissions of greenhouse gases. The EU is also the only economic region in the world where all international flights will be integrated in emissions trading by January 2012, a decision already threatened by the US with trade sanctions (Euractiv, 2008). Current policy backed by Parliament foresees that the sector's emissions will be capped at 97 per cent of average greenhouse gases emitted in the period 2004–2005. The cap will be lowered to 95 per cent for the 2013–2020 trading period, though this is subject to review. Fifteen per cent of allowances will be auctioned. Non-CO_2 emissions from aviation will not be taken into account in the trading scheme, but a proposal has to be put forward before November 2009 to address NO_x emissions (Euractiv, 2008).

In North America, a voluntary trading mechanism exists in the form of the Chicago Climate Exchange (CCX), but while emissions reductions targets in this system are legally binding, the exchange is voluntary to join and still has very limited participation; for instance, airlines are totally absent from the CCX. However, regulatory frameworks are evolving, as many states and provinces have taken action on their own. In the US, two recent legislative decisions have important implications for emissions in the aviation industry. In 2007, the US Senate Committee on Environment and Public Works approved the Lieberman-Warner Climate Security Bill and forwarded it to the full Senate for consideration. This proposed legislation includes an emissions trading scheme. If enacted, the Lieberman-Warner Bill would create a regulatory system similar to the ETS for the American aviation industry. However, airlines and associated organizations have expressed strong opposition to the legislation, and it remains unclear if and when such an ETS will be implemented. In Canada a total of five provinces and in the US eight States have set emissions reduction targets of 10–30 per cent for 2020 (below a 1990 baseline) and six States and two provinces have also set 2050 reduction targets between 75–80 per cent (below a 1990 baseline) (see Gössling et al, 2008). Overall, climate policy may thus be a future challenge for the aviation sector.

With regard to oil prices, the actual cost of jet fuel is a function of different parameters, including long-term contracts and hedging strategies, the global security situation, as well as actual demand, all of which influence prices. The only partial role of actual demand in contrast to supply in affecting oil prices is mirrored in the recent history of fuel price developments. As late as December 2007, the aviation industry did not anticipate the huge increases in oil prices that would have a considerable impact on the sector less than half a year later. As late as December 2007, IATA (2007) projected the price of a barrel of oil at an average of US$87 in 2008, up 6 per cent from the price levels seen in 2007. Just a few months later, IATA corrected its projection of fuel prices to an average of US$106 per barrel for 2008, up almost 22 per cent from its previous estimate. In July 2008 oil prices peaked at US$147 per barrel, and in July IATA corrected its forecast for average oil prices in 2008 to almost US$142 per barrel, a price 75 per cent higher than a year ago

(IATA, 2008b). These developments should also be seen in comparison to the situation just four years ago:

> *by early 2004 airline chiefs around the world were beginning to believe that the worst was over. Traffic levels were up, while many airlines had drastically cut their costs in the preceding two years to try to compensate for the falling yields. They had high hopes, projecting global profits of $4–6 billion for 2004. These hopes were dashed, however, by a new development, the rapid escalation in the price of aviation fuel. IATA's forecast of $4 billion profit in 2004 for its member airlines had been based on an average oil price of $30/barrel. But the average oil price, which had been around $25/barrel in 2002, rose to an average of $28.9 in 2003 and climbed to $45–50 by mid-2004. In the third quarter of 2004 it averaged $43–44/barrel. ...in 2002, [fuel] represented 15.8% of IATA airlines' total operational costs...* (Doganis, 2005, p11)

Fuel costs were approximately 30 per cent of operational costs of airlines in late 2007 (IATA, 2007), a share that has increased since then. With a global average profit margin of just 1.1 per cent, it does not come as a surprise that most airlines have struggled with oil price increases: there have been various buy-outs, airlines have grounded aircraft, and/or have cancelled routes earlier serviced. Even profitable airlines, such as Ryanair, have reported considerable falls in net profits and announced that profit may be negative over the full year (*The Guardian Weekly*, 1 August 2008, p16). These are examples indicating that airlines are highly susceptible to rapid increases in oil prices, questioning the overall economic viability of the sector. So far airlines have economically survived through high passenger volumes and volume growth, but with rising prices for energy and the internalization of the sector's environmental costs, this may no longer be feasible in the future.

Globally, trends towards reduced air transport are not as yet visible. As of 2 July 2008, the UN World Tourism Organization (UNWTO, 2008c) reports 'firm tourism demand', with international tourism growing at 5 per cent over the first four months of the year compared to the same period in 2007, that is 1 per cent higher than the long-term projection. In fact, no region has as yet shown a negative trend in international tourist arrivals. Just a few days earlier, UNWTO (2008d) confirmed its projection of 1.6 billion tourist arrivals by 2020, up from about 900 million in 2007. Similarly, Dotnews reported in virtually each of its weekly June and July 2008 issues on new airline connections being opened. For instance, one July issue contained the news: 'Finnair to Increase Long-Haul Connections Between Asia and Europe', 'Sri Lanka Increases Flights to Support Government's Moves to Woo Middle Eastern Tourists', 'Taiwan Prepares for Wave of Chinese', and 'Tourism Authority of Thailand Targets 20 Percent Growth' (Dotnews, 2008). With oil prices falling to US$124 in mid-July 2008, the question arises of how aviation will be affected in the medium-term future by jet fuel prices – the industry itself certainly prepares for further growth. Overall, it seems likely that low-fare airlines may be lastingly affected by higher oil prices, as they have expanded on the notion of 'free mobility', something that may no longer be feasible with rising oil prices. At the other end of the spectrum, wealthy air travellers may not be concerned at all about oil prices. Short-term long-haul trips from the UK, for instance, are expected to grow from 3.7 million in 2007 to 4.9 million in 2008 (*The Guardian Weekly*, 21 March 2008), and the first US$1 million 7-day holiday is available in Abu Dhabi, much of it based on private jet excursions (*The Independent*, 20 July 2008).

The need for an integrated perspective

The previous sections have shown that the interrelationship of climate change and aviation is a complex one. The rationale for the book is thus that contemporary aviation and its climate impacts can only be properly understood, and responded to fully, if the drivers of aviation growth are themselves properly understood. Rapid growth in air travel is a product of specific and powerful social, economic, cultural, technological and commercial trends as well as a special, often preferential treatment, in politics. Intervention at any one of these levels alone will not suffice to bring air travel within climatic constraints in the short timescale required, though progress in any one aspect may help progress in the others. As mentioned, the latest scientific evidence tells us that within about 10 years the greenhouse gas emissions trends of industrialized nations will need to contract year on year by at least some 4 per cent per annum (on a compound basis) until 2050 (Bows et al, 2007; Upham et al, 2008). However, this is not likely to happen if any economic sector receives special treatment, or is even allowed to grow. Overall, aviation is without doubt significant in terms of climate change. This is because of the comparably expensive options for emissions reductions in this sector, the rapid growth of air travel on a global level, the low price elasticity of many groups of air travellers, as well as its sociocultural and economic importance. The chapters in this book explore these interrelationships in a more detailed manner.

Part I Aviation and Atmosphere

Part I of the book presents its rationale and constitutes an overview of the reasons for concern in relation to rapid growth in aviation emissions. Chapter 2 on climate science comes from one of the foremost specialists in the field. David Lee provides a state-of-the-art overview of the physical and chemical interactions of aviation emissions and the global atmosphere, as currently understood. As Lee points out, research has in recent years moved from the assessment of the effects of emissions from aviation on the climate system towards a focus on how these effects can be reduced. Furthermore, the identification of suitable metrics for the comparison of the contribution made by various greenhouse gases to radiative forcing, as well as the technological and atmospheric trade-offs in mitigation, has been at the forefront of research efforts. David Lee outlines the current knowledge in these areas in great detail, also pointing out uncertainties. Despite various recent and ongoing research projects, many aspects of the interaction between climate change and aviation, such as the role of contrails and aviation-induced cirrus, remain insufficiently understood. The chapter ends with a discussion of technology, air traffic management and policy options for mitigation, acknowledging that even in these fields, there is still uncertainty about how to deal with the complexities of the aviation sector.

Chapter 3 by Paul Peeters and Victoria Williams is a technical discussion of how to calculate the direct emissions of CO_2 by aircraft and how to represent the contribution of the range of other gases and impacts – including nitrogen oxides, contrails, water vapour – on radiative forcing. The discussion covers calculation issues relating to CO_2 emissions for individual flights and national as well as global inventories. For the general reader, perhaps the most important message is that a well-defined and scientifically sound metric for the overall contribution of a single flight to radiative forcing has not yet been agreed upon, as this poses some fundamental theoretical difficulties.

This is problematic for citizens wanting to take responsibility for their emissions, be this by trying to work within a personal emissions budget (e.g. associated with 'one planet living'), or for the purpose of emissions offsetting (discussed in Chapter 15 by John Broderick). We can estimate the CO_2 emissions of a flight more or less accurately (depending on how much we know about the flight), but although we know that the flight will have a warming effect substantially greater than that of CO_2 alone (assuming it is the flight of a jet aeroplane), there is no way of indicating this in an individualized way that has scientific consensus. The key problems are that the impacts are not atmospherically well mixed, that is they have location-specific effects, and that they have widely differing atmospheric lifetimes or durations. The metric of global warming potential deals with the latter by referencing to the atmospheric life time of CO_2. However, this has disadvantages even in a non-aviation context, most notably by rendering the effects of methane arguably less profound than should be the case, given the short time window we have in which to begin deep emissions cuts (see e.g. Jardine et al, 2004 for why we should pay more attention to methane). Nonetheless, the lack of an agreed metric for aviation impacts is politically problematic, especially in terms of public communication. While it is possible to calculate the current contribution of global aviation to radiative forcing based on the radiative forcing index (RFI), first proposed by the IPCC (1999) and updated by Sausen et al (2005), this metric cannot be used to calculate the future impact of one additional flight that is made now. Perhaps partly for this reason, but also perhaps due to a misreading of IPCC (1999), it is not uncommon to find public-oriented emissions estimates, originating from outside the aviation industry (e.g. from offset firms), reporting both CO_2 and the same CO_2 values with a multiplier that, while not scientifically justifiable, does have the advantage of communicating the presence and significance of additional radiative forcing.

Chapter 4 by Alice Bows, Kevin Anderson and Anthony Footitt sets aviation emissions growth scenarios in the context of an aspirational, low-carbon EU. Although there is no scientific consensus for what is considered to be 'dangerous' in relation to climate change, this is generally interpreted at policy levels as relating to the global mean surface temperatures not exceeding 2°C above pre-industrial levels. The European Commission acknowledges that stabilizing long-term greenhouse gas concentrations at 450ppmv CO_2-eq (that is including all GHGs) provides about a 50 per cent chance of ensuring that the 2°C threshold is not exceeded. Thus it has set an aspirational target of reducing EU GHG emissions by 60–80 per cent by 2050, relative to 1990 levels.

Bows et al update earlier work to show the significance of cumulative emissions in relation to specific dates (notably 2050). That is, the authors emphasize that because EU emissions are now high, relative to their required level in 2050, achieving the required emissions reductions means that we must start very soon. This means that we need to shift the policy emphasis away from medium- to long-term targets and technological and system change – which of course we do also need – and refocus on near-term demand reduction. The latter is, of course, a message that the environmental non-governmental organizations (NGOs) have been advocating for many years, with limited success. Even though the authors set out scenarios that assume growth in EU flights and air passengers, while the emissions of other sectors are assumed to contract so that there is net consistency with 450ppmv CO_2, the growth assumptions are substantially lower than those of recent years.

Gaining government and industry acceptance for such lower growth still seems a long way off, making low-growth scenarios appear less plausible than business as usual. Yet isn't that usually the case? What is in front of us is immediately tangible and its continuation into the future is inevitably perceived as more plausible, and to the beneficiaries of a situation, more desirable, than a break with the past. Discontinuities, however, are also a fact of life. Some aspects of aviation business models require growth: most notably, investment in new ground infrastructure (terminals, runways etc.) and investment in airliners at a level beyond replacement. Yet these types of investments are not necessary to maintain a healthy aviation sector. Unless the industry can innovate sufficiently quickly to keep pace with the emissions growth consequent on its traffic growth, the implicit message of Bows, Anderson and Footitt's chapter is that it should not seek growth, nor be permitted it.

Part II Drivers and Trends

In Part II, we look at some of the key industry trends that are driving and facilitating growth. We begin in Chapter 5 with the most obvious change in the sector: that of 'low-cost' airlines, continued in Chapter 6 with a discussion of hypermobile travel patterns and their implications for emissions by Stefan Gössling, Jean-Paul Ceron, Ghislain Dubois and Michael C. Hall. In Chapter 5 Jan Henrik Nilsson provides an overview of the development of low-cost aviation from the late 1970s onwards, a subject continued in Chapter 7, where Nigel Dennis provides a more detailed examination of the network conse-quences of low-cost aviation and an account of how the traditional (legacy) carriers have responded. Major airlines are revising and rationalizing their networks in an attempt to improve financial performance and strengthen their defences against both new entrants and traditional rivals. Dennis shows how the short-haul operations of traditional European airlines such as British Airways and Lufthansa have come under increasing pressure from the growth of low-cost carriers and examines their competitive responses. Despite having to run down secondary hubs, the network strength of the traditional carriers has been largely maintained (Cherie Lu follows up on the emissions implica-tions of point-to-point versus hub travel in Chapter 9).

Estimating the effect of the low-cost airlines on passenger demand is not straightforward and projecting forward is subject to even more uncertainty. Due to the tighter margins within the low-cost model, where fuel costs consti-tute a higher proportion of overall costs, low-cost traffic may be more susceptible to influence by external factors than traffic carried by the tradi-tional airlines. Nonetheless, air passenger growth among the low-costs has patently far outstripped growth in other airline sectors. In the UK, for example, Carey and Newsome cite DfT (2003, p24) as stating, for the period 1998–2002, an increase in passenger numbers of 550 per cent for 'domestic no frills carriers' compared to –11 per cent for 'other domestic' carriers; and +292 per cent for 'international no frills carriers' compared to +5.1 per cent for 'other international' carriers.

However, the low-cost model should not be construed as having opened up aviation to all sectors of industrialized society, and this is a theme developed by Stefan Gössling, Jean-Paul Ceron, Ghislain Dubois and Michael C. Hall in Chapter 6, using the concept of hypermobile travellers. The authors remind us that as little as 2–3 per cent of the world's population fly annually in between any two countries, and that, even in countries where aviation has become a common form of travel, individual travel seems to be unlimited. One study of Swedish air travellers shows for instance that up to 300 return flights per year are possible for individual air travellers. Furthermore, flying appears highly skewed towards the cultural, economic and political elites of the population. Gössling et al provide an overview of studies focusing on the distribution of air travel, and go on to discuss the implications of hypermobile, air-based travel patterns for greenhouse gas emissions. The chapter ends with a discussion of the implications of hypermobile travel patterns for the observed trends towards ever growing mobility (measured in distances travelled) in industrialized countries.

Part III Socio-economics and Politics

Part III considers the politics of aviation expansion at international, national and regional scales. In Chapter 8, David Duval makes a case for the existence of an 'aeropolitics', a term that he uses to refer to and characterize a set of political circumstances specific to aviation. For Duval, aeropolitics emerges from a political economy perspective, in that it attempts to trace the position of economic and political actors and factors within a system. From this perspective, actors are driven by both ideological and commercial interests. Duval envisages a theory of aeropolitics that draws on other theories from international studies, particularly international law and policy, that can be used to explain the ability (and inability) of regional and national governments to fix tariffs, levies or taxes on inbound international aircraft, given existing bilateral/multilateral agreements and conventions. By inference, it is not that those agreements and conventions *necessarily* pose obstacles to effective greenhouse gas emissions control for international aviation. Rather, given the economic, commercial and political interests behind the 1944 Chicago Convention and the array of subsequent agreements, appealing to these as an obstacle makes sense: the main economic actors perceive no advantage to renegotiation, and every advantage to stalling on an international emissions trading system. Surely we are approaching a point at which this view must change, but we are not there yet.

In Chapter 9, Cherie Lu applies an environmental economic approach to environmental charges and their levels. She describes the methods of estimating aircraft engine emissions and noise social costs in practical terms, including the main parameters and inputs for the calculations. The three sets of cost results are derived for different cases, illustrating landing/take-off (LTO) emissions, cruise emissions and, in some cases, the cost of noise nuisance. She then discusses the implications of internalizing these externalities through charges or some other measures, for airline business models, network scenarios, operating costs and passenger demand. Although monetarization of environmental impacts will always be contentious, and rightly so, the chapter provides a clear insight into one approach to 'managing' the environmental impacts of aviation.

In Chapter 10, Cordula Neiberger examines developments in global air freight operations. Applying the conceptual framework of the value chain analysis to air freight, Neiberger looks at the ways in which air freight companies have responded to, and have facilitated, the increasing length of global production chains, while at the same time achieving punctuality and reliability. New large-capacity, long-haul aircraft and worldwide trends to deregulation in the sector have resulted in strong competition but also vertical integration. Transporters, airlines and airports have all responded with new strategies, and global freight logistic corporations have developed. Neiberger illustrates these trends with a case study of the global cut-flower industry.

In Chapter 11, Sally Randles and Sarah Mander examine air transport demand from a sociological perspective. They adapt a metaphor of ratchets originally applied in studies of labour-saving and comfort-providing household appliances, such as the washing machine, dishwasher and air conditioning (Shove, 2003). In the foregoing work, Elizabeth Shove documents how over recent decades in the industrialized world domestic habits have been changing in ways that have led and are leading to escalating and standardizing patterns of consumption. Shove used the term 'ratchets' because ratchets are designed to allow movement in one direction only – in this case in the direction of an increase in energy and water consumption. Randles and Mander also apply the perspective of 'consumption as practice' to an aviation context. Practice theory, developed by Alan Warde and colleagues (e.g. Warde, 2005), conceptualizes consumption in its everyday context of routines and habits. Applying and adapting the concept to frequent flyers, Randles and Mander focus on flying for leisure, examining which processes ratchet up the tendency to fly and which might ratchet it downwards. With regard to the latter, the authors argue that there is hope in the presence of limits to individual consumption of air travel, and refer to the possibilities of modal substitution and the benefits of slower surface travel. However, given the small percentage of the global population who currently fly, such limits clearly have the potential to be negated by a larger number of people flying and cannot possibly be relied upon as an adequate mitigation measure.

In Chapter 12, Sarah Mander and Sally Randles describe a political phenomenon that has facilitated aviation growth in the UK, namely the development of coalitions, partnerships and associated forms of governance, involving the state (local, regional and national) as well as commerce. In common with Duval, Mander and colleagues thus draw attention to the wider backdrop of politico-economic relations that underpin aviation growth, asserting that in the UK this would not have been possible without the pro-growth coalition that involved many partners, and which continues today. As this growth looks likely to add a third runway at Heathrow, such coalitions can have a global influence.

Part IV Mitigation

Part IV focuses on some of the key options for mitigating aviation emissions growth. Containing emissions growth is, of course, possible in principle. In practice the obstacles are substantial, but they are more economic and commercial, and hence political, than technological. Indeed this is, in the view of many observers, true of climate policy in general: we already have a raft of technologies that can assist in reducing GHG emissions, but their implementation is hampered by economic and commercial interests and perceptions.

In Chapter 13, Paul Peeters, Victoria Williams and Alexander de Haan review the potential of technology and air traffic management to reduce emissions and take the view that although there is still room for improvement in technological developments, physical limits are being approached. Nonetheless, they consider the opportunities for improved aerodynamics, materials, structure, propulsion and integrated design optimization. They also consider the potential for increasing operating efficiency by improving air traffic management efficiency and route planning, plus the option of modifying flight paths to avoid contrail formation. Finally, they discuss the role of aircraft capacity, specifically the trade-offs between low-revenue high seat density and high-revenue low seat density strategies, and the role of the low-cost point-to-point model versus hub-and-spoke.

In Chapter 14, Paul Upham, Julia Tomei and Philip Boucher examine the potential for biofuels as a kerosene substitute for global aviation, including the biosequestration potential of forestry and the associated sustainability issues. Kerosene can be manufactured from biomass via the Fischer-Tropsch chemical conversion process and can reduce CO_2 emissions relative to fossil kerosene, providing the land used for the biomass was not previously natural grassland or natural forest. Use of biofuel as a jet A1 substitute or extender has rapidly moved from a relatively niche research topic to mainstream consideration, with Virgin Atlantic publicly announcing plans for tests with one of its 747s. Unfortunately, much current biofuel feedstock production is far from being environmentally or socially sustainable. NGOs cite unacceptable human rights abuses and environmental destruction which will not be prohibited under, for example, UK biofuel regulations.

Upham and his colleagues show that, in principle and in terms of simple land area only, there is sufficient land globally to biologically sequester global aviation emissions in the long term and to supply sufficient wood-based biofuel to cover the needs of projected aviation growth. However, the authors are reluctant to commit to supporting large-scale biofuel production when much of the evidence to date points to environmental harm and poor social conditions involved in its production. Moreover, they argue that even if large-scale production of biofuels can be reconciled with environmental and social benefits, this should be pursued only after the vigorous implementation of demand-side reduction policies. In short, biofuels may well play a future role in aircraft fuel (most plausibly as a kerosene extender), but they cannot be relied on to solve the urgent GHG emissions problem.

In Chapter 15, John Broderick considers the pros and cons of voluntary carbon offsetting as a mitigation option. As greenhouse gas emissions from aviation are increasingly problematized, carbon project retailers have provided the opportunity for individual travellers and businesses to voluntarily 'offset' the impacts of their journey. Indeed, Broderick notes that 'carbon neutral' became the *Oxford American Dictionary* Word of the Year 2006, with high-profile endorsements from Al Gore, The Rolling Stones and BSkyB among others. Offsetting has been particularly associated with air travel because of a reluctance to change to alternative modes of transport or forgo long journeys. The basic structure of this activity is apparently straightforward. After calculating the emissions from aviation and other activities, a sum is paid to finance projects which are intended to reduce an equivalent quantity of emissions from a business as usual baseline. Projects are diverse but may involve forestry, renewable energy, energy efficiency, fuel switching and methane capture. Broderick shows that growth in offset retailing has been substantial, with the World Bank estimating €80 million of carbon credits sales as voluntary offsets in 2006. However, there remain significant objections to the use of carbon offsets in principle and in practice, and for Broderick the problems are more significant than the benefits.

Finally, in Chapter 16 Ben Daley and Holly Preston provide a review and assessment of the main policy approaches open to policy-level decision makers as they tackle the problem of aviation GHG emissions. The options include regulatory measures (standards), market-based measures (taxes, emissions charges, subsidies and tradable permits) and voluntary approaches (carbon offsetting, commitments to achieve carbon neutrality, and other corporate responsibility initiatives). Daley and Preston concur with many when they suggest that any practical policy approach will most likely involve several instruments; that it should ideally be consistent with the precautionary and 'polluter pays' principles; and that it should be integrated with other policies, including sustainable development frameworks and energy, transport and other environmental policies. The authors argue that prompt adoption of such policy options could substantially reduce the impacts of aviation on climate, but that this will require resolve on the part of policy makers, cooperation on the part of industry representatives, and carefully targeted research and monitoring.

In concluding this chapter, it is clear that aviation has only recently received the attention of politicians and the broader public in industrialized countries as a sector relevant to climate change, despite the fact that research has addressed its special role in the chemistry and physics of the atmosphere for at least 30 years (see Fabian, 1974, 1978). It is clear that research still has many questions to answer, not only in the fields of atmospheric physics and chemistry, but also economics, geography and sociology, and it is high time for politics to focus on the aviation sector. This book is an attempt to provide a comprehensive state-of-the-art review of the various issues and interrelationships of aviation and climate change from a variety of perspectives. It is our hope that it will be read widely to increase the interest in and understanding of this important topic.

Note

1   Higher numbers can be found in ICAO (2008a, p6): The total scheduled traffic carried by the airlines of the 190 Contracting States of ICAO amounted to approximately 2260 million passengers and some 41 million tonnes of freight.

References

Airbus (2007) 'Flying by nature', *Global Market Forecast 2007–2026*, available at www.airbus.com/fileadmin/documents/gmf/PDF_dl/00-all-gmf_2007.pdf, accessed 18 February 2008

Boeing (2008) *Summary Outlook 2008–2027,* available at www.boeing.com/commercial/cmo/pdf/boeing_cmo_summary_2008.pdf, accessed 1 August 2008

Bows, A., Anderson, K. and Peeters, P. (2007) 'Technology, scenarios and uncertainties', working paper, Tyndall Centre Manchester, The University of Manchester, available at http://tyndall.web.man.ac.uk/publications/Technology%20Scenarios%20and%20Uncertainties%202007.pdf

Bureau of Transportation Statistics (2008) various documents online, available at www.transtats.bts.gov/, accessed 1 August 2008

DfT (2003) 'The future of air transport', Aviation White Paper and associated fact sheet: 'Key facts: Aviation in the UK', Department for Transport, London, available at www.dft.gov.uk/about/strategy/whitepapers/air/keyfacts/ and www.dft.gov.uk/about/strategy/whitepapers/air/

Doganis, R. (2005) *The Airline Business,* London and New York: Routledge

Dotnews (Destinations of the World News) (2008) 'Travel industry news', available at www.dotwnews.com/TravelHeadlines/tabid/55/Default.aspx, accessed 3 August 2008

EC (2008) 'Questions and answers on the Commission's proposal for effort sharing', Europa Press Releases Rapid, 23 January 2008, item 10, Brussels, available at http://europa.eu/rapid/pressReleasesAction.do?reference=MEMO/08/34&format=HTML&aged=0&language=EN&guiLanguage=en, accessed 8 November 2008

Environment News Service (2007) *Aviation Industry Rejects Europe's Climate Emissions Trading System,* 2 October, available at www.ens-newswire.com/ens/oct2007/2007–10–02–03.asp, accessed 1 March 2008

Euractiv (2008) *Aviation and Emissions Trading,* available at www.euractiv.com/en/climate-change/aviation-emissions-trading/article-139728, accessed 2 August 2008

Fabian, P. (1974) 'Residence time of aircraft exhaust contaminants in the stratosphere', CIAP Contract No. 05–30027, US Department of Transportation, Washington DC, June

Fabian, P. (1978) 'Ozone increase from Concorde operations?', *Nature* 272: 306–307

Gössling, S. and Hall, C. M. (2008) 'Swedish tourism and climate change mitigation: An emerging conflict?', *Scandinavian Journal of Hospitality and Tourism* 8(2): 141–158

Gössling, S. and Peeters, P. (2007) '"It does not harm the environment!" – An analysis of discourses on tourism, air travel and the environment', *Journal of Sustainable Tourism,* 15(4): 402–417

Gössling, S., Peeters, P. and Scott, D. (2008) 'Consequences of climate policy for international tourist arrivals in developing countries', *Third World Quarterly* 29(5): 873–901

Grant, R. G. (2007) *Flight: The Complete History,* New York: DK Publishing

Hansen, J., Sato, M., Kharecha, P., Beerling, D., Berner, R., Masson-Delmotte, V., Pagani, M., Raymo, M., Royer, D.-L. and Zachos, J.-C. (2008) 'Target atmospheric CO_2: Where should humanity aim?', Cornell University Library, available at: http://arxiv.org/abs/0804.1126v2, accessed 11 August 2008

IATA (International Air Transport Association) (2007) *New IATA Financial Forecast Predicts 2008 Downturn,* available at www.iata.org/pressroom/pr/2007–12–12–01, accessed 2 August 2008

IATA (2008a) *2007 Total Passenger Travel Results,* available at www.iata.org/ps/publications/2007-results

IATA (2008b) *Jet Fuel Price Monitor*, available at www.iata.org/whatwedo/economics/ fuel_monitor/index.htm, accessed 2 August 2008

IATA (2008c) *Building a Greener Future*, 2nd Edition, April, available at www.iata.org/NR/rdonlyres/22669B08–918C-4AB7–8D8F-8F9743BA8FE6/ 61062/BuildingaGreenerFutureApril2008.pdf, accessed 2 August 2008

ICAO (International Civil Aviation Organization) (1997) *Kyoto Protocol Emphasizes ICAO's Role in Addressing Greenhouse Gas Emissions from International Aviation*, News Release, 12 December, available at http://72.14.205.104/search?q=cache: yYIz_TuKf2QJ:www.icao.int/icao/en/nr/1997/pio199725_e.pdf+Kyoto+Protocol+ ICAO&hl=en&ct=clnk&cd=1&gl=ca, accessed 1 March 2008

ICAO (2008a) *Annual Report of the Council*, available at www.icao.int/icaonet/ dcs/9898/9898_en.pdf, accessed 7 August 2008

ICAO (2008b) *Environmental Unit*, available at www.icao.int/env/, accessed 8 August 2008

ICAO (2008c) *Aviation and carbon markets*, available at www.icao.int/2008wacm/ Documentation.htm, accessed 8 August 2008

IPCC (Intergovernmental Panel on Climate Change) (1999) *Aviation and the Global Atmosphere*, A special report of IPCC Working Groups I and III, Penner, J. E., Lister, D. H., Griggs, D. J., Dokken, D. J. and McFarland, M. (eds) Cambridge, UK and New York, US: Cambridge University Press

IPCC (2007) *Summary for Policymakers: Intergovernmental Panel on Climate Change: Fourth Assessment Report Climate Change 2007: Synthesis Report*, Bernstein, L., Bosch, P., Canziani, O., Chen, Z., Christ, R., Davidson, O., Hare, W., Huq, S., Karoly, D., Kattsov, V., Kundzewicz, Z., Liu, J., Lohmann, U., Manning, M., Matsuno, T., Menne, B., Metz, B., Mirza, M., Nicholls, N., Nurse, L., Pachauri, R., Palutikof, J., Parry, M., Qin, D., Ravindranath, N., Reisinger, A., Ren, J., Riahi, K., Rosenzweig, C., Rusticucci, M., Schneider, S., Sokona, Y., Solomon, S., Stott, P., Stouffer, R., Sugiyama, T., Swart, R., Tirpak, D., Vogel, C., Yohe, G. Cambridge, UK and New York, US: Cambridge University Press

Jardine, C. N., Boardman, B., Osman, A., Vowles J. and Palmer, J. (2004) *Methane UK*, Environmental Change Institute, University of Oxford, Oxford UK, available at www.eci.ox.ac.uk/research/energy/downloads/methaneuk/methaneukreport.pdf, accessed 8 November 2008

Parry, M., Palutikof, J., Hanson, C. and Lowe, J. (2008) 'Climate policy: Squaring up to reality', *Nature Reports Climate Change* 2: 68–70

Peeters, P. M. and Middel, J. (2007) 'Historical and future development of air transport fuel efficiency', in Sausen, R., Blum, A., Lee, D. S. and Brüning, C. (eds) *Proceedings of an International Conference on Transport, Atmosphere and Climate (TAC); Oxford, United Kingdom, 26–29 June 2006*, Oberpfaffenhoven: DLR Institut für Physic der Atmosphäre, 42–47

Peeters, P., Gössling, S. and Becken, S. (2006) 'Innovation towards tourism sustainability: Climate change and aviation', *International Journal of Innovation and Sustainable Development* 1(3): 184–200

Sausen, R., Isaksen I., Grewe, V., Hauglustaine, D., Lee, D. S., Myhre, G., Köhler, M. O., Pitari, G., Schumann, U., Stordal, F. and Zerefos, C. (2005) 'Aviation radiative forcing in 2000: An update on IPCC (1999)', *Meteorologische Zeitschrift* 14: 555–561

Schneider, S. (2008) 'The Stern review debate: an editorial essay', *Climatic Change* 89: 241–244

Shove, E. (2003) *Comfort, Cleanliness and Convenience*, The Social Organization of Normality, Oxford, UK: Berg Publishers

Stern, N. (2006) *The Economics of Climate Change: The Stern Review,* Cambridge: Cambridge University Press

T&E (Transport and Environment) (2007) *No Fight Plan: How the International Civil Aviation Organization (ICAO) has Blocked Progress on Climate Change for a Decade,* available at www.transportenvironment.org/Pages/aviation/, accessed 2 August 2008

Time (2007) 'China's aircraft industry gets off the ground', available at www.time.com/time/magazine/article/0,9171,1670256,00.html, accessed 1 August 2008

United Nations World Tourism Organization (UNWTO) (2008a) *Historical Perspective of World Tourism,* available at www.unwto.org/facts/eng/historical.htm, accessed 1 August 2008

UNWTO (2008b) *Tourism 2020 Vision,* available at www.unwto.org/facts/eng/vision.htm, accessed 1 August 2008

UNWTO (2008c) *Firm tourism demand,* available at www.unwto.org/media/news/en/press_det.php?id=2532&idioma=E, accessed 3 August 2008

UNWTO (2008d) *Emerging Tourism Markets – The Coming Economic Boom,* available at www.unwto.org/media/news/en/press_det.php?id=2462&idioma=E, accessed 3 August 2008

UNWTO-UNEP-WMO (United Nations World Tourism Organization, United Nations Environment Programme, World Meteorological Organization) (2008) *Climate Change and Tourism: Responding to Global Challenges,* Scott, D., Amelung, B., Becken, S., Ceron, J.-P., Dubois, G., Gössling, S., Peeters, P. and Simpson, M. (eds) Madrid, Spain: UNWTO

Upham, P., Bows, A., Anderson, K. and Broderick, J. (2008) 'Aviation policy options for not exceeding the EU +2°C threshold', in de Jong, D., Kaashoek, B. and Zondag, W.-J. (eds) *Blue Skies or Storm Clouds? Essays on Public Policy and Air Transport,* Scienceguide-Aerlines, NL, pp72–78, available at http://aerlines.nl/page.php?id=261

Warde, A. (2005) 'Consumption and the theory of practice', *Journal of Consumer Culture* 5(2): 131–154

Warren, R. (2006) 'Impacts of global climate change at different annual mean global temperature increases', in Schellnhuber, H. J., Cramer, W., Nakicenovic, N., Wigley, T. and Yohe, G. (eds) *Avoiding Dangerous Climate Change,* Cambridge: Cambridge University Press, 93–131

Part I
Aviation and Atmosphere

2
Aviation and Climate Change: The Science

David S. Lee

Introduction

See that? By this afternoon, those vapor trails will have spread out into thin sheets and you won't be able to tell them from natural cirrus cover formations.

The obvious visible effect that aviation has on the atmosphere is the well-known contrail (condensation trail), first described by meteorologists in work dating back to the 1940s and 1950s by Schmidt (1941), Appleman (1953) and Brewer (1999). Contrails are line-shaped ice crystal clouds formed behind aircraft from the initial emission of water vapour and particles from the engines, which is caught up in the wing-tip vortices into a cold, ice-supersaturated atmosphere. The epigraph above was not from a recent commentator on the effects of aviation on climate, but rather Dr Walter Orr Roberts, the then Director of the National Center for Atmospheric Research in Boulder, in a newspaper interview in *The New York Times*, 23 September 1963.

To date, the potential effects on climate of contrails (linear persistent contrails) and their spreading into cirrus cloud coverage continue to exercise scientists in terms of characterizing their microphysical properties, optical effects, occurrence and ultimate effect on climate. However, persistent linear contrails and aircraft-induced cirrus (AIC) are only two (related) effects that aviation has on climate.

Concern over the emissions of nitrogen oxides (NO_x, where $NO_x=NO+NO_2$) date back to the late 1960s and early 1970s when plans were made in Europe and the US to develop a fleet of supersonic aircraft that would fly in the stratosphere. Emissions of NO_x from aircraft were considered to be a potential problem in terms of stratospheric ozone (O_3) depletion (Johnston, 1971; Crutzen, 1972). In the event, only Concorde was developed and the fleet was small (the former USSR also developed the Tu-144, which only operated on a domestic commercial basis for one year before being taken out of service). Significant steps in our understanding of atmospheric science relating to climate and chemistry were developed over this period (Wayne, 2000) and from these early studies, interest in the effects of the subsonic fleet that flies in the upper troposphere and lower stratosphere (UTLS) was developed and early modelling studies showed that aviation emissions of NO_x could bring about O_3 enhancement in the UTLS where O_3 is a powerful greenhouse gas (GHG) (see, e.g. Hidalgo and Crutzen, 1977; Derwent, 1982).

In the early 1990s, a number of publications dealt with potential impacts of aviation on climate, both NO_x effects on O_3, and contrails and AIC (e.g. Schumann, 1990). Research initiatives such as AERONOX (Schumann, 1995) and the Subsonic Assessment Program (SASS; Friedl et al, 1997) and others were conducted during the early to mid-1990s and culminated in the initiation of a Special Report of the Intergovernmental Panel on Climate Change, *Aviation and the Global Atmosphere* (IPCC, 1999). The IPCC (1999) report was a landmark in terms of developing the science and still remains a valuable reference point, even a decade later. Some of the essential headlines from the report were that aviation represented approximately 3.5 per cent of global anthropogenic radiative forcing (RF; a climate metric, see 'Climate concepts and metrics' below) and that this resulted primarily from emissions of CO_2 and NO_x, and the formation of persistent linear contrails (AIC was excluded from the total RF quantification as no best estimate could be arrived at). This fraction of RF was estimated to increase to 5 per cent in 2050, according to a mid-range growth scenario. The largest uncertainties were associated with AIC (state of knowledge 'very poor'), although significant uncertainties were attached to contrails ('fair') and NO_x effects on O_3 ('fair') and methane (CH_4; 'poor').

Much research effort has been committed since the IPCC (1999) report to further quantify the effects of aviation on climate and in particular, to narrow the uncertainties on contrails and AIC. However, much of this effort has been conducted in Europe since the demise of NASA's aviation-dedicated atmospheric effects research programmes. More recently, there have been initiatives from the US Federal Aviation Administration to investigate aviation's impacts on climate (Brasseur, 2008).

The nature of research efforts on the impacts of aviation on climate has started to shift since the IPCC (1999) report: in and around that period, the question was 'what is the magnitude of the (various) effects?' In more recent years, research has been increasingly focused on such questions as 'how can we reduce the (various) effects?' and 'with what sort of metrics should we compare effects for mitigation?' and 'what are the technological and atmospheric trade-offs in mitigation?'; that is the research questions have become more focused and complex, but nonetheless have frequently run up against a lack of basic scientific knowledge in some areas.

In the following sections, some of the recent science is reviewed and summarized, with respect to: emission trends; climate concepts and metrics; the effects of aviation on radiative forcing and climate; mitigation – technological and policy options; and lastly, some conclusions are drawn.

Emission trends

The civil aviation sector has grown strongly, especially since the advent of the jet age, which made passenger travel over longer distances feasible and more comfortable. In 2006, there were approximately 20,500 civil aircraft in service globally, of which 27 per cent were aircraft of <100 seats, 65 per cent were of >100 seats and 8 per cent were freighters (Airbus, 2007). These statistics represent the bulk of the global fleet in terms of its fuel burn and exclude private jets and general aviation. By 2026, Airbus forecast the fleet to nearly double in numbers to approximately 40,500 aircraft, of which 20 per cent will be aircraft of <100 seats, 70 per cent will be of >100 seats, and 10 per cent will be freighters (Airbus, 2007).

The growth of aviation over time is shown in Figure 2.1, in terms of revenue passenger kilometres (RPKs: i.e. the number of seats flown and occupied, compare with available seat kilometres, or ASKs, which is a metric of capacity). The average year-on-year growth rate over the period 1980–2000 was 5.18 per cent and for the period 1990–2000 was 5.07 per cent. The industry experienced a widely publicized downturn after events such as the 11 September 2001 World Trade Center attack and SARS (severe acute respiratory syndrome) outbreak, post 2000. What has perhaps not been so widely realized is the recovery of the industry to date, prior to fuel prices increasing dramatically in late 2007 and 2008. The growth overall for the period 2000–2006 in terms of RPK was 29.7 per cent, averaging over the period an annual growth rate of 4.8 per cent, only slightly short of longer-term averages, such that the total RPK in 2006 was only 3.6 per cent less than that which might have been expected from the 1990–2000 average annual growth rate, that is less than one year's growth. This is an indication of the resilience of the industry, although how demand will change with changing oil prices remains to be seen – nonetheless, it should be noted that crude oil prices doubled over the period 2003–2006, a period which saw an increase of 30.5 per cent in RPK.

Emissions from aviation do not grow at the same rate as demand for two principle reasons. First, new models of aircraft entering the fleet tend to have better fuel performance as this is a direct driver on operating costs – counterbalancing this, new models of aircraft (or engines) are only produced irregularly because of the investment costs and aircraft have a long lifetime, in the order of 25 years, and while operators with modern fleets roll their fleets over on a shorter timescale than this, older aircraft are usually sold on to other operators. The aircraft that are retired (scrapped) tend to be the very old ones

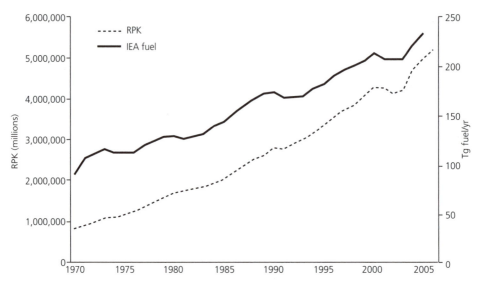

Source: ICAO and IEA

Figure 2.1 *Trends in RPK (millions) and aviation kerosene fuel sales, Tg per year*

that may have been under operation with several airlines. Second, there has been an increase in utilization rate or efficiency in terms of load factors. The contribution of these two terms (technology and load factor) to overall 'traffic efficiency' (i.e. RPK kg^{-1} fuel) is not well known. Nevertheless, a reliable indicator of CO_2 emissions can be taken from the statistics of kerosene fuel sales, as collected by the International Energy Agency (IEA). These data are also shown in Figure 2.1. The growth rate of kerosene sales and use was approximately 2 per cent per year for the period 1990–2005 (last year of IEA data available at time of writing). In 2005, fuel usage was approximately 233Tg per year, or 733Tg CO_2 per year.

The calculation of future emission scenarios was undertaken by the Forecasting and Economic Analysis Sub-Group (FESG, 1998) for the IPCC (1999) report for 2050. More recently, 2050 emission scenarios compatible with the IPCC's Special Report on Emission Scenarios (SRES; IPCC, 2000) have been calculated for SRES A1 and B2 by Owen and Lee (2006) using the same but updated methodology of FESG (1998), which were incorporated into the IPCC Fourth Assessment Report (AR4) WGIII report (Kahn-Ribeiro et al, 2007). These were made using an ICAO forecast of emissions to 2020, and thereafter assuming GDP-driven scenarios with estimated technological improvements over time until 2050. These scenarios, along with other estimations and scenarios are shown in Figure 2.2.

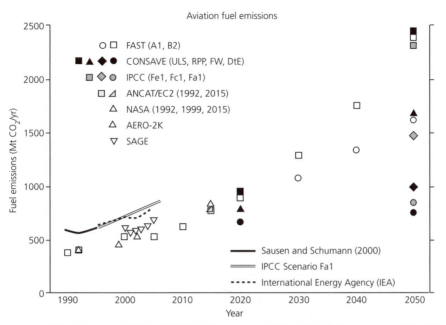

Sources: AERO2K (Eyers et al, 2005), ANCAT/EC2 (Gardner et al, 1998), CONSAVE (Berghof et al, 2005), FAST (Owen and Lee, 2006), IEA (IEA, 2006), IPCC (IPCC, 1999), NASA (Baughcum et al, 1996, 1998, Sutkus et al, 2001), SAGE (Kim et al, 2007), Sausen and Schumann (2000)

Figure 2.2 *Present day, future forecast and scenarios of aviation emissions of CO_2 (Mt per year)*

Climate concepts and metrics

The commonly used metric to quantify the climate impact of some phenomena is 'radiative forcing of climate'. The formal definition adopted by the IPCC is:

> *the change in net (down minus up) irradiance (solar plus longwave; in W m^{-2}) at the tropopause after allowing for strato-spheric temperatures to readjust to radiative equilibrium, but with surface and tropospheric temperatures and state held fixed at the unperturbed values* (see Forster et al, 2007a; Ramaswamy et al, 2001).

The RF metric is used since many climate experiments have found an approximately linear relationship between a change in global mean radiative forcing (RF) and a change in global mean surface temperature (ΔT_s), with some proportionality constant, that is:

$$\Delta T_s \approx \lambda RF \qquad [1]$$

where λ is the climate sensitivity parameter (K (W m^{-2})$^{-1}$), the value of which has been found to be model specific but stable across forcings. However, a number of recent studies have shown that λ may vary between forcing agents that can result in a stronger or weaker temperature change than for other climate gases (e.g. Hansen et al, 1997; Forster and Shine, 1997; Stuber et al, 2005; Hansen et al, 2005).

The reason that the RF concept is so useful is that it can be applied to many forcing agents, for example, a change in GHG concentrations, a change in surface albedo from land-use change, or a change in albedo from cloud cover. In other words, any property of the Earth–atmosphere system that is perturbed, altering the energy budget of long-wave and short-wave fluxes can be quantified using the RF concept. For IPCC purposes, RF is usually quantified as some change since the pre-industrial state of the atmosphere, that is 1750. This date is mostly relevant to long-lived GHGs (LLGHGs) such as CO_2, methane (CH_4) and nitrous oxide (N_2O).

In the case of aviation, its emissions and effects affect RF and as a sector its total RF has been quantified by, for example, the IPCC (1999) for 1992 and a range of 2050 scenarios; Sausen et al (2005) who updated a present-day case for 2000; and Lee et al (2008) who have recently recalculated 2005 forcings and a range of new 2050 scenarios.

In terms of the aviation sector, outside the climate science community, there has been considerable confusion over what RF means, how it is calculated, what its limitations are etc. A number of simple points can be made, some of which are taken up in more detail later in the chapter.

For the long-lived component of aviation RF, that is CO_2, a complete history of emissions is necessary to calculate the RF. For all the other forcings, only a one-year perturbation is necessary to calculate the impact, other than the effect on CH_4 destruction (see 'Effects of aviation on radiative forcing and climate' below), which needs a correction to account for a lifetime of approximately 11 years. Critically, the total RF quantification for aviation is essentially a backward-looking metric (because of the CO_2 component): in other words, it quantifies what the effect has been by the sector to date, or under some emission scenario to its end point. The metric is expressed as a global mean: for some forcings, the pattern is spatially inhomogeneous and here some of the limitations of the concept come in, so if one effect seems to be arithmetically cancelled by another (a positive by a negative), this does not necessarily mean 'no climate effect'. Lastly, and possibly most importantly, RF or its immediate derivatives such as the radiative forcing index (RFI = the sum of aviation RFs divided by the CO_2 RF) cannot be used as emission metrics as the global warming potential (GWP) can (Fuglestvedt et al, 2003; Wit et al, 2005; Forster et al, 2006; Forster et al, 2007a). This is regrettably an ongoing misunderstanding. Some of these points are picked up in later sections.

Effects of aviation on radiative forcing and climate

Overview
Current subsonic aviation affects RF in the following ways:

- emissions of CO_2 result in a positive RF (warming);
- emissions of NO_x result in the formation of tropospheric O_3 via atmospheric chemistry, with a positive RF (warming);
- emissions of NO_x result in the destruction of ambient CH_4 via atmospheric chemistry, with a negative RF (cooling);
- emissions of sulphate particles arising from sulphur in the fuel result in a *direct* negative RF (cooling);
- emissions of soot particles result in a *direct* positive RF (warming);
- emissions of water vapour may cause a small *direct* positive RF (warming);
- persistent linear contrails may form, depending upon atmospheric conditions, that result in both positive and negative RF but overall cause a positive RF effect (warming);
- the formation of aircraft-induced cirrus cloud from spreading contrails results in both positive and negative RF effects but overall is considered to cause a positive RF effect (warming);
- particles emitted from aircraft engines may act as cloud condensation nuclei and seed cirrus cloud formation, which can either increase or decrease the number of ice particles and impact on both the albedo and the emissivity of cirrus clouds. This effect may result in either positive or negative RF effects (warming/cooling) and the sign is rather uncertain.

Carbon dioxide
Carbon dioxide is the only LLGHG emitted in any substantial amount by current aircraft engines. There have been a few measurements of emissions of N_2O and CH_4 in aircraft exhaust but these have demonstrated that these emissions are either very small or not measurable at cruise conditions (Wiesen et al, 1994; IPCC, 1999). (In this respect it is illogical that the IPCC Guidelines for National Greenhouse Gas Inventories (IPCC, 2006) still insist on producing emissions factors for CH_4 and N_2O for aviation, despite a similar note to this effect).

Carbon dioxide is produced in a fixed ratio to fuel consumption in aircraft engines. The bulk of fuel used in civil aviation is kerosene, of which there are two types, with only small amounts of aviation gasoline (AvGas) used for small piston-engined light aircraft. Of the two types of kerosene in common usage, the most prevalent is Jet A1, which has a maximum freezing point of $-47°C$ for which the mean C/H ratio is $C_{12}H_{23}$. Jet A, which has a maximum freezing point of $-40°C$, is in common usage in the US. The emission index (EI, by convention in g kg^{-1} fuel) for CO_2 from kerosene is 3160 ±60 g kg^{-1} fuel for complete combustion. Other minor C-containing gases in the exhaust include CO and various HCs (e.g. Slemr et al, 1998; Anderson et al, 2006) but these are produced in very small quantities as the result of incomplete combustion and as such, their emission indices are greater at lower power conditions.

Emissions of CO_2 from aviation are often quoted in terms of an annual rate, for which it was 733Tg in 2005, according to International Energy Agency statistics of fuel sales. This represents approximately 2–2.5 per cent of total anthropogenic CO_2 emissions. However, here we are concerned with the effect of these emissions, for which a complete history is required, since CO_2 is accumulative in the Earth's atmosphere. Significant aviation activities are generally assumed to have started in 1940; Sausen and Schumann (2000) have reconstructed a historical time series of annual emissions of aviation CO_2 from 1940 to 1995. This time series has been updated to 2005 and the cumulative emissions over the entire 1940–2005 period was 21.3Pg (Lee et al, 2008). If this is compared with current estimates of total CO_2 emissions from fossil fuel burning, cement manufacture and gas flaring (Marland et al, 2007), aviation emissions represent approximately 0.9 per cent over the period 1751–2004, or 1 per cent over the period 1940–2004.

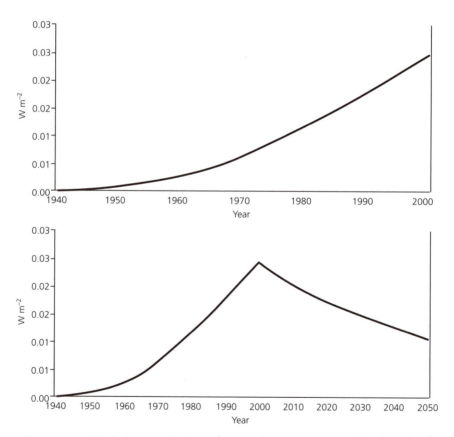

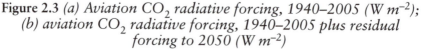

Figure 2.3 *(a) Aviation CO_2 radiative forcing, 1940–2005 (W m^{-2}); (b) aviation CO_2 radiative forcing, 1940–2005 plus residual forcing to 2050 (W m^{-2})*

The aviation contribution to total CO_2 RF can be calculated with a simple C-cycle model (e.g. Hasselmann et al, 1997) to first calculate atmospheric concentrations of CO_2 against background concentrations from observations (or modelled, for futures) and the RF from a simple natural logarithmic fit, which emulates spectral saturation of CO_2 bands (Ramaswamy et al, 2001).

Figure 2.3 below shows the RF from aviation CO_2 over the entire period of emission for 1940–2000. In addition, the lower panel shows the residual RF from these emissions after 2000. This may be looked at in two ways: it represents the time-series of CO_2 RF from aviation, assuming aviation ceased in 2000; or the residual RF left from the cumulative emissions over the 1940–2000 period. The latter view is the more satisfactory and is best represented by the integrated RF that is W m^{-2} per yr. However, this is not a standard climate metric (except for GWPs, see below) but serves to illustrate the behaviour of CO_2, which of course is not specific to aviation CO_2 emissions. However, it gives clues as to why considering short-term forcings (such as O_3, contrails, AIC) versus long-term forcings is a difficult issue in mitigation questions.

Effects of nitrogen oxides on ozone and methane

Overview – formation of NO_x and its atmospheric chemistry

The formation of NO_x in aircraft engines can be via four different routes: the thermal route (thermal NO_x); the prompt route (prompt NO_x); the nitrous oxide route (N_2O) and the fuel-bound nitrogen route (Bowman 1992).

Thermal NO_x arises from the thermal dissociation of nitrogen (N_2) and oxygen (O_2) molecules in combustion air. At high temperatures, N_2 and O_2 dissociate into their atomic states, N and O, and react with N_2 and O_2 to form NO via the Zeldovich mechanism, whereby:

$$N_2 + O \rightarrow NO + N \qquad [2]$$

$$N + O_2 \rightarrow NO + O \qquad [3]$$

The rates of these reactions are dependent upon the stoichiometric ratio (air to fuel ratio) in the primary combustion zone, flame temperature and residence time at the flame temperature. Maximum thermal NO_x production occurs at a slightly lean fuel mix ratio because of excess availability of O_2 for reaction within the hot flame.

Prompt NO_x is produced by the intermediate formation of HCN via the reaction of N_2 and HC radicals. This is a less important mechanism of NO_x formation except in fuel-rich conditions.

Fuel NO_x is produced from the evolution and reaction of fuel-bound N with O_2. The chemical reactions and formation are more complicated than thermal NO_x production. This is relatively unimportant for gas turbines running on kerosene since most distillate fuels have little or no fuel-bound N and essentially most of the NO_x is formed from the thermal route.

The N_2O route involves the reaction of N_2 with atomic O and a third body (M), that is:

$$N_2 + O + M \rightarrow N_2O + M \qquad [4]$$

The N_2O thus formed may react with O, H to form NO, N_2, O_2 or OH via competing reactions. This mechanism can be important in applications where lean premixed combustion is involved. The reaction is also promoted by higher pressures but temperature is less important.

Optimizing combustors for minimal NO_x formation under different engine operating conditions is a major challenge for combustion engineers. For example, lean-burning low-emissions combustors are susceptible to combustion instabilities, caused by the interaction of fluctuating heat with acoustic resonances. Non-uniformities in the fuel–air mixing and combustion process can give rise to hot areas that tend to increase NO_x formation. Keeping the combustion zone fuel–air ratio near to stoichiometry minimizes CO and HC emissions but results in high flame temperatures and increased NO_x production. These are examples of some of the problems that need to be overcome in designing low-NO_x engines.

As a result of the complications of NO_x formation under different conditions, it can be gathered that NO_x emission is not a simple function of fuel consumption, as is the case for the emission of CO_2, but is engine and technology specific. Nonetheless, there are simple algorithms by which fuel flow may be converted to NO_x emission, taking account of upper atmosphere temperature and humidity conditions, such as the so-called Boeing-2 Fuel Flow Method (DuBois and Paynter, 2006).

The effects of the emissions of NO_x from aircraft on the atmosphere involve a large number of reactions (mostly, but not exclusively gas-phase) that ultimately lead to enhancements of O_3 in the UTLS by a few parts per billion (10^9) by volume (ppbv), and the destruction of ambient CH_4 (of the order 1–2 per cent). Thus, the emission of NO_x results in a positive global mean RF from O_3 production and a negative mean RF from CH_4 destruction. Some of the basic chemistry is as follows.

Emissions of NO_x from current subsonic air traffic alter tropospheric chemistry and have an impact on the coupling of the NO_x–HO_x chemical reaction chains. Ozone is constantly being formed and photolysed in the cycle:

$$O(^3P) + O_2 + M \rightarrow O_3 + M \qquad [5]$$

$$O_3 \xrightarrow{h\upsilon} O(^3P) + O_2 \qquad [6]$$

where $O(^3P)$ is atomic oxygen in the ground state formed from the photo-dissociation of O_2 (mostly in the stratosphere >16km) where the wavelength of the incoming radiation is <243nm, and M represents a third body. This system is perturbed in the troposphere and lower stratosphere by the presence of CO,

CH_4 and other non-methane hydrocarbons (NMHCs). Carbon monoxide from natural and humanmade sources reacts with the hydroxyl radical to form the hydroperoxy radical HO_2:

$$OH + CO \rightarrow H + CO_2 \hspace{4cm} [7]$$

$$H + O_2 + M \rightarrow HO_2 + M \hspace{4cm} [8]$$

This HO_2 may then react with NO to form NO_2 which is subsequently photolysed to reform NO, and produce $O(^3P)$, which may then participate in reaction [5]:

$$HO_2 + NO \rightarrow NO_2 + OH \hspace{4cm} [9]$$

$$NO_2 \xrightarrow{h\nu} NO + O(^3P) \hspace{4cm} [10]$$

Methane and other NMHCs may also contribute to the formation of HO_2:

$$CH_4 + OH \rightarrow CH_3 + H_2O \hspace{4cm} [11]$$

$$CH_3 + O_2 + M \rightarrow CH_3O_2 + M \hspace{4cm} [12]$$

$$CH_3O_2 + NO \rightarrow CH_3O + NO_2 \hspace{4cm} [13]$$

$$CH_3O + O_2 \rightarrow HCHO + HO_2 \hspace{4cm} [14]$$

and then reacting as in equation [9]. NMHCs can also participate as in [11] to [14], where, by convention, the NMHC is designated RH, taking the place of CH_4 and its derivative species above. The formaldehyde (HCHO) thus formed can also react with OH to form HO_2 and its photolysis products contribute towards HO_2 formation:

$$HCHO + OH(+O_2) \rightarrow HO_2 + H_2O + CO \hspace{3cm} [15]$$

$$HCHO \xrightarrow{h\nu} H_2 + CO \hspace{4cm} [16]$$

and

$$HCHO + 2O_2 \xrightarrow{h\nu} 2HO_2 + CO \hspace{4cm} [17]$$

Ozone is lost from the system, either by dry deposition to the earth's surface, or by chemical destruction, principally from photolysis to form $O(^1D)$ (the electronically excited state of atomic oxygen) which reacts with water vapour to form OH, this reaction being the principal source of OH in the atmosphere:

$$O_3 \xrightarrow{h\upsilon} O(^1D) + O_2 \qquad\qquad [18]$$

$$O(^1D) + H_2O \rightarrow 2OH \qquad\qquad [19]$$

two other major routes of chemical destruction of O_3 are reaction with OH and HO_2:

$$O_3 + OH \rightarrow HO_2 + O_2 \qquad\qquad [20]$$

$$O_3 + HO_2 \rightarrow OH + 2O_2 \qquad\qquad [21]$$

However, any injection of NO competes for the HO_2 and therefore reduces the rate of loss of O_3 by HO_x ($OH+HO_2$). Evidently, any NO_x present in the chemical system acts as a catalyst for O_3 production. Nitric oxide also reacts with O_3 to form NO_2, but since the NO_2 is photolysed during the day [10], no net formation of O_3 results on the timescale of ~1 day except in polar winters. The catalysis is terminated when NO_x is removed from the system which can occur either in the day by reaction with OH:

$$NO_2 + OH + M \rightarrow HNO_3 + M \qquad\qquad [22]$$

or by night to form HNO_3 which is adsorbed on existing aerosol:

$$NO_2 + O_3 \rightarrow NO_3 + O_2 \qquad\qquad [23]$$

$$NO_3 + NO_2 \rightarrow N_2O_5 \qquad\qquad [24]$$

$$N_2O_5 + H_2O \rightarrow 2HNO_3 \qquad\qquad [25]$$

However, NO_2 may be regenerated by photolysis of HNO_3:

$$HNO_3 \xrightarrow{h\upsilon} NO_2 + OH \qquad\qquad [26]$$

or by reaction with OH:

$$HNO_3 + OH \rightarrow H_2O + NO_3 \qquad\qquad [27]$$

and subsequent photolysis of NO_3:

$$NO_3 \rightarrow NO + O_2 \qquad\qquad [28]$$

or:

$$NO_3 \xrightarrow{h\upsilon} NO_2 + O(^3P) \qquad\qquad [29]$$

The role of HO_x is critical: the pathways of OH and HO_2 generation having been given above. In addition, however, acetone $((CH_3)_2CO)$, hydrogen peroxide (H_2O_2) and other peroxides may provide additional sources of HO_x (Wennberg et al, 1998). Hydroperoxy radicals are removed from the system by three (net, i.e. not showing intermediate reactions) main pathways:

$$OH + HO_2 \rightarrow H_2O + O_2 \tag{30}$$

$$2OH + NO_2 \rightarrow H_2O + NO_3 \tag{31}$$

$$OH + HO_2 \rightarrow H_2O + O_2 \tag{32}$$

It has been known for some time that NO_x emissions result in a reduction of ambient CH_4. Emissions of NO_x result in enhanced concentrations of the hydroxyl radical, OH:

$$NO + HO_2 \rightarrow NO_2 + OH \tag{9}$$

The O_3 increase associated with NO_x emissions is accompanied by a shift in the concentrations of HO_2 to OH. The increased OH concentrations from aircraft NO_x emissions then result in a reduction in CO concentrations from the reactions:

$$OH + CO \rightarrow H + CO_2 \tag{33}$$

$$H + O_2 + M \rightarrow HO_2 + M \tag{8}$$

The lifetime of CO is of the order months, so that decreased CO concentrations from increased OH may spread from cruise altitudes down to lower altitudes and latitudes (bearing in mind that most NO_x emissions from aircraft occur at 8–12km in northern mid-latitudes). Much of the CH_4 oxidation in the troposphere occurs at tropical and sub-tropical latitudes and because CO levels are reduced, OH is higher (CO being a sink for OH) and as a result, more CH_4 is oxidized, reducing CH_4 concentrations:

$$CH_4 + OH \rightarrow CH_3 + H_2O \tag{11}$$

Thus, as CH_4 concentrations are reduced as a result of aircraft NO_x emissions, the RF effect from ambient CH_4 is reduced, such that a negative RF from CH_4 can be attributed to NO_x emissions from aviation.

The above is an outline sketch of aviation's impacts on the coupled chemistry of the tropospheric NO_x–O_3–CH_4 system but the main point in terms of GHGs is the enhancement of O_3 in the UTLS that tends to occur on a hemispherical scale and the subsequent depletion of background CH_4 concentrations at a global scale.

Modelling of aircraft impacts on tropospheric chemistry

The models with which such perturbations are calculated are complex. Initial models that examined this were very simplified one-dimensional models with very basic descriptions of chemistry. In the early 1970s these progressed to two-dimensional (usually latitude by height) and ultimately to the three-dimensional models that are currently in use, having been developed since the early 1990s. Such state-of-the-art models are usually referred to as chemical transport models (CTMs) or climate chemistry models (CCMs). The former are driven by meteorological data either from global climate models (GCMs) that solve the primitive equations of motion, or reanalysis/operational data from, for example the European Centre for Medium-Range Weather Forecasts (ECMWF). The latter (CCMs) may be conventional GCMs with added chemistry, or coupled climate-chemistry models, where the changing chemistry feeds back on the radiation and dynamical schemes. There is a trend towards such a highly integrated 'Earth system modelling', which incorporates atmosphere, ocean feedbacks, chemistry and biosphere. Zhang (2008) gives a recent overview of such modelling.

Such CTM/CCM models are usually run for a period of one to five years (integration period) as they are computationally expensive, often running on supercomputers. They typically have a resolution of 2–5° (latitude by longitude) with a vertical discretization of a few kilometres up to altitudes of 20–30km on a hybrid pressure scale (uneven by height). The meteorological data are usually read every three to six hours with an interpolated advection time step. Chemical schemes are often quite complex (up to 100 chemical species) for CTMs but often slightly more simplified for CCMs where the additional computational expense of the underlying GCM needs to be accounted for. In addition, the models must incorporate parameterized processes of convection, aerosol processes, emissions and wet and dry deposition (removal). Such complex models need careful evaluation in terms of their performance and this is a subject of study itself (e.g. Brunner et al, 2003, 2005; Eyring et al, 2005). Wild (2007) provides an overview of performance of CTMs on the tropospheric O_3 budget from a modelling perspective, and Singh et al (2007) examine the performance of CTMs with respect to a specific large-scale field campaign and point to persistent discrepancies between models and observations, which suggests that modelling the impacts of NO_x emissions (in general) is still far from providing great confidence in the outputs.

Recent assessments of aviation's impacts on present-day O_3 have been conducted under a number of research programmes, notable 'TRADEOFF' in Europe (Isaksen, 2003) and more recently 'QUANTIFY'. The results of the TRADEOFF project were summarized by Sausen et al (2005) and include more detailed studies by Gauss et al (2006). Figure 2.4 is taken from Gauss et al (2006) and shows fairly typical NO_x, NO_y (reactive nitrogen), OH and O_3 perturbations in two dimensions (from a three-dimensional model), in terms of latitude versus height.

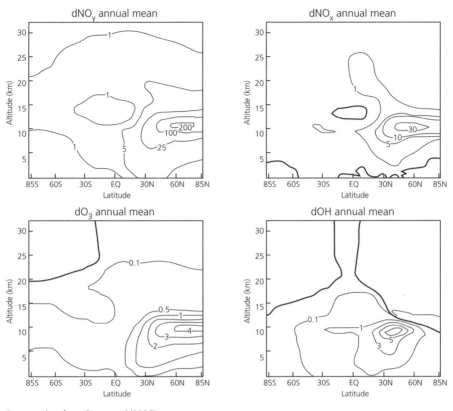

Source: taken from Gauss et al (2006)

Figure 2.4 *Change in zonal-mean NO$_y$ (top left, pptv); NO$_x$ (top right, pptv); O$_3$ (bottom left, ppb); and OH (bottom right, 10^4 molecules cm^{-3}) from aircraft emissions (year 2000 emissions)*

Radiative forcing from ozone and methane perturbations

The chemical modelling described above of aircraft NO$_x$ emissions usually results in enhancements of NO$_x$, NO$_y$, OH and O$_3$ in the main air traffic corridors, as shown in Figure 2.4.

The O$_3$ production efficiency per molecule of NO$_x$ is greater at these altitudes than anywhere else in the atmosphere (IPCC, 1999). Moreover, the RF produced by a unit change on O$_3$ is proportional to the temperature difference between the radiation absorbed and the radiation emitted, such that the RF efficiency is greatest for O$_3$ changes near the tropopause (Lacis et al, 1990; Forster and Shine, 1997). The O$_3$ production efficiency and RF efficiency of O$_3$ at the tropopause conspire to produce RF effects from aviation that are larger per unit NO$_x$ emission than for surface sources.

It is also thought that O$_3$ produced at these altitudes may have a greater efficacy than 1, that is a departure from equation [1]. The efficacy gives the ratio of global-mean surface temperature change for a 1W m^{-2} forcing from a given forcing mechanism compared with the surface temperature change for a 1W m^{-2} forcing from a change in CO_2 (e.g. Joshi et al, 2003; Hansen et al, 2005). Ponater et al (2006) recently calculated an efficacy for O_3 changes at these altitudes of 1.37 and for CH_4 of 1.18.

The reduction in CH_4 concentrations and lifetime (since aviation NO_x emissions result in extra OH, the principal sink/destruction term for CH_4) are global because of its lifetime, being in the order of 8–11 years. However, the arithmetic subtraction of the negative CH_4 RF and the positive O_3 RF arising from aircraft NO_x emissions may not translate to corresponding *climate* effects. The IPCC (1999) report (Chapter 6) cautioned against such a simple interpretation. Other work (Stuber et al, 2005) has also indicated that a northern hemisphere forcing from O_3 in the UT may cause a stronger temperature *response* than from the same forcing distributed globally.

Given the additional findings on efficacy and latitudinal differentials of RF on temperature response, the issue of aviation NO_x emissions on climate remains an open one.

In the absence of any refinements of using an efficacy >1 for O_3 and CH_4 changes, the magnitude of the O_3 RF from aviation NO_x emissions estimated by the IPCC for 1992 was 23mW m^{-2}, with a CH_4 RF of –14mW m^{-2}. Over the intervening years, the global atmospheric models used to calculate the chemical responses have been much improved. Sausen et al (2005) reassessed overall aviation RF for the year 2000 and found that the O_3 RF response had not increased in line with CO_2 emissions over the period 1992–2000, which was attributed to improvements in the atmospheric models, probably because of better vertical and horizontal resolution, resulting in less artificial mixing. Their assessment resulted in an O_3 RF of 21.9mW m^{-2} and a CH_4 RF of –10.4mW m^{-2}.

Outlook and uncertainties

Two recent initiatives reviewing aviation impacts, ATTICA in Europe (Lee et al, 2009) and ACCRI in the US (Brasseur, 2008) have identified a number of research issues relating to modelling aviation NO_x impacts. Clearly, models and observations do not match well for some critical species such as HO_2; representation of processes such as convection and lightning NO_x remain a problem in terms of the overall O_3 budget and attribution of it to particular NO_x emissions (e.g. Singh et al, 2007). There is also an unresolved issue over the role of heterogeneous chemistry in that any fast transformation to 'sink' species (i.e. species that do not significantly take part in further catalytic production of O_3) will reduce the O_3-forming potential of NO_x emissions. It has been speculated that this may occur on contrails and cirrus cloud, although there are no reliable assessments of this: furthermore, bromine species may also provide a 'denoxification' process, although similarly, the extent to which this occurs on the global scale is not well studied, with only one paper on this subject (Hendricks et al, 2000).

Plume-scale processes also remain an issue. Most CTMs/CCMs treat the NO_x emission as directly injected. However, there is some evidence for plume-scale processing which may reduce the overall O_3 impact calculated (e.g. Kraabol et al, 2000, 2002): such parameterizations, however, require additional assumptions over conditions that critically affect the outcome, such as the emission of OH, mixing times of the plume under a variety of conditions and background concentrations of chemical species.

Given the above issues of the ability of CTMs/CCMs to reproduce observations and uncertainties over basic chemical and physical processes, one can conclude that there are good indications and evidence that aircraft NO_x emissions affect climate through O_3 formation and CH_4 destruction but the magnitude of this effect still remains uncertain.

Water vapour

Emissions of H_2O from subsonic aviation affect RF and climate in two ways: directly, through the RF from additional H_2O vapour, and indirectly, through the initial emission of H_2O resulting in contrails and AIC. Here, we deal with the direct effect.

Similarly to CO_2, H_2O is produced as a fixed ratio to fuel, with an emission index of $1230 \pm 20g$ kg^{-1} fuel for complete combustion of kerosene. The IPCC (1999) report assessed that the RF of H_2O vapour was rather small ($1.5mW$ m^{-2}, some 3 per cent of the total aviation effect in 1992), since the addition from aircraft exhaust represented only a small addition to the natural hydrological cycle. A small amount of H_2O vapour will be directly deposited into the drier lowermost stratosphere, but given the exchange times, this will have only a small effect. This is in agreement with earlier studies (Fortuin et al, 1995; Ponater et al, 1996; Rind et al, 1996), and little or no effort has been committed to studying this impact since the IPCC (1999) report.

However, should supersonic flight in the mid-stratosphere become an issue again, it could well be that the RF effects from H_2O vapour would be significant, as was found by the IPCC's (1999) 2050 supersonic scenario and more recent work (Grewe et al, 2007), with H_2O vapour dominating the total RF. Currently, the prospects for the development of a fleet of large supersonic aircraft seems remote.

Particles – sulphate, black carbon, organic
Overview

Sulphate and black carbon (BC) particles, or soot, are also involved in the formation of contrails along with water vapour. In addition, the existence of organic particles has been postulated that also may contribute to contrail/AIC formation (e.g. Kärcher et al, 1998; Yu and Turco, 1999). Here, however, we are concerned with the direct radiative effect that these particles may have.

Similar to H_2O vapour, there has been little, if any, work on the direct radiative effects of these particles since the IPCC (1999) report, although much research has been committed to their role in contrails and AIC.

Sulphur emissions

Sulphur is present in aviation kerosene in low concentrations, at a typical concentration of 400µg g^{-1} fuel. The S is oxidized to sulphur dioxide (SO_2) and is subsequently oxidized to sulphur trioxide (SO_3) and gaseous sulphuric acid (H_2SO_4) in the engine and near-field of the plume, converting approximately 3 per cent of the initial $S^{(IV)}$ to $S^{(VI)}$. The rest of the S (mostly SO_2) is converted slowly in the atmosphere to H_2SO_4, probably on pre-existing particles.

Only two recent global modelling studies have been identified which treat aircraft S emissions explicitly (Kjellström et al, 1999; Lucas and Akimoto, 2007). Both of these studies assess the contribution of aircraft S emissions to be approximately 1 per cent of the total tropospheric burden: Lucas and Akimoto (2007) estimate that in the UT northern hemisphere, aircraft S is about 3 per cent of the S burden. The direct RF of sulphate particles was examined by the IPCC (1999) and found to be a small negative term of –3mW m^{-2}. Subsequent assessments have simply scaled this value with fuel usage (e.g. Sausen et al, 2005).

Black carbon emissions

Black carbon is formed as a result of incomplete combustion of kerosene and ultimately from the coagulation of complex C-containing species such as polyaromatic hydrocarbons (PAHs) in the combustor. 'Smoke' is one of the regulated emission standards for aircraft engines and much has been accomplished since the development of early jet engines to eliminate dark visible smoke emissions. Particles of BC typically have aerodynamic diameters of approximately 30–60nm (e.g. Petzold et al, 2003). The average BC emission factor decreases with altitude from about 0.08g kg^{-1} fuel at altitudes near take-off and landing to 0.02g kg^{-1} fuel at 16 km (Hendricks et al, 2004). The 2002 fleet average was estimated to be 0.025g kg^{-1} fuel (Eyers et al, 2005) although more modern engines emit much less, 0.01g soot kg^{-1} fuel. Of the order of 10^{14}–10^{15} kg^{-1} fuel of soot particles are emitted, depending on engine type and power setting (Petzold et al, 1999).

The IPCC (1999) estimated the direct RF from aviation BC to be 3mW m^{-2}. Hendricks et al (2004) updated global calculations of the contribution of aviation to BC abundance and found it to be smaller than the IPCC's (1999) estimates and suggested (although did not calculate) that the RF was accordingly smaller.

Organic particle emissions

There is evidence that low-volatility hydrocarbons including oxygenated hydrocarbons and organic acids may be emitted from aircraft engines that form particles (Kiendler et al, 2000; Wohlfrom et al, 2000). Such evidence primarily comes from experiments that cannot explain the large apparent remaining number of volatile particles for low-fuel sulphur contents (e.g. Schröder et al, 1998; Schumann et al, 2002). However, the chemical composition of such particles has not yet been elucidated, so no emission index is given here.

Persistent linear contrails and aircraft-induced cirrus
Background and definitions

As was alluded to in the introduction, much of the recent aviation-related climate research has focused on persistent linear contrails and AIC; yet there has also been awareness of this potential impact for some decades, including mention of contrail impacts in early assessments (e.g. SMIC, 1971).

Here we discriminate between a number of effects of aircraft on cloudiness:

1 short-lived contrails that are likely to have little or no impact on climate;
2 persistent (30 minutes or more) linear contrails that because of sheer numbers and frequency of occurrence may impact climate;
3 spreading contrails from line-shaped structures into cirrus cloud coverage that is likely to impact upon climate;
4 seeding of the upper atmosphere with cloud condensation nuclei (particle emissions) that trigger cirrus cloud coverage.

For convenience and simplicity, the terms 'linear contrails' and aircraft-induced cirrus (AIC) are used here, which incorporate the above effects (2–4). Short-lived contrails form when the atmosphere is dry, with relative humidity below ice-supersaturation. Persistent linear contrails form when the ambient atmosphere's humidity is greater than saturation humidity over ice surfaces (RHi >100 per cent). The difference between 2 and 3 is really an operational one, where satellites are mostly used to detect such linear structures and from which computations of contrail coverage are derived. Spreading contrails are, by nature, more difficult to attribute to air traffic with satellite data because of the non-linear structures, but it is clear that this occurs. The fourth effect is theoretically possible by quite conventional cloud physics but has not been directly isolated and observed to be caused by air traffic.

Contrail formation

Persistent linear contrails are formed from the emission of particles and water vapour from the aircraft exhaust into a cold (typically −40°C), ice-supersaturated atmosphere. The water condenses on the particles which freeze within milliseconds after being emitted into the atmosphere, and ambient water vapour deposits on these tiny particles, which grow in size. A common misconception is that the mass of water (ice) observed on a persistent contrail is from the exhaust: this is incorrect and approximately 98 per cent of the water (ice) mass originates from the ambient atmosphere. Thus, it can be seen that the formation of contrails is critically dependent upon the state of the background atmosphere.

The conditions under which contrails form may be defined quite well with a knowledge of the emission index of H_2O, the combustion heat of kerosene, the ambient temperature and pressure, the specific heat capacity of air, and the propulsion efficiency of the aircraft. Formal derivations may be found in a number of publications, including Schumann (1996, 2000, 2005), who provides excellent overviews and detail. The definition of conditions under which a contrail may be formed is often referred to as the Schmidt-Appleman criterion (Schumann, 1996) because of their foundational work in understanding the physics of contrail formation.

Experiments have confirmed that more fuel-efficient aircraft with greater propulsive efficiencies cause contrails to form at higher temperatures (Schumann, 2000; Schumann et al, 2000). Moreover, it has also been shown that changes in the fuel S content or soot emission only make small differences (less than 0.4K) to the threshold temperature for contrail formation (Schumann et al, 2002).

The formation of contrails, as described above, is dominated by thermodynamics such that as long as particles are present, their composition or size seems to matter little. In addition to sulphate, soot and organic particle emissions, chemi-ions (e.g. Arnold et al, 2000) and small amounts of metal particles (from mechanical wear) (Petzold et al, 1998) are also emitted. However, even in the absence of any particles emitted, theoretical calculations imply that contrails would be formed on particles from the background atmosphere passing through the engine (Kärcher et al, 1998). If this were the case, in theory for liquid hydrogen (LH_2)-powered aircraft, the ice crystals would be likely to be larger and have different optical properties (Schumann, 1996).

Radiative effect of contrails

Contrails and AIC may affect the radiative balance of the atmosphere in two ways: first, they reflect back solar radiation to space (a cooling effect) and second, they reduce the long-wave radiation leaving Earth to space (a warming effect). Currently, radiative transfer calculations imply an overall warming from contrails, especially at night (Meerkötter et al, 1999; Myhre and Stordal, 2001; Stuber et al, 2006). Evidently the balance between the two radiative effects is a critical one and affects the overall RF signal of contrails and AIC.

One of the critical parameters in determining the overall radiative balance of contrails and AIC is the optical depth, τ (a dimensionless measure of the transparency of the cloud for the solar range of wavelengths), which is dependent on the size and ice water content (IWC) of the ice crystals, the latter varying over several orders of magnitude. Estimates of τ range from 0.05 to 0.5 with a best estimate of 0.3 according to Schumann (2005) based on an evaluation of Lidar measurements.

Estimating contrail coverage and radiative forcing

The basic methodology for this was established by Sausen et al (1998), which in turn was based on the method by which high cloud is parameterized in a GCM. In this methodology, first the propensity of the atmosphere to cause contrails is determined, the 'potential contrail coverage', which is taken from climatological data of relative humidity and temperature over some long time period, if done on a statistical basis, such as the ERA-40 reanalysis data from

ECMWF (Uppala et al, 2005). By taking these data a cirrus cloud coverage can be calculated (correcting for a local critical humidity threshold, see Sausen et al, 1998) a potential contrail coverage distribution is obtained, which is then weighted by a global air traffic movement database to get actual contrail coverage. In a final step, the coverage is normalized by some independent observational area from satellite data. The methodology to calculate contrail coverage 'on line' within a GCM framework is similar; see Ponater et al (2002).

To calculate the RF, a radiative transfer code must be employed which utilizes data on fractional coverage and assumptions over ice particle size and shape etc. Examples of such calculations are given by Minnis et al (1999), Myhre and Stordal (2001), Marquart et al (2003), Stuber and Forster (2007) and Rädel and Shine (2008). Despite the number of calculations now performed, considerable uncertainties remain over the contrail coverage, the observational normalization area utilized, the assumed value of τ etc. As Schumann (2005) points out, the computed RF is the difference between two large values, and small errors in either term can have a large effect on the net RF. Thus more effort is required to study sensitivities to data and assumptions. The overall result of more recent studies is that a smaller net RF is generally computed, of the order 3–10mW m^{-2}, than was done by Minnis et al (1999), whose value of 20mW m^{-2} for 1992 traffic was adopted by the IPCC (1999).

Examples of the steps of cirrus cloud coverage, potential contrail coverage, actual contrail coverage and contrail RF are illustrated in Figure 2.5.

Trends in aircraft-induced cirrus

While much progress has been made to investigate contrail formation from aspects of microphysics through to modelling and satellite observation (to which this chapter cannot do full justice because of the vast body of literature), understanding and quantifying the extent to which aviation affects cirrus cloud coverage and its consequential effects on RF has proved to be difficult. Justifiable efforts have been expended on understanding and better quantifying basic physical properties of the atmosphere including cirrus cloud microphysics and water vapour distributions (a surprisingly difficult and poorly defined parameter in the UTLS). For details of such work, the overviews by Schumann (2002, 2005) are recommended.

Given the increase in air traffic over the last few decades, and aviation's obvious propensity to alter cloudiness (from many satellite images, e.g. NASA's 'Visible Earth' project at http://visibleearth.nasa.gov/, accessed August 2008), one might expect to find trends in cirrus clouds as a result of increased aviation activities. However, this has been difficult to prove unequivocally.

The principle difficulty is the lack of suitable, robust, long-term observational data sets. Such data sets can be derived from ground-based and satellite observations, and several observational platforms and projects have been established, such as the International Satellite Cloud Climatology Project (ISCCP;

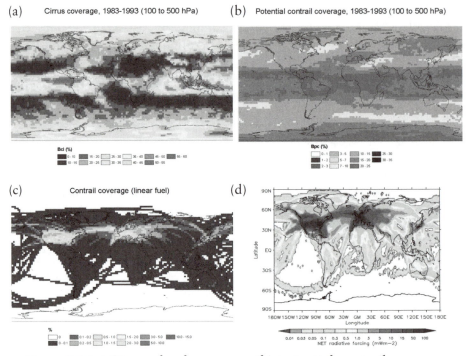

(a) Cirrus coverage, 1983-1993 (100 to 500 hPa)

(b) Potential contrail coverage, 1983-1993 (100 to 500 hPa)

(c) Contrail coverage (linear fuel)

(d)

Figure 2.5 *(a) Cirrus cloud coverage; (b) potential contrail coverage; (c) actual contrail coverage calculated with ECMWF data; and (d) contrail radiative forcing*

Rossow and Schiffer, 1999) which provides a 20+ year archive of daily observations. Similarly the High Resolution Infrared Radiometer Sounder (HIRS) instruments have been flown on a number of satellites over a 20+ year period. The results seem to conflict with each other: Wylie et al (2005) analysed 20 years of HIRS data and compared the findings with ISCCP data, and found that while ISCCP data show a decrease in total and high cloud amounts, high clouds from HIRS show a small but statistically significant increase in the tropics and northern hemisphere. Evan et al (2007), however, have recently claimed that apparent trends in the ISCCP data set are attributable to viewing geometry artefacts and are not related to physical changes in the atmosphere; they suggest that the ISCCP data are unsuited for studies of trends.

A number of studies have attempted to extract an aviation-related signal to cirrus cloud trends using satellite data (Minnis et al, 2001; Zerefos et al, 2003; Minnis et al, 2004; Stordal et al, 2005; Stubenrauch and Schumann, 2005; Zerefos et al, 2007; Eleftheratos et al, 2007), although this was not the focus of the last study. All these studies used the ISCCP data set with the exception of Stubenrauch and Schumann (2005), who used eight years of TOVS data (TIROS-N Operational Vertical Sounder).

- Zerefos et al (2003) used the ISCCP (D2) data set for the period 1984–1998 to examine changes in cirrus cloud cover (CCC) after first removing the influences of the El Niño Southern Oscillation (ENSO), the quasi-biennial oscillation (QBO) and North Atlantic Oscillation (NAO) and found a statistically significant increasing trend of >2 per cent per decade in certain high traffic density regions in the North Atlantic and North America in summer. Adjacent low traffic density regions had insignificant trends, mostly negative.
- Stordal et al (2005) used data from the METEOSAT area of the ISSCP D2 data set, recognizing that errors may be introduced from changing satellite viewing geometry. They estimated that the trend in high cloud cover that might be associated with air traffic density was 0.23 per cent (range 0.07–0.41 per cent), giving a trend in cirrus of 1–2 per cent per decade.
- Stubenrauch and Schumann (2005) used data from the TOVS path B satellite and estimated relative humidity at aircraft cruise altitudes for conditions under which contrail formation was likely and calculated an increase in cloud cover of 0.2–0.25 per cent per decade over Europe and an increase of 0.08–0.24 per cent per decade over the North Atlantic flight corridor during the period 1987–1995, which may be attributable to air traffic.
- Eleftheratos et al (2007) also used ISCCP D2 data from 1984–2004. After de-seasonalizing the data and using regression to remove the NAO, they found a trend in CCC in the western part of the North Atlantic flight corridor of 1.6 per cent per decade and a trend of –0.5 per cent per decade in the eastern part of the North Atlantic.

What is clear from all these analyses is that it is very difficult to pick out a signal in CCC from aviation and that it is almost impossible to do this unequivocally, since the inherent assumption is one of a relationship between high cloud amount and air traffic density: this is not unreasonable but there are many other physical factors other than air traffic that affect CCC. Despite this, there is some evidence for a correlation between high cloud amount and high air traffic density in regions where the formation of CCC is less likely to be influenced by dynamics, for example in the tropics where convection dominates. Nonetheless, such correlation analyses cannot attribute causality between CCC and air traffic. Furthermore, the recent findings of Evan et al (2007) bring into question the usage of ISCCP data for such trend analysis.

Radiative effects of aircraft-induced cirrus

The first estimate of global AIC RF was given by the IPCC (1999) who estimated a range from 0–40mW m^{-2} for air traffic in 1992. Stordal et al (2005), using their analysis of additional CCC from aviation, arrived at a mean of 30mW m^{-2} (range 10–80mW m^{-2}) assuming that AIC has similar optical properties to linear contrails. Minnis et al (2004) did not discriminate between linear contrails and AIC and estimated a range of RF of 6–25mW m^{-2}. The uncertainties remain large in estimating AIC RF and more progress is likely only to come through thorough analyses of particular situations and process-based modelling, which is in its infancy.

The above analyses essentially contain all the aircraft-induced cloudiness estimates from contrails and spreading contrail-cirrus. The other mechanism by which aircraft may contribute to CCC is through the seeding of cirrus clouds through particle emissions, which is dealt with in the next section.

At the moment, all one can conclude is that the RF from AIC could be large (there seems to agreement of a minimum RF of around 5–10mW m^{-2}); larger than any of the other aviation-induced forcings but there are also great uncertainties that need to be resolved.

Soot cirrus

The expression 'soot cirrus' refers to cirrus cloud formed from aircraft particle emissions that have not made a contrail first. There is some limited circumstantial evidence for this occurring through the measurements of Ström and Ohlsson (1998) and Kristensson et al (2000), who found an increase in ice particle concentrations in cirrus clouds which had elevated soot concentrations assumed to be associated with aviation. This is sometimes referred to as an indirect effect.

However, the effect is not straightforward and the addition of particles can in theory either increase or decrease ice crystal concentrations. Cirrus clouds may form by either homogeneous or heterogeneous freezing: homogeneous freezing is when pure water droplets freeze without the presence of a substrate; heterogeneous freezing is when a solid is immersed inside a droplet (immersion freezing), or in contact with its surface (contact freezing); the solid are termed ice nuclei (IN). The presence of IN allows freezing to occur at higher temperatures than homogeneous freezing. While both mechanisms may be in operation, in practice one tends to dominate over the other. If IN are present in low concentrations, then water vapour may be depleted, inhibiting homogeneous freezing, which may reduce the ice crystal concentrations compared with what might have been expected for homogeneous freezing. Conversely, if IN are present at high concentrations, they may increase ice crystal concentrations (Kärcher et al, 2007). Hendricks et al (2005) attempted to model these processes in a global model and found that in both cases of aviation either increasing or decreasing ice crystal concentrations were possible, depending upon whether homogeneous or heterogeneous freezing was assumed to dominate.

Recently, Penner et al (2008) have presented a modelling study, using two different physically based parameterizations of ice nucleation to calculate ice crystal number concentration (Liu and Penner, 2005, Kärcher et al, 2006), which represent the competition between homogeneous and heterogeneous freezing processes. The net RF from the addition of aircraft soot was found to range between –160mW m^{-2} and –20mW m^{-2} (Penner et al, 2008). The different responses arose from the two parameterizations used and also whether the model was operated in a three-size distribution mode, or a 'mass mode' that calculated mass concentrations and then number concentrations were assumed from a size distribution, giving rise to four combinations of model versions. Only one model version gave an overall positive global mean RF. However, for the two figures demonstrated by the Kärcher et al (2006) parameterization (three-mode and mass), while both showed negative global mean and northern hemisphere RFs, positive forcing was also found in the northern hemisphere between 30°N and 60°N, possibly indicating heterogeneous freezing processes dominating in the main air traffic corridors.

Clearly, the potential effect of aviation soot on cirrus cloud needs further work in terms of the physical effect and the overall RF response from both measurements and modelling perspectives.

Overall RF and climate response from aviation

Using the information compiled from the preceding subsections, we may now arrive at an overall picture of aviation impacts. As outlined, the conventional way in which this is done is to use RF. Such an overall assessment was probably first compiled by the IPCC (1999) for a base year of 1992, and updated by Sausen et al (2005) for 2000 (see Figure 2.6). The overall RF for 2000 was approximately the same as that estimated by the IPCC (1999) for 1992 despite traffic increases. The main reason for this was the reduction in the linear contrail RF. The linear contrail RF changed largely because of assumptions over the optical depth of contrails (Sausen et al, 2005). Moreover, the O_3 and CH_4 RFs did not change linearly with increases in fuel. This is probably because the CTMs/CCMs used for the TRADEOFF research project were more refined than those used in the IPCC (1999) report, in particular the horizontal and vertical resolutions were improved, such that the models became less numerically diffusive; although this explanation was not rigorously tested.

The IPCC (2007) reassessed all background anthropogenic RFs and estimated the RF for 2005 to be 1.6W m^{-2} (range 0.6–2.4W m^{-2}) (Forster et al, 2007a). In doing so, aviation RFs were reconsidered since the IPCC's base year was 2005; however, at that time, aviation RFs from Sausen et al (2005) were considered probably to be within 10 per cent of the 2000 value. In the event, this proved not to be the case, as might be guessed from the aviation growth rates for the period 2000–2005 referred to earlier in this chapter, and the RF for 2005 aviation has been recalculated by Lee et al (2008) and was found to be 14 per cent greater (excluding AIC).

Assuming the values for aviation RF presented by IPCC AR4 WGI (IPCC, 2007; Forster et al, 2007a), WGIII (in conjunction with WGI) assessed the potential contribution to overall RF to account for approximately 3 per cent of the total anthropogenic RF (range 2–8 per cent). This 90 per cent confidence range is skewed towards lower percentages and does not account for uncertainty in the aviation forcings. Work is currently under way to perform a more comprehensive uncertainty assessment that also accounts for the uncertainties in the aviation RFs.

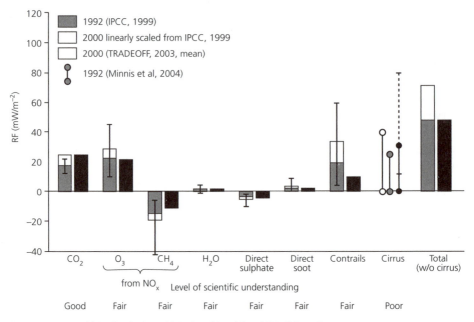

Source: Sausen et al (2005), Minnis et al (2004) and Stordal et al (2005) for AIC

Figure 2.6 *Aviation RFs for the various components for the year 2000 (dark grey bars), mW m⁻². Also shown are the IPCC (1999) values for 1992 (light grey bars) and the values that would have been implied with a simple linear scaling of RFs by fuel (open boxes superimposing light grey bars)*

An alternative way of looking at aviation's climate impacts is to approximate the temperature response induced by individual forcings via a simplified analytical climate response model (e.g. Lim et al, 2007). This is somewhat closer to a tangible physical effect than RF. In addition, by calculating temperature response, one can account from departures to the proportionality in equation [1] by utilizing the efficacies of different non-CO_2 RFs. This is illustrated in Figure 2.7, in which the temperature response for 2000 RFs (using Sausen et al, 2005 RFs) is shown with and without accounting for efficacies for UTLS O_3 RF, CH_4, H_2O and contrail RFs taken from Ponater et al (2006). The climate response model is tuned to the fourth-generation atmospheric general circulation model (ECHAM4) and coupled ocean general circulation model (OPYC3) (Roeckner et al, 1999). Such calculations are of more relevance to 'effects' but introduce additional uncertainties owing to the differences in temperature response of various climate models.

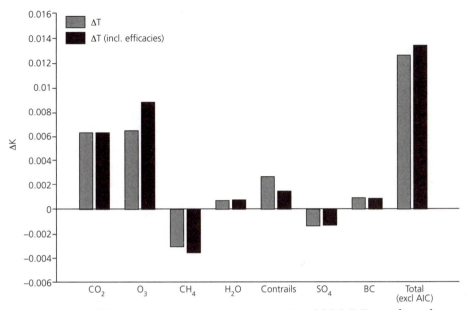

Figure 2.7 *Temperature response to aviation 2000 RFs with and without efficacies for O_3, CH_4, H_2O and contrails, in K*

Mitigation: Technological and policy options and the complication of the atmosphere

Technological and policy options for mitigation of aviation's impacts on climate change are dealt with in other chapters of this book and the reader is directed to those chapters for an overview. However, from a science perspective, it is important to point out some of the limitations to mitigation that the atmosphere imposes, which are not universally understood from the standpoint of engineering, air traffic management or policy communities.

In terms of technology, this may be divided between the engine/airframe, the fuel and aircraft operations. For policy measures, while this may not at first be seen to be an atmospheric science issue, the complication of how the atmosphere responds and how science quantifies impacts necessitates some interaction between the science and technology/policy communities in terms of quantifying mitigation prospects.

Technology

In terms of the engine/airframe, and what can be done from an engineering point of view to mitigate against aviation's climate impacts, this largely comes down to the combustion/propulsion system in terms of atmospheric science questions, other than small incremental improvements from aerodynamics to fuel burn rate and more radical new airframe configurations such as the blended wing body.

There is broad understanding that currently both NO_x and CO_2 emissions are causing climate impacts through their effect on RF. In terms of emissions reductions, the critical questions for the engineering community are 'by how much?' and 'to what extent for each?' Such questions are asked since there is a potential technological trade-off between CO_2 and NO_x reductions. The reduction of fuel usage, and hence CO_2, is part of the engineering community's ongoing requirement to reduce operating costs for airlines and this is the primary motivation for such developments. The reduction of NO_x emissions is entirely for environmental purposes and principally to comply with ICAO's certification requirements, the original purpose of which was to reduce local air quality impacts around airports.

In developing engines that have better fuel consumption characteristics, the tendency has been towards the development of high bypass-ratio turbofan engines (which have also helped with noise reductions). However, this has led to higher pressures and temperatures at the combustor inlet – conditions that favour NO_x formation – such that extra effort has had to be focused on combustor development in order not to increase NO_x emissions. Potentially, there is a point at which NO_x emissions reductions could be at the expense of CO_2 (although it is not clear that this has happened yet), hence the question of 'which pollutant and by how much?' The answer to this has generally been along the lines of 'both' but any clear weighting of one over the other has not been forthcoming from the science community.

The reason for the difficulty of stressing the reduction of one pollutant over the other is that they have different lifetimes. The lifetime of CO_2, as has been mentioned, is long, while the lifetime of O_3 (from NO_x emissions) is of the order months in the LS. Moreover, there is the further complication of the magnitude of ambient CH_4 concentration reductions to NO_x emissions. Such questions also broach the complex area of science metrics for policy purposes, as essentially the same questions are being asked.

There are two ways of looking at the atmospheric response: one is from the standpoint of 'now' and looking backwards to see how one got to 'now' – this in essence is the nature of the RF metric as it assumes some time-dependent development; the other standpoint is forward-looking and asks the question 'what happens in the future as a result of an additional unit of emissions?'

Unfortunately, these are not straightforward questions and the outcome is entirely dependent upon the way in which such calculations are made and the metric chosen. So, for the forward-looking question, one might use a GWP but, for the short-lived species such as NO_x, a number of issues have to be addressed such as: is the 100-year time horizon (as in Kyoto) appropriate? Should a pulse or sustained GWP be used? Are the responses spatially dependent as well as temporally? This is a complex topic beyond the scope of this chapter and a detailed discussion would be a chapter in itself, but some of the complications are dealt with by Fuglestvedt et al (2003, 2009) and Shine et al (2005, 2007). However, some clear messages are emerging in that it is relatively easy to formulate the metrics, for example a GWP or GTP (global temperature change potential), but that the choices of parameters are not entirely natural science issues. Also, the latest work of Fuglestvedt et al (2009) reveals that in formulating GWPs or GTPs for NO_x, the results from CTM/CCMs in this mode of operation are more disparate than had hitherto been revealed by the rather more straightforward scenario-type calculations that are more often performed with such models. This implies that more work on the CTM/CCMs is required in order to resolve the discrepancies in the results, which even extend to a change in overall signs of forcing from additional aviation emissions (Stevenson et al, 2004).

In terms of the fuel used and mitigation possibilities, the discussion is largely over so-called alternative fuels. This topic then basically breaks down into kerosene substitutes in terms of biofuels and future alternative fuels such as LH_2. Biofuels are dealt with elsewhere in this book and the issues are largely to do with feasibility of production but there are also ethical (Wardle, 2003; Lovett, 2007) and GHG-balance issues (Crutzen et al, 2008) for some agroproduction methods, as well as technological difficulties associated with usage in gas turbine engines (Daggett et al, 2008).

In terms of future alternative fuels, LH_2 is the fuel that has been most investigated. There are system, technological and atmospheric issues all involved for LH_2. The technological issue is that LH_2 requires different airframe structures/configurations because of LH_2's lower energy density (per unit volume) than kerosene, and that uptake of such an airframe by airlines would depend not only on availability of such aircraft but on the widespread availability of the fuel (a system issue). Similarly, at a system level, it would be necessary to demonstrate that the production of the LH_2 fuel was in favour of overall CO_2 emissions reductions, since energy is required to make the fuel. The atmospheric issues related to the adoption of LH_2-powered aircraft have been examined by Ponater et al (2006). Overall, Ponater et al (2006) find a favourable outcome with the introduction of an LH_2-powered fleet of aircraft, with RF reductions arising from CO_2, NO_x emissions and contrails under the caveat that the overall CO_2 emission (including fuel production) is reduced but that some uncertainties remain over AIC.

Air traffic management

Mitigation in terms of air traffic management (ATM) is usually discussed in terms of contrail reduction, although ATM also has a role to play in terms of CO_2 reductions though improved operational efficiency, for example point-to-point operation, continuous descent approach, and improved route structures/flight altitudes. Such system efficiencies should, of course, be striven for but do not represent a substantial contribution to ongoing emissions mitigation, since improvements of 6–12 per cent are discussed as a possibility (IPCC, 1999), but in any such system improvements, the last few percentage points will come at high cost, and at current growth rates, this represents around four years' growth (using longer-term emissions growth rates). Thus, while non-negligible and clearly beneficial, improvements in ATM do not represent a means of ongoing emissions reductions, once the system is optimized.

It has been recognized for some time that contrails are a function of the atmosphere for the current subsonic fleet, with technology (propulsion efficiency) changes being a second-order influence that tends to increase contrails (Schumann, 2000). Thus, in order to reduce contrails for the current subsonic fleet, it would be necessary to avoid those regions of the atmosphere which have the propensity to cause contrails (cold, ice-supersaturated).

There are two associated questions with contrail avoidance: first, does avoidance of such contrail-causing regions make a difference? Second, if so, is it worth it? This latter question addresses the state of knowledge and also climate trade-offs, which will become apparent.

Contrail avoidance has been discussed by a number of researchers (Schumann, 1996; Sausen et al, 1998; Williams et al, 2002; Fichter et al, 2005; Mannstein et al, 2005; Rädel and Shine, 2008) and recently reviewed by Gierens et al (2008), to which the reader is directed for a comprehensive overview. Reduction of cruise altitudes, which offers more options since increases in cruise altitude are less feasible, will tend to both increase and decrease contrails, depending on latitude. This latitudinal dependency (see Figure 2.5) is associated with the height of the tropopause and thus temperature and ice-supersaturation. For the overall current-day fleet, reduction in cruise altitude offers a means of reducing contrails and their RF in an approximately linear manner, as shown by the parametric study of Fichter et al (2005). However, as pointed out by Mannstein et al (2005), blanket reductions in cruise altitudes would not be necessary (and indeed could be potentially counterproductive because CO_2 emissions would be increased, as shown by Fichter et al, 2005), since areas of ice-supersaturation are non-homogeneous and occur in relatively thin layers such that 'tactical avoidance' would be sufficient to reduce contrails. The study by Mannstein et al (2005) showed that in their field of study, contrail-forming layers of the atmosphere averaged 510m in depth (with a standard deviation of 600m). However, because of the restricted spatial analysis of Mannstein et al (2005) no rules can be inferred from their study. Cirrus cloud layers in mid-latitudes can often be 1–2km thick, such that much larger altitudinal deviations by aircraft may be necessary than suggested by Mannstein et al (2005). Clearly, there is a need for better basic atmospheric data to take such tactical avoidance further and generalizations are still rather premature.

An additional strategy for limiting the warming effect of contrails may also be effected by avoidance of night flights since contrails are a balance of short-wave and long-wave radiation. Night-time contrails warm, exclusively, so avoiding such flights has been suggested (Meerkötter et al, 1999; Myhre and Stordal, 2001; Stuber et al, 2006), although this would present substantial operational difficulties and constraints for airlines.

Other strategies have been suggested, including changing fuel properties and engine architecture (Gierens, 2007; Haglind, 2008). Gierens (2007) concluded that changing fuel properties by a hypothetical fuel additive that reduced the hygroscopic nature of emitted particles did not represent a realistic prospect, and the changes in engine architecture suggested by Haglind (2008) would require substantial changes in engine design, equivalent to a 1.5K change in threshold temperature, or approximately a change of one flight level.

The second question posed above was if contrails could be reduced, would it be worth it? Quite simply, it is impossible to state whether such tactical avoidances of contrails would be worthwhile. The costs involved require a contrail forecasting system and it is unclear whether numerical weather prediction models can provide sufficiently reliable data of ice-supersaturation at the required high-resolution scales, as this is a notoriously difficult parameter to simulate. Moreover, a contrail prediction system would need to be integrated into both the flight planning regime and the actual real-time management of flights, which would represent a significant infrastructural and implementation cost. Additionally, there is a question over the overall effect on fuel consumption. If fuel consumption were to be increased overall, even by small amounts, there is the potential complexity once again of increasing long-term CO_2 impacts at the expense of short-term impacts such as contrails. Lastly, the state of knowledge over actual radiative impacts of contrails and AIC is still too uncertain to conclude whether the costs of such a contrail-avoidance flight planning system would be justified.

Policy options

Policy options range from market-based instruments (e.g. emissions trading) to regulation and are not discussed here in any detail. The main atmospheric science inputs to such options are once again related to choices of climate metrics. Here, it is simply noted that there is not yet a consensus metric for such policies suitable for aviation although there is consensus that RF and its derivatives that involve historical estimations are unsuitable (Wit et al, 2005; Forster et al, 2006, 2007b). Forward-looking metrics such as GWPs and GTPs are the most suitable, but issues over time horizons, formulation and input data (from CTM/CCMs for the coupled NO_x–O_3–CH_4 system) remain an issue.

Conclusions

Aviation activity has increased six-fold in terms of ASK (eight-fold in terms of RPK) over the period 1970–2005 with an increase in CO_2 emissions by a factor of 2.6 over the same period. Long-term growth rates over the last 20 years average approximately 5 per cent per year in RPK. The fleet of aircraft is expected to double over the period 2006–2026. The annual CO_2 emission rate from civil aviation is 2–2.5 per cent of total global CO_2 emissions and aviation CO_2 emissions have increased by about 2 per cent per year over the last 15 years. Despite some dramatic external factors which have temporarily slowed or reversed the growth rate of aviation, the industry has proven to be remarkably resilient to these events with consistent recovery to long-term growth rates. Fuel price increases have also had little effect over the period 2003–2006 but it remains to be seen how more recent changes will affect long-term viability of the industry. Nonetheless, aviation emissions are projected to increase into the middle of the 21st century by factors of three to four over current emission rates.

Because of the strong growth rate of aviation and its resultant CO_2 emissions, coupled with the fact that its climate effect is greater than that from its CO_2 emissions only, aviation effects on the atmosphere are of policy concern in combating climate change and are the subject of scientific research. Aviation exerts effects on radiative forcing of climate through its emissions of CO_2, NO_x, particles and water vapour, and affects cloudiness of the Earth's upper atmosphere through contrails and aircraft-induced cirrus. The effects of contrails and aircraft-induced cirrus remain scientific challenges with large uncertainties remaining. Some studies using long-term satellite data (ISCCP data) show weak but significant increases in cirrus cloud coverage over some heavily trafficked areas. However, recent work has cast doubt upon the usefulness of long-term satellite data from the ISCCP data set. Newly researched effects of aviation particles seeding new cirrus clouds in the absence of contrails and contrail-cirrus show that depending upon the prevalent physical processes, cirrus cloud ice particles can be either increased or decreased, and the subsequent radiative effect is of uncertain sign and magnitude. The effects of aviation NO_x on O_3 and CH_4 are clearer, although much remains to be done on improving the modelling at global and regional scales. Investigations of the climate effect of aviation NO_x emissions on O_3 and CH_4 indicate that a stronger temperature response occurs as a result of O_3 formed at aircraft cruise altitudes and when the northern hemisphere (where aviation dominates) is forced alone (compared with a control experiment where the atmosphere was forced evenly across the hemispheres by O_3). These factors considered together imply that NO_x emissions from aircraft remain an issue for climate change.

Mitigation of aviation emissions is increasingly discussed but there are complex technological and atmospheric trade-offs to be considered, which also impinge on choices and decisions relating to potential policy instruments. Core to this issue is how to balance the long-term effects from CO_2 against shorter-term effects such as those from O_3, contrails and aviation-induced cirrus that have equal or greater radiative magnitude than CO_2. Particular focus has been given to the potential for reducing contrail radiative forcing by modifying flight altitudes. However, it is not clear that this is advantageous, since an increase in fuel usage is generally implied (and thus the short-term versus long-term forcing issue arises), nor is it clear that we have sufficient knowledge and predictive capability of the atmosphere to justify implementing a contrail avoidance system for air traffic. Similarly, technological trade-offs between NO_x and CO_2 emissions need to be considered from an atmospheric science standpoint and the models that provide the input data to comparative metrics still provide large variations in results.

Acknowledgements

The author gratefully acknowledges funding from various research activities that have allowed him to be active in this field, in particular: the UK Department for Transport (DfT); the UK Department for Environment, Food and Rural Affairs (DEFRA); and the European Commission (projects 'Quantify', 'ATTICA' and 'ECATS'). Dr Ling Lim and Dr Ruben Rodriguez de Leon of MMU are thanked for providing material for Figure 2.5. Dr Dave Fahey of NOAA is thanked for redrafting Figure 2.2.

References

Airbus (2007) *Global Market Forecast 2006–2026,* France: Airbus

Anderson, B. E., Chen, G. and Blake, D. R. (2006) 'Hydrocarbon emissions from a modern commercial airliner', *Atmospheric Environment* 40: 3601–3612

Appleman, H. (1953) 'The formation of exhaust condensation trails by jet aircraft', *Bulletin of the American Meteorological Society* 34: 14–20

Arnold, F., Kiendler, A., Wiedemer, V., Aberle, S. and Stilp, T. (2000) 'Chemi-ion concentration measurements in jet engine exhaust at the ground: Implications for ion chemistry and aerosol formation in the wake of a jet aircraft', *Geophysical Research Letters* 27: 1723–1726

Baughcum, S. L., Henderson, S. C., Tritz, T. G. and Pickett, D. C. (1996) *Scheduled Civil Aircraft Emission Inventories for 1992: Database Development and Analysis,* NASA CR4700, NASA, Hampton, VA, US: Langley Research Center

Baughcum, S. L., Sutkus Jr, D. J. and Henderson, S. C. (1998) *Year 2015 Aircraft Emission Scenario for Scheduled Air Traffic,* NASA-CR-1998–207638, National Aeronautics and Space Administration, Hampton, VA, US: Langley Research Center

Berghof, R., Schmitt, A., Eyers, C., Haag, K., Middel, J., Hepting, M., Grübler, A. and Hancox, R. (2005) *CONSAVE 2050,* Final Technical Report, Köln, Germany: DLR

Bowman, C. T. (1992) 'Control of combustion-generated nitrogen oxide emissions: Technology driven by regulation', *Twenty-Fourth Symposium (International) on Combustion,* Pittsburgh: The Combustion Institute, pp859–878

Brasseur, G. (ed) (2008) 'A report on the way forward based on the research gaps and priorities', *Aviation Climate Change Research Initiative* (ACCRI), Sponsored by the Environmental Working Group of the US NextGen Joint Planning and Development Office, available at www.faa.gov/about/office_org/headquarters_offices/aep/aviation_climate/, accessed August 2008

Brewer, A. (1999) *The Stratospheric Circulation: A Personal History,* available at www.aero.jussieu.fr/~sparc/News15/15_Norton.html, accessed August 2008

Brunner, D., Staehelin, J., Rogers, H. L., Kohler, M. O., Pyle, J. A., Hauglustaine, D., Jourdain, L., Berntsen, T. K. , Gauss, M., Isaksen, I. S. A., Meijer, E., van Velthoven, P., Pitari, G., Mancini, E., Grewe, V. and Sausen, R. (2003) 'An evaluation of the performance of chemistry transport models by comparison with research aircraft observations. Part 1: Concepts and overall model performance', *Atmospheric Chemistry and Physics* 3: 1609–1631

Brunner, D., Staehelin, J., Rogers, H. L., Kohler, M. O., Pyle, J. A., Hauglustaine, D., Jourdain, L., Berntsen, T. K. , Gauss, M., Isaksen, I. S. A., Meijer, E., van Velthoven, P., Pitari, G., Mancini, E., Grewe, V. and Sausen, R. (2005) 'An evaluation of the performance of chemistry transport models – Part 2: Detailed comparison with two selected campaigns', *Atmospheric Chemistry and Physics* 5: 107–129

Crutzen, P. J. (1972) 'SSTs: A threat to the earth's ozone shield', *Ambio* 1: 41–51

Crutzen, P. J., Mosier, A. R., Smith, K. A. and Winiwarter, W. (2008) 'N_2O release from agro-biofuel production negates global warming reduction by replacing fossil fuels', *Atmospheric Chemistry and Physics* 8: 389–395

Daggett, D., Hendricks, R. C., Walther, R. and Corporan, E. (2008) *Alternate Fuels for Use in Commercial Aircraft,* NASA/TM—2008-214833, ISABE-2007-1196, available at www.boeing.com/commercial/environment/pdf/alt_fuels.pdf

Derwent, R. G. (1982) 'Two-dimensional model studies of the impact of aircraft exhaust emissions on tropospheric ozone', *Atmospheric Environment* 16: 1997–2007

DuBois, D. and Paynter, G. C. (2006) '"Fuel Flow Method2" for estimating aircraft emissions', *SAE Transactions* 115(1): 1–14

Eleftheratos, K., Zerefos, C. S., Zanis, P., Balis, D. S., Tselioudis, G., Gierens, K. and Sausen, R. (2007) 'A study on natural and manmade global interannual fluctuations of cirrus cloud cover for the period 1984–2004', *Atmospheric Chemistry and Physics* 7: 2631–2642

Evan, A. T., Heidinger, A. K. and Vimont, D. J. (2007) 'Arguments against a physical long-term trend in global ISCCP cloud amounts', *Geophysical Research Letters* 34

Eyers, C. J., Addleton, D., Atkinson, K., Broomhead, M. J., Christou, R., Elliff, T., Falk, R., Gee, I., Lee, D. S., Marizy, C., Michot, S., Middel, J., Newton, P., Norman, P., Plohr, M., Raper, D. and Stanciou, N. (2005) *AERO2k Global Aviation Emissions Inventories for 2002 and 2025,* QINETIQ/04/01113, Farnborough, Hants, UK: QinetiQ

Eyring, V., Harris, N. R. P., Rex, M., Shepherd, T. G., Fahey, D. W., Amanatidis, G. T., Austin, J., Chipperfield, M. P., Dameris, M., Forster, P. M. De F., Gettelman, A., Graf, H. F., Nagashima, T., Newman, P. A., Pawson, S., Prather, M. J., Pyle, J. A., Salawitch, R. J., Santer, B. D. and Waugh, D. W. (2005) 'A strategy for process-oriented validation of coupled chemistry-climate models', *Bulletin of American Meteorological Society* 86: 1117–1133

FESG (1998) *Report 4. Report of the Forecasting and Economic Analysis Sub-Group (FESG): Long-Range Scenarios,* Canberra, Australia: International Civil Aviation Organization Committee on Aviation Environmental Protection, Steering Group Meeting, January

Fichter, C., Marquart, S., Sausen, R. and Lee, D. S. (2005) 'The impact of cruise altitude on contrails and related radiative forcing', *Meteorologische Zeitschrift* 14(4): 563–572

Forster, P. M. and Shine, K. (1997) 'Radiative forcing and temperature trends from stratospheric ozone changes', *Journal of Geophysical Research* 106: 10841–10855

Forster, P. M., Shine, K. P. and Stuber, N. (2006) 'It is premature to include non-CO_2 effects of aviation in emission trading schemes', *Atmospheric Environment* 40: 1117–1121

Forster, P. M., Ramaswamy, V., Artaxo, P., Berntsen, T., Betts, R., Fahey, D. W., Haywood, J., Lean, J., Lowe, D. C., Myhre, G., Nganga, J., Prinn, R., Raga, G., Schulz, M. and Van Dorland, R. (2007a) 'Changes in atmospheric constituents and in radiative forcing', in *IPCC Climate Change,* Fourth Assessment Report of Working Group I of the Intergovernmental Panel on Climate Change, Cambridge, UK: Cambridge University Press

Forster, P. M., Shine, K. P. and Stuber, N. (2007b) Corrigendum to 'It is premature to include non-CO_2 effects of aviation in emission trading schemes', *Atmospheric Environment* 40: 1117–1121

Fortuin, J. P. F, van Dorland, R., Wauben, W. M. F., and Kelder, H. (1995) 'Greenhouse effects of aircraft emissions as calculated by a radiative transfer model', *Annales Geophysicae* 13: 413–418

Friedl, R. R., Baughcum, S. L., Anderson, B., Hallett, J., Liou, K.-N., Rasch, P., Rind, D., Sassen, K., Singh, H., Williams, L. and Wuebbles, D. (1997) 'Atmospheric effects of subsonic aircraft: Interim assessment of the advanced subsonic assessment program', *NASA Reference Publication* 1400, Washington DC, US

Fuglestvedt, J. S, Berntsen, T. K., Godal, O., Sausen, R., Shine, K. P. and Skodvin, T. (2003) 'Metrics of climate change: assessing radiative forcing and emissions indices', *Climatic Change* 58: 267–331

Fuglestvedt, J. S., Shine, K. P., Cook, J., Berntsen, T., Lee, D. S., Stenke, A., Skeie, R. B., Velders, G. and Waitz, I. A. (2009) 'Assessment of transport impacts on climate and ozone: metrics', *Atmospheric Environment* (submitted)

Gardner, R. M., Adams, J. K., Cook, T., Larson, L. G., Falk, R. S., Fleuti, E., Förtsch, W., Lecht, M., Lee, D. S., Leech, M. V., Lister, D. H., Massé, B., Morris, K., Newton, P. J., Owen, A., Parker, E., Schmitt, A., ten Have, H. and Vandenberghe, C. (1998) *ANCAT/EC2 Aircraft Emissions Inventories for 1991/1992 and 2015: Final Report,* Produced by the ECAC/ANCAT and EC Working Group, European Civil Aviation Conference

Gauss, M., Isaksen, I. S. A., Lee, D. S. and Søvde, O. A. (2006) 'Impact of aircraft NO_x emissions on the atmosphere – tradeoffs to reduce the impact', *Atmospheric Chemistry and Physics* 6: 1529–1548

Gierens, K. (2007) 'Are fuel additives a viable contrail mitigation option?', *Atmospheric Environment* 41: 4548–4552

Gierens, K., Lim, L. and Eleftheratos, K. (2008) 'A review of various strategies for contrail avoidance', *The Open Atmospheric Science Journal* 2: 1–7

Grewe, V., Stenke, A., Ponater, M., Sausen, R., Pitari, G., Iachetti, D., Rogers, H., Dessens, O., Pyle, J., Isaksen, I. S. A., Gulstad, L., Søvde, O. A., Marizy, C. and Pascuillo E. (2007) 'Climate impact of supersonic air traffic: An approach to optimize a potential future supersonic fleet – results from the EU-project SCENIC', *Atmospheric Chemistry and Physics* 7: 5129–5145

Haglind, F. (2008) 'Potential of lowering the contrail formation of aircraft exhausts by engine re-design', *Aerospace Science and Technology* 12: 490–497

Hansen, J., Sato, M. and Ruedy, R. (1997) 'Radiative forcing and climate response', *Journal of Geophysical Research* 102: 6831–6864

Hansen, J., Sato, M., Ruedy, R., Nazarenko, L., Lacis, A., Schmidt, G. A., Russell, G., Aleinov, I. and Bauer, M. (2005) 'Efficacy of climate forcings', *Journal of Geophysical Research* 110

Hasselmann, K., Hasselmann, S., Giering, R., Ocana, V. and von Storch, H. (1997) 'Sensitivity study of optimal CO_2 emission paths using a simplified Structural Integrated Assessment Model (SIAM)', *Climatic Change* 37: 345–386

Hendricks, J., Lippert, E., Petry, H. and Ebel, A. (2000) 'Implications of subsonic aircraft NO_x emissions for the chemistry of the lowermost stratosphere: Model studies on the role of bromine', *Journal of Geophysical Research* 105: 6745–6759

Hendricks, J., Kärcher, B., Dopelheuer, A., Feichter, J., Lohmann, U. and Baumgardner, D. (2004) 'Simulating the global atmospheric black carbon cycle: A revisit to the contribution of aircraft emissions', *Atmospheric Chemistry and Physics* 4: 2521–2541

Hendricks, J., Kärcher, B., Lohmann, U. and Ponater, M. (2005) 'Do aircraft black carbon emissions affect cirrus clouds on the global scale?', *Geophysical Research Letters* 32

Hidalgo, H. and Crutzen, P. J. (1977) 'The tropospheric and stratospheric composition perturbed by NO_x emissions of high-altitude aircraft', *Journal of Geophysical Research* 82: 5833–5866

IEA (2006) *Oil Information 2006,* Paris: International Energy Agency, Table 9

IPCC (1999) *Aviation and the Global Atmosphere,* Penner, J. E., Lister, D. H., Griggs, D. J., Dokken, D. J. and McFarland, M. (eds), Cambridge University Press: Intergovernmental Panel on Climate Change

IPCC (2000) *Emission Scenarios. A Special Report of Working Group III of the Intergovernmental Panel on Climate Change,* Cambridge, UK: Cambridge University Press

IPCC (2006) *2006 IPCC Guidelines for National Greenhouse Gas Inventories,* Eggleston, S., Buendia, L., Miwa, K., Ngara, T and Tanabe, K. (eds), Hyama, Japan: Intergovernmental Panel on Climate Change, Institute for Global Environmental Strategies (IGES)

IPCC (2007) *Climate Change 2007, The Physical Science Basis,* Contribution of Working Group I to the Fourth Assessment Report of the Intergovernmental Panel on Climate Change, Solomon, S., Qin, D., Manning, M., Chen, Z., Marquis, M., Averyt, K. B., Tignor, M. and Miller, H. L. (eds), Cambridge, UK: Cambridge University Press

Isaksen, I. S. A. (ed) (2003) *Aircraft Emissions: Contributions of Various Climate Compounds to Changes in Composition and Radiative Forcing – Tradeoff to Reduce Atmospheric Impact (TRADEOFF),* Final report to the Commission of European Communities, European Commission DG XII, Brussels

Johnston, H. S. (1971) 'Reduction of stratospheric ozone by nitrogen oxide catalysts from supersonic transport exhaust', *Science* 173: 517–522

Joshi, M., Shine, K. P., Ponater, M., Stuber, N., Sausen, R. and Li, L. (2003) 'A comparison of climate response to different radiative forcings in three general circulation models: Towards an improved metric of climate change', *Climate Dynamics* 20: 843–854

Kahn-Ribeiro, S., Kobayashi, S., Beuthe, M., Gasca, J., Greene, D., Lee, D. S., Muromachi, Y., Newton, P. J., Plotkin, S., Wit, R. C. N. and Zhou, P. J. (2007) 'Transportation and its infrastructure', in IPCC *Mitigation of Climate Change* Fourth Assessment Report Working Group III, Intergovernmental Panel on Climate Change, Cambridge, UK: Cambridge University Press

Kärcher, B., Busen, R., Petzold, A., Schröder, F. P., Schumann, U. and Jensen, E. J. (1998) 'Physicochemistry of aircraft-generated liquid aerosols, soot, and ice particles. 2: Comparison with observations and sensitivity studies', *Journal of Geophysical Research* 103: 17129–17147

Kärcher, B., Hendricks, J. and Lohmann, U. (2006) 'Physically based parameterization of cirrus cloud formation for use in global atmospheric models', *Journal of Geophysical Research* 111

Kärcher, B., Möhler, O., Demott, P. J., Pechtl, S. and Yu, F. (2007) 'Insights into the role of soot aerosols in cirrus cloud formation', *Atmospheric Chemistry and Physics* 7: 4203–4227

Kiendler, A., Aberle, S. and Arnold, F. (2000) 'Positive ion chemistry in the exhaust plumes of an aircraft jet engine and a burner: Investigations with a quadrupole ion trap mass spectrometer', *Atmospheric Environment* 34: 4787–4793

Kim, B. Y., Fleming, G. G., Lee, J. J., Waitz, I. A., Clarke, J.-P., Balasubramanian, S., Malwitz, A., Klima, K., Locke, M., Holsclaw, C. A., Maurice, L. Q. and Gupta, M. L. (2007) 'System for assessing Aviation's Global Emissions (SAGE), Part 1: model description and inventory results', *Transportation Research Part D* 12: 325–346

Kjellström, E., Feichter, J., Sausen, R. and Hein, R. (1999) 'The contribution of aircraft emissions to the atmospheric sulfur budget', *Atmospheric Environment* 33: 3455–3465

Kraabol, A. G., Konopka, P., Stordal, F. and Schlager, H. (2000) 'Modelling chemistry in aircraft plumes. 1: Comparison with observations and evaluation of a layered approach', *Atmospheric Environment* 24: 3939–3950

Kraabol, A. G., Bemsten, T. K., Sundet, J. K. and Stordal, F. (2002) 'Impacts of NO_x emissions from subsonic aircraft in a global three-dimensional chemistry transport model including plume processes', *Journal of Geophysical Research* 107, D22

Kristensson, A., Gayet, J.-F., Ström, J. and Auriol, F. (2000) 'In situ observations of a reduction in effective crystal diameter in cirrus clouds near flight corridors', *Geophysical Research Letters* 27: 681–684

Lacis, A. A., Wuebbles, D. J. and Logan, J. A. (1990) 'Radiative forcing of climate by changes in the vertical distribution of ozone', *Journal of Geophysical Research* 95(D7): 9971–9981

Lee, D. S., Fahey, D. W., Forster, P. M., Newton, P. J., Wit, R. C. N., Lim, L. L., Owen, B. and Sausen, R. (2008) 'Aviation and global climate change in the 21st century', *Atmospheric Environment* (submitted)

Lee, D. S., Pitari, G., Grewe, V., Gierens, K., Penner, J. E., Petzold, A., Prather, M., Schumann, U., Bais, A., Berntsen, T., Iachetti, D., Lim, L. L. and Sausen, R. (2009) 'Scientific assessment of the impacts of aviation on climate change and ozone depletion', *Atmospheric Environment* (submitted)

Lim, L. L., Lee, D. S., Sausen, R. and Ponater, M. (2007) 'Quantifying the effects of aviation on radiative forcing and temperature with a climate response model', in Sausen, R., Lee, D. S. and Fichter, C. (eds) *Transport, Atmosphere and Climate*, proceedings of an international conference, Oxford, 26–29 June 2006, European Commission Air Pollution Report

Liu, X. and Penner, J. E. (2005) 'Ice nucleation parameterization for a global model', *Meteorologische Zeitschrift*, 14: 499–514

Lovett, J. C. (2007) 'Biofuels and ecology', *African Journal of Ecology* 45: 117–119

Lucas, D. D. and Akimoto, H. (2007) 'Contributions of anthropogenic and natural sources of SO_2, H_2SO_4(g) and nanoparticle formation', *Atmospheric Physics and Chemistry Discussions* 7: 7679–7721

Mannstein, H., Spichtinger, P. and Gierens, K. (2005) 'A note on how to avoid contrail cirrus', *Transportation Research Part D* 10: 421–426

Marland, G., Boden, T. A. and Andres, R. J. (2007) 'Global, regional, and national CO_2 emissions', in Carbon Dioxide Information Analysis Center's *Trends: A Compendium of Data on Global Change*, US Department of Energy, Oak Ridge, TN, US: Oak Ridge National Laboratory, available at http://cdiac.ornl.gov/trends/emis/tre_glob.htm, accessed August 2008

Marquart, S., Ponater, M., Mager, F. and Sausen, R. (2003) 'Future development of contrail cover, optical depth and radiative forcing: Impacts of increasing air traffic and climate change', *Journal of Climate* 2: 890–904

Meerkötter, R., Schumann, U., Doelling, D. R., Minnis, P., Nakajima, T. and Tsushima, Y. (1999) 'Radiative forcing by contrails', *Annales Geophysicae* 17: 1080–1094

Minnis, P., Schumann, U., Doelling, D. R., Gierens, K. M. and Fahey, D. W. (1999) 'Global distribution of contrail radiative forcing', *Geophysical Research Letters* 26: 1853–1856

Minnis, P., Ayers, J. K., Palikonda, R., Doelling, D. R., Schumann, U. and Gierens, K. (2001) 'Changes in cirrus cloudiness and their relationship to contrails', *Proceedings American Meteorology Society* 11(9): 239–242

Minnis, P., Ayers, J. K., Palikonda, R. and Phan, D. (2004) 'Contrails, cirrus trends, and climate', *Journal of Climate* 17: 1671–1685

Myhre, G. and Stordal, F. (2001) 'On the tradeoff of the solar and thermal infrared radiative impact of contrails', *Geophysical Research Letters* 28: 3119–3122

Owen, B. and Lee, D. S. (2006) *Allocation of International Aviation Emissions from Scheduled Air Traffic – Future Cases, 2005 to 2050*, Centre for Air Transport and the Environment, Manchester Metropolitan University, CATE-2006-3(C)-3, UK

Penner, J. E., Chen, Y., Wang, M. and Liu, X. (2008) 'Possible influence of anthropogenic aerosols on cirrus clouds and anthropogenic forcing', *Atmospheric Chemistry and Physics Discussions* 8: 13903–13942

Petzold, A., Ström, J., Ohlsson, S. and Schröder, F. P. (1998) 'Elemental composition and morphology of ice-crystal residual particles in cirrus clouds and contrails', *Atmospheric Research* 49: 21–34

Petzold, A., Döpelheuer, A., Brock, C. A. and Schröder, F. (1999) 'In situ observation and model calculations of black carbon emission by aircraft at cruise altitude', *Journal of Geophysical Research* 104: 22171–22181

Petzold, A., Stein, C., Nyeki, S., Gysel, M., Weingartner, E., Baltensperger, U., Giebl, H., Hitzenberger, R., Döpelheuer, A., Vrchoticky, S., Puxbaum, H., Johnson, M., Hurley, C. D., Marsh, R. and Wilson, C. W. (2003) 'Properties of jet engine combustion particles during the PartEmis experiment: Microphysics and Chemistry', *Geophysical Research Letters* 30(13): 1719

Ponater, M., Brinkop, S., Sausen, R. and Schumann, U. (1996) 'Simulating the global atmospheric response to aircraft water vapour emissions and contrails: A first approach using a GCM', *Annales Geophysicae* 14: 941–960

Ponater, M., Marquart, S. and Sausen, R. (2002) 'Contrails in a comprehensive global climate model: Parameterization and radiative forcing results', *Journal of Geophysical Research* 107

Ponater, M., Pechtl, S., Sausen, R., Schumann, U. and Hüttig, G. (2006) 'Potential of the cryoplane technology to reduce aircraft climate impact: A state-of-the-art assessment', *Atmospheric Environment* 40: 6928–6944

Rädel, G. and Shine, K. (2008) 'Radiative forcing by persistent contrails and its dependence on cruise altitudes', *Journal of Geophysical Research* 113

Ramaswamy, V., Boucher, O., Haigh, J., Hauglustaine, D., Haywood, J., Myhre, G., Nakajima, T., Shi, G. Y. and Solomon, S. (2001) 'Radiative forcing of climate change', in Houghton, J. T. (eds) *Climate Change 2001: The Scientific Basis*, contribution of Working Group I to the Third Assessment Report of the Intergovernmental Panel on Climate Change, Cambridge, UK: Cambridge University Press

Rind, D., Lonergan, P. and Shah, K. (1996) 'Climatic effect of water vapour release in the upper troposphere', *Journal of Geophysical Research* 101: 29,395–29,405

Roeckner, E., Bengtsson, L., Feichter, J., Lelieveld, J. and Rodhe, H. (1999) 'Transient climate change simulations with a coupled atmosphere-ocean GCM including the tropospheric sulfur cycle', *Journal of Climate* 12: 3004–3032

Rossow, W. B. and Schiffer, R. A. (1999) 'Advances in understanding clouds from ISCCP', *Bulletin of the American Meteorological Society* 80: 2261–2287

Sausen, R. and Schumann, U. (2000) 'Estimates of the climate response to aircraft CO_2 and NO_x emissions scenarios', *Climatic Change* 44: 27–58

Sausen, R., Gierens, K., Ponater, M. and Schumann, U. (1998) 'A diagnostic study of the global distribution of contrails part I: Present day climate', *Theoretical and Applied Climatology* 61: 127–151

Sausen, R., Isaksen, I., Grewe, V., Hauglustaine, D., Lee, D. S., Myhre, G., Köhler, M. O., Pitari, G., Schumann, U., Stordal, F. and Zerefos, C. (2005) 'Aviation radiative forcing in 2000: An update of IPCC (1999)', *Meteorologische Zeitschrift* 14: 555–561

Schmidt, E. (1941) 'Die Entstehung von Eisnebel aus den Auspuffgasen von Flugmotoren', *Schriften der Deutschen Akademie der Luftfahrtforschung* 44: 1–15

Schröder, F., Kärcher, B., Petzold, A., Baumann, R., Busen, R., Hoell, C. and Schumann, U. (1998) 'Ultrafine aerosol particles in aircraft plumes: In situ observations', *Geophysical Research Letters* 25: 2789–2792

Schumann, U. (ed) (1990) *Air Traffic and the Environment,* Lecture Notes in Engineering, 60, Berlin: Springer

Schumann, U. (1995) *The Impact of NO$_x$ Emissions from Aircraft Upon the Atmosphere at Flight Altitudes 8–15 km* (AERONOX), Commission of the European Communities, Brussels

Schumann, U. (1996) 'On conditions for contrail formation from aircraft exhausts', *Meteorologische Zeitschrift* 5: 4–23

Schumann, U. (2000) 'Influence of propulsion efficiency on contrail formation', *Aerospace Science and Technology* 4: 391–401

Schumann, U. (2002) 'Contrail cirrus', in Lynch, D. K., Sassen, K., O'C. Starr, D. and Stephens, G. (eds) *Cirrus,* Oxford, UK: Oxford University Press

Schumann, U. (2005) 'Formation, properties and climatic effects of contrails', *Comptes Rendus Physique* 6: 549–565

Schumann, U., Busen, B. and Plohr, M. (2000) 'Experimental test of the influence of propulsion efficiency on contrail formation', *Journal of Aircraft* 37: 1083–1087

Schumann, U., Arnold, F., Busen, R., Curtius, J., Kärcher, B., Kiendler, A., Petzold, A., Schlager, H., Schroder, F. and Wohlfrom, K. H. (2002) 'Influence of fuel sulfur on the composition of aircraft exhaust plumes: The experiments SULFUR 1–7', *Journal of Geophysical Research* 107: 1–28

Shine, K. P., Berntsen, T. K., Fuglestvedt, J. S. and Sausen, R. (2005) 'Scientific issues in the design of metrics for inclusion of oxides of nitrogen in global climate agreements', *Proceedings of the National Academy of Sciences of the United States of America* 102: 15768–15773

Shine, K. P., Berntsen, T. K., Fuglestvedt, J. S., Bieltvedt Skeie, R. and Stuber, N. (2007) 'Comparing the climate effect of emissions of short- and long-lived climate agents', *Philosophical Transactions of the Royal Society* A, 365: 1903–1914

Singh, H. B., Salas, L., Herlth, D., Kolyer, R., Czech, E., Avery, M., Crawford, J. H., Pierce, R. B., Sachse, G. W., Blake, D. R., Cohen, R. C., Bertram, T. H., Perring, A., Wooldridge, P. J., Dibb, J., Huey, G., Hudman, R. C., Turquety, S., Emmons, L. K., Flocke, F., Tang, Y., Carmichael, G. R. and Horowitz, L. W. (2007) 'Reactive nitrogen distribution and partitioning in the North American troposphere and lowermost stratosphere', *Journal of Geophysical Research* 112

Slemr, F., Giehl, H., Slemr, J., Busen, R., Haschberger, P. and Schulte, P. (1998) 'In-flight measurements of aircraft nonmethane hydrocarbon emission indices', *Geophysical Research Letters* 25: 321–324

SMIC (1971) *Inadvertent Climate Modification,* Report of the Study of Man's Impact on Climate, Cambridge, MA, US: MIT Press

Stevenson, D., Doherty, R. M, Sanderson, M. G., Collins, W. J., Johnson, C. E. and Derwent, R. G. (2004) 'Radiative forcing from aircraft NO$_x$ emissions: Mechanisms and seasonal dependence', *Journal of Geophysical Research* 109: 1–13

Stordal, F., Myhre, G., Stordal, E. J. G., Rossow, W. B., Lee, D. S., Arlander, D. W. and Svendby, T. (2005) 'Is there a trend in cirrus cloud cover due to aircraft traffic?',

Atmospheric Chemistry and Physics 5: 2155–2162

Ström, J. and Ohlsson, S. (1998) 'In situ measurements of enhanced crystal number densities in cirrus clouds caused by aircraft exhaust', *Journal of Geophysical Research* 103: 11355–11361

Stubenrauch, C. J. and Schumann, U. (2005) 'Impact of air traffic on cirrus coverage', *Geophysical Research Letters* 32

Stuber, N. and Forster, P. (2007) 'The impact of diurnal variations of air traffic on contrail radiative forcing', *Atmospheric Chemistry and Physics* 7: 3153–3162

Stuber, N., Ponater, M. and Sausen, R. (2005) 'Why radiative forcing might fail as a predictor of climate change', *Climate Dynamics* 24: 497–510

Stuber, N., Forster, P., Rädel, G. and Shine, K. (2006) 'The importance of the diurnal cycle of air traffic for contrail radiative forcing', *Nature* 441: 864–867

Sutkus, D. J., Baughcum, S. L. and DuBois, D. P. (2001) *Scheduled Civil Aircraft Emission Inventories for 1999: Database Development and Analysis*, National Aeronautics and Space Administration, Glenn Research Centre, NASA CR-2001/211216

Uppala, S. M. and 45 co-authors (2005) 'The ERA-40 re-analysis', *Quarterly Journal of the Royal Meteorological Society* 131: 2961–3012

Wardle, D. A. (2003) 'Global sale of green air travel supported using biodiesel', *Renewable and Sustainable Energy Reviews* 7, 1–64

Wayne, R. P. (2000) *Chemistry of Atmospheres*, 3rd edn, Oxford, UK: Oxford University Press

Wennberg, P. O., Hanisco, T. F., Jaeglé, L., Jacob, D. J., Hintsa, E. J., Lanzendorf, E. J., Anderson, J. G., Gao, R. S., Keim, E. R., Donnelly, S., Del Negro, L., Fahey, D. W., McKeen, S. A., Salawitch, R. J., Webster, C. R., May, R. D., Herman, R., Proffitt, M. H., Margitan, J. J., Atlas, E., McElroy, C. T., Wilson, J. C., Brock, C. and Bui, P. (1998) 'Hydrogen radicals, nitrogen radicals and the production of ozone in the upper troposphere', *Science* 279: 49–53

Wiesen, P., Kleffmann, J., Kortenbach, R. and Becker, K. H. (1994) 'Nitrous oxide and methane emissions from aero engines', *Geophysical Research Letters* 21: 2027–2030

Wild, O. (2007) 'Modelling the global tropospheric ozone budget: Exploring the variability in current models', *Atmospheric Chemistry and Physics* 7: 2643–2660

Williams, V., Noland, R. B. and Toumi, R. (2002) 'Reducing the climate change impacts of aviation by restricting cruise altitudes', *Transportation Research Part D* 7: 451–464

Wit, R. C. N., Boon, B. H., Velzen, A. van, Cames, M., Deuber, O. and Lee, D. S. (2005) *Giving Wings to Emission Trading, Inclusion of Aviation under the European Emission Trading System (ETS): Design and Impacts*, Delft, The Netherlands: CE

Wohlfrom, K.-H., Eichkorn, S., Arnold, F. and Schulte, P. (2000) 'Massive positive and negative ions in the wake of a jet aircraft: Detection by a novel aircraft-based large ion mass spectrometer (LIOMAS)', *Geophysical Research Letters* 27: 3853–3856

Wylie, D., Jackson, D. L., Menzel, W. P. and Bates, J. J. (2005) 'Trends in global cloud cover in two decades of HIRS observations', *Journal of Climate* 18: 3021–3031

Yu, F. and Turco, R. P. (1999) 'Evolution of aircraft-generated volatile particles in the far wake regime: potential contributions to ambient CCN/IN', *Geophysical Research Letters* 26: 1703–1706

Zerefos, C., Eleftheratos, K., Balis, D. S., Zanis, P., Tselioudis, G. and Meleti, C. (2003) 'Evidence of impact of aviation on cirrus cloud formation', *Atmospheric Chemistry and Physics* 3: 1633–1644

Zerefos, C., Eleftheratos, K., Zanis, P., Balis, D. S. and Tselioudis, G. (2007) 'Search for man-made cirrus contrails over Southeast Asia', *Terrestrial, Atmospheric and Oceanic Sciences* 18: 459–474

Zhang, Y. (2008) 'Online coupled meteorology and chemistry models: History, current status, and outlook', *Atmospheric Chemistry and Physics* 8: 2895–2932

3
Calculating Emissions and Radiative Forcing

Paul Peeters and Victoria Williams

The quest for metrics and data

Airlines, governments, NGOs, scientists, consultants and aviation organizations involved in the discussion on climate change try to provide estimates of the impact of aviation on the climate. The metrics used describe CO_2 emissions or use a proxy for the net climate impact. However, there is large variability, linked to problems with defining average flight conditions and to difficulties describing how emissions and their atmospheric impacts evolve.

Estimates for the average CO_2 emissions per passenger km (pkm), referred to as the emission factor, vary widely. For long haul, values can be as low as 0.080–0.100kgCO_2/pkm (Roos et al, 1997) or up to 0.140kgCO_2/pkm (Dubois and Ceron, 2006). Peeters et al (2005b) give 0.111kgCO_2/pkm, which is consistent with the value of 0.110kgCO_2/pkm proposed by the United Nations Environment Programme (UNEP) (Thomas et al, 2000). For short haul, emission factors are higher. UNEP proposes 0.180kgCO_2/pkm (Thomas et al, 2000). Åkerman (2005) uses 0.140kgCO_2/pkm for both short and long haul, based on Penner et al (1999). For very short routes (less than 500km), Brand (2005) suggests 0.240kgCO_2/pkm.

One problem with selecting an appropriate value for the emission factor is that the specific conditions for which each estimate is valid are seldom given. Occupancy rate, distance flown, take-off weight (including freight for example), atmospheric conditions and operational conditions such as speed and cruise altitude all have significant impacts on energy use and emissions. A further problem with measuring the impact of aviation on the climate system is the need for relevant metrics to describe the combined effect of emissions and impacts with different lifetimes and operating over different spatial scales. One approach is to use radiative forcing (a measure of the change in the balance between the incoming energy from the sun and the energy radiated from the Earth).

Climatically relevant emissions cause a chain of impacts: emission change → concentration change → radiative forcing change → temperature change → climate impacts → societal and ecosystem impacts → economic impacts (see Shine et al, 2005b, p282). Societal, ecosystem and economic impacts will be the ultimate focus of most climate policy studies, but the number and magnitude of uncertainties increases sharply when moving up the chain. Metrics for emissions can be relatively simple and more reliable, but will lack the detail often required by policy makers. This paper seeks to present a method for calculating the contribution of tourism air transport to climate change, focusing on the radiative forcing index as a compromise between reliability and usefulness.

Civil aviation contributed 1.8 per cent of all CO_2 emissions from burning fossil fuels in 2002 (based on Nakicenovic et al, 2000; Eyers et al, 2004). The future share depends both on the air transport scenario and the world emissions scenario. For a medium aviation growth scenario, the share in 2025 will be between 1.7 per cent and 3.5 per cent (based on comparing AERO2K aviation emissions estimates with the highest and lowest SRES scenarios (Nakicenovic et al, 2000)). When low and high aviation growth scenarios are considered, the aviation share of total annual CO_2 emissions is expected to be between 1.6 per cent and 8.7 per cent (Prather and Sausen, 1999, p195). However, all these numbers exclude the impact of non-carbon emissions. These non-carbon impacts are short lived – most less than ~10 days (Forster et al, 2006). They also have different impacts depending on where they are released (Shine et al, 2005a), which makes it difficult to assess non-carbon impacts with the politically accepted global warming potential (GWP) concept. GWP is defined as the 'time integrated commitment to climate forcing from the instantaneous release of 1kg of a trace gas expressed relative to that of 1kg of the reference gas CO_2' (Fuglestvedt et al, 2001). Typically, a time horizon of 100 years is used. In a recent paper Graßl and Brockhagen (2007) compare the metrics radiative forcing index (RFI), emission weighting factor (EWF) and GWP and find RFI to be more meaningful for aviation policy analysis because it reflects the true impact on the climate in a specified year and given assumptions for the emissions path to this year. Often the terms 'equivalence factor' or 'CO_2-equivalent' are used to indicate and include the contribution of greenhouse gas emissions other than CO_2 to radiative forcing. The problems associated with such an approach will be discussed in the following paragraphs.

Carbon dioxide emissions

Two methods exist to estimate CO_2 emission factors for aviation. A bottom-up (aggregate) approach assesses the properties of individual aircraft and aggregates these based on the composition of the global fleet and the movements undertaken by each aircraft. In contrast, a top-down (compound) approach starts with the total fuel consumption for aviation based on worldwide statistics (e.g. by the International Energy Agency, IEA), transforms this into emissions and divides the result by global transport performance measured in passenger kilometres (pkm) or seat kilometres (skm) (e.g. data provided by IATA and ICAO). For the global level both methods can be applied, although the aggregate method requires huge amounts of data on individual flights. The compound method can also be very useful to assess the fuel or emission efficiency of an airline by simply dividing the airlines' overall fuel consumption by its overall transport performance.

Emission inventories

Henderson and Wickrama (1999) use three-dimensional (latitude, longitude and altitude) global inventories of civil and military aircraft fuel burned. The inventory is prepared by Boeing and published in NASA reports and by DLR (see references in Henderson and Wickrama, 1999; see also the Dutch AERO model, Pulles et al, 2002). These emission inventories are based on summing the emissions from individual flights, using the following general approach: transport demand + technology → transport supply → flights per aircraft type → flight paths per aircraft type → fuel consumption and emissions. In the AERO model, emissions are calculated from a standard flight profile (including aircraft movements on the ground), using ten generic aircraft types to represent a range of seat capacities, capabilities and aircraft ages.

The Boeing/NASA method is based on flight timetable data from the Official Airline Guide (OAG) database. The database is corrected for double counted flights and unplanned changes from the schedule. The database is then used with 'airplane performance data files' to calculate fuel burn and emissions. These files provide:

> *time, fuel burned and distance flown as a function of aircraft gross weight and altitude for climb out, climb, and descent conditions. They also provide tables of fuel mileage (nautical miles per pound of fuel burned) as a function of gross weight, cruise Mach number and altitude for cruise conditions'* (Baughcum et al, 1996b, p11)

The number of aircraft types directly described in the performance data files has increased from 27 in 1976. By 1992, 76 of the 250 aircraft in the OAG database had directly defined performance data. If performance data for the specified aircraft are unavailable, an alternative aircraft with similar operating characteristics is used (Baughcum et al, 1996b).

The emissions of CO_2 are directly related to the amount of fuel: every kg of fuel (kerosene; Jet A) used will lead to 3.155kg of CO_2 emitted to the atmosphere (Baughcum et al, 1996a).

Some accuracy issues exist: 'Total fuel consumption calculated as part of the NASA 1992 scheduled inventory was, on the average, 17 per cent below that reported ... for the ten major passenger air carriers considered' (Daggett et al, 1999, pi). The fuel efficiency attained in practice is lower than the one calculated with idealized flight cycles. Daggett et al (1999) mention wind, higher aircraft weight and aircraft aging as reasons for the differences between calculated and measured fuel consumption.

The most recent IPCC report on mitigation (IPCC, 2007) gives an overview of emission inventories, estimating total air transport CO_2 emissions to be 480Mt in 2000 and 482Mt in 2005. The report predicts these emissions will be up to 584Mt in 2010, 860Mt in 2020, 1262Mt in 2030 and 2377Mt in 2050 (Metz et al, 2007, pp334–335). These estimates are based on the FAST-A1 scenario (Metz et al, 2007, Figure 5.6) and consider only scheduled air transport. The SAGE (System for assessing Aviation's Global Emissions) project, which includes charter flights as well as scheduled services, gives an estimate of 640MtCO$_2$ for global commercial aviation in 2005 (Kim et al, 2005 [updated 2006]: Figure 20). These data include all commercial aviation (i.e. freight transport and passenger transport; Eyers et al, 2004; Kim et al, 2007; Lee et al, 2007). For an alternative estimate see Chapter 2 of this volume.

Another difficulty arises when assessing the emissions for passenger and freight transport. If aircraft are used either entirely for freight or entirely for passengers (most low-cost carrier aircraft, many short-haul jets), a distinction is easy, but as most medium- and long-haul aircraft carry both passengers and freight, emissions have to be allocated between the two. This requires a conversion factor between freight and passengers. In air transport statistics, the total work performed is often given in revenue passenger kilometres (rpkm) and revenue tonne kilometres (rtkm). Assuming between 88 and 100kg per passenger, a total in rtkm can be calculated (see Peeters et al, 2005a, Annex III). However, passenger cabins add more to the 'empty weight' of the aircraft, due to fixtures including seats, air conditioning and safety equipment. Comparing passenger and freight versions of the same aircraft type, the freight-only version has a freight capacity of 150–220kg for every seat in the high-density passenger-only version (Peeters et al, 2005a). These factors are probably lower in aircraft that combine freight and passenger capabilities so 160kg/passenger (Wit et al, 2002) might be a convenient average, though the actual value depends on whether the constraint for a specific flight is weight or volume.

For a flight carrying both passengers and freight, the emissions attributable to passengers $E_{X_{pax}}$ can now be derived from:

$$E_{X_{pax}} = E_X \frac{V_{pax}}{V_{pax} + \dfrac{1000 \times V_{fr}}{\overline{C_{W_{pax}}}}} \qquad [1]$$

where E_X is the total emissions from the flight, V_{pax} is the number of passengers, V_{fr} is the amount of freight (in tonnes) and $\overline{C_{W_{pax}}}$ is the average weight in kg per passenger (thus the mass of the passenger, baggage and fixtures such as the seat are taken into account).

Equation [1] can also be applied to more than one flight, by expressing V_{pax} and V_{fr} in terms of total activity (revenue passenger kilometres and revenue tonne kilometres). Using data for 1997–2010 (Pulles et al, 2002) and assuming a value of 160kg/passenger for $\overline{C_{W_{pax}}}$, suggests freight accounts for 19.5 per cent emissions. 80.5 per cent of emissions can be attributed to passenger trips.

Fleet or route emission

The basic method to calculate emissions uses the product of the amount of work performed (e.g. seat kilometres) and the average emissions per unit of work (the emission factor):

$$E_X = \beta_X \times V \qquad [2]$$

However, the traffic volume (V) and the emission factor β_X may be expressed using seat km or passenger km, so one value may need to be converted. For a specific flight or route, the available data may indicate only the number of passengers and the great circle distance d_{gc} between origin and destination. Using the number of passengers needs an adjustment for average seat occupancy rate (η_{sor}) to calculate the work performed in seat km. The great circle (direct) distance also requires correction factors to reflect diversions imposed by air traffic control (η_{ATC}) and the effects of wind on the flight time (η_{win}). Another distance correction may be required to account for passengers choosing interconnecting rather than direct flights (η_{det}).

Aircraft are generally most efficient at medium distances, as at short distances the energy-intensive take-off and climb sections comprise a relatively large share, while at long-haul distances the amount of fuel to be carried at take-off and climb-out requires extra energy. This impact of distance flown on emissions per km can be taken into account by a correction factor $C_{dist}(\overline{d})$ (see Table 3.1).

Table 3.1 *Relation between emission factor and distance flown*

Distance flown (km)	Distance correction factor
<500	1.86
750	1.39
1250	1.18
1750	1.09
2000–5000	1.00
>5000	1.05

Source: derived from data for medium-range, medium-size aircraft given by de Ceuster et al, 2004

Combining these adjustments, the fleet emissions for N flights can be calculated using:

$$E_X = \beta_{X\_LH_{seat}} \times \sum_{n=1}^{N} C_{dist_v}(\overline{d}_n) \times V_{seat_n}$$

$$d_n = \eta_{ATC} \times \eta_{det} \times \eta_{win} \times d_{gc_n}$$

$$V_{seat_n} = \frac{d_n \times n_{pax_n}}{\eta_{sor_n}} \qquad [3]$$

The value used for the emission factor β_X or $\beta_{X\_LH_{seat}}$ should be chosen carefully as it depends strongly on aircraft type. A flight from Amsterdam to Stockholm (1152 km) has an emission factor of 0.091kg/pkm for a Boeing 737–800, but 44 per cent higher (0.131kg/pkm) for a Boeing MD81 (SAS Group, 2004). If the aircraft types are known, these should be used, with corrections for wind and detours (see Table 3.2). If no specific emission factor is known a generalized factor can be found using the following equation:

$$E_I = E_{I_0} + \frac{C_{E_t}}{1 + \left(\dfrac{(Y - Y_{ref}) - C_1}{C_2} \right)^{\gamma}} \qquad [4]$$

Where E_I is the energy intensity (MJ/ASK) and $(Y-Y_{ref})$ the number of years between a base year Y_{ref} (i.e. the year of introduction of a new technology or the starting year of the database) and the year of introduction to the market of the specific aircraft, E_{I_0} is a theoretical minimum energy intensity and C_{E_t}, C_1, C_2 and γ are constants. See further explanation in Chapter 13. Equation [4] calculates energy intensity (EI), not an emission factor. However, these are directly proportional for CO_2 emissions (and water vapour, but not for all other emissions), so the ratio of the energy intensity to that of an aircraft with a known emission factor (Table 3.3) will also give the ratio of emission factors. The ratio will be greater than 1.0 for aircraft older than the reference aircraft type and less than 1.0 for newer aircraft.

Table 3.2 *The use of the different factors*

Parameter	When to apply
η_{ATC}	if only the number of passengers for each origin–destination pair is known
	if emission factors are based on individual trips
η_{det}	if emission factors are based on individual trips
	if only the number of passengers for each origin–destination pair is known
η_{win}	if emission factors are based on standard atmospheric conditions excluding wind effects
η_{sor}	if the passenger flows are known and not the capacity of seat kilometres supplied

The additional distance travelled due to air traffic control inefficiencies (e.g. the use of ground-based navigation points rather than direct routes) increases the distance travelled by a factor of 1.15 for short haul and 1.05 for long haul (Peeters et al, 2004). However, another issue is the way tourists use the air transport system. Tourists may make detours for at least three reasons: (1) hub-and-spoke systems encourage travellers to interchange at major airports, rather than offering direct routes between smaller destinations; (2) it may be cheaper to complete a journey in two legs with a low-cost airline than to take a direct route with a conventional carrier; and (3) large alliances compete on long-haul travel via their hubs, seeking to attract passengers by offering lower prices for the combined feeder flight and main flight. These detours can add up to 10–15 per cent to total distances travelled and even more to total fuel consumed,

Table 3.3 *Factors for calculating emissions*

Parameter	Values	Reference
η_{ATC}	Short haul (SH) 1.15	Air France-KLM, 2005
	Long haul (LH) 1.05	
η_{det}	SH/LH: <1.10[a]	DeRudder et al, 2005
η_{win}	LH: 1.05	Daggett et al, 1999
η_{sor}	LH: 0.75	Peeters et al, 2005a,
	SH: 0.70	Peeters et al, 2005b
β_X	Average for all flights worldwide, 2005: 0.097kg/skm	UNWTO-UNEP-WMO,
	Average domestic: 0.116kg/skm	2008
	Average LH: 0.090kg/skm	
$\beta_{X\_LH_{seat}}$	B737-800: 0.0581kg/skm @ 2400km/70%[b]	SAS Group, 2004[c]
	A320: 0.0567kg/skm @ 2400km/70%	
	A330-300: 0.0873–0.0655kg/skm @ 5900km/90%	
	A340-300: 0.1062–0.0797kg/skm @ 5900km/90%	

Notes:
a Recent unpublished research at the NHTV Centre for Sustainable Tourism and Transport, Breda, the Netherlands, has shown the average detour to add only 2.2 per cent for EU travel and 5.3 per cent for intercontinental CO_2 emissions, based on a survey of the Dutch population (n=545; 2211 reported journeys). As the Netherlands is a small country with an important European hub and thus a relatively large number of direct connections, these figures can be considered a minimum.
b The percentages in the last line give the load factor assumed, as this determines the flying weight and thus the fuel consumption per aircraft kilometre.
c SAS does not correct for freight on board. For long haul they state up to 25 per cent of payload will be freight. The range gives values between 25 and 0 per cent freight.

because detours split flights up into shorter flights, which are less efficient per passenger km (DeRudder et al, 2005).

Radiative Forcing

The climate effect of CO_2 emissions from aviation since 1945 can be described as a change in the balance between incoming solar radiation and outgoing terrestrial radiation (a radiative forcing) of $25.3mWm^{-2}$. Aviation also has the following non-CO_2 impacts on the climate (mWm^{-2} in 2000; Sausen et al, 2005):

- NO_x induces the forming of O_3, that has a short-lived warming effect ($21.9mWm^{-2}$);
- NO_x also induces a reduction of CH_4 thus creating a longer lived cooling effect ($-10.4mWm^{-2}$);
- Direct short-lived H_2O emissions ($2.0mWm^{-2}$);
- direct short-lived sulphate emissions ($-3.5mWm^{-2}$);
- direct short-lived soot ($2.5mWm^{-2}$);
- very short-lived contrails ($10.0mWm^{-2}$); and
- very short-lived contrail-induced cirrus (best estimate: $30mWm^{-2}$, upper limit $80mWm^{-2}$).

These impacts on radiative forcing (excluding CO_2 and cirrus) amount to $22.5mWm^{-2}$. To add CO_2 and non-CO_2 impacts, differences in their characteristics must be considered. For most non-aviation emissions, global warming potential (GWP) can be used to compare the impact of 1kg of a gas with that of 1kg of CO_2 (see Section 'GWP' below). However, this measure is less suitable for the non-CO_2 impacts of aviation as they are dependent on the altitude and location of emission (see Prather and Sausen, 1999, p199). An alternative metric, the radiative forcing index (RFI) has been proposed, which compares total radiative forcing due to aviation with that due to aviation CO_2 (Prather and Sausen, 1999, p200; see also Section 'RFI' below). Many authors within tourism/transport scenario studies incorporate the additional warming from non-CO_2 impacts using a constant factor of 2.7, often imprecisely referred to as an 'equivalence factor' (Åkerman, 2005; Gössling et al, 2005; Peeters et al, 2005b; Dubois and Ceron, 2006; Peeters et al, 2007a). RFI is also often used to compare the impacts of different transport modes. Unfortunately, the use of RFI as an indicator of future emissions is fundamentally flawed and should be avoided (Forster et al, 2006; Forster et al, 2007; Graßl and Brockhagen, 2007). This is because the RFI is based on the cumulative effect of past emissions and is dependent on background atmospheric concentrations – the value of RFI is not constant. It does not describe the future impact of an extra pulse of emissions (such as an extra flight). Therefore RFI is suitable for global policy studies taking into account the cumulative emission from 1945 to the scenario end-year, but not suitable for use as a multiplier for individual emissions (e.g.

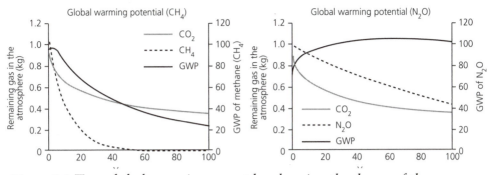

Figure 3.1 *Two global warming examples showing the decay of the gas after an impulse emission in year zero and the resulting GWP*

for carbon off-setting). For this, an adapted form of GWP would be more suitable to consider the future impacts.

GWP

The GWP is 'the time-integrated radiative forcing due to a pulse emission of a given gas, over some given time period (or horizon) relative to a pulse emission of CO_2 (Shine et al, 2005b, p281). Generally, somewhat arbitrarily, a period of 100 years is chosen. With GWP all emissions can be recalculated to 'equivalent CO_2 emissions' (CO_2-eq). Figure 3.1 gives two examples, for a relatively short-lived gas (CH_4: 12 years) and a long-lived one (N_2O: 114 years). The value of the GWP heavily depends on the time horizon chosen: the GWP of short-lived gases decreases rapidly over time, while it increases more slowly for a long-lived one. Still, for one time horizon the value is unequivocal and gives a good approximation of the impact of the emissions of a unit mass of gas as compared to a unit mass of CO_2.

This approach works only for long-lived impacts, where the gas will be well mixed and its impact will not depend on the altitude or location of emission. As the method compares the response to a unit mass of emission, it is also not applicable to contrail and cirrus cloud impacts as these cannot be quantified in that way.

RFI

RFI (radiative forcing index) is defined as the ratio between the total aviation-related radiative forcing (RF) in year n divided by the RF in the same year that is caused by the accumulated emissions of CO_2 since 1945. The value of RFI is unique for each year in the history (and the future) of aviation. Generally, definitions of RFI exclude contrail-induced cirrus due to uncertainty about the magnitude of cirrus radiative forcing. Therefore, RFI should be considered a minimum value.

Peeters et al (2007b) describe two detailed methods to determine RFI for both current and future situations. The first method is analytical and, to be

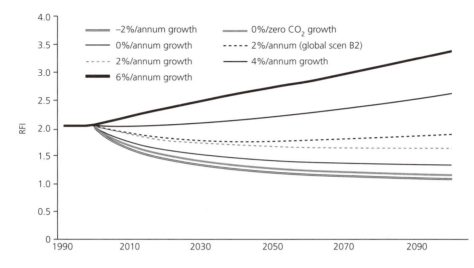

Figure 3.2 *The relations between RFI (excluding the impact of cirrus), future year, aviation emission growth rates and global emissions scenario*

solvable, had to assume constant exponential growth paths for global CO_2 concentrations, aviation CO_2 emissions, transport volume and technological progress. Figure 3.2 gives the results for this analytical approach for several aviation growth rates and two IPCC SRES global emissions scenarios. The second method is a numerical approach that avoids the mathematical problems and allows more flexibility in the design of scenarios. It has been programmed in a spreadsheet. Both methods are based on data given by Prather and Sausen (1999) and Sausen et al (2005).

Figure 3.2 shows that the aviation growth rate has a large impact on RFI, causing the impact of non-carbon radiative forcing to be greater at high aviation emission growth rates, and smaller at lower growth rates. This means that the non-CO_2 impact would decrease if growth in aviation CO_2 emissions ceased. Furthermore, global scenarios with slower growth of total CO_2 concentrations cause the RFI to reduce (see B2 and zero CO_2 growth scenarios). For 2100, the RFI value ranges from 1.1 to 3.4.

The numerical method allows for periods with different growth rates for aviation (see Bows et al, 2006, pp37–88) and varying rates for technological efficiency improvement (see Peeters and Middel, 2007). Figure 3.3 shows an example of a low global carbon emissions scenario aiming at a maximum of 550ppmv CO_2 concentration. Such a scenario was previously thought to prevent a global average temperature increase of more than 2°C – currently it seems more stringent targets need to be realized to avoid dangerous climate change (less than 475ppmv see Meinshausen et al, 2006). Several assumptions relating to aviation growth and efficiency improvements have been made, which do not necessarily fit into the global scenario. The figure shows clearly

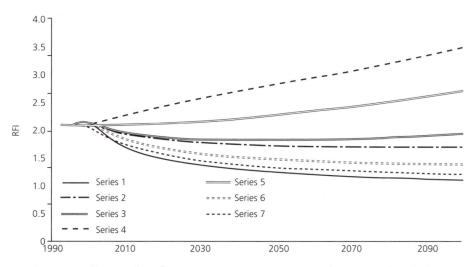

Figure 3.3 *Example of some non-constant growth rate and aviation scenarios combined with a 'sustainable' global emission scenario aiming at 550ppmv*

how RFI varies with growth rates of emissions. As also shown in Figure 3.2, a low global emissions scenario tends to reduce RFI values.

While forecasts of CO_2 emissions are intrinsically linked to fuel consumption, growth in radiative forcing is sensitive to assumptions regarding the distribution of air traffic, as contrails, O_3 and CH_4 and their impacts are dependent on local atmospheric conditions along the trajectory of the flight. Another dimension to this issue is that for the same radiative forcing, the impact on global average temperature of an ozone increase depends upon the altitude and location at which it occurs (Joshi et al, 2003).

AGWP

There is a need for a metric for aviation that is comparable to GWP: one that gives the non-CO_2 RF of a pulse emission integrated over a period of 100 years. First, many carbon compensation schemes offer to offset full impacts alongside CO_2-only. Furthermore, politicians discuss incorporating aviation in other mitigation policies, such as emissions trading, and need a comparable way to account for non-CO_2 impacts. Several authors state that the impacts of very short-lived greenhouse gases can only be accurately compared with long-lived ones using sustained emissions (see Shine et al, 2005a; Wit et al, 2005). This approach equals the RFI for a zero aviation CO_2 emissions growth within a zero growth of atmospheric CO_2 concentration global scenario (see Figure 3.2). This does not tell us much about the impact of adding one flight (or rather, within mitigation policies, removing one).

As GWP compares the integrated future radiative forcing of 1kg of the emitted gas with that of 1kg of CO_2, it is unsuitable for describing the non-

CO_2 impacts of aviation due to the dependence of impacts on the altitude of emission and on background conditions. Specifically, O_3 is very short lived and so acts locally, unlike the 'well-mixed trace gases' GWP was meant for (see Green, 2003, p336). There is also no directly analogous treatment for contrail or cirrus cloud (which cannot be quantified per kg of emission). This has been overcome by using total contrail radiative forcing and total aviation CO_2 to derive a measure of contrail radiative forcing per kg of CO_2 emission (Forster et al, 2006, 2007), termed the absolute global warming potential (AGWP). A similar approach has been used to derive an AGWP value for aircraft NO_x for which a conventional GWP cannot be defined due to the sensitivity of its impacts to altitude and background conditions. Forster et al (2006, 2007) derive an emissions weighting factor (EWF) for aviation (i.e. the total approximated global warming potential divided by the CO_2 global warming potential) of 1.2 for a 100-year timescale.

The values for EWF provided by Forster et al (2007) provide a method for comparing the impact of the emission of 1kg of CO_2 from aviation (including the associated non-CO_2 impacts) with 1kg of CO_2 emitted with no other associated impacts. These represent a lower bound, as the considerable uncertainties associated with determining the radiative forcing of contrail-induced cirrus cloud led the authors to exclude those impacts from their analysis. Here, an approximation of contrail-induced cirrus impacts is included to derive an estimated range of EWF values. Sausen et al (2005) give a best estimate of radiative forcing in 2000 from contrail-induced cirrus of $30mWm^{-2}$, with an upper bound of $80mWm^{-2}$, compared with a radiative forcing for contrail of $10mWm^{-2}$. For both contrail and contrail-cirrus, impacts are short-lived, so the value for GWP does not change with time. Scaling the contrail AGWP values (of 1.8) gives a best estimate of 5.6 and an upper limit of 14.4 for contrail-induced cirrus.

These values can be used to identify a range of values for the emissions weighting factor (Table 3.4). For the case without cirrus this results in a weighting factor of 1.2, for a 100-year timescale. Including average cirrus raises this to 1.8 and with maximum cirrus it would be 2.8. Clearly, the uncertainty associated with the radiative impact of contrail-induced cirrus has significant consequences for reporting aviation impacts and for designing effective mitigation policies. There are further uncertainties associated with NO_x impacts.

Even if these uncertainties can be resolved, these values for EWF must be used with caution, as there are several key assumptions implicit in the definition of the metric. In selecting a single value for EWF, it is assumed that there is an agreed timescale over which the impacts should be considered. Expressing NO_x and contrail-integrated radiative forcing in units per kg of CO_2 emitted also assumes a linear relationship between aviation CO_2 emissions and non-CO_2 impacts. This could distort the comparison between impacts, particularly when applied for a single flight.

Table 3.4 CO_2 *and approximate non-CO_2 AGWPs (radiative forcing integrated over time) at different time horizons for a pulse emission in 2000*

Time horizon	Absolute global warming potential ($10^{-14}W\ m^{-2}\ kgCO_2^{-1}$ year)				EWF[d] (range)
(years after 2000)	CO_2[a]	CH_4 and O_3 NET[a]	Contrail[a]	Cirrus[b] (range)[c]	
1	0.25	1.94	1.8	5.6 (0–14.4)	37.6 (16.0–73.6)
20	2.65	0.34	1.8	5.6 (0–14.4)	3.8 (1.8–7.2)
100	9.15	−0.038	1.8	5.6 (0–14.4)	1.8 (1.2–2.8)
500	29.9	−0.038	1.8	5.6 (0–14.4)	1.2 (1.1–1.5)

Notes: a Values from Forster et al (2007); the RF of contrails is constant as long as the emissions of aviation are constant.
b Derived from Sausen et al (2005); the RF of cirrus is constant as long as the emissions of aviation are constant.
c Minimum values in range correspond to zero impact from contrail-induced cirrus, maximum values correspond to the cirrus radiative forcing upper limit in Sausen et al (2005).
d Emission-weighting factor for aviation defined as the sum of AGWP values divided by the CO_2 AGWP.

When a weighting factor for current pulse emissions is needed, it is suggested to use (with caution) the values for EWF in Table 3.4, which includes average cirrus. These values (subject to agreement of an appropriate timescale; for GWP calculations a scale of 100 years is most commonly used) could be used to include all impacts for offset schemes. For policy making, the (variable) RFI should be taken for the year under investigation. This is consistent with the conclusions by Graßl and Brockhagen (2007). Further verification, particularly of the treatment of NO_x impacts, is required, as calculations of net NO_x impacts are highly sensitive to modelling assumptions (Forster et al, 2007). For the ETS (Emissions Trading Scheme) as proposed by the European Commission to start in 2012, the EWF is a simple way to include non-CO_2 impacts. A more precise way to handle the total radiative forcing for ETS is to base it on RFI and re-evaluate the actual world global value at regular times (e.g. every five years). As Figure 3.2 shows, then the ETS system will also act in a way to dampen high growth rates as RFI will increase with high emission growth.

For both EWF and RFI, the design of the metric has some significant consequences for its application. The first is that the distribution of traffic is intrinsically assumed to be fixed. If a change in traffic significantly alters the share of night-time or winter flights or focuses demand increases in particular areas, the equivalence factor should be re-evaluated. Similarly, the value should be reviewed if specific measures are introduced to address an individual impact, such as cruise altitude changes to reduce NO_x impacts or contrail formation.

In addition to problems in determining its value, there is also a fundamental problem in applying any multiplier to emissions for aviation. To do so implies that the non-CO_2 impacts can be countered, for example by making increased carbon reductions in another area. However, this ignores the different spatial and temporal patterns. The use of a constant multiplier value can also distort policy goals by focusing attention on CO_2 emission reductions, which could increase NO_x emissions or contrail formation.

Methodological recommendations

This paper discussed methods to calculate air transport emissions and impacts on radiative forcing and several metrics to incorporate non-carbon impacts in policy analysis or in carbon offset schemes. The methods for CO_2 principally give the same results. The choice depends on data availability and the purpose of the calculations. For the non-carbon impacts, more difficulties arise. Due to the very different nature of the main non-carbon impacts (contrails and NO_x emission-induced methane and ozone concentrations) several theoretical and practical problems were encountered. The commonly accepted metric of global warming potential (GWP) cannot be used as the basic assumptions – medium- to long-lived trace gases that are well-dispersed over the atmosphere – do not sufficiently apply to the aviation non-carbon climate impacts. Therefore several alternative metrics have been proposed (see section on radiative forcing above). These alternatives (RFI and EWF derived from AGWP) both have advantages and disadvantages. Therefore the most appropriate metric should be chosen based on the purpose of the calculation (see Table 3.5).

Based on Table 3.5 it can be concluded that no method covers all purposes. For practical reasons of data availability, the compound method can as a second choice also be used for calculations regarding emissions trading. Using RFI for carbon offset schemes is not recommended as it looks at the history, not the future of additional emissions. The proposed AGWP-derived emissions weighting factor for a 100-year time horizon, calculated as a factor 1.8 is more suitable.

Current plans for inclusion of aviation in the EU Emissions Trading Scheme do not yet provide for non-carbon emissions, but 'by the end of 2008, the Commission will put forward a proposal to address the nitrogen oxide emissions from aviation after a thorough impact assessment' (European Commission, 2006, p7). Implementation of the planned trading scheme could thus increase radiative forcing if the aviation industry becomes a net purchaser of permits from other sectors (Lee and Sausen, 2000). This stresses the importance of incorporating non-carbon impacts. Though its volatile character complicates the use of RFI, it still is well defined at a given year, now or in the future. Therefore using RFI with a regular (e.g. every five year) update of the value could be seen as the best solution. Using an AGWP-derived emissions weighting factor is more complicated as it requires the arbitrary choice of a time horizon, which has a very large impact on the result.

Table 3.5 *Overview of methods to find emissions of CO_2 and impacts on radiative forcing of non-carbon greenhouse gases*

Method	Short description	Most appropriate use for tourism studies (note reference)
Emissions of CO_2		
Compound	The compound method directly couples traffic volumes to emissions by using generalized emission factors (EF) and transport demand. Relatively low level of data demand.	a, b, c
Aggregate	The aggregate method finds total emissions by summing the emissions for all full three-dimensional flight paths required for the transport volume under consideration.	d, e
Non-carbon impacts on radiative forcing and climate change		
RFI	Is the ratio of all aviation-related RF in a specific year to that of RF caused by cumulated aviation CO_2 emissions since 1940.	a, b, d
AGWP	Absolute global warming potential is the integrated RF impact of a pulse emission expressed for a certain period (usually 100 years). Impacts are scaled to the mass of aviation CO_2 emitted. From this, an emissions weighting factor (EWF) is derived by dividing the sum of AGWP values by the CO_2 AGWP.	c, e

Notes:
a Determine current share of historic (cumulative) aviation's impact on climate change.
b Aviation's impact on climate change in scenario studies.
c Impact of current emissions for the future.
d Multiplication factor for emission trade systems.
e Multiplication factor for carbon offsetting schemes.

The use of radiative forcing as a measure to compare climate impacts of aviation also has implications for the identification and prioritization of mitigation policies. For example, measures to eliminate contrail and cirrus cloud formation through changes in cruise altitude or routing away from ice-supersaturated zones would force aircraft to fly less efficient trajectories and so incur a CO_2 penalty (Williams et al, 2003). Using radiative forcing to compare impacts would suggest that this policy would have significant climate benefits as contrail-induced radiative forcing would be eliminated with only a marginal increase in radiative forcing from CO_2 (a small increase in annual CO_2 emissions would have a much smaller impact on the cumulative CO_2 concentration). A full comparison would, however, also need to take into account the future climate impacts of the additional CO_2 emitted, using a metric like EWF, and the evaluation of whether a net climate benefit would be achieved would depend on the time horizon chosen for analysis.

Conclusions and research recommendations

The chapter has shown the differences between current models to calculate aviation's emissions and radiative impacts. The chapter discussed both top-down (compound) and bottom-up (aggregate) approaches to emission calculations, and sought to recommend ways to include non-carbon radiative effects in calculations of emissions. From the calculations it becomes clear that the inclusion of both carbon and non-carbon radiative forcing is important, though difficult to integrate. In the future, calculations of aviation-related emissions should be made in a consistent way to better understand the changing role of aviation in climate change and to identify suitable mitigation and compensation measures. The methods described are intended to give some standardization for calculating the impact of tourism-related air transport, both for CO_2 and non-carbon impacts.

The main conclusion of the chapter is that current metrics can be used if the caveats around them are taken into consideration and if the right metric is chosen for the right purpose as shown in Table 3.5. Further development of metrics for non-carbon impacts is still required. One cause for uncertainty is the relatively poor understanding of the impact of contrails and contrail-induced cirrus on radiative forcing and the feedback loops between climate change and the local and global occurrence of these aviation-related impacts. This requires further research and may affect the conclusions of this chapter.

Finally an interesting conclusion from the RFI evaluation is that, for aviation CO_2 emission growth scenarios of above 2 per cent per year, the total future radiative forcing of aviation will increase faster than this rate due to an increase in RFI. When growth is less than 2 per cent the reverse will happen. This means that controlled growth of aviation emissions has a more than proportional impact on reducing radiative forcing.

References

Air France-KLM (2005) *Sustainability Report 2004/05,* Roissy: Air France Secretary Generalship – Environment and Sustainable Development

Åkerman, J. (2005) 'Sustainable air transport – on track in 2050', *Transportation Research Part D* 10 (2): 111–126

Baughcum, S. L., Henderson, S. C. and Tritz, T. G. (1996a) *Scheduled Civil Aircraft Emission Inventories for 1976 and 1984: Database Development and Analysis,* NASA CR-4722 Washington DC: NASA

Baughcum, S. L., Tritz, T. G., Henderson, S. C. and Pickett, D. C. (1996b) *Scheduled Civil Aircraft Emission Inventories for 1992: Database Development and Analysis,* NASA CR-4700 Washington DC: NASA

Bows, A., Anderson, K. and Upham, P. (2006) *Contraction and Convergence: UK Carbon Emissions and the Implications for UK Air Traffic,* technical report 40: Tyndall Centre

Brand, C. (2005) *Integrated Travel Emissions Profiles,* methodology report, Oxford: Transport Studies Unit Environmental Change Institute, University of Oxford

de Ceuster, G., van Herbruggen, B., Logghe, S. and Proost, S. (2004) *TREMOVE 2.0 Model Description,* Leuven: Transport and Mobility Leuven

Daggett, D. L., Sutkus, D. J., DuBois, D. P. and Baughcum, S. L. (1999) *An Evaluation of Aircraft Emissions Inventory Methodology by Comparisons with Reported Airline Data,* CR-1999–209480, Seattle: NASA

DeRudder, B., Devriendt, L. and Witlox, F. (2005) *Flying Where You Don't Want to Go: An Empirical Analysis of Hubs in the Global Airline Network,* Ghent: Ghent University

Dubois, G. and Ceron, J.-P. (2006) 'Tourism/leisure greenhouse gas emissions forecasts for 2050: Factors for change in France', *Journal of Sustainable Tourism* 14(2): 172–191

European Commission (2006) *Proposal for a Directive of the European Parliament and of the Council Amending Directive 2003/87/EC so as to Include Aviation Activities in the Scheme for Greenhouse Gas Emission Allowance Trading within the Community,* unofficial advanced version, available at http://ec.europa.eu/environment/climat/pdf/aviation_ets_com_2006_818–21273_en.pdf, accessed 22 December 2006

Eyers, C. J., Norman, P., Middel, J., Plohr, M., Michot, S., Atkinson, K. and Christou, R. A. (2004) *AERO2K Global Aviation Emissions Inventories for 2002 and 2025,* Farnborough, UK: QinetiQ Ltd

Forster, P. M. d. F., Shine, K. P. and Stuber, N. (2006) 'It is premature to include non-CO_2 effects of aviation in emission trading schemes', *Atmospheric Environment* 40(6): 1117–1121

Forster, P. M. d. F., Shine, K. P. and Stuber, N. (2007) Corrigendum to 'It is premature to include non-CO_2 effects of aviation in emission trading schemes', *Atmospheric Environment* 41: 3941

Fuglestvedt, J. S., Berntsen, T. K., Godal, O., Sausen, R., Shine, K. P. and Skodvin, T. (2001) *Assessing Metrics of Climate Change: Current Methods and Future Possibilities,* CICERO Report 2001:04, Oslo: CICERO Center for International Climate and Environmental Research

Gössling, S., Peeters, P. M., Ceron, J.-P., Dubois, G., Patterson, T. and Richardson, R. B. (2005) 'The eco-efficiency of tourism', *Ecological Economics* 54(4): 417–434

Graßl, H. and Brockhagen, D. (2007) 'Climate forcing of aviation emissions in high altitudes and comparison of metrics', online documents at www.mpimet.mpg.de/fileadmin/download/Grassl_Brockhagen.pdf, accessed 10 November 2008, Hamburg: Max Planck Institute for Meteorology

Green, J. E. (2003) 'Greener by design', in Sausen, R., Fichter, C. and Amanatidis, G. (eds) *Proceedings of the AAC-Conference, 30 June–3 July,* Friedrichshafen: European Commision, pp334–342

Henderson, S. C. and Wickrama, U. K. (1999) 'Aircraft emissions: Current inventions and future scenarios', in Penner, J. E., Lister, D. H., Griggs, D. J., Dokken, D. J. and McFarland, M. (eds) *Aviation and the Global Atmosphere; A Special Report of IPCC Working Groups I and III,* Cambridge: Cambridge University Press, pp185–215

IPCC (2007) *Climate Change 2007. The Physical Science Basis. Contribution of Working Group I to the Fourth Assessment Report of the International Panel on Climate Change,* Cambridge: International Panel on Climate Change

Joshi, M., Shine, K. P., Ponater, M., Stuber, N., Sausen, R. and Li, L. (2003) 'A comparison of climate response to different radiative forcings in three general circulation models: Towards an improved metric of climate change', *Climate Dynamics* 20(7–8): 843–854

Kim, B. Y., Fleming, G. G., Balasubramanian, S., Malwitz, A., Lee, J. J., Waitz, I. A., Klima, K., Locke, M., Holsclaw, C. A., Morales, A., McQueen, E. and Gillette, W.

(2005) *System for Assessing Aviation's Global Emissions (SAGE), Version 1.5, Global Aviation Emissions Inventories for 2000 through 2004*. FAA-EE-2005–02, Washington DC: Federal Aviation Administration

Kim, B. Y., Fleming, G. G., Lee, J. J., Waitz, I. A., Clarke, J.-P., Balasubramanian, S., Malwitz, A., Klima, K., Locke, M., Holsclaw, C. A., Maurice, L. Q. and Gupta, M. L. (2007) 'System for assessing Aviation's Global Emissions (SAGE), Part 1: Model description and inventory results', *Transportation Research Part D* 12: 325–346

Lee, D. S. and Sausen, R. (2000) 'New directions: Assessing the real impact of CO$_2$ emissions trading by the aviation industry', *Atmospheric Environment* 34: 5337–5338

Lee, J. J., Waitz, I. A., Kim, B. Y., Fleming, G. G., Maurice, L. and Holsclaw, C. A. (2007) 'System for assessing Aviation's Global Emissions (SAGE), Part 2: Uncertainty assessment', *Transportation Research Part D* 12(6): 381–395

Meinshausen, M., Hare, B., Wigley, T. M. M., Van Vuuren, D., Den Elzen, M. G. J. and Swart, R. (2006) 'Multi-gas emissions pathways to meet climate targets', *Climatic Change* 75(1): 151–194

Metz, B., Davidson, O., Bosch, P., Dave, R. and Meyer, L. (2007) *Climate Change 2007: Mitigation of Climate Change*, contribution of Working Group III to the Fourth Assessment Report of the International Panel on Climate Change, Cambridge: International Panel on Climate Change

Nakicenovic, N. and Swart, R. (eds) (2000) *Special Report on Emission Scenarios: Summary for Policymakers*, Cambridge: Intergovernmental Panel on Climate Change

Peeters, P. M. and Middel, J. (2007) 'Historical and future development of air transport fuel efficiency', in Sausen, R., Blum, A., Lee, D. S. and Brüning, C. (eds) *Proceedings of an International Conference on Transport, Atmosphere and Climate (TAC); Oxford, United Kingdom, 26–29 June 2006*, Oberpfaffenhoven: DLR Institut für Physic der Atmosphäre, pp42–47

Peeters, P. M., van Egmond, T. and Visser, N. (2004) *European Tourism, Transport and Environment*, final version. Breda: NHTV CSTT

Peeters, P. M., Middel, J. and Hoolhorst, A. (2005a) *Fuel Efficiency of Commercial Aircraft: An Overview of Historical and Future Trends*, NLR-CR-2005–669 Amsterdam: Peeters Advies/National Aerospace Laboratory NLR

Peeters, P. M., Szimba, E. and Duijnisveld, M. (2005b) 'European tourism transport and environment', *European Transport Conference, 3–5 October*, Strasbourg: PTRC

Peeters, P., Szimba, E. and Duijnisveld, M. (2007a) 'Major environmental impacts of European tourist transport', *Journal of Transport Geography* 15: 83–93

Peeters, P., Williams, V. and Gössling, S. (2007b) 'Air transport greenhouse gas emissions', in Peeters, P. M. (ed) *Tourism and Climate Change Mitigation: Methods, Greenhouse Gas Reductions and Policies*, Breda: NHTV, pp29–50

Penner, J. E., Lister, D. H., Griggs, D. J., Dokken, D. J. and McFarland, M. (eds) (1999) *Aviation and the Global Atmosphere: A Special Report of IPCC Working Groups I and III*, Cambridge: Cambridge University Press

Prather, M. and Sausen, R. (1999) 'Potential climate change from aviation', in Penner, J. E., Lister, D. H., Griggs, D. J., Dokken, D. J. and McFarland, M. (eds) *Aviation and the Global Atmosphere: A Special Report of IPCC Working Groups I and III*, Cambridge: Cambridge University Press, pp185–215

Pulles, J. W., Baarse, G., Hancox, R., Middel, J. and van Velthoven, P. F. J. (2002) *AERO Main Report: Aviation Emissions and Evaluation of Reduction Options*, The Hague: Ministerie van Verkeer en Waterstaat

Roos, J. H. J., Bleijenberg, A. N. and Dijkstra, W. J. (1997) *Energy and Emission Profiles of Aircraft and Other Modes of Passenger Transport Over European Distances,* Delft: CE

SAS Group (2004) *Emission Calculator,* available at http://sasems.port.se/emissioncalc.cfm?sid=Calculate, accessed April 2004

Sausen, R., Isaksen, I., Grewe, V., Hauglustaine, D., Lee, D. S., Myhre, G., Köhler, M. O., Pitari, G., Schumann, U., Stordal, F. and Zerefos, C. (2005) 'Aviation radiative forcing in 2000: An update on IPCC (1999)', *Meteorologische Zeitschrift* 14(4): 555–561

Shine, K. P., Berntsen, T. K., Fuglestvedt, J. S. and Sausen, R. (2005a) 'Scientific issues in the design of metrics for inclusion of oxides of nitrogen in global climate agreements', *PNAS* 102(44): 15768–15773

Shine, K. P., Fuglestvedt, J. S., Hailemariam, K. and Stuber, N. (2005b) 'Alternatives to the global warming potential for comparing climate impacts of emissions of greenhouse gases', *Climate Change* 68: 281–302

Thomas, C., Tennant, T. and Rolls, J. (2000) *The GHG Indicator: UNEP Guidelines for Calculating Greenhouse Gas Emissions for Businesses and Non-Commercial Organizations,* Geneva: UNEP

UNWTO-UNEP-WMO (2008) *Climate Change and Tourism: Responding to Global Challenges,* Madrid: UNWTO

Williams, V., Noland, R. B. and Toumi, R. (2003) 'Air transport cruise altitude restrictions to minimize contrail formation', *Climate Policy* 3(3): 207–219

Wit, R. C. N., Dings, J., Mendes de Leon, P., Thwaites, L., Peeters, P. M., Greenwood, D. and Doganis, R. (2002) *Economic Incentives to Mitigate Greenhouse Gas Emissions from Air Transport in Europe,* 02.4733.10, Delft: CE

Wit, R. C. N., Boon, B. H., van Velzen, A., Cames, M., Deuber, O. and Lee, D. S. (2005) *Giving Wings to Emission Trading. Inclusion of Aviation under the European Emission Trading System (ETS): Design and Impacts,* 05.7789.20, Delft: CE

4

Aviation in a Low-carbon EU

Alice Bows, Kevin Anderson and Anthony Footitt

Introduction

European nations agree they must tackle escalating greenhouse gas emissions arising from energy consumption. In response, several nations have set emission reduction targets for future years. In theory at least, these targets are chosen to correspond with stabilizing emissions at levels that are likely to avoid 'dangerous climate change'.

Global climate targets

Although there is no scientific consensus for what is considered to be 'dangerous' in relation to climate change, it is broadly accepted by the policy community that this relates to global mean surface temperatures not exceeding 2°C above pre-industrial levels. The European Commission acknowledges that stabilizing long-term greenhouse gas concentrations at 450ppmv CO_2-eq provides around a 50 per cent chance of ensuring global mean temperatures do not exceed the 2°C threshold. In response it has set an aspirational target of reducing greenhouse gas emissions by 60–80 per cent by 2050 from 1990 levels by apportioning global emissions to EU nations.

By selecting a target related to global CO_2-eq concentrations, governments have, perhaps inadvertently, accepted such targets must include all greenhouse gas-producing sectors. Furthermore, aiming for a target percentage reduction by a particular date neglects the crucial importance of cumulative emissions. By addressing these two issues, this analysis quantifies the contribution of the aviation industry to future EU climate change targets. Moreover, it assesses the implications of including aviation within the EU's Emissions Trading Scheme. Results indicate that unless the scheme adopts both an early baseline year and an overall cap designed to be in keeping with a 450ppmv cumulative emission pathway, the impact on aviation emissions will be minimal.

Aviation trends

The air transport market within the EU25 nations continues to grow rapidly. Passenger numbers in 2005 exceeded 700 million, with an 8.5 per cent increase on the previous year's figures (De La Fuente Layos, 2007),[1] illustrating a resurgence of the industry following the events of 11 September 2001. Inseparable from this resurgence are the continued high levels of growth in CO_2 emissions from the industry. Although nations are not required under Kyoto to publish their CO_2 emissions from international aviation within their national inventories, this data is submitted alongside as a memo. Combining the CO_2 emissions from domestic and international aviation provides an estimated CO_2 emission growth rate for the EU's aviation industry of 7 per cent between 2003 and 2004 and 6 per cent between 2004 and 2005. These rates of growth are similar to those produced by the industry since 1993, with the exception of the period affected by the events of 11 September 2001. This rapid growth in emissions, coupled with limited opportunities for other than incremental improvements in fuel efficiency, at least in the short- to medium term, gives rise to the concern that as EU nations strive to reduce CO_2 emissions, aviation will be responsible for an increasing share of the EU's total.

EU Emissions Trading Scheme

The EU's Emissions Trading Scheme (EU ETS) began operating in 2005, with the first phase of the scheme complete by the end of 2007. The scheme initially involved some 12,000 installations covering energy activities that exceeded 20MW, as well as a number of process emission activities together amounting to around 45 per cent of the EU's CO_2 emissions. The second and expanded phase of the EU ETS began in 2008, and, in recognizing the growing issue of emissions generated by the aviation industry, the EU have proposed to include aviation within the scheme by 2012.

The proposal suggests including all departures and arrivals from EU nations with the aim of internalizing some of the costs of the environmental impact of the aviation sector. To explore the implications of aviation's inclusion within the scheme, this chapter presents a suite of aviation emission scenarios and compares them with the EU's overall carbon budget.

Carbon budgets

One of the key variables of interest to those involved in climate change mitigation and adaptation is the global mean temperature change due to the increase in atmospheric greenhouse gas concentrations. However, there is both confusion and uncertainty as to the relationship between greenhouse gases and the likely resultant temperature change. Some of this confusion stems from errors in the translation of the science into policy. For example, many UK policy documents refer to 550ppmv CO_2 'alone' being related to the 2°C threshold, when in fact the original work carried out by the UK's Royal Commission on Environmental Pollution (RCEP) linked 550ppmv CO_2 equivalent[2] (CO_2-eq) to this temperature change (RCEP, 2000). Uncertainty, on the other hand, stems from the inherent range of outputs given by climate models in assessing the impact of altering the atmospheric concentration of greenhouse gases, and the variety of model results available. The methods used in the analysis presented here are consistent with those within *'Living within a Carbon Budget'* (Bows et al, 2006b), and relate an atmospheric concentration of CO_2 alone and the 2°C temperature threshold, based on the work of Meinshausen (2006).[3]

The EU has adopted a target of global mean surface temperatures not exceeding a 2°C rise above pre-industrial levels. To achieve this, recent studies illustrate that a 450ppmv CO_2-eq stabilization level will provide a reasonable probability of not exceeding this 2°C threshold (Meinshausen, 2006). There are therefore a number of important issues to be addressed in relation to the EU's climate change target and in turn how such targets relate to the aviation industry.

The first point to be considered is the ultimate aim of the target – that is for temperatures to not exceed the 2°C threshold. This threshold is associated with atmospheric CO_2-eq levels relating to different probabilities of exceeding 2°C. This type of methodology therefore assumes that all greenhouse gas-producing sectors are included, as the atmosphere does not 'see' what is or is not accounted for. The Kyoto Protocol and the UK's climate change bill omit international aviation and shipping from their targets. For the EU, it is ambiguous as to whether or not these sectors are or are not included. If these sectors currently contribute insignificant amounts of greenhouse gases, it might be reasonable to omit them at this stage. However, the data strongly indicate that this is not the case for the aviation sector. Therefore, to institute climate policy that is both proportionate and sufficient to address the issues, there is a need to account for the emissions from international sectors that are, or may in the future represent, a significant proportion of a nation's total emissions.

Second, in considering how best to develop a carbon trajectory for a 2°C target, it is important not to become overly focused on choosing a convenient percentage reduction by a future date. It is the cumulative emissions that are more influential in reaching a desired greenhouse gas concentration than the emission pathway taken (Jones et al, 2006). This is a point that, although very significant, is often overlooked by governments. Accordingly, delaying action to mitigate emissions requires more stringent measures to avoid exceeding the 2°C threshold than is generally recognized (Bows et al, 2006b; Stern, 2006). The danger of failing to adequately account for the cumulative emissions issue in policy making is that the resulting policies will be overly focused on the longer-term issues (and hence address energy supply), when in fact it is the short to medium term (and hence energy demand) that is of crucial importance (Bows et al, 2006b: 20). Clearly, a policy that is out of balance with the

Table 4.1 *Global and EU cumulative carbon budgets*

Scenario	Global cumulative emissions[a] $GtCO_2$ (1990–2100)[b]	EU cumulative emissions $GtCO_2$
(1990–2100)		
450 Low	1431	160
450 High	2257	212

Notes: a not including forestry.
b taken from IPCC, 2007, p17.

variables which it seeks to regulate will not be an efficient policy and may fail.

A third point relates to carbon-cycle feedbacks. These feedback mechanisms have only recently, and still partially, been incorporated in climate change emission budget studies, and are shown to have a very significant effect on the carbon budgets available (IPCC, 2007, p17). Carbon budgets that include feedback mechanisms can be some 20 per cent smaller than those that omit feedbacks (Matthews, 2005).

To derive a cumulative carbon budget range for the EU, it is necessary to apportion the global cumulative CO_2 emissions to nations using a modified form of the contraction and convergence (Meyer, 2000) approach. The results are presented in Table 4.1.

This provides a cumulative carbon budget range for the EU, but it is also desirable to be able to understand the impact of this budget on the EU's pathway to a low-carbon future. This is achieved by first considering those emissions released for the years 2000–2005, incorporating current EU emission trends, and finally by constraining the pathway to remain within budget. The importance of using empirical data for the period between 2000–2005 cannot be overstated. When considering the cumulative carbon budget, nations emitting at high levels today are 'spending' their budgets very rapidly. As such, those emissions occurring between 2000 and 2005, and also for the short-term future, will have a significant impact on the range of pathways available into the longer term. For example, in the case of the '450 High' scenario in Table 4.1, the emissions represent ~14 per cent of the total budget in just 4 of the 50 years (i.e. 14 per cent spent over only 8 per cent of the timescale).

Emission pathways for the cumulative emissions for the EU from Table 4.1 are presented in Figure 4.1; the higher the cumulative target, the easier it is to manoeuvre in later years with the converse true for lower cumulative targets. Hence any policy aiming for levels at or lower than '450 Low' must both stabilize emissions urgently and maintain significant year-on-year reductions for three decades, to allow sufficient 'room for manoeuvre'.

Aviation emission scenarios

It has been widely publicized that the aviation sector's emissions are growing more rapidly than any other sector in the UK. This is also true for the EU25.

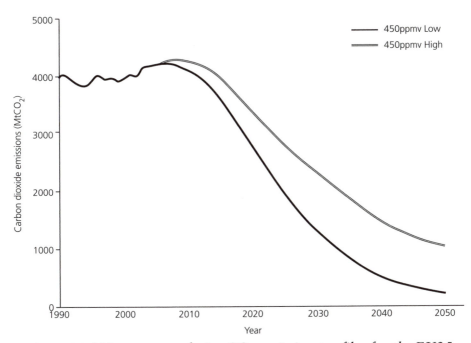

Figure 4.1 *450ppmv cumulative CO_2 emission profiles for the EU25*

Figure 4.2 presents the CO_2 emissions from the aviation sector in the EU25 from 1993 to 2005.

The emissions from international flights clearly dominate. CO_2 emissions from domestic flights have increased at an average of 2.5 per cent per year since 1990 while the corresponding figure for international flights is 4.5 per cent. However, the events of 11 September 2001 had a marked impact on the growth rate of aviation emissions, as illustrated. If the period between 1990 and 2000 is assessed, domestic aviation's annually averaged CO_2 growth was 3.2 per cent, with international air travel at 5.6 per cent.[4] From 2003 to 2004, and 2004 to 2005, the total amount of CO_2 from the EU25's aviation industries increased by 7 per cent and 6 per cent respectively.

In addition to emitting CO_2, aircraft release soot and water vapour that lead to the formation of contrails and cirrus clouds, and NO_x emissions that form ozone and deplete methane. All these emissions alter the radiative properties of the atmosphere either globally, in the case of well-mixed greenhouse gases, or at a local level in relation to contrails and cirrus clouds. However, there is much debate over the appropriate metric to account for these additional impacts. One metric that has been used to calculate the total impact on the climate of these emissions (in addition to CO_2) is radiative forcing. Radiative forcing is the sum of the globally and annually averaged impact of anthropogenic emissions on the climate in terms of watts per square metre (W m^{-2}) in relation to an assumed 0W m^{-2} in pre-industrial years (1750). For total

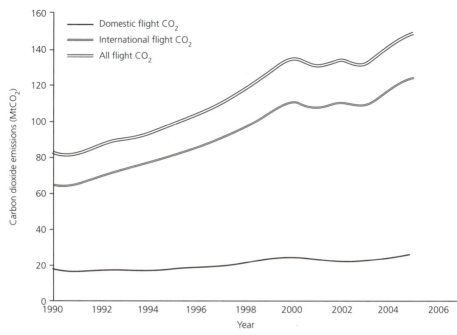

Note: The data incorporates estimates for Greece and Malta in 2005 due to an absence of data. Although not all the EU25 were in the EU from 1990, all the nations have been included in the totals from the outset.

Figure 4.2 *CO_2 emissions from the EU25's aviation sectors, from data submitted to the UNFCCC in 2007*

global anthropogenic activities – that is from all sources, the figure stands at 1.6W m^{-2} (IPCC, 2007). If this metric is applied to the aviation sector, the emissions of CO_2, NO_x and contrails amount to a total radiative forcing impact in the year 2000 of around 0.048W m^{-2} (Sausen et al, 2005).[5]

While this metric has a clear role to play in the scientific analysis of climate change, it has limitations for developing current and future mitigation policies. Radiative forcing is often used to relate the CO_2 impact to the impact from NO_x and contrails through the use of an 'uplift factor' developed initially by the IPCC (Penner et al, 1999) and since updated (Sausen et al, 2005). However, radiative forcing compares the impact of emissions from 1750 to date to illustrate the historical impact of the different sectors on the overall temperature rise. When using it to look at future impacts, this measure can lead to inappropriate policy messages if it guides policy mitigation. Furthermore, the metric could lead to unhelpful policy conclusions in certain situations. For example, if applied to shipping emissions, the policy conclusion may be to increase the sulphur emissions from ships to mitigate the warming caused by their release of CO_2 emissions. Consequently, the cumulative approach is more useful in the context of this research, given its importance in policy terms. Therefore, to be consistent with the cumulative carbon budget approach being taken here, the analysis of the aviation sector will address CO_2 alone, requiring no additional metric.

Aviation emission baselines

To include aviation within the EU ETS, the Commission propose the baseline above which the industry must buy emission allowances be placed at the 2004–2006 level. In other words, any CO_2 emitted above the 2004–2006 level will need to be purchased by the industry from the market. However, the UK Government has also explored the possibility of employing alternative baseline dates.

To illustrate the impact of the baseline date choice, three different baselines are explored here – one for 1990, one for 2000 and one for 2005. Aviation scenarios for the short-term period 2006–2012 are compared with these baselines to illustrate the levels of emissions needed to be purchased if all departing and arriving flights are included within the scheme. Following on from this, a suite of aviation scenarios from 2013 to 2050 commensurate with a world striving to live within the 450ppmv carbon budget are developed. These scenarios incorporate a range of growth rates and assumptions related to fuel efficiency and, in the longer term, the inclusion of alternative low-carbon fuels. The cost implications of these different scenarios under a range of carbon allowance prices are considered for selected exemplar flights. Finally, the aviation scenarios are compared with the overall 450ppmv carbon budget for the EU25.

To develop the scenarios, the baselines must be quantified. One important distinction to make at this stage is the difference between the CO_2 baselines for emissions submitted to the United Nations Framework Convention on Climate Change (UNFCCC), and the emissions that will be included in the EU ETS. For the UNFCCC, domestic aviation's CO_2 is submitted separately from the CO_2 from international aviation. The latter broadly approximates to 50 per cent of all flights to and from each nation within the EU to either another EU nation or an extra-EU nation. Therefore, the total domestic and international CO_2 for aviation submitted to the UNFCCC is an estimate of the CO_2 associated with all domestic flights within the EU25 and 50 per cent of international flights to and from EU nations, giving a baseline for 2005 of $150MtCO_2$: $25MtCO_2$ from domestic and $125MtCO_2$ from international. However, to incorporate aviation within the EU ETS, the Commission proposes that CO_2 emissions from *all* departures and arrivals from and to EU nations should be included. It is not appropriate to simply double the CO_2 emissions submitted to the UNFCCC to account for these additional flights, as double counting for domestic and intra-EU flights would occur. The EU ETS baseline is therefore higher than the 2005 UNFCCC baseline, standing at some $225MtCO_2$ in 2005. The method used to derive this alternative baseline uses empirical data in addition to some model data (Wit et al, 2005). The breakdown of EU aviation CO_2 emissions are presented in Table 4.2 for baselines in 1990, 2000 and 2005. For more information on the method see Anderson et al (2007, section 3.1).

Table 4.2 *CO_2 emissions from all flights that either depart or arrive in the EU*

| | Data type | Emissions (MtCO$_2$) | | |
		1990	2000	2005
UNFCCC international aviation bunker CO_2,[a]	Empirical	64.8	111.0	124.3
UNFCCC domestic aviation CO_2	Empirical	17.8	24.2	25.3
Intra EU flight CO_2 (EU to EU, not domestic)	Modelled	19.3	36.0	40.2
EU to EU ultra peripheral regions CO_2	Modelled	4.8	8.9	8.1
EU to EU overseas countries and territories CO_2	Modelled	0.5	0.9	0.9
Derived starting aviation CO_2 value	Empirical and model	122.8	200.4	224.7

Note: a 2007 submission.

Short-term

Following the baseline quantification, aviation scenario development requires quantification of the aviation CO_2 from now until the estimated commencement date of the revised scheme (2012). A number of assumptions are made leading to a range of growth rates. In addition to available passenger number and CO_2 data, factors influencing the choice of scenarios include:

- the current continued success of the low-cost air model;
- access to a network of growing regional airports;
- the low-cost model extending in modified form to medium and longer-haul routes;
- no significant economic downturn between the 2005 data and 'today' (2007); and
- high growth routes between the EU and industrializing nations.

For the years from 2006 to 2012, recent and longer-term trend data significantly influence the choice of scenarios. According to the submissions to the UNFCCC, there has been a long-term trend of increasing CO_2 emissions from EU25 nations in the order of 6 per cent per year. More recent emissions have also increased at 6 per cent per year, once allowance is made for the period affected by the events of 11 September 2001. Reinforcing this 6 per cent figure is EUROCONTROL's forecast of strong growth for 2007–2008 (EUROCONTROL, 2007). The range of scenarios considered for the period from 2006 to 2012 therefore uses 6 per cent annual emission growth as a mid-range value, with 4 per cent for the lower range and 8 per cent for the higher range. Assuming no radical step changes in the short-term, the scenarios all use a 1 per cent per year improvement in fuel efficiency across the fleet for this short-term period.

Based on these scenarios, by the end of 2011, the aviation sector's emissions range between around 284 and 355MtCO$_2$ (Figure 4.3). Of the three

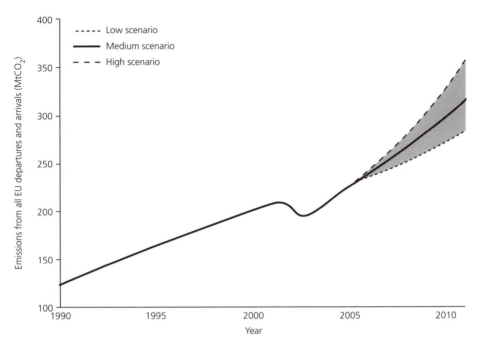

Note: This range is the same as the data submitted to the UNFCCC in 2007. The data incorporates estimates for Greece and Malta in 2005 due to an absence of available data. Although not all the EU25 were in the EU from 1990, all the nations have been included in the totals from the outset.

Figure 4.3 *Aviation CO_2 emissions for all departures and arrivals under a range of growth rates*

initial baselines of 1990, 2000 and 2005 for aviation emissions considered here (Table 4.2), Table 4.3 presents the allowances that need to be purchased in 2012.

The earlier the baseline year, the more allowances must be purchased by the industry. In fact, the aviation sector has grown so significantly since 1990 that the emissions allowances required by 2005 under the 1990 baseline are in excess of the total amount of emissions released in 1990. The range is somewhat lower for the 2005 baseline, where between 59 and 130 million allowances must be purchased by the industry. The cost to the industry will depend on the price of carbon on the market and will be discussed in the next section.

Medium to long term

In considering aviation emission scenarios for the medium (2017–2030) to long term (2031–2050), not only must a range of assumptions be made in relation to the aviation industry, but attention must also be paid to the over-arching EU policy climate.

Table 4.3 *Emissions allowances to be purchased in 2012 under the range of Tyndall scenarios*

Baseline year	Emissions in baseline year (MtCO$_2$)	Emissions in 2012 (MtCO$_2$)	Emissions to be purchased (MtCO$_2$)
1990	123	284–355	161–232
2000	200	284–355	84–155
2005	225	284–355	59–130

In aiming for a 450ppmv stabilization level, it is assumed that:

• The EU adopts a comprehensive and scientifically literate basis for its climate policy derived from a cumulative carbon budget approach.
• It has a complete account of all sectors.
• It uses a contraction and convergence regime for emission apportionment.

From 2011 onwards, three suites of scenarios commensurate with 450ppmv are considered alongside one illustrative suite outside the 450ppmv regime. Given that the core scenarios are required to be commensurate with the cumulative emissions budget for 450ppmv, the sooner the EU responds, the less demanding will be the emissions pathway from that point onwards.

Future aviation emissions are subject to a number of factors including the rate of growth in the short, medium to long term (i.e. after 2012) and the rate of introduction of new technologies and operational measures that may improve the efficiency and carbon intensity of the industry. Accordingly, building on the three near-term scenarios to 2012 (Figure 4.3), a series of scenarios that reflect the range of reasonable and optimistic possibilities for the short, medium and long term are developed. These scenarios are called *Indigo*, *Aqua*, *Violet* and *Emerald*.

In each case, the four scenarios are divided into three time periods after 2012:

• Short term: start of 2012 to the start of 2017.
• Medium term: start of 2017 to the start of 2031.
• Long term: start of 2031 to the start of 2051.

All but the *Emerald* scenario are based on an assumption that the EU is committed to a meaningful 450ppmv carbon budget, and that aviation will play its part in that process. Consequently, all these scenarios assume the significant reductions in the CO$_2$ emitted per passenger km flown (CO$_2$/pax), as presented in Table 4.4; these combine to give a reduction in CO$_2$/pax for 2012–2050 of 68.5 per cent. The overarching context of this reduction in carbon intensity is society's explicit and genuine commitment to a 450ppmv pathway.

Table 4.4 CO_2/pax improvement per period

	Short	Medium	Long
Mean annual improvement in CO_2/pax	1.5%	2%	4%
Total improvement of the period	7% in 5 yrs	23% in 14 yrs	56% in 20 yrs

The study *Greener by Design* (Greener by Design, 2005) highlights a number of areas that could offer substantial improvements in terms of the fuel burn saved per seat km. For example, in the short to medium term, air traffic management improvements could offer an 8 per cent reduction in fuel burn, open rotor engines could improve fuel efficiency by some 12 per cent and the use of lighter materials such as carbon fibre could offer an additional 15–65 per cent improvement. In the longer term, laminar flow-type aircraft designs could reduce fuel burn by over 50 per cent and alternative fuels, although generally believed unlikely to be used across the fleet prior to 2030, could play a role in reducing aviation's CO_2 emissions, if the drive towards a low-carbon economy were strong enough. What is of key importance is the timescale over which the gains in fuel efficiency and the incorporation of low-carbon fuels into the mix can be achieved.

In terms of these Tyndall scenarios, technological improvements in efficiency coupled with a variety of air traffic management and operational changes provide the principal components of the reducing CO_2/pax during the first two periods (2012–2017 and 2018–2030). Typical changes include continued incremental jet-engine improvements and the incorporation of rear-mounted open rotor engines particularly for shorter-haul flights. In addition, improvements are made through airframe modifications to wing design, to improve air flow and reduce fuel burn, and use of increasing amounts of lighter materials. It is assumed there will be additional load-factor increases, and a series of efficiency gains across the air traffic management system through more direct routing, reduced taxiing, waiting and circling, and reduced use of the auxiliary power unit.

Fuel switching is considered to be a minor component within the two earlier periods. In the long-term period, fuel efficiency improvements across the fleet continue to be of the order of 2 per cent per year, with the remaining 2 per cent being derived from fuel switching to a low-carbon fuel such as biofuel or hydrogen, for example. In considering these assumed efficiency savings and the introduction of low-carbon fuels, it must be noted that these reflect a situation where the aviation industry goes well beyond its achievements over the previous two decades. However, such significant improvements to the technical, operational and managerial efficiency of aviation are only considered possible when driven by a concerted effort on the part of the industry (and society) to deliver them.

In terms of drivers for such a change, the three scenarios reflect a society whose focus is very different from that of today. Within this society, low-carbon innovation receives very significant funding and policies would be in place to regulate low-carbon behaviour and operation within companies. The difference in emphasis between this world and ours is central to these scenarios. Therefore it is worth reiterating that the carbon intensity improvements envisaged are well in excess of what has occurred within most fleets in recent times, yet in keeping with what is physically possible (Green, 2005) if the right suite of incentives were in place.

In terms of the other variables reflected in the scenarios, while three of the scenarios all have the same level of carbon intensity improvement, each differs in the rate of passenger growth. These factors combine to produce different emission changes between 2012 and 2050 which, in combination with the range of short-term scenarios, produce a range of possible net CO_2 emissions from aviation.

A fourth scenario (*Emerald*) differs from the others in terms of both passenger growth and technological efficiency improvements. This scenario reflects only partial commitment to both curbing passenger growth rates and instigating the technological efficiency improvements described above, and is highly unlikely to be compatible with a 450ppmv pathway.

The scenario emission growth rates are presented in Table 4.5. *Indigo* is the most responsive to the climate change issue and the EU ETS, and shows a significant, comprehensive and early drive towards a low-carbon aviation industry within the EU. The net aviation emission change between 2012 and 2050 equates to a 45 per cent reduction, though compared with 1990 it still represents a 24–55 per cent increase.

In *Aqua*, aviation responds more slowly to the EU ETS scheme, compensated by slightly larger reductions by other sectors. Net aviation emission change between 2012 and 2050 equates to a 16 per cent reduction, though compared with 1990 it represents a 95–144 per cent increase.

In *Violet*, the aviation industry continues to grow its emissions at a higher rate than in the *Indigo* and *Aqua* scenarios at the expense of the other sectors in the EU ETS. The net aviation emission change between 2012 and 2050

Table 4.5 *Scenario passenger km growth and carbon intensity improvements*

Parameter	Scenario	Short	Medium	Long
Annual passenger km growth	INDIGO	3%	1.5%	1%
	AQUA	4%	3%	2%
	VIOLET	5%	4%	3%
	EMERALD	6%	5%	3%
Annual CO_2/pax improvement	INDIGO/AQUA/VIOLET	1.5%	2%	4%
	EMERALD	1%	1.5%	2%
Annual emissions change	INDIGO	1.5%	−0.5%	−3%
	AQUA	2%	1%	−2%
	VIOLET	3.5%	2%	−1%
	EMERALD	5%	3.5%	1%

equates to a 26 per cent increase, and compared with 1990 a 184–256 per cent increase.

Emerald is an additional scenario used to illustrate a future where the current rhetoric on climate change is only partially converted into meaningful action. Such a future would be more attuned to cumulative emissions associated with much higher CO_2 concentrations and a failure to respond to the 2°C commitment. In this case, the net aviation emission change between 2012 and 2050 equates to a 146 per cent increase, and compared with 1990 a 278–373 per cent increase. Assumptions behind these growth rates include new EU nations expanding their aviation industries towards per capita rates of old EU nations, and a modified version of the low-cost model assumed to extend to medium- and long-haul flights. Point-to-point aircraft, in combination with the expansion of regional airports, are assumed to provide much quicker and convenient air travel for all. Security becomes less of an obstacle to flying and big improvements in check-in improve the quality of experience for the traveller. Increasing globalization stimulates more migration and consequently international travel to maintain family ties. In economic terms, world GDP growth continues and the EU's economy grows at 2.5–3 per cent per annum. Although it is impossible to paint an accurate picture of a business as usual future for aviation emissions, the *Emerald* scenario represents the closest to an extrapolation of current trends of all the scenarios.

When combined with the three near-term growth scenarios (Figure 4.3), the full scenarios result in nine core scenarios, with a further three for the *Emerald* set. The resulting net CO_2 emissions for all twelve scenarios are provided in Figure 4.4.

To compare the scenarios with total emissions consistent with a 450ppmv budget, the scenario assumptions are applied to the UNFCCC baseline figure of 150MtCO_2 (Figure 4.5).

Unless very low growth rates and substantial improvements to carbon efficiency are achieved, aviation emissions could exceed the 450ppmv 'low' pathway by the late 2040s. For the 450ppmv 'high' pathway, the emissions from aviation account for at best 10 per cent and at worst 29 per cent of the total budget for all sectors and all emissions.

All the aviation industry scenarios, within a world striving to achieve a 450ppmv future, reflect an increase in CO_2 levels in 2050 compared with 1990. This is in sharp contrast to the other sectors of the economy, where 75–90 per cent reductions from 1990 levels have been required to remain within budget.

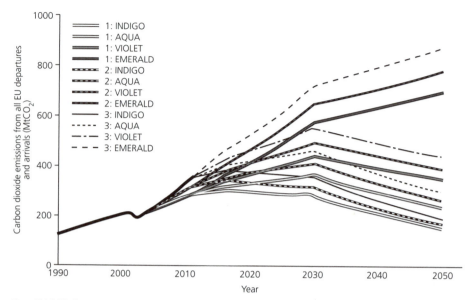

Note: Thick black represents the *Indigo* scenarios, thick grey the *Aqua* scenarios, thin black the *Violet* scenarios and thin grey the *Emerald* scenarios. Within each scenario set, the solid lines represent the low scenarios, dotted lines the medium scenarios and dash-dot-dash the high scenarios.

Figure 4.4 CO_2 *emissions from the nine core scenarios (Indigo, Aqua and Violet for pre-2012 near-term growth scenarios low-1, medium-2 and high-3) and the three illustrative higher growth scenarios (Emerald for pre-2012 near-term growth scenarios low-1, medium-2 and high-3*

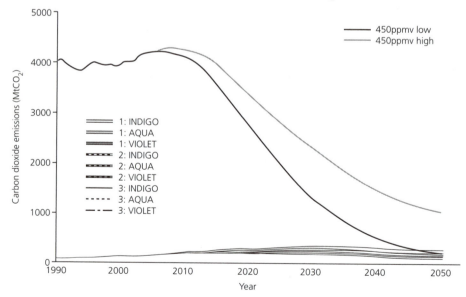

Figure 4.5 CO_2 *emission budgets for 450ppmv compared with aviation emissions scenarios based on the UNFCCC data to account for 50 per cent of international flights and all domestic and intra-EU flights*

Economic analysis

To investigate the likely scale of carbon price necessary to bring about the growth and efficiency changes embedded in the scenarios, a basic and illustrative analysis is presented in relation to three different emission baseline levels, for three typical flight lengths. The price of carbon is varied to provide a range of possible impacts on flight price.

The first stage compares the emissions over different time periods with the baseline results for 1990, 2000 and 2005. The choice of baseline significantly impacts the amounts of carbon permits required. For example, by the end of 2011, between 57 per cent and 65 per cent of emissions must be purchased if 1990 is to be the chosen baseline. Whereas, 21–37 per cent would need to be purchased if 2005 were the baseline (Table 4.6). The carbon intensity improvements are assumed to be the same across all types of flight.[6]

To estimate the additional cost of a typical flight (assuming that all costs are passed on to the passenger) a range of carbon prices for these permits is considered. Although carbon prices above €50 have yet to materialize, the premise of this report is that the EU is genuinely committed to 450ppmv. With this in mind, it is assumed that between 2012 and 2017 carbon prices are €50–€100, increasing in the longer term to €100–€300. These prices broadly reflect the higher ranges of values discussed within the literature (Stern, 2006, p323; Uyterlinkde et al, 2006).

Typical emissions per passenger data is used to provide indicative costs per passenger for flights. As carbon intensity improves over time in line with the figures presented in Table 4.5, so the carbon emissions per passenger will fall for the same flight. For three exemplar flights, Table 4.7 presents the carbon emissions over time relating to the carbon efficiency improvements.

To estimate the typical indicative cost per passenger, the percentage of a flight's carbon emissions for which permits are required to be purchased can be applied to the data in Table 4.7 for the lowest growth scenario, *Indigo*, and the

Table 4.6 *Percentage of permits that would need to be purchased for the lowest,* Indigo, *and highest,* Violet, *scenarios*

INDIGO Baseline dates	Percentage of the carbon on a flight that needs to be purchased		
	End 2011	*End 2016*	*End 2050*
1990	57%	60%	20%
2000	29%	34%	–31%
2005	21%	26%	–47%
VIOLET Baseline dates	Percentage of the carbon on a flight that needs to be purchased		
	End 2011	*End 2016*	*End 2050*
1990	65%	71%	72%
2000	44%	52%	54%
2005	37%	46%	49%

Table 4.7 *Tonnes of CO_2 per passenger for three example flights in 2005, 2011 and 2050 with carbon efficiencies taken from Table 4.5*

One-way flight	2005	End 2011	End 2050
Short haul (e.g. London–Barcelona)	0.25	0.235	0.073
Medium haul (e.g. London–Washington)	1	0.941	0.291
Long haul (e.g. London–Sydney)	2	1.883	0.582

highest growth scenario, Violet. Using the percentages, the typical costs per flight are presented in Table 4.8 for Indigo and Violet.

Table 4.8 illustrates the typical additional costs per passenger for a one-way flight under the *Indigo* and *Violet* scenarios. Again, the earlier the baseline, the higher the additional cost.

Even in the case of the higher growth scenario (*Violet*) and even assuming that all costs were passed on to the passenger, the additional €8–€15 for a short-haul flight is unlikely to significantly influence passenger growth rates (the €15 figure equates to a carbon price of €100 per tonne).

Table 4.8 *Typical prices for exemplar flights over different periods and baselines for the lowest,* Indigo, *scenario and highest,* Violet, *scenario*

Carbon prices for different types of typical flights

INDIGO

Carbon price	Baseline years	End 2011 1990	End 2011 2005	End 2016 1990	End 2016 2005	End 2050 1990	End 2050 2005
€50	Short haul	€7	€2	€7	€3	–[a]	–
	Medium haul	€27	€10	€26	€11	–	–
	Long haul	€53	€20	€52	€23	–	–
€100	Short haul	€13	€5	€13	€6	€1	–€3
	Medium haul	€53	€20	€52	€23	€6	–€14
	Long haul	€107	€39	€104	€46	€11	–€27
€300	Short haul	–	–	€39	€17	€4	–€10
	Medium haul	–	–	€156	€69	€17	–€41
	Long haul	–	–	€313	€138	€34	–€82

VIOLET

Carbon price	Baseline years	End 2011 1990	End 2011 2005	End 2016 1990	End 2016 2005	End 2050 1990	End 2050 2005
€50	Short haul	€8	€4	€8	€5	–	–
	Medium haul	€31	€17	€31	€20	–	–
	Long haul	€62	€35	€62	€41	–	–
€100	Short haul	€15	€9	€15	€10	€5	€4
	Medium haul	€62	€35	€62	€41	€21	€14
	Long haul	€123	€69	€124	€81	€42	€28
€300	Short haul	–	–	€46	€30	€16	€11
	Medium haul	–	–	€185	€122	€63	€42
	Long haul	–	–	€371	€243	€125	€85

Note: a Values indicated by '–' illustrate that within a 450ppmv budget a value of €50 per tonne is unrealistic post-2030; similarly, much higher carbon prices of €300 are unlikely in the period prior to 2012.

For the longer-haul flights, the maximum additional premium would be €371 if 1990 were to be the baseline. The permit price in this case is €300 – an order of magnitude higher than other studies typically expect in the future. Only at such a level, and with an early baseline, is there likely to be a sufficient price signal to significantly curb the growth in emissions from the aviation sector. When considering the 2005 emission baseline, it is probable that carbon prices would have to rise well above €300 per tonne to have a significant influence on growth.

The *Violet* scenario adds an additional €30 to a short-haul flight by the end of 2016, €122 to a medium-haul flight and €243 to a long-haul flight (all at €300 per tonne). The respective figures are €5, €20 and €41 at the lower carbon price of €50 per tonne. Here, again, price signals from even high estimates of carbon prices would not seem to be sufficient to produce the required effect.

Discussion and conclusions

In March of 2008 the EU reaffirmed its commitment to not exceeding the 2°C target. Drawing on this commitment, this chapter illustrates the EU's associated emission-reduction pathway over the next 50 years, with particular focus on what this means for the aviation sector. Three of the scenario suites presented reflect emission pathways for the aviation sector that, although representing a growing share of the EU's emissions, could nevertheless be reconciled with a 450ppmv CO_2 pathway. However, in all cases, these scenarios reflect the situation where there is a concerted effort to produce not only very significant increases in the carbon efficiency of aviation, but a curbing of passenger km growth rates. Furthermore, even though the aviation emissions pathways implied by the scenarios can be reconciled with the 450ppmv CO_2 pathway, the other sectors would have to significantly compensate for aviation to remain within the carbon budget available. While these scenarios are, in principle, achievable, they also represent an urgent and radical departure from the current level of aviation's emission growth and the majority of analyses and passenger growth forecasts for the future of aviation.

Current aviation emissions are significant

In 2005 aviation emissions were approximately 150MtCO$_2$, representing 4 per cent of the EU's total CO_2 emissions. It is such percentages that give rise to the repeated and dangerously misleading claim that 'aviation is not a major greenhouse gas polluter' (IATA, 2007). Making simplistic comparisons with other emissions sources conveniently chosen to underplay aviation's contribution to total emissions only serves to confuse an already confusing issue (see IATA, 2007, p12). The same basis of analysis would suggest that the UK's total transport and power station emissions are not major sources when compared with global totals; similarly the emissions from nations such as Belgium, Portugal and the Netherlands are too small to be the focus of concerted low-carbon action. Unfortunately, this view is all too prevalent in discussions over climate change. The UK's proportion of world emissions is often cited as only 2 per cent of the global total and, so the argument goes, whatever the UK does in terms of carbon emissions is of little relevance. Similarly, Beijing, New York, Delhi, Paris and all the other major cities of the world are respectively less than 2 per cent of total emissions. This apparent logic would suggest there is little benefit in their implementing stringent carbon-reduction strategies. *All* emissions are inevitably the aggregate of smaller percentages; using this as an excuse for relative inaction will collectively lead to individual, sectoral, national and, ultimately, global apathy. The aviation sector's 4 per cent of EU emissions is therefore already a significant proportion of total EU emissions, and it is essential this is recognized.

EU aviation scenarios within a 450ppmv budget

Most of the scenarios presented within this chapter, unlike many existing aviation scenarios, are expressly designed to be compatible with a 450ppmv CO_2 pathway. Understanding the importance of this emphasis is essential if the scenarios are to provide a useful heuristic for policy makers and other stakeholders. Seriously exacerbating the aviation sector's already significant level of emissions is the sector's rate of growth. While emissions from most sectors are broadly stable,[7] the latest EU aviation data show increases in emissions of between 6 and 7 per cent per annum, consistent with long-run trends. Such growth rates are often ignored or underestimated by those with a vested interest in the sector's continued prosperity. Currently, the limited constraints on the expansion of the EU's aviation sector are being dwarfed by the drivers for expansion. In the absence of explicit and coordinated action to both constrain growth and increase efficiency it is difficult to envisage the current situation changing appreciably. Previous Tyndall scenarios demonstrated the dangers of relative inaction in relation to emissions growth (Anderson et al, 2005; Bows et al, 2006a); by contrast these scenarios illustrate what viable aviation emission pathways may look like, provided radical policies are implemented to constrain emissions growth as a matter of urgency.

These latest scenarios contain reductions in carbon intensity per passenger km well above those assumed within all but the industry's more optimistic predictions. This is a consequence of the latest scenarios being developed for an explicit 450ppmv CO_2 future. There is a raft of opportunities for reducing the carbon intensity at levels not dissimilar to those used within this report. However, the scope and scale of policies necessary to bring about such changes and the more immediate and short-term benefits of behavioural and operational adjustments are often ignored.

The analysis presented within this chapter begins to sketch out the necessary scope and scale of policies; with an inevitably conditional conclusion being that, if price is to be the principal driver, the € per tonne carbon prices currently being discussed are an order of magnitude too low. Carbon prices of €50–€100 per tonne in 2012 equate to a typical short-haul flight price increase of €2–€15 per passenger, medium-haul €10–€60, and flights from, for example, the UK to Australia, €40–€120. It is difficult to envisage such small price signals having other than marginal impacts on the rate of growth of aviation emissions. In relation to the more demanding of the report's scenarios (*Indigo*), the €300 carbon price in 2017 equates to a per passenger supplement for typical short-, medium- and long-haul flights of €15–€40, €70–€155 and €140–€310 respectively. Given the radical departure from aviation's current high emission growth represented by the *Indigo* scenario, these additional costs are still likely to be insufficient. Current discussions often refer to carbon prices well below €50/tonne, with the latest IATA report (IATA, 2007, p3) focusing on values per tonne of CO_2 of between €15 and €33. Such low prices are considered inconsistent with a genuine drive towards an EU 450ppmv CO_2 pathway, and consequently the prices are revised upwards significantly. Only with carbon prices an order of magnitude higher than those currently being considered by the industry (i.e. €100–€300 per tonne as opposed to €15–€33 per tonne), and with an early baseline year, can the scheme have sufficient impact on reducing current levels of emission growth.

Aviation remains privileged

On first reading, the scenarios in this chapter may appear to place undue constraints on the aviation sector. However, even under the most demanding scenario (*Indigo*), aviation remains highly privileged in relation to emissions. The 450ppmv CO_2 pathway demands aggregate emission reductions from all sectors, compared with 1990, of approximately 75–90 per cent by 2050. By contrast, even the *Indigo* scenario has an emissions increase from the aviation sector in 2050 of between 23 per cent and 53 per cent compared with 1990. This growth is despite the exceptionally high levels of efficiency and unprecedented reduction in passenger km growth assumed within the scenario. Such findings illustrate the scale of the challenge facing the EU and its member states and reveal the failure of existing policy instruments to address the rapid growth in aviation emissions. Moreover, it exposes the politically expedient rather than scientifically literate basis of discussions informing and framing the scale of forthcoming policy instruments. It is imperative that this reluctance to actively engage in evidence-based analysis of current and future emissions be reversed if the EU is to meet even the higher 450ppmv emission pathway, let alone the EU's own 2°C commitment.

Conclusion

From the relatively simple 'what if' economic analysis presented in this chapter, a series of options for reconciling aviation with a 450ppmv CO_2 pathway are evident. First, the EU ETS cap must be designed in keeping with a cumulative 450ppmv pathway. A reconsideration of an early baseline year should be a prerequisite for aviation's inclusion in the EU ETS and early inclusion in the scheme is highly desirable, with stringent constraints on the sector's emission growth implemented in the interim. In relation to the carbon price, the overall

EU ETS cap needs to be sufficiently tight that carbon prices well in excess of €300/tonne are achieved. Finally, in relation to non-CO_2 climate change impacts, additional and substantial flanking instruments must be implemented. Constrained and responsible growth of the aviation sector can be reconciled with a 450ppmv CO_2 future, but the carbon price currently being discussed is an order of magnitude too low to stimulate the necessary changes.

For the EU to achieve its climate targets, all sectors require mitigation policies. If a realistically high carbon price is considered unachievable, there are a number of alternative mechanisms available for consideration. For example, the aviation sector could operate within a sector-specific cap; either for aviation only, or for all transport modes, based on the sector making its fair contribution to a 450ppmv cumulative CO_2 pathway. Or, a very high carbon-related price could be placed on the industry in the form of a fuel tax, air passenger duty, or some other innovative charging instrument. One other mechanism is for a stringent carbon-rationing regime to be introduced, such as personal carbon allowances, with the quantity of allowances in line with a cumulative 450ppmv CO_2 pathway. If a stringent policy mechanism is not chosen, the EU must prepare to adapt to climate change impacts in excess of a +2°C future. The transition from the EU's rhetoric on climate change to a scientifically literate policy agenda demands a reframing of the debate in terms of cumulative carbon budgets and accompanying carbon-reduction pathways. Within such a framing, addressing urgently aviation's rapidly escalating emissions becomes a prerequisite of any meaningful carbon-reduction strategy.

Notes

1   The latest figures for passenger growth are for the EU27 nations, and are therefore not comparable with the EU25 figures. However, these indicate a 5 per cent growth compared with the previous year (De La Fuente Layos, 2008).
2   Equivalent relates to the inclusion of the basket of six greenhouse gases.
3   The reasoning behind investigating CO_2 alone can be found in section 2.1 of Anderson et al (2007).
4   This period also incorporated the first Gulf War, which understandably impacted on the industry.
5   This figure does not include contrail-induced cirrus cloud.
6   Tables 12 and 14 in Anderson et al (2007) give more details.
7   Seldom increasing or decreasing at more than 1–2 per cent per annum.

References

Anderson, K., Shackley, S., Mander, S. and Bows, A. (2005) *Decarbonising the UK: Energy for a Climate Conscious Future,* Manchester: The Tyndall Centre for Climate Change Research

Anderson, K., Bows, A. and Foottit, A. (2007) *Aviation in a Low-Carbon EU*, Report for Friends of the Earth, Manchester: Tyndall Centre for Climate Change Research

Bows, A., Anderson, K. and Upham, P. (2006a) *Contraction and Convergence: UK Carbon Emissions and the Implications for UK Air Traffic,* Tyndall Centre Technical Report, Norwich: Tyndall Centre for Climate Change Research

Bows, A., Mander, S., Starkey, R., Bleda, M. and Anderson, K. (2006b) *Living within a Carbon Budget*, Report commissioned by Friends of the Earth and the Co-operative Bank, Manchester: Tyndall Centre

De La Fuente Layos, L. (2007) *Air Transport in Europe in 2005: Statistics in Focus*, European Communities: EU

De La Fuente Layos, L. (2008) *Air Transport in Europe in 2006: Statistics in Focus*, European Communities: EU

EUROCONTROL (2007) *Flight Movements 2007–2008*, Short-Term Forecast, EUROCONTROL, STATFOR

Green, J. E. (2005) 'Future aircraft: greener by design?', *Meteorologische Zeitschrift*: 583–590

Greener by Design (2005) *Mitigating the Environmental Impact of Aviation: Opportunities and Priorities*, London: Royal Aeronautical Society

IATA (2007) *Financial Impact of Extending the EU ETS to Airlines*, available at www.iata.org/economics, accessed May 2008

IPCC (2007) *Climate Change 2007: The Physical Science Basis*, Report of Working Group 1 to the Fourth Assessment Report of the Intergovernmental Panel on Climate Change

Jones, C. D., Cox, P. M. and Huntingford, C. (2006) 'Impact of climate-carbon cycle feedbacks on emissions scenarios to achieve stabilisation', in Schellnhuber, H. J., Cramer, W., Nakicenovic, N., Wigley, T. and Yohe, G. (eds) *Avoiding Dangerous Climate Change*, Cambridge: Cambridge University Press, pp323–331

Matthews, H. D. (2005) 'Decrease of emissions required to stabilise atmospheric CO_2 due to positive carbon cycle-climate feedbacks', *Geophysical Research Letters* 32(L21707)

Meinshausen, M. (2006) 'What does a 2°C target mean for greenhouse gas concentrations? A brief analysis based on multi-gas emission pathways and several climate sensitivity uncertainty estimates', in Schellnhuber, H. J., Cramer, W., Nakićenović, N., Wigley, T. and Yohe, G. (eds) *Avoiding Dangerous Climate Change*, Cambridge: Cambridge University Press, pp253–279

Meyer, A. (2000) *Contraction and Convergence: the Global Solution to Climate Change*, Devon: Green Books

Penner, J. E., Lister, D. G., Griggs, D. J., Dokken, D. J. and McFarland, M. (eds) (1999) *Aviation and the Global Atmosphere*, a special report of IPCC Working Groups I and III, Cambridge: Cambridge University Press

RCEP (2000) *Energy – The Changing Climate*, 22nd Report, CM4749, London: The Stationery Office

Sausen, R., Isaksen, I., Grewe, V., Hauglustaine, D., Lee, D. S., Myhre, G., Kohler, M. O., Pitari, G., Schumann, U., Stordal, F. and Zerefos, C. (2005) 'Aviation radiative forcing in 2000: An update on IPCC (1999)', *Meteorologische Zeitschrift* 14(4): 555–561

Stern, N. (2006) *Stern Review on the Economics of Climate Change*, Her Majesty's Treasury, Cambridge: Cambridge University Press

Uyterlinkde, M. A., Martinus, G. H., Rösler, H., Van der Zwaan, B. C. C. and 23 co-authors (2006) *The Contribution of Nuclear Energy to a Sustainable Energy System*, CASCADE MINTS project policy brief, Netherlands: Energy Resource Centre

Wit, R. C. N., Boon, B. H., van Velzen, A., Cames, A., Deuber, O. and Lee, D. S. (2005) *Giving Wings to Emissions Trading: Inclusion of Aviation under the European Trading System (ETS): Design and Impacts*, Delft: CE

Part II
Drivers and Trends

5
Low-cost Aviation

Jan Henrik Nilsson

Introduction

In late spring 2008, Brivibas Iela (Liberty Street) in central Riga is crowded
with tourists, mainly from Britain, Germany and Scandinavia. Only a couple of
years ago, there were not many tourists around, just a few businessmen and
tram spotters. If known at all, the old Hanseatic city was considered dangerously eastern. Now people have come here for a few days extra holiday, for a
city break. Despite expensive accommodation, it is an affordable experience
for many Europeans – thanks to low-cost aviation.

The Latvian capital is only one of many cities and regions where tourism
has grown at a rate never seen before. The development of low-cost aviation
has radically changed European travel patterns. New landscapes of mobility
and interaction are emerging. The figures speak for themselves: in 2007,
European low-cost carriers had around 150 million passengers, and in 2000
they were less than 20 million (LFV, 2005; York Aviation, 2007; ELFAA, 2008;
note that these numbers differ depending on definitions). At such a scale, low-
cost aviation not only moves millions of people and Euros around; it affects
social life, patterns of mobility and the environment.

The purpose of this chapter is thus to describe and explain the development
of low-cost aviation and to analyse some of its effects. The 'low-cost revolution' has been totally dependent on the deregulation of aviation. Initially in this
chapter the changes in the institutional framework surrounding aviation are
therefore accounted for. This forms a background for the next section where
the actual development of low-cost aviation is described. By describing the
low-cost business model, the next section explains the reasons for its success.
In the latter part of the chapter, the effects of low-cost aviation on mobility,
destinations and the environment are described and analysed.

From regulation to open skies

International civil aviation commenced in the wake of World War I. Since then, it has been a concern for national authorities: for economic reasons, for the sake of national pride, and above all due to military considerations. From the beginning, national interests made aviation highly regulated and heavily subsidized (*Kunskapens Bok*, 1945). With the Chicago Convention of 1944 and the setting up of the International Civil Aviation Organization (ICAO), an international regulatory framework was imposed on aviation in which governments remained the central group of actors. The Chicago Convention covered most aspects of aviation. In practice it meant that commercial operations were based on bilateral service agreements which regulated international traffic rights. Capacity was regulated by governments and national carriers, and price levels controlled (Doganis, 2002, pp19–43). This system remained basically unchanged during most of the post-war period until 1978. In the following 30 years international aviation has gradually been liberalized. The system of bilateral service agreements is, however, still practised in many parts of the world.

Prior to 1978, US aviation was just as regulated as anywhere else, despite market competition and privately owned airlines. The 1978 Aviation Deregulation Act brought an end to all regulation of the domestic aviation market in the US. US deregulation influenced developments both in domestic markets in Europe and in international aviation (Doganis, 2002; Button, 2004). Simply speaking, the liberalization of international aviation since 1978 has been carried out in steps. The first two stages, which built on renegotiated bilateral agreements, were mainly promoted by the US. 'Open market' agreements, in the period 1978–1991, allowed for more airlines to access the market and compete on international routes, thereby reducing the monopoly status of flag carriers. 'Open skies' agreements, after 1991, abolished restrictions on traffic frequencies and price levels. These liberalized bilateral agreements were first introduced on the US–European and intra-European markets but have later spread to other parts of the world, such as Southeast Asia and the Pacific (Doganis, 2006).

In the European Union, aviation was deregulated following three 'packages' of reforms by the Council of Ministers. The third package, of 1992–1997, was an effect of the 'single market'. This transformed the European Union into a domestic market for aviation, with free market access for all European airlines and no restriction on capacity and pricing. State subsidies are gradually to be removed (Button, 2004). With the expansion of the European Union the domestic market has grown from the original 15 states to 30 in 2007 (adding 12 new members, in addition to Norway, Iceland and Switzerland, which remain outside the EU).

An important argument behind the liberalization has been that aviation ought to be treated like any other line of business. However, one interesting restriction still remains from the old regulatory framework. In the Chicago Convention, the signing nations agreed not to put taxes on air fuel used for international aviation (ICAO, 2006, clarified in ICAO, 2000). An attempt by the European Union to change this policy, at the ICAO 2007 assembly, was a failure (ICAO, 2007). As opposed to the case of ground transport, national governments have agreed not to use taxes as a way to adjust the negative impacts of this specific kind of consumption. Since fuel and other forms of energy are heavily taxed in most countries, aviation in practice enjoys substantial indirect subsidies (Meijers, 2005). Consequently, aviation is thus not treated as any other business.

To conclude, the process of deregulation has had major effects on market access, pricing and other aspects of airline activity. Domestic and international deregulation has also been a necessary prerequisite for the development of low-cost carriers; it has made new business models possible. On the other hand, in its efforts to cope with the negative effects of increased aviation, the public sector is still bound up by the post-war system of bilateral service agreements based on the Chicago Convention.

The emergence of low-cost carriers

Southwest Airlines (SWA) is generally considered to be the first low-cost carrier (Doganis, 2006). Deregulation allowed the airline to develop an entirely new business model, radically changing the aviation market. In the decades following 1978 it grew from being a minor Texan airline to becoming one of the major US carriers. In 2005, it had a 16 per cent share of the US market (Knorr, 2007, p79) and has consistently stayed profitable for the last 35 years, an achievement no other US airline can match.

Following a strategy based on high efficiency, large cost reductions and price levels radically lower than its competitors', it opened up new markets. SWA concentrated its business on short-distance traffic, using secondary airports and offering very basic services. Its main target group was price-sensitive leisure travellers. Thereby, its main competitors were not other airlines in the first place, but ground traffic. The low price levels also acted as a stimulus to increased traffic in general (see Calder, 2006). SWA has had a dramatic influence on competition, price levels and aggregate demand (Knorr, 2007). This so-called 'Southwest effect' was used to describe the positive change in the numbers of emplacements plus the induced decrease of the average fare at the airports and/or the specific markets SWA had entered (Knorr, 2007, p91). The airline's competitive force affected not only the city pairs which it was trafficking but also others from nearby airports (Knorr, 2007, pp91–93). The spread of its innovative business model came to have global effects.

In the beginning of the deregulation process, in the period 1987–1995, European deregulation resulted in the development of privately owned airlines who tried to compete with the state-owned flag carriers by using traditional business models. These airlines, for example British Midlands, paved the way for the low-cost carriers by pushing deregulation forward through the political and administrative systems (Calder, 2006). Low-cost operations in Europe commenced in the mid-1990s with Great Britain and Ireland taking the lead (Francis et al, 2006). At around the same time, late 1995, easyJet started operations between Luton and Glasgow while Ryanair commenced its Stansted–Prestwick connection. EasyJet was a start-up low-cost carrier, while Ryanair had been running the London–Dublin connection for some years, gradually transforming itself into a low-cost carrier. Since then, these two airlines have been leading the development of low-cost aviation in Europe. SWA has clearly been a role model for the European low-cost carriers (Knorr, 2007). The front figures of Ryanair and easyJet, Michael O'Leary and Stelios Haji-Ioannou, both explicitly point at SWA as their main source of inspiration (Creaton, 2007; Jones, 2007). From their strong positions on the British Isles, Ryanair and easyJet gradually built up strong networks. They started bases on the continent in 1999, from which expansion could grow even further. After that their market position has become increasingly dominant. Apart from these two carriers, the low-cost market has been highly volatile. Several new carriers have set up, but a lot of them have failed or have been bought up by competitors (Francis et al, 2006).

Since the enlargement of the European Union in 2004, the most dynamic development of low-cost carriers has taken place in east-central Europe. For instance, the Hungarian carrier Wizz Air, founded in 2003, is today operating 70 routes from its six bases in Poland, Hungary, Rumania and Bulgaria. Katowice in the south of Poland is its best-connected base, serving 25 destinations, of which nine are in Britain alone (Wizz Air, 2008). This route pattern is an interesting reflection of the changing geographies of employment, migration and travel in post-2004 Europe.

However, as of 2008, Ryanair and easyJet dominate the European low-cost market, with Air Berlin, Germanwings and other competitors all being significantly smaller (Bjelicic, 2007; ELFAA, 2008). The two dominant airlines have divided the market between themselves: they clearly avoid competing. EasyJet is mainly flying between big cities using major airports, while Ryanair is targeting secondary airports and regional centres and thereby opens up new regions for international scheduled aviation (Calder, 2006; easyJet, 2008; Ryanair, 2008). In this respect, the route patterns of the two airlines follow different geographical logics.

One of the most important aspects of low-cost aviation is its impact on traditional airlines whose operations have come under severe pressure, especially on their short-haul routes. The traditional airlines' strategies to handle the competition have included both cost-reducing and productivity-increasing measures. Some have also started low-cost subsidiaries to get into the low-cost market. The results have so far been mixed (Dennis, 2007; see also Chapter 7, this volume). The low-cost carriers have definitely put a downward pressure on fares and on service quality. In general, the European airline market has the appearance of going through a reconstruction process in which probably only the strongest business groups will survive, those with the most well-developed intercontinental connections.

From its Western origins low-cost aviation has since the turn of the century spread to other parts of the world. Australia and New Zealand made an early start following deregulations in the 1980s and early 90s. Other markets developed later, following a second wave of deregulation in 1998–2003 (Francis et al, 2006). The Malaysian low-cost carrier Air Asia, which began operating in 2001 and went international in 2004, was the pioneer low-cost airline in Southeast Asia. Apart from Southeast Asia, its route network today includes Indonesia, Australia and China (Air Asia, 2008; see also Forsyth et al, 2006). Since then, low-cost aviation has spread to other parts of the region and to India and the Gulf States as well. Outside Asia, South Africa and Brazil have become important markets for low-cost carriers. For example, the Brazilian low-cost carrier Gol has in a few years become a major domestic and international operator (Evangelho et al, 2005; Francis et al, 2006; Gol, 2008; *Peanuts*, 2008).

To summarize, since the beginning of the 21st century, low-cost aviation has spread to many parts of the world. It is, however, difficult to get an accurate overview of its global development due to the rapidly improving market opportunities. Low-cost aviation has shown very high growth rates in the markets where the business model has been introduced; market shares typically amount to between 20 and 40 per cent. There has therefore been extensive academic and professional discussion about the expansion of low-cost aviation and its impact on the aviation market and on traditional airlines in particular (see Vowles, 2000; Dennis, 2007; Mason and Alamdari, 2007; Pitfield, 2007). On the other hand, from a climate change perspective market shares are of minor importance. What is important is how low-cost aviation affects the total growth rates of global aviation, and thereby the total increase of greenhouse gas emissions.

Since the recovery after the terrorist attacks in 2001 global growth rates of aviation have been impressive. In annual revenue passenger kilometres, global aviation increased by 29 per cent between 2001 and 2006 (Boeing, 2007). During this period, low-cost aviation grew from being a Western niche market issue to changing world aviation. To establish exactly to what extent these growth rates depend on low-cost aviation is difficult. Simply disaggregating traffic and passenger growth by airline type, to observe growth differentials, is not sufficient to indicate what proportion of growth is 'new', what proportion has been shifted from surface transport modes and what proportion has been taken from traditional airlines by the low-costs (itself a presumption in terms of direction).

So far, there is little evidence of any slowdown in the growth of global aviation. Expectations are also high: Boeing (2007) counts on a 5 per cent average annual growth rate in passenger numbers until 2026, which in total would mean a 271 per cent increase from 2006 figures. Many business analysts regard low-cost aviation to be an important growth engine in the future, especially if the business model expands into new markets such as intercontinental traffic. In this context, Boeing's latest market outlook concludes that:

> *The strongest features of low-cost airlines, such as ruthless attention to productivity, minimal complexity, highly efficient distribution (sales) systems, and maximum potential for ancillary revenues ... will be increasingly applied in a long-haul context. The operational practicality of this approach has been demonstrated for years by charter and inclusive tour airlines around the world. However, only now is the regulatory environment becoming liberal enough for potentially successful application of these strategies* (Boeing, 2007, p9)

Keeping this forecast in mind, the next section will try to explain some of the reasons behind the success of low-cost aviation.

The business model of low-cost airlines

The development described above has been possible because low-cost carriers have significant competitive advantages. Above all, they run some very simple operations compared to those of the traditional network airlines. By only running point-to-point routes they avoid costs associated with network operations, that is the transfer of passengers and luggage at hubs, connection management, revenue dilution etc (Doganis, 2006, pp181–183). Indeed, their competitive advantages are based on measures taken in all fields of airline management, operational and non-operational. The business model of low-cost airlines is well described in the aviation literature (Doganis, 2002, 2006; Calder, 2006; Groß and Schröder, 2007). The model below is aimed at summarizing the most important aspects of the low-cost business model. It describes cost and revenues, both internal and external. The difference between internal and external is here defined as based on whether or not the measures in question are managed directly by the carrier or by external actors.

As shown in the model in Figure 5.1, cost-reducing measures are clearly an important part of the low-cost carriers' efforts to gain advantage. Using a cascade analysis, the aviation analyst Rigas Doganis (2006, pp170–181) concludes that the cost advantages of low-cost carriers in operations, services and distribution, are in the range of 50 per cent. The area where low-cost carriers have been the most innovative is in distribution. By using 'simple' one-way, single class tickets they made it possible for costumers to purchase tickets directly from the airline (for details see Bley and Büermann, 2007). Direct online sales were encouraged through innovative web interfaces combined with advantages and discounts for those booking online. This way, agents and global distribution systems (GDS) could be circumvented, and commissions avoided. Introducing ticketless travel further reduced costs. When the use of traditional distribution channels was abandoned, large efforts had to be put into other forms of marketing. Advertising has become very important as a way of reaching the public directly. The use of spectacular slogans and posters in public places have been combined with events and different forms of

INTERNAL	• Point to point • Homogenous fleet • High fleet utilization • Fast turnarounds • No frills • Lower crew costs • Smaller administration • No frequent flyers programs • Direct sales, web discount • Ticketless travel • No agent, GDS, costs	• Dense, single class seating • Yield management • In-flight sales • Inventive price information eg, wheelchair • Inventive advertising eg, "marketing in court"
EXTERNAL	• Secondary airports • Outsourced handling • Lower station costs	• "Marketing support" by airports and regions • Web marketing of connected services

Figure 5.1 *The business model of low-cost airlines, competitive measures*

guerrilla marketing, that is marketing where unconventional methods are used. The media have been a major contributor in this respect; not least, Ryanair has been clever in using lawsuits and other controversies as a means of attracting public attention (Calder, 2006). This tactic might be called 'marketing in court'.

In the cascade analysis, Doganis (2006) shows that higher seating densities (shorter distances between seats) used by low-cost carriers is their most important cost-reducing tool. This example shows that the business model is just as much about increasing revenues as it is about cutting costs. Promotion of in-flight sales is another example of turning cost reductions into revenues. The no-frills approach means that catering is not offered for free; instead people have to pay for food and drinks. These revenues are important: some estimates suggest that in-flight sales account for between 10 and 20 per cent of revenues (Bley and Büermann, 2007; Calder, 2006). Although these figures seem exaggerated, the importance of these sales is stressed by the fact that stewards and hostesses in some cases are partly paid by commission based on individual sales records (Bley and Büermann 2007). A reason for the possible exaggeration is that in-flight sales are blurred with revenues coming from web marketing of connected services sold by other businesses, such as hotels, cars or travel insurance (Doganis, 2006). Together, these non-ticket revenues are becoming increasingly important for low-cost carriers.

Sophisticated yield management is used, aimed at adapting prices to meet demand at the right level at all times and thereby optimizing load factors. The flexibility to adjust prices upwards tends to make average price levels a lot higher than the bargains advertised. This is by no means uncommon; airlines normally put on an extra charge for taxes and unexpected rises in fuel prices. The advertised price is thus rarely what the passenger pays. But, since price is clearly their most important competitive advantage, low-cost carriers use more 'innovative' price information than other airlines (Bley and Büermann, 2007). Ryanair's quotation, as shown in Table 5.1, illustrates this.

Table 5.1 *Quotation (in SEK) for a Ryanair return flight*
Gothenburg–Prestwick, April 2008

Item	Price	Cumulative
Advertised price 1 (outward)	299.00	299.00
Advertised price 2 (return)	199.00	498.00
Taxes and ticket charges	423.55	921.55
Insurance, wheelchair levy, aviation insurance	107.12	1028.67
Charge for 1 bag and airport check-in	254.00	1288.67
Credit card fee	Up to 95.00	1385.67

Source: Ryanair.com, 15 April 2008

This calculation is based on the services a normal passenger would use, that is to bring a bag, check in at the airport and pay with a credit card (for which there is no alternative); all other extras are excluded. Thus, taxes, charges and fees amount to SEK887.67, 178 per cent of the advertised price. Apart from the generally high percentage, some figures are striking. All passengers have to pay a wheelchair levy (see Calder, 2006, p104) and a credit card fee is charged for each trip, although only one transaction is taking place. Keeping the advertised price down is clearly the preferred marketing strategy; other fees and charges are supposedly brought on by other actors. The problem is though that hardly any other businesses than airlines use this kind of quotation structure, thus preventing a fair comparison with other modes of transport.

The original SWA business model included the use of secondary, regional airports as a way of reducing costs. In Europe, this strategy has been adopted to a varying degree by different airlines. Ryanair almost exclusively uses secondary airports, while other airlines tend to use a mix of hubs and secondary airports. Secondary airports offer a number of advantages, primarily lower operating costs, that is lower landing charges and cheaper handling of passengers and luggage. The risk of congestion at secondary airports is negligible; so turnaround times are reduced and aircraft utilization is improved. The downside is of course that secondary airports tend to be located at a distance from major metropolitan market areas.

Another reason for the lower costs at airports, apart from cheaper facilities, is an oversupply of airport capacity in Europe and the US. Airport congestion and capacity problems, which have been widely discussed during the last decade, only refer to a few of the largest airports, such as Heathrow and Frankfurt. One reason behind this oversupply is the conversion of former military airfields after 1989. For example, in 1969 the Swedish Air Force had 19 active airbases, today only four remain (*Nationalencyklopedien*, 1991; Flygvapnet, 2008). On this buyer's market, the bargaining power of low-cost carriers is quite strong.

At major hub airports many airlines compete, but in many cases single carriers have a huge impact on the business of regional airports themselves and on the surrounding region. When a low-cost carrier opens up connections to a small or medium-size airport the amount of traffic normally grows significantly. Most research suggests that low-cost aviation has a significant positive impact on regional development. Various reports point at increasing growth in employment, incoming investments and tourism (ELFAA, 2004; Turismens Utredningsinstitut, 2005; Pantazis and Liefner, 2006; Widmann, 2007). There is less agreement on the nature and degree of the impact. Obviously, the differences between airports and regions are large, for instance depending on how competition between neighbouring airports looks (Francis et al, 2004).

The owners of converted airfields are anxious to attract traffic; the competitive situation clearly pushes landing and service charges down. Furthermore, to attract low-cost carriers, airport owners and regional authorities on a number of occasions have agreed to give the carrier different kinds of marketing support. In Europe, direct subsidies have been banned by the European Commission, but support is instead disguised as payment for some promotional services. In some cases the regions have ended up paying for each passenger brought into the region (Calder, 2006, pp98–100). The ambition by low-cost carriers to push costs onto other actors has become more pronounced recently. At the time of writing (2008), the price of kerosene has increased quite significantly. In order to retain their price advantage, low-cost carriers have to cut costs even more. This will certainly affect airports and Ryanair's CEO Michael O'Leary leaves no room for misunderstandings: 'Those airports who are not willing to work with us to cut costs will face a reduction in traffic' (*Travel News*, April 2008, p11).

Taken together, the radical efforts to cut costs and improve revenues summarized in this section have changed practice in many parts of the aviation management process. Thereby, low-cost aviation has also changed the market for aviation.

Effects on demand and traffic

Internationally, aviation has seen rapid expansion during the last 50 years with average annual growth rates of between 5 and 10 per cent (SIKA, 2007). It is most likely that aviation would have continued to grow, although at a slower rate, without the massive structural change that has taken place since deregulation. Nevertheless, the development of low-cost aviation has without doubt been a major stimulus to the recent growth in aviation. The dynamic effects of low-cost aviation are apparent on both supply and demand. Low-cost carriers have opened up routes to airports and regions that earlier had few, if any, international connections. Competition has also been improved on established routes, giving passengers more alternative connections. These issues will be discussed further in the following section.

The most important effects of low-cost aviation can be seen on the demand side. The low-cost business model has resulted in reduced fares that have increased demand for flights. Low-cost aviation influences demand both directly and indirectly. Lower fares encourage the public to travel more. They also divert consumers away from competitors and other forms of transport. These effects are in line with standard micro-economic models; if the price of a service decreases, the demand will increase. The increasingly dense network of point-to-point connections has also become an important demand booster. The indirect influences on demand come from increased competition. Low-cost carriers have put severe pressure on traditional airlines. They have been forced to adapt to the new, more competitive market environment. Some airlines have started their own low-cost subsidiaries. Most airlines have adapted parts of the low-cost business model. In the end, traditional airlines have had to reduce fares as well, in order not to lose passengers. The success of low-cost carriers has also encouraged new entrants into aviation, which has added to competition (Doganis, 2006; Knorr, 2007).

When discussing the impact of low-cost aviation on the growth of aviation in general it is important to notice that there is no exact definition of what a low-cost carrier is. Few, probably only Ryanair, follow all aspects of the business model presented above. And, as traditional airlines copy parts of that model, the distinction between low-cost and full-service airlines becomes increasingly blurred (Hvass, 2006). Regardless of problems of definitions, it is very difficult to estimate the influence of low-cost aviation dynamics on the aggregate increase in aviation in quantitative terms. Macário et al (2007, pp39–40) are probably right in their statement, in a report to the European Parliament, that 'there is no scientific grounds to establish a correlation between the LCA [Low Cost Airline] offer and the increase of travel and change of travel patterns'. On the other hand, in the same paragraph they conclude that 'there is evidence the LCA have brought major changes in European travel patterns. They have generated new traffic in many cases for tourism purpose by people who otherwise would either not travel or choose other modes of transport.' It might thus be the case that solid statistical evidence is lacking, but it is a fair conclusion that there is substantial circumstantial evidence for the case that the development of low-cost aviation has been vital for the recent growth in aviation.

Hence, in order to inform the discussion about low-cost aviation and climate change, it is necessary to try to discuss numbers. Regarding direct influences on growth, the most important issue concerns the percentage of low-cost passengers who would not have travelled by air if there were no low-cost aviation available. Reports by stakeholders mention that 'around 60 per cent of traffic is stimulated and around 40 per cent is substitution' (York Aviation, 2007). The problem is that these percentages are based on one survey only (ELFAA, 2004). However, based on what we know about low-cost passengers (see the next section), the percentages mentioned seem to be a reasonable estimate. It is also reasonable to think that the percentage is higher in mid-income countries in Asia and Latin America, where price matters more. All analysis agrees that the greater part of low-cost aviation is 'new' traffic (ELFAA, 2004; Doganis, 2006; Knorr, 2007).

As mentioned before, the definitions of low-cost aviation are far from straightforward. But based on figures from stakeholder organizations (ELFAA, 2008; *Low Cost Monitor*, 2007) it is reasonable to conclude that low-cost carriers in 2007 carried approximately 150 million passengers in Europe alone. In that case, low-cost carriers represent a contribution of 90 million extra air passengers in Europe, a figure that is likely to grow if current trends continue. This is probably a very moderate estimate since it does not take indirect effects into consideration. These 12–15 per cent of European passengers represent a substantial contribution of greenhouse gas emissions.

Low-cost carriers argue that low-cost aviation is in fact more environmentally friendly (or less harmful) than other forms of aviation. Most importantly they emphasize the relatively higher efficiency of low-cost carriers. They have higher average load factors than traditional airlines, which makes emission levels lower per passenger kilometre. They also use more modern fleets than most traditional airlines. Modern aircraft cause lower emission levels than older ones, per flight, and there is significant technological progress taking place. Further, the use of secondary airports will decrease the impacts of ground congestion and noise compared to the situation of major airports (ELFAA, 2004). Each of these arguments is true as such, although the latter does not concern climate change. However, they do not take the most important point into consideration, namely low-cost aviation's impact on the total increase of aviation and thereby on the emission of greenhouse gases. The most important conclusion here is that the dynamics, directly and indirectly created by low-cost aviation, and resulting from increased traffic levels, eliminate all mitigation from improved technical and logistic efficiencies.

The destination perspective

When looking at the European low-cost network from a geographical perspective, some dominant patterns emerge. First, one important part of the route network goes between major metropolitan regions in western Europe. These routes are complementary to and competing with the main routes of traditional airlines, although they are not necessarily using the same airports. Second, there are numerous new connections between northern Europe and the Mediterranean. Much of this is related to vacation travel and the growing market for second homes in the sun. Third, following the enlargement of the EU and the related deregulation of east-central European aviation, a large number of east–west connections have emerged. For example, the Polish city of Katowice is today connected to 22 western European cities, half of them in Great Britain and Germany. There are today hundreds of thousands of people from east-central Europe who are working for longer or shorter periods in western Europe; some even 'commute' to work. Most of them work in the service industries. Growth of low-cost traffic to places such as Katowice can therefore be seen as a sign of the migratory geography of post-2004 Europe. Fourth, there are relatively few new connections between the different parts of central Europe; the internal connectivity in the region has not improved much. This category of traffic is mostly business related and taken care of by traditional airlines.

Increased demand for travel combined with improved connectivity, resulting in rapidly rising numbers of passengers, has had a substantial impact on (tourist) destinations. In this context we must reconsider the meaning of a destination. Generic tourism system models (see Hall, 2000, pp42–53) build on a dichotomy between a sending region, home, and a receiving region, the destination. At a time when most tourism was thought of as going to the seaside, the Mediterranean, the Alps or to capital cities, this way of thinking came quite naturally. However, as a consequence of European integration, higher income levels, improved connectivity and lower fares, this dichotomy is no longer valid. New patterns of travel and tourism are emerging. People from regions that were mostly considered as destinations are today increasingly travelling to traditional sending regions; people from Spain are visiting Scandinavia and people from central Europe are going to the west. Low-cost carriers do, as opposed to traditional charter, bring people in both directions. With rapidly increasing numbers of people travelling, this transforms most airport regions into tourist destinations.

In absolute numbers, it is the best connected metropolitan regions, such as London, that are gaining most visitors from low-cost travelling. The impact is, however, much more pronounced in more peripheral regions and cities. In some cities in east-central Europe the change has been remarkable. A swift analysis of timetables confirms this. During the first week in June 2008 53,755 seats (the actual number of passengers flying is confidential) left Riga airport for international destinations within Europe; the comparable figure in 2001 was 11,297 (Riga Airport, 2008; Nilsson, 2003). This means an increase in traffic of 478 per cent. It could of course partly be explained by the membership of the European Union, economic integration etc. However, low-cost carriers entered this market in 2001. Ryanair has opened up ten connections to Riga, and the domestic airline, Air Baltic, has transformed itself into a low-cost carrier. Riga's growth rate is not unique; there are other comparable cities in other parts of east-central Europe (Flick, 2007).

When discussing the regional economic effects of low-cost aviation, one aspect must be considered first. There is always a balance between gains from incoming visitors and losses caused by increased numbers of people going away from their home region. This relation between incoming and outgoing differs substantially between different connections (see Turismens Utredningsinstitut, 2005; Widmann, 2007).

This said, increasing numbers of connections and incoming passengers stimulate the regional economies in a number of ways. Direct employment at the airport and in aviation-related businesses increases. In some cases this effect is substantial; for example, the German low-cost airport at Hahn has around 2300 persons employed at the airport alone (Widmann, 2007, p182). Regions may also gain from improved connectivity. This does not only mean that the region is more easily accessible to visitors, it also affects the working conditions of internationally oriented businesses and it might improve the supply of labour.

Destination spending by visitors is in most cases considered to be the main economic benefit from low-cost aviation. Airports themselves are the first to profit. The long check-in hours and the no-frills concept tend to make people eat and drink at the airport and spend some time shopping. Secondary airports are often located far away from cities and regular communications. Many passengers use shuttle buses or choose to hire a car. Spending patterns are closely related to the characteristic features of low-cost passengers. They tend to be relatively young and well-educated, individual travellers on leisure trips or visiting friends and relatives (Candela Garriga, 2004; Nilsson, 2008). Young, educated people are more likely to be able and willing to make arrangements on their own than other groups. It should, however, be noted that the use of the internet today has penetrated all age groups apart from those over 65, at least among western Europeans (Nilsson, 2008). Young people are also more likely to have developed international friendships, for example through studies and exchanges.

Most evidence suggests that leisure is the most important reason for travelling with low-cost airlines. There are of course large differences in proportions between 'classical' resorts and average destination regions. There are also some people using low-cost travel for business purposes, but the inflexible ticket systems, prolonged check-in times and more time-consuming connections make this group relatively small. On some connections, mainly involving east-central Europe, a distinct proportion of passengers travel to work. A large and under-researched group is visiting friends and relatives. In a survey (473 respondents) conducted at Malmö Airport, Sweden, 60 per cent of the foreign visitors indicated visiting friends and relatives as one of their reasons for visiting the region, 46 per cent put it as their main reason. For some, visiting friends and relatives was combined with either leisure or work (Nilsson, 2008).

Low-cost travellers tend to stay on average between four and seven days at the destination, that is longer than most business travellers. Weekend trips are also rather common. Naturally, people working or visiting friends and relatives often stay longer and are generally more frequent visitors. Passengers using low-cost carriers tend to spend less money at the destination than other travellers. Their accommodation preferences distinguish them. They tend to prefer relatively cheap lodgings: small hotels, bed-and-breakfasts or hostels. In the Malmö survey, 55 per cent stayed with friends and relatives. Of course, they also use surface transport, eat and drink at restaurants, go shopping and visit attractions. Although perhaps being small spenders on average, their numbers make them profitable for the destination regions. After all, low-cost aviation is a business model for mass transportation.

In the Malmö survey, which was conducted at a time when some of the connections to the airport were endangered (Ryanair stopped operations a few month later), a number of respondents said they were 'dependent' on low-cost aviation to Malmö. Since Copenhagen Airport is only 40 kilometres away, these statements suggest that flying at a low cost has become a natural part of their lives. They don't only use aviation for fun or business, but above all to stay in touch with friends and relatives. Different kinds of transborder social networks are created and reinforced by low-cost aviation (see Larsen et al, 2007). With this in mind, the importance of low-cost aviation on general patterns of mobility becomes clear. Tendencies like those mentioned here are signs that low-cost aviation has changed the way we look at aviation. To many people, to fly has become a common practice of mobility – almost an everyday thing.

Conclusion: Low-cost aviation – a Janus-faced business

The low-cost revolution described in this chapter has changed the face of both aviation and travel patterns in general. But like the Roman god Janus, low-cost aviation shows a different face depending on one's viewpoint.

To passengers, low-cost carriers have reduced fares and improved opportunities to travel. New groups of people have become able to afford air travel. Declining service quality is obviously something people are prepared to accept, if the price is right. For destinations, low-cost aviation has become equally successful. Many destination regions have seen a growth in incoming tourism, in some cases radical growth. The downsides are of course a growing dependency on single low-cost carriers and, depending on the mix of routes, a risk of large outflows of tourism, a decline in the tourism home market. To the aviation industry in general, low-cost aviation is a huge success story. The range of service innovations put forward by low-cost carriers is an injection to the business and has been a major contributor to the last decade's impressive growth rates.

Most aviation analysts would probably not hesitate to call low-cost aviation a great success story. All stakeholders seem to be happy – this is exactly the problem. The business success of low-cost aviation might very well be the most forceful booster of aviation demand ever. But, as shown elsewhere in this book, aviation is the fastest growing and most problematic mode of transport, causing ever growing amounts of greenhouse gas emissions. Thus, from a global, environmental perspective the development of low-cost aviation is nothing less than disastrous.

References

Air Asia (2008) Airline information website, available at www.airasia.com, accessed 1 April 2008

Bjelicic, B. (2007) 'The business model of low-cost airlines: Past, present, future', in Groß, S. and Schröder, A. (eds) (2007) *Handbook of Low-cost Airlines. Strategies, Business Processes and Market Environment,* Berlin: Erich Schmidt Verlag, pp11–30

Bley, K. and Büermann, T (2007) 'Business processes and IT solutions in the low-fare environment', in Groß, S. and Schröder, A. (eds) (2007) *Handbook of Low-cost*

Airlines: Strategies, Business Processes and Market Environment, Berlin: Erich Schmidt Verlag, pp51–76

Boeing (2007) *Current Market Outlook*, report available at www.boeing.com

Button, K. (2004) *Wings Across Europe: Towards an Efficient European Air Transport System,* Aldershot: Ashgate

Calder, S. (2006) *No Frills. The Truth Behind the Low-Cost Revolution in the Skies,* London: Virgin Books

Candela Garriga, J. (2004) *Low-cost, A Regional Affair*, Proceedings of the Airport Regions Conference

Creaton, S. (2007) *Ryanair: The Full Story of the Controversial Low-Cost Airline,* London: Aurum

Dennis, N. (2007) 'End of the free lunch? The responses of traditional European airlines to the low-cost threat', *Journal of Transport Management* 13: 311–321

Doganis, R. (2002) *Flying Off Course: The Economics of International Airlines,* 3rd edn, London: Routledge

Doganis, R. (2006) *The Airline Business,* 2nd edn, London: Routledge

easyJet (2008) Airline information website, available at www.easyjet.com, accessed 1 April 2008

ELFAA (European Low Fares Airline Association) (2004) *Liberalisation of European Air Transport: The Benefits of Low Fares Airlines to Consumers, Airports, Regions and the Environment*, report available at www.elffa.com

ELFAA (2008) Association information website, available at www.elfaa.com, accessed 26 March 2008

Evangelho, F., Huse, C. and Linhares, A. (2005) 'Market entry of a low-cost airline and impacts on the Brazilian business travellers', *Journal of Air Transport Management* 11: 99–105

Flick, B. M. (2007) 'Air Baltic: The dynamic market in the eastern parts of the European Community', in Groβ, S. and Schröder, A. (eds) (2007) *Handbook of Low-cost Airlines: Strategies, Business Processes and Market Environment,* Berlin: Erich Schmidt Verlag, pp111–122

Flygvapnet (2008) Website of the Swedish Air Force, available at www.flygvapnet.mil.se, accessed 17 April 2008

Forsyth, P., King, J. and Rodolfo, C. L. (2006) 'Open skies in ASEAN', *Journal of Air Transport Management* 12: 143–152

Francis, G., Humphreys, I. and Ison, S. (2004) 'Airports' perspectives on the growth of low-cost airlines and the remodelling of the airport-airline relationship', *Tourism Management* 25: 507–514

Francis, G., Humphreys, I., Ison, S. and Aicken, M. (2006) 'Where next for low-cost airlines? A spatial and temporal comparative study', *Journal of Transport Geography* 14: 83–94

Gol (2008) Airline information website, available at www.voegol.com.br, accessed 1 April 2008

Groβ, S. and Schröder, A. (eds) (2007) *Handbook of Low-cost Airlines: Strategies, Business Processes and Market Environment,* Berlin: Erich Schmidt Verlag

Hall, C. M. (2000) *Tourism Planning: Policies, Processes and Relationships,* Harlow: Prentice Hall

Hvass, K. (2006) 'Fra LCC til FSC: Forretningsmodellernes nuancer og deres inflydelse på profitabiliteten' [From LCC to FSC: the business models' nuances and their influence on profitability], Presentation, Copenhagen Business School, available at www.cbs.dk/content/download/41559/612613/file/Fra%20LCC%20til%20FSC.pdf, accessed 28 May 2008

ICAO (International Civil Aviation Organization) (2000) *ICAO's Policies on Taxation in the Field of International Air Transport*, available at www.icao.int/icaonet/dcs/8632/8632_3ed_en.pdf, accessed 25 March 2008

ICAO (2006) *Convention on International Civil Aviation (Chicago Convention)*, 9th edn, available at www.icao.int/icaonet/arch/doc/7300/7300_9ed.pdf, accessed 25 March 2008

ICAO (2007) *ICAO Journal 5*, available at www.icao.int, accessed 25 March 2008

Jones, L. (2007) *EasyJet: The Story of Britain's Biggest Low-cost Airline*, London: Aurum

Knorr, A. (2007) 'Southwest airlines: The low-cost pioneer at 35', in Groβ, S. and Schröder, A. (eds) (2007) *Handbook of Low-cost Airlines: Strategies, Business Processes and Market Environment*, Berlin: Erich Schmidt Verlag, pp77–110

Kunskapens Bok [Book of Knowledge] (1945) Stockholm: Natur och Kultur

Larsen, J., Urry, J. and Axhausen, K. W. (2007) 'Networks and tourism: Mobile social life', *Annals of Tourism Research* 34: 244–262

LFV (2005) Luftfartsverket, Swedish Aviation Authority

Low Cost Monitor (2007) 'Deutsches Zentrum für Luft- und Raumfart, Arbeitsgemeinschaft Deutscher Verkehrsflughäfen', Issue 2/2007, available at www.adv.aero, accessed 14 April 2008

Macário, R., Reis, V., Viegas, J., Meersman, H., Monteiro, F., van de Voorde, E., Vanelslander, T., Mackensie-Williams, P. and Schmidt, H. (2007) *The Consequences of the Growing European Low-cost Airline Sector*, European Parliament, Directorate-General for Internal Policies of the Union, PE 397.234

Mason, K. J. and Alamdari, F. (2007) 'EU network carriers, low cost carriers and consumer behaviour: A delphi study of future trends', *Journal of Air Transport Management* 13: 299–310

Meijers, D. (2005) 'Tax Flight: An Investigation into the Origins and Developments of the Exemptions from Various Kinds of Taxation of International Aviation', Working paper I05-E001, Universiteit Maastricht, International centre for Integrative Studies

Nationalencyklopedien (1991) Höganäs: Bra Böcker

Nilsson, J. H. (2003) *Östersjöområdet: Studier av Interaktion och Barriärer* [Baltic Sea Region: Studies of Interactions and Barriers], Communications from Lund University's Geographic Institute, thesis no 152, Lund: Sisyfos Förlag

Nilsson, J. H. (2008) 'Lågprisflygets Passagerare som Regional Resurs' [Low-cost aviation's passengers as a regional resource], Report, Department of Service Management, Lund University

Pantazis, N. and Liefner, I. (2006) 'The impact of low-cost carriers on catchment areas of established international airports: The case of Hanover Airport, Germany', *Journal of Transport Geography* 14: 265–272

Peanuts (2008) Low-cost airline news, available at http://peanuts.aero, accessed 1 April 2008

Pitfield, D. E. (2007) 'Ryanair's impact on airline market share from the London area airports: A time series analysis', *Journal of Transport Economics and Policy* 41: 75–92

Riga Airport (2008) Airport website, available at www.riga-airport.com, accessed 12 June 2008

Ryanair (2008) Airline information website, available at www.ryanair.com, accessed 1 April 2008

SIKA (Statens institut för kommunikationsanalys) (2007) *Luftfart 2006* [Air travel 2006], Östersund

Travel News (2008) Swedish travel trade magazine, April

Turismens Utredningsinstitut (2005) *Lågkostnadsflyget: en Möjlighetsrevolution för den Svenska Rese- och Besöksnäringen* [The low-cost flight, a revolution in possibilities for the Swedish travel and visitor economy], Stockholm

Vowles, T. M. (2000) 'The effect of low fare air carriers on airfares in the US', *Journal of Transport Geography* 8: 121–128

Widmann, T. (2007) 'The contribution of low-cost carriers to incoming tourism as exemplified by Frankfurt-Hahn Airport and the Rhineland Palatinate destination of the Moselle region', in Groβ, S. and Schröder, A. (eds) (2007) *Handbook of Low-cost Airlines: Strategies, Business Processes and Market Environment,* Berlin: Erich Schmidt Verlag, pp171–184

Wizz Air (2008) Airline information website, available at http://wizzair.com, accessed 1 April 2008

York Aviation LLP (2007) *Social Benefits of Low Fare Airlines in Europe*

6
Hypermobile Travellers

*Stefan Gössling, Jean-Paul Ceron, Ghislain Dubois
and Michael C. Hall*

Introduction

The contribution of aviation to climate change is, with a global share of just 2 per cent of emissions of CO_2 (see Chapter 2, this volume), often regarded as negligible. This perspective ignores, however, the current and expected growth in air traffic, as well as its sociocultural drivers. Aviation is a rapidly growing sector, with annual passenger growth forecasts of 4.9 per cent in the coming 20 years (Airbus, 2008). In a carbon-constrained world with the ambition to reduce absolute levels of greenhouse gas emissions and limited options to technically achieve these (see Chapter 13, this volume), the growth in air traveller numbers thus indicates an emerging conflict (see also Chapter 4, this volume). Moreover, it becomes increasingly clear that aviation is an activity in which comparably few people participate. With regard to international aviation, it can be estimated that only about 2–3 per cent of the world's population fly in between any two countries over one consecutive year (Peeters et al, 2006), indicating that participation in air travel is highly unequally distributed on a global scale. The vast majority of air travellers currently originate from industrialized countries, even though there are some recent trends, particularly in China and India, showing rapid growth in air travel (see UNWTO, 2007). There is also evidence that air travel is unevenly distributed *within* nations, particularly those with already high levels of individual mobility. In industrialized countries there is evidence of a minority of highly mobile individuals, who account for a large share of the overall kilometres travelled, especially by air. These travellers are 'hypermobile' in terms of participation in frequent trips, often over great distances. The following chapter sets out to describe hypermobile travellers and their mobility patterns from both statistical and sociological perspectives. It also presents a case study of the distribution of mobility in France, and discusses the importance of hypermobile lifestyles for emissions of greenhouse gases and climate change more generally.

Evidence of hypermobility

The terms 'hypermobile' and 'hypermobility' were introduced into the transport and cognate literature in the 1980s and 1990s (Hepworth and Ducatel, 1992; Lowe, 1994; van der Stoep, 1995) as well as related literature on the geography and sociology of globalization and regional change (e.g. Damette, 1980; Shields, 1996; Cox, 1997). Whitelegg (1993), for example, in looking at the connections between sustainability and transport contrasted the hypermobility of those in the North with the chronic underprovision of transport accessibility in the South. Adams' (1999) contribution to an OECD report on sustainable transport is widely referred to with respect to the term 'hypermobility', but he does not go beyond the statement that, 'The term hypermobility is used in this essay to suggest that it may be possible to have too much of a good thing' (Adams, 1999, p95). For the purpose of this chapter, Khisty and Zeitler's (2001, p598) definition of hypermobility as 'the maximization of physical movement' is more suitable to characterize the vast growth in temporary mobility by a relatively small number of individuals (Hall, 2005a; Bell and Brown, 2006). The chapter has thus a focus different from the perspectives of earlier works on hypermobility in that it seeks to describe highly mobile travellers rather than just the consequences of hypermobility for society (the focus of C. Jotin Khisty, P. S. Siraja and John Adams). In this chapter, the term should be understood to include a quantitative and qualitative dimension, and comprises a range of temporary mobilities, including leisure- and business-related mobility, both of which will be reviewed in more detail.

Leisure travel in industrialized countries has changed substantially in recent years, with a trend towards more frequent, but shorter trips to more distant locations, which increasingly involve air travel (e.g. Peeters et al, 2006). Within Europe and the US, this development is characterized by the emergence of low-fare carriers, now carrying some 150 million passengers per year in the European Union alone (Nilsson, Chapter 5 this volume). However, there is also a rapidly increasing leisure class of people travelling to distant or relatively peripheral destinations, often for considerably short periods of time (*The Guardian*, 21 March 2008). Similar developments can be observed in business travel, where a considerable number of people may now be commuting on a daily or weekly basis between their places of residence and work by air. Clearly, over the last 20 years, there has thus been a transition from aviation being a luxury form of mobility for the wealthy few to being a self-evident and often cheap means of mass transportation for large parts of society in industrialized countries, including both leisure and business travellers. It seems equally clear that these changes in the availability and affordability of air travel have also fundamentally changed perceptions of distance, place and space (e.g. Janelle, 1969; Urry, 2000; Gössling, 2002a; Adey et al, 2007); including what is regarded as routine and non-routine environments (Hall, 2005a, b; Coles and Hall, 2006). For example, Hall (2005a) criticizes the notion of tourism being a break from routine for the hypermobile, given that for them mobility as well as frequent visitation to the same locations is the norm.

> *The routinized space–time paths of those living in 2004 are not the same as those of people in 1984 when Giddens was writing or in the 1960s when Hägerstrand was examining routine daily space–time trajectories. Instead, because of advances in transport and communication technology, for a substantial proportion of the population in developed countries or for elites in developing countries, being able to travel long distances to engage in leisure behaviour (what one would usually describe as tourism) is now a part of their routine activities.* (Hall, 2005a, p24)

As yet, little is known about hypermobile travellers (see Hall, 2005a). Statistically, some 390 million tourists trips have been made between any two countries by air in 2007 (UNWTO, 2008) – out of a global population of about 6.7 billion (UN, 2008). However, as the same individuals will often have made multiple international flights over one year, it is estimated that the percentage of the world's population participating in international air travel is in the order of just 2–3 per cent (Peeters et al, 2006). This implies that a very minor share of humanity accounts for a large part of the overall kilometres travelled and consequent impacts. From a global point of view, all international air travellers may thus be seen as 'hypermobile travellers', as they usually account for vastly greater travel distances than the rest of the global population, but there are substantial differences in individual distances travelled as well as motivations for frequent travel. This demands a more thorough analysis of hypermobile travel. However, while the term is widely used with respect to the scale, magnitude and frequency of travel, there are only a very limited number of published studies that provide an empirical basis for this.

One of the first to look at a group of frequent travellers were Høyer and Næss (2001). In studying conference tourism, they report on at least three important insights with regard to hypermobile travellers. First, Høyer and Næss (2001, p452) summarize a Norwegian travel survey by Denstadli and Rideng (1999):

> *According to a recent Norwegian travel survey, job-related trips account for about 60 per cent of all flights, domestic as well as flights to and from foreign countries. Five per cent of air travellers make more than 15 return flights annually. This group of customers alone accounts for a quarter of all domestic flights.*

Most of their flights are made in connection with their job. ...
Among the 60 per cent of flights characterised as job-related,
courses and conferences account for about one-third (a little
more for domestic flights and a little less for foreign trips), while
service/consulting makes up about one-seventh.

This study indicates that the distribution of air travel may be highly skewed within industrialized countries, that is countries where overall mobility is high, and that a considerable share of mobility may be work-related, with 'courses and conferences' accounting for a significant share of travel motives. The respective shares of personal and professional mobility in air travel are, however, still debated in the absence of reliable global data sets on travel motives. Høyer and Næss (2001) go on to report on the case of scientist 'H' as a case study of a hypermobile citizen. Over the course of one year, H travelled on average 124km per day, which can be compared to the average daily mobility of 42km per Norwegian. As indicated in Table 6.1, almost 65 per cent of H's annual mobility is a result of air travel.

Høyer and Næss (2001, p460) also present the results of a survey of conference participants (n = 128, conference: 'Traffic Days 1999', Aalborg University):

The participants included researchers as well as public and
private sector practitioners. The respondents all lived in
Scandinavia. On average, they had attended 2.7 conferences
during the latest 12 months. Of these, 43 per cent were in the
home region (within 100km distance of the workplace), 39 per
cent elsewhere in Scandinavia, 15 per cent in Europe outside
Scandinavia, and 3 per cent in the rest of the world. The confer-
ence participation of the researchers was considerably higher
than among the practitioners... On average, each researcher had
travelled by plane to 1.4 conferences during the latest 12 months,
compared to a mean of 0.5 among the practitioners.

Table 6.1 *Annual accounts for a conference tourist:*
mobility and energy use

	Mobility km/year	Mobility km/day	Energy use kWh/year
Residential energy			7000
Private car	16,000	44	6130
Domestic scheduled flights	8000	22	6450
International scheduled flights	13,000	36	8670
Charter flights	8000	22	3400
Total	45,000	124	31,650

Source: Høyer and Næss, 2001

They conclude that scientists are highly mobile travellers, and, consequently, an important group contributing significantly to the overall amount of air miles flown within a given society. While these results seem to indicate that business travellers may be an important group of hypermobile travellers, leisure travel can be as important.

In a study of 252 international leisure tourists in Zanzibar, Tanzania, carried out in October 2003, Gössling et al (2006 and unpublished data) found that the average distance flown for leisure in 2002 and 2003 (i.e. over 22 months, air travel only) was 34,000pkm per tourist, excluding the trip to Zanzibar. The 10 most frequent travellers in this case study had covered almost 180,000pkm each for leisure travel by air in 2002/2003, with a maximum of 24 countries visited by one traveller in this period. Together, the 10 most frequent travellers had covered 20 per cent of the total distances travelled. Averaged per year, the study thus indicates that leisure travellers can cover vast distances, with an average of 17,000pkm travelled by air by each respondent over the course of one year, corresponding to 46.5km per day (a conservative estimate, as the trip to Zanzibar was not included and the study did not address the last two months of 2003). As various studies of individual mobility patterns in industrialized countries show, this is about the *total average distance* or about twice the *average leisure distance* travelled per capita in industrialized countries (see Gössling, 2002b). Furthermore, the study indicates that within the group of these highly mobile leisure travellers, there is a subgroup of hypermobile travellers, covering 90,000pkm each within a period of 12 months, that is effectively travelling more than twice around the globe within a year, corresponding to 246pkm per person per day, which can be compared to the global average distance of 298pkm flown per person *per year* (see Gilbert and Perl, 2008, p67). The study thus suggests that there is a group of long-distance leisure travellers who are responsible for a considerable share of the distances travelled for leisure-related purposes. Their demographic characteristics suggest that they are 20–50 years old, well educated and wealthy, while their awareness of environmental problems caused by energy-intense lifestyles is low (Gössling et al, 2006).

Another more recent study of air travellers at Gothenburg Airport, Sweden (Gössling et al, 2009) reveals that among all air travellers, mobility may be highly skewed. While about 28 per cent of the air travellers in the study had made one or two domestic or international return flights in the past 12 months (including the present flight; similar figures are reported by Lethbridge (2002) for the UK), and another 23 per cent between 3 and 5 flights, the situation was different at the higher end of the spectrum, where about 12 per cent of the respondents had flown at least 30 times (return) over the past 12 months, with a maximum of 300 return flights made by two respondents over one year.

The results thus indicate that a minority of air travellers accounts for a large share of the overall number of trips made. In this survey, the 3.8 per cent of hypermobile air travellers (>50 return flights per year) accounted for about 28 per cent of all trips made by the sample. Even this survey thus confirms that

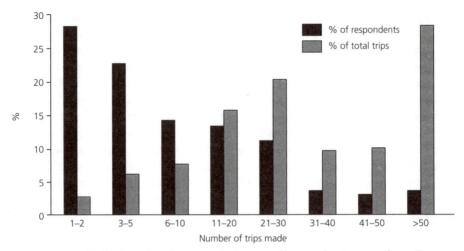

Figure 6.1 *Relationship between air traveller and trip number shares*

there is a small group that could be termed 'hypermobile hypermobiles', that is a minority in each population accounting for a comparably large share of trips and overall mobility.

Finally, a survey by Lassen (2006) investigating the travel behaviour of employees of the company Hewlett-Packard Denmark (n = 600) and Aalborg University (n = 1200) revealed that the average employee of Hewlett-Packard took 3.8 international trips within the last year, covering on average of 17,000pkm, with 94 per cent of international trips being made by air (the share of respondents in the sample was 32 per cent, i.e. 193 out of 600 employees) However, 25 per cent of the sample did not make any trips at all, while the most frequent traveller made 43 international trips. With regard to the distances travelled, 26 per cent of all trips were to Scandinavian countries, 67 per cent to other European countries, and 7 per cent outside Europe. A similar situation was found at Aalborg university (n = 547, representing a 46 per cent response rate), where on average only two international trips were made in one year, but the distance covered was higher at 22,000pkm, with aircraft being the transport mode in 85 per cent of all trips. Even in the case of Aalborg University, more than 30 per cent of employees did not make work-related trips at all, while the most frequent traveller had made 22 trips within the last year. Of all trips, 22 per cent were to Scandinavian countries, 56 per cent to other European countries, and 22 per cent to countries outside Europe. Lassen (2006) concludes that in both the case of Hewlett-Packard Denmark and Aalborg University, mobility is significantly higher than for the average Danish citizen, even though the study also suggests that mobility is unevenly distributed among employees, that is confirming the existence of a group of 'hypermobile hypermobiles'.

Essentially, the latter two studies, though not representative, indicate that some elite air travellers may account for a large share of the overall trips made, raising the question of how hypermobile travellers can be sociologically characterized. Reasons for high mobility may generally be professional, that is work-related, as for instance indicated in an interview with the manager of a large international company: 'I divide my time between [...] headquarters in San Francisco and a flat in New York' (*Metro*, 14 November 2005), indicating that he is commuting to work over a distance of more than 4000km. Likewise, the lead singer of a Swedish pop band stated in an interview that, 'In 1989–1991, we have been sitting on aircraft 260 days per year' (*Metro*, 8 September 2005). While these members of the cultural and economic elites (Bauman, 1998) may thus be seen as 'hypermobile hypermobiles', other societal groups may also be highly mobile. An example may be traveller 'A', a 25–30-year-old woman coincidentally encountered on a train in southern Sweden during the time of writing of this chapter. 'A' has worked for five years in the US for a research institute, then for another two years for an aid organization in Afghanistan. During the years abroad, she flew home at least twice a year. She has presently come from Bangkok, via a stopover in Istanbul, to visit her sister in Malmö, Sweden. She will travel to the low-cost airport Nyköping some 300km further north, where she bought a free flight (tax only) to Paris, and then continue from there to Israel (both trips to visit friends). After that she will move to New York, where she plans to study law. This example illustrates the importance of visiting friends and relatives (VFR) travel motives in increasingly global social worlds, as well as the global socio-economic structures in which people increasingly become embedded. Leisure-related travel motives may also greatly enhance distances travelled, however. The *Guardian Weekly* (21 March 2008) reports, for instance, that:

> *Cash-rich/time-poor travellers ... are indulging in ever more ambitious mini-breaks to wildly exotic locations... These 'break-neck breaks' will increase by more than a third this year, with the number of Brits travelling to destinations including Hong Kong, New York and Rio de Janeiro for just a few days rising from 3.7m to 4.9m in 2008.*

While these studies and quotes can provide some sociological insight into the group of hypermobile travellers, that is those participating in frequent and often long-distance air travel, no systematic study seems as yet to exist that allows for a better characterization of hypermobile travellers and their contribution to the distances travelled as well as the emissions of greenhouse gases caused. In the following, French studies will be presented in order to gain further insight into the group of hypermobile travellers.

Who are the hypermobile travellers? A case study in France

The following results are based on the representative monthly survey 'Suivi des déplacements touristiques' (SDT, including 30,000 households and 53,000 individuals), a tourism travel survey focusing on domestic and international travel of French residents, which excludes international tourists in France as well as French living abroad. All travel of distances >100km is included. Regarding the calculation of emissions, the French ADEME[1] provides emission coefficients in its 'Bilan carbone' (carbon account) database. The figures used here include indirect emissions from energy production but exclude energy linked to infrastructure building and maintenance, as well as a life-cycle analysis (ADEME, 2006) For air travel, ADEME uses an uplift factor (radiative forcing index, RFI) of 2. Each tonne of CO_2 is thus doubled in this calculation to account for the radiative forcing impact caused by non-CO_2 emissions (see Chapters 2 and 3 this volume).

The combination of the two databases allows the calculation of travel patterns and emissions for 4510 individuals. Based on hierarchical clustering, which is a process used to obtain groups through an iterative process aggregating the two nearest individuals (finally resulting in clusters that are as homogeneous as possible), six groups of travellers can be distinguished:

Cluster 1: frequent travellers who prefer short (less than 3 nights) or day trips;
Cluster 2: travellers who tend to use trains, favouring French destinations;
Cluster 3: travellers who tend to use cars, favouring French destinations;
Cluster 4: travellers used to travelling by plane, favouring French/European destinations;
Cluster 5: frequent travellers in France and abroad, including to long-haul destinations, using all modes of transport;
Cluster 6: immobiles, that is those staying at home.

Figure 6.2 associates each of these groups with greenhouse gas emissions, expressed in $kgCO_2$-equivalent per individual. The results show that the cluster immobile individuals (cluster 6) cause virtually no travel emissions, while the cluster of long-stay car travellers (cluster 3) as well as train travellers (cluster 2) and the short-stay travellers (cluster 1) cause comparably low emissions. Of greater importance for overall emissions are travellers in France and the rest of Europe (cluster 5), using different transport modes, and the frequent flyers to French and European destinations (cluster 4).

Figure 6.2 also shows that in terms of trip numbers, clusters 1 and 5 are fairly similar with an average of 6.5 and 6.2 trips per individual per year. However, in terms of emissions, an individual in cluster 1 emits on average $536kgCO_2$-eq, while an individual in cluster 5 causes $4300kgCO_2$-eq (Table 6.2).

Emissions are correlated with distances travelled, with a range of 150 to 19,153pkm per individual traveller per year between clusters. Long-distance travellers (cluster 5) mostly rely on air travel, raising per capita per day travel distances related to tourism to more than 52pkm, compared with just over 4pkm per day for the group of 'immobile' travellers (cluster 6).

Figure 6.3 shows that there are considerable differences between clusters 1, 2, 3, 4 and 6 with regard to individual emissions and distances travelled.

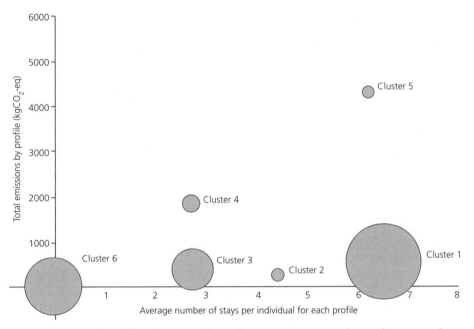

Figure 6.2 *Traveller clusters, based on average number of trips and emissions per individual*

However, cluster 5 clearly emerges in terms of distances travelled and emissions caused, indicating the importance of this hypermobile group of air travellers in generating emissions. While even individuals in cluster 4 use aircraft for a significant part of their travel, the main difference between the two groups is the number of trips made during a year, with cluster 5 individuals making on average 6.2 trips per year, 38 per cent of these by air.

From the above analysis, further attention should be given to clusters 1, 4 and 5. Cluster 1 represents frequent travellers engaging in quite short journeys. Cluster 4 comprises travellers travelling less frequently, but often by air. Cluster 5 represents the hypermobile travellers engaging in frequent trips, with a large share of these made by air. As these clusters are not entirely homogeneous, a more detailed analysis is follows (see Table 6.3).

Table 6.2 *Emissions per individual and cluster*

Cluster	Emissions ($kgCO_2$-eq)	Distance travelled (pkm)	Share of each cluster in national emissions
Cluster 1	536	3898	32%
Cluster 2	231	4265	2%
Cluster 3	344	2371	11%
Cluster 4	854	4041	11%
Cluster 5	4300	19,153	42%
Cluster 6	34	150	2%
Average all clusters	570	3452	

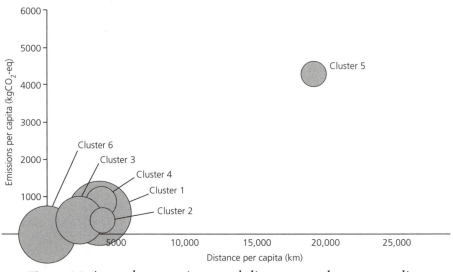

Figure 6.3 *Annual per capita travel distances and corresponding emissions per capita*

In the analysis of the three selected clusters, figures are expressed as deviations from the average values in the whole sample; unless otherwise indicated they refer to tourism.

Cluster 1 can be characterized as follows:

- frequent travellers in France both for leisure- and business-related reasons (the number of stays is 80 per cent and 40 per cent above average), with a high share of day trips (+87 per cent);
- stay mostly in France (97 per cent fewer visits to remote countries and 58 per cent fewer visits to Europe and the Mediterranean than the French average);
- visiting friends and relatives is a predominant travel motive (+149 per cent), while leisure travel is less important (33 per cent less than on national average);
- use of the car is predominant (57 per cent higher than average) as well as conventional trains (+106 per cent), even though not the TGV (high-speed train) (54 per cent less than average) or aircraft (70 per cent less than average);

Table 6.3 *Average number of trips and use of aircraft*

	Average number of trips	Share of aircraft as means of transport in all trips made (%)
Cluster 1	6.5	2
Cluster 4	2.7	35
Cluster 5	6.2	38
Average (clusters 1 to 6)	3.6	6

- own more second homes than French population on average (+25 per cent).

Individuals with medium–high income levels (€3000–7500 net income per month) are well represented in this cluster, as are citizens in management positions and workers with higher education. Citizens aged 30–39 are overrepresented in this cluster, including a higher share of 50–69 year olds as well. With regard to family structures, couples with one or two children are overrepresented. Geographically, the cluster is balanced, with people living in cities of all sizes. Overall, the results would thus indicate that family structure, social structure (visiting friends and relatives), age and income are defining travel patterns in this group.

Cluster 4 can be characterized as follows:

- travellers heavily focus on trips to Europe and the Mediterranean (+741 per cent);
- the use of the plane is dominant (+518 per cent);
- travellers focus on long stays (4 nights and more, +82 per cent).

Medium–high income groups (€3000–7500 per month) are overrepresented in this cluster, as well as citizens working in management positions, workers with higher education, craftsmen, traders and farmers. Household size is generally smaller in this cluster, with two-person households and households with one child being overrepresented. Households with 2–3 children are on the other hand underrepresented, while those with 4–6 children are overrepresented. Younger citizens (<20 years) are overrepresented in this group, as are elderly people. Individuals in this group live more often in medium or large cities, as well as the French capital, Paris. In conclusion, this cluster may mostly contain 'new conventional' holidaymakers, who have substituted the French coast for 'more southern' Mediterranean coastlines, usually favouring the plane as the means of transport. This group also contains immigrants visiting friends and relatives in their country of origin (southern Europe, North Africa).

Cluster 5 can be characterized as follows:

- travellers focus on distant destinations far more than the average (+1762 per cent), which is also reflected in distances travelled (1730 per cent farther than average);
- travellers make more trips both for leisure (+74 per cent) and for business (+150 per cent);
- length of stay is greater for both long stays (4 nights and more, +56 per cent) and short stays (fewer than 4 nights, +17 per cent);
- travel motives include leisure (+57 per cent) and visiting friends and relatives (+10 per cent);
- the use of aircraft is far greater than on average (+558 per cent).

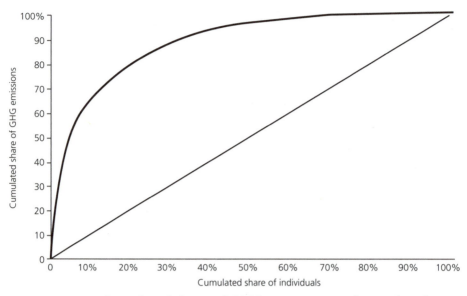

Figure 6.4 *Cumulated share of GHG emissions and cumulated shares of individuals*

The individuals in this cluster could be considered as the hypermobile share of the population. Citizens with higher income levels (>€7500 per month) are overrepresented in the cluster. With regard to profession, management positions and workers with higher education are dominant in this group. Elderly people (50–69) are overrepresented in this cluster. Singles dominate this cluster, as well as couples without children, and they often live in Paris.

With regard to the relationship between individual travel patterns and their contribution to overall distances travelled (as well as emissions), Figure 6.4 shows that half the emissions of greenhouse gas emissions caused by the mobility of French citizens are caused by just 5 per cent of the population, indicating the major importance of hypermobile travellers in addressing transport-related emissions.

The results of this case study suggest that average values for a society's mobility patterns appear less applicable in a climate change context. Clearly, there are many groups in society whose lifestyles are, with regard to transport, quite sustainable. At the other end of the spectrum, there may be a minority of hypermobile travellers with highly unsustainable mobility patterns, who account for the majority of distances travelled, predominant use of the most energy- and emission-intense transport mode, that is aircraft, and, consequently, a high share of national emissions. However, the results of the French study also show that air travellers are not necessarily frequent travellers, confirming the findings of Gössling et al (2009) that a considerable share of air travellers may only take one or two return trips per year, and often over comparably short distances. This group is of interest, as their air-based mobility may be substitutable by high-speed trains (Ceron and Dubois, 2006; Dubois and Ceron, 2007). Of similar interest is the group of frequent travellers not using aircraft. Here, results indicate that stage in life as well as family structure has important implications for mobility patterns.

The emergence of hypermobile travel patterns

This chapter has presented evidence that air travellers may generally be seen as a highly mobile part of society (with regard to the distances travelled), even though a further distinction of a small class of hypermobile hypermobiles, that is both frequent and long-distance (air) travellers, can be made in Western societies – and possibly in every society – who account for a major share of the distances travelled by society as a whole. These seem more generally to correspond to Zygmunt Bauman's (1998) cultural, capital and communication elites, or, as national travel surveys indicate, to the well-educated, high-income parts of society, to which men belong more often than women (e.g. Carlsson-Kanyama and Lindén, 1999; Carlsson-Kanyama and Räti, 2008). For example, in a study of census night patterns of temporary mobility away from permanent place of residence in Australia, Bell and Brown (2006) reported that the Australian evidence does suggest clear differences in the characteristics that predispose individuals to travel for particular purposes. For production-oriented work-related travel outside the local area, the most significant predictors were being male, maritally unattached, in a high-income job, and working either in mining, agriculture, or government administration and defence. In contrast, travel for leisure and tourism consumption demonstrated more balanced sex ratios, but was selective of older age groups and those who are unemployed or outside the labour force, although it also indicated a strong relationship with income.

It has long been recognized that it is the wealthier elements of a society, those with the greatest economic budget and, to a great extent, time budget, who are the most mobile (Hall, 2005a). However, with global changes in transport systems, and particularly the rise of low-cost airlines, new groups of hypermobile travellers have come into existence. These may for instance include health migrants and medical tourists (Connell, 2006; Ramírez de Arellano, 2007), second-home commuters (often to remote parts of the world, such as Swedes in Thailand or the French in Africa) (Hall and Müller, 2004), short-break long-distance travellers ('break-neck breaks') (Williams and Montanari, 1995), frequent low-fare holidaymakers (Connell and Williams, 2005), as well as longer-distance commuters (Green et al, 1999) and long-haul business travellers (Swarbrooke and Horner, 2001). This also includes opportunities to take 'a break' or 'sabbatical' in life, while flying around the world including various stopovers and/or participating in volunteer projects as part of the 'OE' (Overseas Experience) or 'gap year' has become a new rite of passage for wealthier and middle-class youths in industrialized countries (Williams and Hall, 2002; Simpson, 2005). The emergence of these new highly mobile

Table 6.4 *Typology of hypermobility*

	Production-oriented		Consumption-oriented	
	Permanent employment	Seasonal and short-term contract employment	Personal consumption	Leisure and tourism
Reason/ motivation	• International business travel • Long-distance commuting • Expatriate employment	• Seasonal work travel	• Health and medical travel • Educational travel	• Vacations, including development of international weekend and short-break market • Second-home commuting • Sunbirding / snowbirding • VFR
Primary characteristics	• High income • Professional / managerial • Specific sectors and industries • Males	• Low and medium income • Often relatively low skilled but meeting labour shortages at destinations • Specific sectors and industries	• Medium and high income • Professional	• Medium and high income • Low constraints on travel

societal groups is facilitated by increasing incomes, with disproportional growing incomes in the upper classes of society, as well as cheap and even declining fares for air travel and the perception of no-cost mobility created by low-fare airlines. Airline marketing strategies may also be relevant to the process, as for instance in the case of low-cost airlines targeting youth markets (Shaw and Thomas, 2006) and the impact of frequent flyer programmes on the demand for air travel (Chin, 2002). Just as significantly, new flexible labour strategies and the reduction of international barriers in the mobility of skilled and, in some cases, relatively unskilled workers (such as crop pickers) also substantially contribute to production-oriented hypermobility (Hall and Coles, 2008).

The recognition of consumption and production-oriented forms of hypermobility is significant as it helps identify different reasons and characteristics of hypermobility that may, in turn, assist the development of mitigation strategies. Some of these forms of hypermobility are outlined in Table 6.4.

Overall, several trends are influencing the rise of hypermobile travellers, including the emergence of low-fare airlines, introducing cheap mass travel and perceptions of no-cost mobility, as well as frequent and often short long-distance flights to more remote destinations. The social and economic importance of these trends is twofold. First, high-speed transport systems lead to increasing travel distances, because the average daily amount of time spent travelling, as well as the average share of personal income spent for travel seems constant (Schafer, 1998; Schafer and Victor, 2000). When average incomes increase, the absolute amount of money spent for transport will also grow. Likewise, with faster means of transport, absolute travel distances increase. The important implication here is that faster transport systems will not be used to reduce transport time, that is to reduce the share of time spent travelling, rather than to travel to more distant locations. This would indicate that there are few limits to mobility with regard to the distances travelled by individuals, except via the constraints of the aviation transport network, while there may also be a trend towards more energy-intense forms of travel, as mirrored in the rapidly growing number of private and increasingly luxurious aircraft. For example, news agency Reuters reported in December 2007 that the first A380, the world's largest passenger aircraft, had been sold to a private customer, a member of the Saudi royal family (*USA Today*, 2007). This coincides with Miller's (2007) conclusion that growth in mobility may not primarily be a result of new parts of society becoming air travellers, rather than affluent people travelling more, with average household income for leisure passengers departing by air from London airports Gatwick, Luton and Stansted being over £50,000 (about €74,000 as of June 2008) per year (Miller, 2007, based on UKERC, 2006 and CAA, 2006). While individual hypermobile travel patterns as yet only comprise a very small share of the world's population, there is evidence that a rapidly increasing number of people is becoming highly mobile. For instance, while 50 per cent of adult UK residents flew at least once in 2001 (Lethbridge, 2002), this share is substantially lower in China and India (see UNWTO, 2007) but appears set to catch up if the context (sociocultural and economic) remain the same (Arlt, 2006).

Although changes in technology are important for hypermobility it must also be acknowledged that the demand for increased long-distance mobility is socially and economically constructed within processes of contemporary globalization (Hall, 2005a). For example, along with advances in communications, aviation is contributing to time–space convergence via 'space–time compression' (see Harvey, 1989), in the sense that vast distances can now be covered in comparably short periods of time, and 'space–time distantiation' is contributing to increased extensibility, in the sense that social and economic relations are now stretched over time and space. Time–space convergence therefore unites concepts of hypermobility as used in the transport literature to describe the maximization of physical mobility by a relatively small number of people, with those of Damette (1980) to describe the accelerated switching of investment between locations as the turnover time of fixed capital is reduced. Both forms of hypermobility each contribute to and are affected by contemporary globalization.

Hypermobility is therefore embedded in reflexive and recursive social and economic practices that serve to reinforce acceptance and demand for global work and play. This is, in part, argued by some as being responsible for the emergence of a global cosmopolitan society of people (Giddens, 2003), culturally tolerant and who are increasingly at home anywhere in the world (Urry,

2000), while the wish to experience new places may be reinforced through travel (Gössling, 2002a). Aviation is thus, more than any other means of transport, reconfiguring perceptions of distance, space and time towards cosmopolitan identities and new global social networks. As this process involves primarily young people, the consequences may be far-reaching. As Shaw and Thomas remark, '... "global lifestyle" aspirations acquired in their [the youths'] formative years may well establish travel patterns for 50 years or more...' (Shaw and Thomas, 2006, p210). Various, as yet little researched processes support these developments, as high mobility is both associated with and often even a precondition for social status (Høyer and Næss, 2001), while high mobility is simultaneously rewarded with even greater individual mobility, for instance through bonus systems (frequent flyer miles). These processes may in turn lead to the expectation of cheap and readily available mobility that may be perceived as both a norm and a human right (see UNWTO, 2000; Shaw and Thomas, 2006). Further complicating the picture is the extent to which processes of work and play are increasingly being defined in global terms. For example, Jones (2008, p14) observes that, 'Contemporary work is becoming less constituted through localized, physically proximate relations and increasingly constituted through distantiated relations. These multiple spatial associations increasingly extend to the planetary scale.' The reconfiguration of work in global terms also creates its own dynamic in terms of 'how individuals and groups of individuals are empowered (or not) in relation to global capitalism, and the future life chances and opportunities which workers have open to them' (Jones, 2008, p13). In order to compete in the global workplace it is therefore not surprising that not only is increased value based on the experience derived from hypermobility but also the willingness of individuals to continue to engage in such mobility for corporate benefit.

Conclusions: Hypermobility and climate change

The chapter has presented evidence that hypermobility is a process driven by a relatively small part of society, but increasingly comprising new societal groups with 'new' mobility motives. Visiting friends and relatives, frequent business trips, second homes in more remote locations, long-haul short breaks for leisure, as well as low-cost short breaks all boost the distances travelled in industrialized societies. While aviation as such is in fact an important contributor to global emissions of greenhouse gases (see Chapter 2, this volume), it deserves mention that these emissions are primarily caused by a small share of highly mobile and hypermobile travellers. In a world with a global trend towards higher, more energy-intense mobility, emissions will vastly increase. This process may be fostered by air travellers in general and in particular by the 'hypermobile hypermobiles' identified in this chapter. These findings also underline the current dichotomy between Kyoto- and post-Kyoto emissions reduction needs and the reproduction of mobility through various, as yet little researched social processes. This should deserve the attention of policy makers in industrialized countries, as individual emissions associated with food consumption may vary by a factor of 2–5, by a factor of 5–10 for housing, but possibly by a factor of 100–1000 for mobility.

Societal trends towards hypermobile, aviation-based travel patterns as currently observed may seem increasingly irreversible, both because of the symbolic power associated with this transport mode in terms of a 'human right of mobility' and 'freedom to travel', as well as very real need to travel arising in globalized social networks, where for instance 'visiting friends and relatives' travel motives seem on the increase. From a climate policy point of view, hypermobile travellers appear to be the group with the largest potential to achieve substantial reductions in greenhouse gas emissions, even though this may be difficult, as they usually represent the political, economic and cultural elites of society. It may thus be equally important to dissuade other groups of presently less frequent travellers to enter carbon-intensive hypermobile lifestyles.

Note

1   Agence de l'environnement et de la maîtrise de l'énergie.

References

Adams, J. (1999) *The Social Implications of Hypermobility*, OECD Project on Environmentally Sustainable Transport, Paris: OECD

ADEME (2006) *Bilan Carbone. Calcul des Facteurs d'Emissions et Sources Bibliographiques Utilisées* (version 4.0), Paris: ADEME, MIES

Adey, P., Budd, L. and Hubbard, P. (2007) 'Flying lessons: Exploring the social and cultural geographies of global air travel', *Progress in Human Geography* 31(6): 773–791

Airbus (2008) *Flying by Nature: Global Market Forecast 2007–2026*, available at www.airbus.com/fileadmin/documents/gmf/PDF_dl/00-all-gmf_2007.pdf, accessed 18 February 2008

Arlt, W. G. (2006) *China's Outbound Tourism*, London: Routledge

Baumann, Z. (1998) *Globalization: The Human Consequences*, Cambridge, UK: Polity Press

Bell, M. and Brown, D. (2006) 'Who are the visitors? Characteristics of temporary movers in Australia', *Population, Space and Place* 12: 77–92

CAA (2006) *2005 Air Passenger Survey*, available at www.caa.co.uk/default.aspx?catid=81&pagetype=90&pageid=7640, accessed 9 July 2008

Carlsson-Kanyama, A. and Lindén, A.-L. (1999) 'Travel patterns and environmental effects now and in the future: Implications of differences in energy consumption among socio-economic groups', *Ecological Economics* 30: 405–417

Carlsson-Kanyama, A. and Räti, R. (2008) *Kvinnor, Män och Energi: Makt, Produktion och Användning* [Women, men and energy: Power production and use], Stockholm: Totalförsvarets Forskningsinstitut

Ceron, J.-P. and Dubois, G. (2006) *Demain le Voyage. La Mobilité de Tourisme et de Loisirs des Français Face au Développement Durable. Scénarios à 2050*, Paris: Ministère des transports, de l'équipement, du tourisme et de la mer

Chin, A. T. H. (2002) 'The impact of frequent flyer programmes on the demand for air travel', *Journal of Air Transportation* 7(2): 53–86

Coles, T. and Hall, C. M. (2006) 'The geography of tourism is dead: Long live geographies of tourism and mobility', *Current Issues in Tourism* 9(4–5): 289–292

Connell, J. (2006) 'Medical tourism: Sea, sun, sand and ... surgery', *Tourism Management*, 27(6): 1093–1100

Connell, J. F. and Williams, G. (2005) 'Passengers' perceptions of low-cost airlines and full service carriers: A case study involving Ryanair, Aer Lingus, Air Asia and Malaysia Airlines', *Journal of Air Transport Management* 11(4): 259–272

Cox, K. R. (ed) (1997) *Spaces of Globalization: Reasserting the Power of the Local*, New York: Guilford Press

Damette, F. (1980) 'The regional framework of monopoly exploitation: New problems and trends', in Carney, J., Hudson, R. and Lewis, J. R. (eds) *Regions in Crisis*, London: Croom Helm, pp76–92

Denstadli, J. M. and Rideng, A. (1999) 'Flere reiser med fly, og vi flyr oftere og lengre' [More people make flights, and we fly more frequently and longer], *Samferdsel* 9: 16–7

Dubois, G. and Ceron, J.-P. (2007) 'How heavy will the burden be? Using scenario analysis to assess future tourism greenhouse gas emissions', in Peeters, P. (ed) *Tourism and Climate Change Mitigation: Methods, Greenhouse Gas Reductions and Policies*, Breda: NHTV Breda University of Applied Science, pp189–207

Giddens, A. (2003) *Runaway World: How Globalization is Reshaping Our Lives*, 2nd edn, New York: Routledge

Gilbert, R. and Perl, A. (2008) *Transport Revolutions: Moving People and Freight Without Oil*, London: Earthscan

Gössling, S. (2002a) 'Human-environmental relation with tourism', *Annals of Tourism Research* 29: 539–556

Gössling, S. (2002b) 'Global environmental consequences of tourism', *Global Environmental Change Part A*, 12: 283–302

Gössling, S., Bredberg, M., Randow, A., Svensson, P. and Swedlin, E. (2006) 'Tourist perceptions of climate change', *Current Issues in Tourism* 9(4–5): 419–435

Gössling, S., Hultman, J., Haglund, L, Källgren, H. and Revahl, M. (2009) 'Voluntary carbon offsetting by Swedish air travellers: Towards the co-creation of environmental value?' *Current Issues in Tourism*, in press

Green, A. E., Hogarth T. and Shackleton, R. E. (1999) 'Longer distance commuting as a substitute for migration in Britain', *International Journal of Population Geography* 5: 49–68

Hall, C. M. (2005a) *Tourism: Rethinking the Social Science of Mobility*, London: Pearson Education

Hall, C. M. (2005b) 'Reconsidering the geography of tourism and contemporary mobility', *Geographical Research* 43(2): 125–139

Hall, C. M. and Coles, T. (2008) 'Introduction: Tourism and international business – tourism as international business', in Coles, T. and Hall, C. M. (eds) *Tourism and International Business*, London: Routledge, pp1–25

Hall, C. M. and Müller D. (eds) (2004) *Tourism, Mobility and Second Homes: Between Elite Landscape and Common Ground*, Clevedon: Channelview Publications

Harvey, D. (1989) *The Condition of Postmodernity*, Oxford: Blackwell

Hepworth, M. and Ducatel, K. (1992) *Transport in the Information Age: Wheels and Wires*, London: Belhaven Press

Høyer, K. G. and Næss, P. (2001) 'Sustainable tourism or sustainable mobility? The Norwegian case', *Journal of Sustainable Tourism* 8: 451–470

Janelle, D. G. (1969) 'Spatial reorganization: A model and concept', *Annals of the Association of American Geographers* 59: 348–364

Jones, A. (2008) 'The rise of global work', *Transactions of the Institute of British Geographers*, NS 33: 12–26

Khisty, C. J. and Zeitler, U. (2001) 'Is hypermobility a challenge for transport ethics and systemicity?', *Systemic Practice and Action Research* 14: 597–613

Lassen, C. (2006) 'Aeromobility and work', *Environment and Planning A* 38: 301–312

Lethbridge, N. (2002) *Attitudes to Air Travel*, London: Office of National Statistics

Lowe, M. D. (1994) 'The global rail revival', *Society*, 31(5): 51–56

Miller, G. (2007) *Public Understanding of Sustainable Leisure and Tourism*, a research report completed for the Department for Environment, Food and Rural Affairs by the University of Surrey, Surrey, UK: University of Surrey

Peeters, P., Gössling, S. and Becken, S. (2006) 'Innovation towards tourism sustainability: climate change and aviation', *International Journal of Innovation and Sustainable Development*, 1(3): 184–200

Ramírez de Arellano, A. B. (2007) 'Patients without borders: The emergence of medical tourism', *International Journal of Health Services* 37 (1): 193–198

Schafer, A. (1998) 'The global demand for motorized mobility', *Transportation Research Part A* 32(6): 445–477

Schafer, A. and Victor, D. G. (2000) 'The future mobility of the world population', *Transportation Research Part A* 34: 171–205

Shaw, S. and Thomas, C (2006) 'Social and cultural dimensions of air travel demand: Hyper-mobility in the UK?', *Journal of Sustainable Tourism* 14(2): 209–215

Shields, R. (1996) 'Flow', *Space and Culture* 1: 1–5

Simpson, K. (2005) 'Dropping out or signing up? The professionalisation of youth travel, *Antipode* 37(3): 447–469

Swarbrooke, J. and Horner, S. (2001) *Business Travel and Tourism*, Oxford: Butterworth-Heinemann

UKERC (UK Energy Research Centre) (2006) *Predict and Decide*, Oxford: UKERC

UN (2008) *World Population Prospects: The 2006 Revision Population Database*, available at: http://esa.un.org/unpp/, accessed 9 July 2008

UNWTO (United Nations World Tourism Organization) (2000) *Global Code of Ethics for Tourism*, Madrid: UNWTO

UNWTO (2007) *Compendium of Tourism Statistics*, Madrid: UNWTO

UNWTO (2008) *Facts and Figures*, available at www.unwto.org/index.php, accessed 9 July 2008

Urry, J. (2000) *Sociology Beyond Societies: Mobilities For The Twenty-First Century*, London: Routledge

USA Today (2007) 'Saudi Prince Alwaleed buys his own A380 jumbo jet', available at www.usatoday.com/money/industries/travel/2007–11–12-prince-alwaleed-a380_N.htm, accessed 9 July 2008

van der, Stoep, J. (1995) 'Hypermobility as a challenge for systems thinking and government policy', *Proceedings 39th Annual Meeting International Society for the Systems Sciences*, Louisville, pp402–411

Whitelegg, J. (1993) *Transport for a Sustainable Future: The Case for Europe*, London: Belhaven Press

Williams, A. M. and Hall, C. M. (2002) 'Tourism, migration, circulation and mobility: The contingencies of time and place', in Hall, C. M. and Williams, A. M. (eds) *Tourism and Migration: New Relationships Between Production and Consumption*, Dordrecht: Kluwer, pp1–52

Williams, A. M. and Montanari, A. (1995) 'Tourism regions and spaces in a changing social framework', *Tijdschrift Voor Economische en Sociale Geografie* 86(1): 3–12

7
Airline Trends in Europe: Network Consolidation and the Mainstreaming of Low-cost Strategies[1]

Nigel Dennis

Introduction

The early years of the 21st century have been uncomfortable ones for many of the world's major airlines. The downturn in demand for air travel that followed the terrorist attacks of 11 September 2001, coupled with intensive competition – especially from new entrants based on the 'low-cost/no-frills' model – resulted in several years of severe losses. The Iraq war and the SARS epidemic further suppressed demand while high fuel prices, magnified by the weakening economic conditions in many Western economies lead to little optimism at the time of writing either.

For almost the first time, demand for air travel cannot be assumed to follow an ever rising trend. Airlines have reacted by cutting back the weaker parts of their network and operations and aiming for more cooperation and consolidation within the industry to curb excess capacity. The major airlines have moved to strengthen their position in the marketplace by consolidating operations under one brand. In some cases this involved the merger or takeover of an independent rival (for example, Scandinavian Airlines (SAS) acquired its Norwegian rival Braathens, and American Airlines absorbed the ailing Trans World Airlines (TWA)). Franchising, whereby one airline licenses its product and identity to another is an alternative method for the major carriers to extend their brand presence while leaving the commercial risk with the franchisee (Denton and Dennis, 2000). Other secondary forms of collaboration include joint operations and code-sharing agreements, which may be organized on an ad-hoc, route-by-route basis.

One of the most important developments in the global arena is the emergence of international airline alliances (Hanlon, 1999). Examples are the Star Alliance, which includes Lufthansa and United among others or SkyTeam, based around Air France and Delta. These aim to extend the reach of an individual airline network by linking it with services of partner carriers. This increases the number of city pairs that can be served compared to the airlines operating individually, enables joint scheduling and marketing, combination of frequent flyer programmes, combined purchasing and sharing of services and infrastructure. In a downturn of demand, alliances also enable consolidation of capacity, at both the route and network level.

Alliances, mergers, franchising and code-sharing arrangements all have the effect of reducing the number of carriers operating at an airport which has the potential to diminish competition and increases the risk to airport operators and communities should the dominant operator change strategy or go out of business. The impact of this reshaping of the airline industry on airline networks in Europe is addressed below.

The commercial strategies adopted by the major airlines in reaction to the competitive threat from low-cost carriers are then considered. These include means of reducing labour costs or increasing productivity within the mainline airline operation. There is also the possibility of transferring services to regional partners, franchises or alliances and even setting up a low-cost carrier subsidiary. Services and procedures have also come under scrutiny. Areas such as distribution costs have been brought closer to the low-cost airline model by reducing or scrapping commission payments to travel agents. British Airways (BA) and British Midland Airways (bmi) have revised their fare structures to remove minimum stays on the cheaper tickets for most European sectors. Catering in economy class is generally on a downward spiral with airlines such as Aer Lingus, bmi and SAS moving to paid-for refreshments and some others offering only non-alcoholic beverages. Charter airlines such as Monarch have moved into the scheduled business while Thomsonfly offers seat-only charters on a range of new routes.

The success of these approaches has been rather variable. In particular, few of the low-cost subsidiaries have been very successful, suggesting it is difficult to run two brands under the same roof. British Airways is generally accredited with having the most realistic strategy for dealing with the low-cost airlines, perhaps alongside Aer Lingus who are the only real example of a traditional network airline converting much of the way into a low-cost carrier (*Aviation Strategy*, 2004b). Others have done the minimum by changing strategy only where head-to-head with either a low-cost airline or BA. Some have adopted aggressive tactics through legal procedures or control of slots, facilities or capacity to keep new entrants out.

Changes in long-haul coverage

The most unstable demand in recent years has come in intercontinental markets such as the North Atlantic and Europe–Middle East. This has accelerated the rationalization by many airlines of their long-haul services. In Europe, too many small countries have attempted to maintain a national 'flag carrier' with an intercontinental presence. The larger airlines often had several airports in their home country from which they flew long-haul. It is generally less efficient to split long-haul services between hubs, and airlines had already started addressing this problem prior to 11 September, with Swissair moving long-haul routes from Geneva to Zurich and British Airways (BA) deciding to concentrate on Heathrow at the expense of Gatwick (Halstead, 2001).

Tables 7.1 and 7.2 consider the change in long-haul service at European airports from summer 2000 (the high-point of the traditional airline industry) to summer 2003. Table 7.1 takes only the cities with a daily service by the major hub airline (including code-shares). This is a good yardstick of the principal route network, being the minimum frequency necessary in most

Table 7.1 *Daily long-haul services by major hub airline in first week of July (including code-shares)*

Airport (Airline)	Year	North America	Latin America	Africa	Asia Pacific	Total
London Heathrow (BA)	2000	14	-	3	17	34
	2003	18	1	6	17	42
London Gatwick (BA)	2000	11	1	2	-	14
	2003	4	1	-	-	5
Paris CDG (AF)	2000	15	2	6	11	34
	2003	15	8	9	14	46
Amsterdam (KL)	2000	16	1	4	10	31
	2003	18	6	7	14	45
Frankfurt (LH)	2000	18	2	3	15	38
	2003	20	3	3	17	43
Munich (LH)	2000	5	-	-	-	5
	2003	7	-	-	1	8
Zurich (SR/LX)	2000	12	1	1	9	21
	2003	9	1	1	7	18
Milan Malpensa (AZ)	2000	8	-	1	1	10
	2003	7	1	1	2	11
Rome Fiumicino (AZ)	2000	4	-	1	1	6
	2003	4	-	1	1	6
Madrid (IB)	2000	3	5	-	1	8
	2003	4	11	-	1	16
Brussels (SN)	2000	7	-	1	1	9
	2003	1	-	1	-	2
Copenhagen (SK)	2000	4	-	-	4	8
	2003	4	-	-	2	6
Vienna (OS)	2000	2	-	-	1	3
	2003	2	-	-	4	6

Source: Compiled from OAG data

markets to compete with the strongest airlines (including those with hubs outside Europe). Multistop services are included as long as there is no aircraft change involved.

It can be seen that four major airline hubs dominate long-haul services in Europe (BA-London Heathrow, Air France-Paris CDG, Royal Dutch Airlines (KLM)-Amsterdam and Lufthansa-Frankfurt). These have all strengthened their position and now have a very similar level of service with between 40 and 50 daily long-haul flights by the local airline. In some cases, smaller aircraft are used than previously. BA has run down London Gatwick and moved services to London Heathrow with no net growth. Air France has expanded rapidly at Paris CDG, particularly increasing the frequency of services to Latin America. KLM has likewise at Amsterdam Schiphol upgraded a number of sub-daily routes (mainly to Africa and Latin America) to a daily frequency. Lufthansa remains heavily focused on the North Atlantic and Asia. Zurich has conventionally been the 'number five' long-haul hub and Swiss has gradually reinstated much of the old Swissair long-haul network. Iberia at Madrid is the strongest gateway to Latin America. Of the remaining airports, Brussels has suffered badly following the demise of Sabena and Copenhagen also appears to be declining. Munich and Vienna have shown modest expansion.

Table 7.2 includes all long-haul points served, which offers a broader perspective. In some cases these are services by other airlines, elsewhere they are sub-daily routes by the hub major. Many secondary Asian points are served only by the foreign carrier and Caribbean points are often served by quasi-charter airlines, especially in Germany, Italy and the Netherlands. It can be seen that the total long-haul network has not increased much, as airlines are tending to focus on higher frequencies to major points rather than maximizing the number of places with direct service. Total network coverage has declined everywhere except London Heathrow and Munich over the last three years. Munich is still growing albeit slowly. London Heathrow has benefited from the decimation of London Gatwick long-haul operations – where the total network has halved, the biggest decline of any featured airport including Brussels (where Sabena went bankrupt). Brussels' network to Africa has been maintained but with many small foreign airlines often providing low-frequency multistop service. Asian and North Atlantic coverage has been badly hit however. Zurich and Rome have also seen significant declines.

Some airlines have benefited more than others from cutbacks by the weaker players. This has enabled Air France and Lufthansa to gain market share, as part of the traffic that used to pass through Gatwick, Brussels, Zurich, Copenhagen and Rome is spilled elsewhere.

Lufthansa has launched an innovative means of providing long-haul service away from its main hub airports in Germany. This involves using a long-range Airbus A320 configured in an all business-class layout. Routes have included Düsseldorf–New York and Düsseldorf–Chicago. Such a strategy will only work where there is sufficient high-yield business traffic to maintain a reasonable load factor on an everyday basis, however.

Table 7.2 *Long-haul points served by all airlines at any frequency in first week of July*

Airport (Airline)	Year	North America	Latin America	Africa	Asia Pacific	Total
London Heathrow	2000	19	5	15	49	88
	2003	24	14	20	47	105
London Gatwick	2000	29	17	17	8	71
	2003	19	9	5	3	36
Paris CDG	2000	20	14	30	40	104
	2003	18	15	27	43	103
Amsterdam	2000	20	22	14	42	98
	2003	24	20	14	37	95
Frankfurt	2000	30	20	18	57	125
	2003	33	18	20	51	122
Munich	2000	10	6	7	12	35
	2003	10	4	9	15	38
Zurich	2000	13	4	19	27	63
	2003	11	3	17	19	50
Milan Malpensa	2000	10	13	13	17	53
	2003	8	14	11	17	50
Rome Fiumicino	2000	10	11	14	30	65
	2003	8	6	11	29	54
Madrid	2000	8	19	5	8	40
	2003	8	16	5	8	37
Brussels	2000	9	-	22	11	42
	2003	6	-	20	5	31
Copenhagen	2000	6	2	2	10	20
	2003	6	2	2	9	19
Vienna	2000	4	-	4	24	32
	2003	4	-	3	23	30

Source: Compiled from OAG data

Dependence upon a single airline or alliance group

Rather than negotiating with a number of airlines on an equal basis, airports are increasingly likely to find they now have one very powerful customer. Hub airports have for some years tended to become natural monopolies as the hub airline captures almost all the transfer demand and hence will be able to support much higher frequencies than would be justified by the local traffic alone – in some cases the routes would not exist if it were not for the connection traffic. This makes it very difficult for a competitor to survive unless they are flying from a hub at the other end of the route. For example, Lufthansa accounts for 61 per cent of scheduled flights at Frankfurt. In the US, more extreme concentrations are to be found, particularly at the medium-sized hubs: US Airways has 88 per cent of flights at Charlotte and Northwest 80 per cent at Detroit (Airline Business, 2000). Taking a route example, Lufthansa and Alitalia operated one daily flight each between Frankfurt and Turin in 1989. By 2003 this had increased to five flights per day but they are all by Lufthansa.

This trend has been exacerbated by airline alliance development (Morrish and Hamilton, 2002). The key hub-to-hub trunk links are seeing a rapid increase in operations. For example, Amsterdam–Detroit, which was not served at all prior to the KLM/Northwest Alliance, now has four flights per day by Boeing 747 or DC10; Frankfurt–Chicago has gone from two flights per day to four and Copenhagen–Munich from three to six. Airports and routes which do not fit neatly into the alliance groupings are liable to see their service reduced. For example, United has pulled off Washington–Zurich to concentrate on its links with Lufthansa at Frankfurt while Delta, an Air France partner, has similarly axed Washington–Frankfurt. SAS used to serve Hong Kong (now a oneworld hub) from Copenhagen but this has lost service altogether in favour of Star Alliance connections via Bangkok using Thai, or Frankfurt using Lufthansa. Duplication is also likely to be eliminated over time (for example, Delta dropped its Frankfurt mini-hub to concentrate on links with partner Air France at Paris CDG instead). The net result is that the share of traffic held by the dominant alliance at a particular airport tends to be growing rapidly while rival alliances redeploy output elsewhere.

This poses a potential problem for airport operators. Many airports have traditionally been proud of the range of airlines serving their facility and will make great effort to attract another brightly coloured tailfin onto their apron. In the US, airport expansion has often hinged around airline requirements. Airlines have also been successful in extracting generous terms from airports by playing them off against each other to be the chosen location for hub expansion. With many airports under local government control, there is a vested interest in bringing employment to the area and obtaining the greatly improved communication links that could never be justified on the basis of local demand but can be supported on the back of the hub traffic (Small, 1997).

In Europe, airlines are trimming the large number of point-to-point services they historically operated from places other than their major hub. Even at the major hubs, the number of intercontinental points receiving a direct service is often diminishing as airlines restructure around high-frequency links to the key overseas hubs, with secondary cities reached through connections on partner airlines. For example, 20 years ago, SAS used to serve 36 intercontinental points from Copenhagen, many only once or twice a week with several intermediate stops; it now serves only 8 but as most of these operate at least daily, more flights are made in total.

Potential winners and losers among European cities and airports from international airline alliance formation

Most of the global alliances contain one partner in each major region of the world, which consequently defines the key hubs. In Europe, however, there is much more duplication within each alliance's coverage. The presence of many international boundaries and the historic constraints these posed to traffic rights have created a different pattern of airline networks from the US. Many

Table 7.3 *Change in European coverage of major hubs 1999–2002;*
number of European airports with at least three services per weekday
from each hub

Hub	1999 routes	2002 routes	Change
Frankfurt (Star)	53	65	+12
Paris CDG (SkyTeam)	49	61	+12
Amsterdam (KLM)	69	51	−18
Munich (Star)	42	49	+7
Copenhagen (Star)	36	42	+6
Madrid (oneworld)	29	40	+11
London LHR (oneworld)	31	36	+5
Zurich (Swiss)	41	36	−5
Stockholm (Star)	36	35	−1
Barcelona (oneworld)	a	34	NA
Brussels (SN)	50	31	−19
Lyon (SkyTeam)	20	31	+11
Milan MXP (SkyTeam)	30	30	0
Vienna (Star)	28	30	+2
Rome FCO (SkyTeam)	26	29	+3
London LGW (oneworld)	28	27	−1
Paris ORY (SkyTeam)	24	24	0
London LHR (Star)	20	22	+2
Düsseldorf (Star)	a	20	NA
Helsinki (Star)	21	20	−1
EuroAirport (Swiss)	21	a	NA

Note: a less than 20 routes operated 3x per weekday.
Source: Compiled from OAG data

airlines have ended up dominating a number of airports in their home country, although these are not necessarily all operated as hubs. There is thus considerable repetition in existing airline networks (e.g. Lufthansa can carry a passenger from Italy to the US via Frankfurt, Munich or Düsseldorf) before one starts looking at the impact of alliances. US experience would suggest there are too many secondary hubs or 'focus cities' in Europe and the financial performance of these is generally poor compared to the primary hubs. The only rationale for major airlines to maintain these dispersed operations is because of capacity constraints at the major airports (e.g. London Heathrow, Frankfurt), which prevent consolidation of operations there, or as a defensive tactic to deter a rival from invading their 'backyard'. The alliance groupings have led to further overlap and together with expansion by low-cost new entrants such as Ryanair are likely to spell the end for some of the weaker hubs.

Table 7.3 amplifies the changing position in the short-haul coverage of the major European hubs. Frankfurt and Paris CDG are forging well ahead while Amsterdam slips back. Munich and Madrid are rising in importance at the expense of Brussels and Zurich, although it is noticeable that the overall picture in short-haul markets is one of growth despite the current parlous state of the aviation industry.

Future of the global alliances and implications for European hubs

The future development of the global airline alliances has potentially significant implications for the role of different hub airports in Europe and around the world. To date, the alliance groupings have been in a continual state of flux and we are unlikely to have reached the final form yet (Agusdinata and de Klein, 2002). The level of integration within many of the alliances is far from perfect, however, and it is quite possible that airlines within the same alliance will continue to compete in the way they have always done, paying little regard to the strategies of their supposed partners.

Within the current alliances, Continental is unhappy with their position in SkyTeam following Delta/Northwest merger proposals and is talking to the alternative groupings. The Star Alliance has gained US Airways which has restructured fairly successfully (*Travel Trade Gazette*, 2003). This is likely to strengthen the hand of Lufthansa in Europe as more North Atlantic capacity is flown to Star hubs. However, the future of Virgin Atlantic is one of the big unknowns. Despite being 49 per cent owned by Star member Singapore Airlines, Virgin has remained resolutely outside the major groupings, instead favouring a block space agreement with Continental. Current interest focuses on the scope for a bmi–Virgin merger which would give Star a serious presence at London Heathrow and create a formidable rival to BA (Noakes, 2003). The potential sale of Iberia may change its alliance arrangements while SAS has questioned whether it should be continuing in the long-haul market. Some of the smaller European flag carriers may reduce to a purely short-haul network, feeding other alliance partners with longer distance traffic (Campbell, 2003).

It is difficult to see an obvious route to two global alliances from the current position. This would seem to require the failure of one of the six US international carriers. A more likely scenario where mergers start to occur between major airlines is that some airlines will then find themselves in two alliances, and to overcome competition concerns or local monopolies in certain parts of the world (e.g. Australasia where Qantas is likely to dominate), the fair and easy solution is to merge the alliances so that we return to one industry alliance (IATA by any other name), where all the carriers cooperate with each other. This avoids smaller airlines being disadvantaged and would favour the smaller hubs and the less coordinated or multi-airline hubs such as London over the one-airline dominant hubs such as Frankfurt. Similar outcomes can be seen in other industries where rival networks have existed (e.g. banking and railways).

Airline service at second-tier cities

It is probable that less air service will be provided at the medium-sized cities by the traditional national flag carriers in the future. These do not offer the network synergies of the main hubs and are exposed to competition from low-cost airlines when traffic is mainly 'point-to-point'. Where there is room for conventional service, it is increasingly likely to be provided by foreign airlines, for whom it is a spoke point, or specialist regional operators using small aircraft.

The low-cost airlines will maintain a reasonable level of direct air service from such cities at competitive fares. They may not be profitable to the airport operator, however, due to their unwillingness to pay normal airport charges. The other shortcoming is that they do not provide the global accessibility of a conventional hub link as flights cannot be booked through the global distribution system (GDS), there is no through pricing or schedule coordination. This makes low-cost services almost unusable for connecting journeys.

The traditional airlines have favoured airports that have kept the low-cost carriers out – this usually requires either a restricted runway or high user charges. For example, British Airways launched services in spring 2003 from London City and it remains the only London airport other than Heathrow to be served by most of the European national carriers. London City's runway is too short to handle 737 jets. Other examples include Southampton, chosen for expansion by Flybe who have been chased out of many of their traditional markets, and Manchester, where there is only a limited low-cost presence, receiving new foreign carrier services.

Airline restructuring

The established European airlines have taken other steps to improve performance in the last few years, with a collapse in profitability and doubt cast over their traditional business model. Meanwhile, there has been dramatic growth by the low-cost airlines and other new entrants. Although much has been written of the low-cost carriers' performance – for example, see Lawton (2002), Gudmundsson et al (2005), Doganis (2006), Civil Aviation Authority (2006) – relatively little research has taken place on the reactions of the traditional airlines.

Some of the European majors such as British Airways, Aer Lingus and Lufthansa face low-cost competition across a substantial part of their short-haul network. Others such as Air France, Austrian or TAP Air Portugal only have significant exposure on routes to the UK at the present time.

Raising labour productivity and outsourcing more services

One area where the low-cost airlines have made significant savings over the traditional carriers is in terms of labour costs. The major airlines have tried to revise their wage costs downwards through various measures, including increasing productivity, freezing or reducing salaries or benefits, hiring new staff on less generous terms and conditions, and outsourcing more activities, including selling off or transferring to third parties support services that were previously done in-house (catering, ground handling, etc). Employment with

Table 7.4 *Change in traffic and employment levels for European airlines 1999–2004*

Airline	Change 1999–2004			2004
	Traffic (RPK) % change	Employees % change	RPK/employee % change	RPK/employee
Ryanair	+330	+78	+142	8765
easyJet	+356	+117	+110	6685
GB Airways	+70	+34	+27	3808
Virgin Atlantic	+3	+5	−2	3657
Aer Lingus	+27	−36	+99	3131
Lufthansa	+17	−9	+29	3011
British Airways	−8	−21	+17	2077
Iberia	+15	−2	+17	1745
bmi	+56	−40	+162	1686
Alitalia	−18	−1	−18	1639
KLM/AirFrance	+10	+23	−10	1592
Flybe	+85	+26	+46	1233

Note: RPK = revenue passenger km.
Source: Compiled from IATA, *Flight International* and Airline Business data

the major airlines was historically a comfortable existence. Once easyJet and Ryanair and others found there were staff willing to work in the airline industry for much less, it became difficult to justify maintaining these generous conditions. Table 7.4 shows the changes over the last five years for major UK scheduled airlines and a selection of other European carriers.

It can be seen that traffic has generally grown faster than employee numbers. In many cases the number of staff on the books has actually gone down. This has led to a superficially improved productivity indicator (RPK/employee). These have to be treated with caution, however. Stage length is a critical factor in determining the absolute RPK/employee figures. Some of the largest changes have been achieved by selling off whole departments (e.g. ground handling at bmi). EasyJet and Ryanair have achieved their dramatic growth in productivity by taking on the bare minimum of extra flight and cabin crew to support their vastly expanded operations. This has spread administrative staff over more passengers, while everything else is contracted out. The UK and Irish airlines have generally moved further in this direction than their European counterparts. The KLM/Air France figures are hard to explain and may be down simply to changes of definition.

Unlike the low-cost carriers, the major airlines have not generally tried to shift any flight and cabin crew to lower cost economies. They still put a large number of crew in expensive accommodation away from home to operate early morning flights from other countries, rather than setting up a local crew base. BA even does this on domestic sectors where a particular fleet is based at the opposite end of the route (e.g., 737 crews overnight away from Gatwick at Edinburgh).

Support services such as catering, cleaning and ground handling have come under much more severe pressure (Stewart and Michaels, 2003). These providers may rue the day they did a deal with Ryanair or easyJet on a marginal cost basis. At that time, these airlines were small players and it was seen as useful incremental extra business. The assumption was that the traditional airlines would continue paying 'normal rates' which covered the full cost of the service plus a profit margin. However, the majors have been forced to renegotiate their contracts to remain competitive, in some cases reducing service standards as well. Caterers are in the bleakest position as food provision has generally fallen across the board. Gate Gourmet's revenue fell 30 per cent from 2000–2004 despite a growth in passenger numbers (Ott, 2005). Low-cost airlines now account for a large part of the market and, along with those traditional carriers selling refreshments, have complicated procedures while shifting the risk of wastage onto the suppliers. The high-profile dispute at Gate Gourmet which crippled BA's Heathrow operation in summer 2005 is indicative of the problems in the industry. Contract prices have fallen well below costs as supply exceeds demand leading to huge losses. Staff – many of whom may have once worked for BA's own catering operation under much better terms and conditions before it was outsourced – have taken the brunt of the pain. Handling companies are barely in a healthier position (witness recent industrial disputes at Aviance, for example). Aircraft maintenance is in somewhat better shape. The going rate for routine maintenance is fairly static as skilled engineers in a country such as the UK come at a price and everyone has to pay up. The main area where maintenance costs can be cut is through conducting heavy maintenance in lower cost economies, particularly eastern Europe. Lufthansa Technik, for example, now has a base in Budapest for such activities.

Growth provides an alternative means for traditional airlines to improve productivity without reducing staff numbers. Lufthansa have favoured this course of action, adding new capacity faster than average in recent years (Flottau, 2005). BA on the other hand has been more ruthless in holding capacity down and conceding market share in an aim to avoid yields plummeting further. It is debatable as to how sustainable lower cost levels are. The majors are likely to be blighted by industrial action if they try to cut further, while if the third-party providers go out of business, contracts will have to be retendered at a higher level – which may turn the pressure onto the low-cost airlines. Rising fuel prices are also undermining many of the efforts airlines have made on cutting their internal costs. Nevertheless, it is still viewed as essential for the major carriers to reduce their cost base if they are to stand any chance of remaining competitive in the future commercial environment (Franke, 2004).

More use of regional aircraft

In the US, one of the most noticeable impacts of the increased competition faced by the 'legacy' carriers has been the transfer of many short-haul routes to

Table 7.5 *Unit costs of regional jets and Boeing 737*

Aircraft type	Typical seats	Cost per available seat mile, US cents	Cost per flight US$ (averaged to 500 miles)
Canadair CRJ-200	48	7.86	1592
Embraer 145	50	6.93	1590
Boeing 737-300	126	4.09	2912

Note: Stage length varies from 330 to 640 miles.
Source: costs from Avmark Aviation Economist/Airline Monitor (based on US DoT data)

regional partner airlines. There are two main reasons behind this. Where market share has been eroded by low-cost carriers such as Southwest it enables the major airline to maintain frequency – an important competitive weapon, especially when linked to frequent flyer programmes (FFPs) – while reducing capacity. In theory, this also enables yields to be maintained as it is the less valuable passengers on lower fares that will be turned away. The second reason is that the regional partners operate under a much lower labour cost regime than the majors have been able to achieve. Thus although aircraft such as the CRJ200 inherently have higher unit costs than a Boeing 737, for example, this has distorted the market, making the regional jets lower-cost to operate overall (Table 7.5). The recent surge in fuel prices means that many of these routes would be more efficiently served with a turboprop or large jet but the amount of regional jet flying has grown too large to unwind.

In Europe, there has been much less shift to regional jets due to capacity constraints at the major hub airports. The opportunity cost of using a precious slot for a 50-seater aircraft is enough to tip the balance in favour of the larger jets. At locations such as Manchester, however, which have seen their traffic base for traditional scheduled services eroded by low-cost operations at nearby airports, particularly Liverpool, there has been a considerable amount of trading down to smaller aircraft. This has been facilitated by the extra runway capacity available since the opening of a second runway in 2001.

Revising pricing and removing minimum stays on low fares

Traditional airlines developed a very sophisticated system of yield management that aimed to minimize consumer surplus and divide the market according to different degrees of willingness and ability to pay (Tretheway, 2004). The consequence was a wide range of different fares for essentially the same product. The cheaper fares were surrounded with conditions, the most onerous of which was the requirement to spend a Saturday night away in order to obtain a discount tariff. The cheaper fares were hence sold only on a round-trip basis. This neatly divided the market on the assumption that anyone returning before the weekend must be a business passenger and so have low elasticity to price as they would not be paying their own fare. Cheap fares were hence reserved for leisure passengers who stayed away over the weekend. Flexibility was only available at the higher fares, again making cheap tickets unattractive to business passengers whose travel plans may change frequently.

The low-cost airlines, particularly easyJet in Europe, started offering one-way fares. They still operated differential pricing but the only relevant factors now were the time of travel (peak/off-peak etc.) and how far ahead the ticket was purchased. Initially the major carriers lived in denial, believing that business passengers would continue to buy expensive full-fare tickets in order to benefit from high-frequency service from convenient airports with FFP credit. Business passengers started leaching away to the low-cost airlines, as did leisure passengers who wanted the ability to make a cheap midweek trip. When the damage could be contained to one or two routes, the risks of dilution (business passengers who would have paid a full fare trading down) outweighed the traffic being lost. Once British Airways was facing low-cost competition on most of its short-haul network, however, this couldn't be ignored any longer. In 2002, BA abandoned the minimum stay requirement for cheap fares on short-haul travel originating in the UK. They did not go as far as the low-cost airlines, however. BA still requires a return journey which enables some sophistication in changing the fare of the return flight depending on the outward flight that has been chosen. It also means that the cheap flights are not necessarily the same for passengers starting at opposite ends of the route. For example, an 0800 flight on Wednesday morning may be cheap if booked as a return sector but high as an outbound sector. A 1700 return flight on Monday evening may be cheap if the passenger flew out the previous week but high if flying out the same Monday morning. BA still requires a minimum stay of two nights for cheap fares from certain European countries, where it is effectively matching the local carrier (e.g. Iberia or Swiss) rather than easyJet. The low-cost airlines generally base their aircraft in Britain and so cannot offer competitive timings for short trips from Europe to the UK. Bmi went a step further by pricing on a single journey basis. This means that on routes where BA and bmi compete the one-way fares are often more expensive on BA (as constrained by the highest pricing quoted as part of a return journey). BA made some one-way seats available at lower fares through consolidators – typically on routes from Gatwick where they go head-to-head with easyJet (e.g. Gatwick–Amsterdam; Unijet were quoting a one-way fare of £59 on BA in January 2005 as against a published fare of £158). Cheaper one-way fares are now available on ba.com – but typically only on off-peak or Gatwick flights. From Heathrow, to discourage mixing a one-way with the foreign airline to get the preferred timings, single flights at business times remain high.

The response of the other European airlines on pricing has been variable. Table 7.6 summarizes the latest position on short-haul international routes within Europe. Some, such as Air France, have matched BA for bookings in the UK but continue to cling to their beloved Saturday night rules and no flexible tickets other than business class on the rest of their European network. Others, such as KLM, haven't even matched BA where they are head-to-head.

Table 7.6 *Conditions attached to cheapest round-trip excursion fares on traditional European airlines, March 2007*

| Airline | From UK | | Most other markets within Europe | |
	Minimum stay (nights)	Changes possible (fee)	Minimum stay (nights)	Changes possible (fee)
British Airways	0	Yes	0	Yes
Air France	0	No	Sat	No
Lufthansa	0	Yes	2 or Sat[a]	Yes
KLM	2 or Sat	No	3 or Sat	No
SAS	0	No	0	No
Iberia	0	Yes	Sat	Yes
Swiss	0	No	2 or Sat	Yes
Alitalia	0	Yes	Sat[a]	Yes
Aer Lingus	0	Yes	0	Yes

Note: a 0 nights to UK.
Source: airline websites

Lufthansa has some cheap flights on Germany–UK routes without a minimum stay requirement but typically at very poor times. SAS has recently moved towards pricing the legs of a return journey separately (*Travel Trade Gazette*, 2005) but this is hardly the achievement it is made out to be – merely emulating BA's structure; it is still not possible to buy cheap one-way tickets. EasyJet made all tickets flexible as a response to the lower fares with fixed reservations introduced by the major airlines. However, the difference in price still has to be paid between the original fare and the selling rate on the new flight at the time the change is made, as well as an administration charge. As fares are increased dramatically close to departure this is not a realistic option for many passengers. British Airways, Aer Lingus, Lufthansa, Iberia and Alitalia have now adopted similar tactics, as it represents a means of increasing revenue from low-fare passengers rather than simply having them not travel or buy a new ticket elsewhere.

Table 7.7 provides a snapshot of pricing strategies for a midweek day-return trip, booked three weeks ahead on routes to or from London. This was chosen to see where the major carriers have become more competitive for advance booking on short duration midweek trips and where they still have minimum stay rules in place. Restricted tickets were permitted in the analysis, although in some cases only an unrestricted ticket at a very high fare was offered. On London–Amsterdam, the KLM fare is over £300 without a two-night minimum stay. VLM on the City Airport route is much below KLM. BA or bmi are available for just over £100 return. EasyJet offers a significant price advantage over all the other airlines on this route (around half the BA rates). It is difficult to see who would choose KLM for a day trip unless the company is paying and they want the FFP miles or they require a flexible ticket and the KLM flight is at the most convenient time.

On London–Paris there is less inter-airline competition. Air France matches BA and bmi from Heathrow. The main alternative comes from the train

Table 7.7 *Cheapest GBP fares for a day-return trip[a] on Wednesday 31 August 2005 (booking Wednesday 10 August 2005)*

London–Amsterdam–London		Amsterdam–London–Amsterdam	
KL-LCY	354	KL-LCY	335
KL-LHR	308	KL-LHR	256
VG-LCY	128	VG-LCY	134
BA-LGW	117	BA-LHR	105
BA-LHR	112	BD-LHR	102
BD-LHR	94	BA-LGW	100
U2-STN	55	U2-LGW	59
U2-LGW	53	U2-LTN	48
U2-LTN	53		
London–Paris–London		**Paris–London–Paris**	
AF-LCY	136	AF-LHR	270
BA-LHR	126	BA-LHR	150
AF-LHR	105	U2-LTN	68
BD-LHR	91		
U2-LTN	78		
London–Geneva–London		**Geneva–London–Geneva**	
LX-LCY	218	LX-LCY	519
BA-LHR	178	BA-LHR	395
LX-LHR[b]	166	BA-LCY	395
BA-LCY	144	BA-LGW	395
U2-LGW	115	LX-LHR[b]	220
BA-LGW	112	U2-LGW	119
U2-LTN	95		
London–Madrid–London		**Madrid–London–Madrid**	
IB-LHR	188	IB-LHR	697
BA-LHR	148	BA-LHR	688
IB-LGW[b]	147		
U2-LTN	140		
U2-LGW	125		
BA-LGW	112		

Notes: a Outbound flight must depart by 0900 and return flight must leave from 1700; Tickets may be non-refundable/non-changeable; rounded to nearest GBP.
Abbreviations: AF-Air France, BA-British Airways, BD-bmi, IB-Iberia, KL-KLM, LX-Swiss, U2-easyJet, VG-VLM (Flemish Air Transport Company), b operated by BA.
Source: airline websites

(Eurostar). If one books at least three weeks ahead, Eurostar offers £59 return to 'leisure travellers only' (what happens if you turn up with a suit and brief-case?). Otherwise they don't go below £199 return for a day-trip midweek, making the airlines potentially cheaper. Air France makes no attempt to match BA out of Paris and easyJet offers less price advantage – presumably no one chooses Luton to travel to Paris unless it is more convenient than the other airports and Waterloo, in which case they have a captive market. Bmi (and also Air France on the London City Airport route) cannot offer a viable day-trip schedule if starting in Paris. Airline pricing behaviour in the London–Paris market was studied in more detail by Pels and Rietveld (2004).

For London–Geneva the most interesting feature is BA's differential pricing depending whether one starts from the London or the Geneva end of the route. Swiss have a medium fare of £220 return from Geneva – the flight is ironically operated by BA who charge at least £395. EasyJet is not much cheaper for London-originating passengers – indeed BA beats them by £3 out of Gatwick.

Finally, Madrid–London perhaps raises the greatest competition concerns. BA has an alliance with Iberia and for Madrid residents making a day-trip to London, it is still the good old days here for the airlines with BA charging £688 and Iberia £697. EasyJet can only offer a day-trip if starting from London and once again they are more expensive than BA out of Gatwick. Bmi only offers one flight per day.

Charging for catering or reducing free provision

Economy class passengers making international journeys within Europe have traditionally been served a hot or cold meal depending on the time of day and length of route. The first attempt to adapt this came when BA introduced the separate Club and Tourist products more than 20 years ago. Club passengers received upgraded catering while Tourist had a carry-on sandwich bag on longer flights and nothing on short hops. Few carriers matched BA's provision (indeed British Midland made a virtue out of its 'diamond service' for all), so for competitive reasons, the airline was forced to return to a conventional food service in economy. Non-alcoholic beverages have always been free and during the 1980s the move towards free drinks across the network meant that most European airlines started offering complimentary wine or beer as well. Domestic catering has traditionally been minimal in some countries (France, Spain, Italy). In the UK, BA only operated one cabin and so enhanced catering with hot meals was available to all passengers. Until recently, most of these routes were dominated by business traffic.

It was not until the last five years that the growth of the low-cost carriers, which either offered no catering or a basic paid-for service ('no frills'), forced a revaluation of the short-haul product by the traditional airlines. The difference over the 1980s was that passengers then saw no price incentive for forgoing the food and drink. Now with fares half or less those of the major airlines available from Ryanair or easyJet, the free catering (which many passengers never much liked anyway) suddenly became the most visible symbol of difference between the two sectors.

There has since been a gradual drift to reducing provision in economy class by the traditional airlines. As well as saving money, this has the added benefit of allowing the business class product to become more differentiated, encouraging the 'service seekers' to trade up. The argument is that no one buys an air ticket because of the food. Therefore if the ticket price can be cut by £5 through cutting out the food, that will be more commercially successful. The danger for the traditional airlines, however, is that they can never match the cost levels – and hence the average fares – of Ryanair or easyJet. If inclusive economy class catering is eliminated, passengers may then see no reason for using these airlines.

The evidence, however, is less supportive of traditional services. In the US, all the legacy carriers have rushed to strip out catering provision on short-haul flights. They believe the frequent flyer programme is the only 'frill' valued by the passenger (and perhaps in-flight entertainment on longer routes, a major selling point of Jet Blue). Most of these airlines have been doing extremely badly, however, not helped by the negative passenger perception that comes from no in-flight service, disillusioned staff and fares that are still often higher than Southwest or Jet Blue.

In Europe, Aer Lingus has gone to paid-for catering only. Prices are reasonable and the menu comprehensive compared to the low-cost carriers. A full Irish breakfast is available until 10.00 hours at €7. At other times a hot ham and cheese panini is €5 (Aer Lingus, 2005). Maersk of Denmark (now part of Sterling) was another airline that made an early move in this direction, their style being copied shortly afterwards by SAS. Iberia, Swiss, Brussels Airlines and Austrian subsequently shifted to paid-for food and drink also.

The problem with paid-for catering, however, is that it is a rather inefficient process. Axing all food saves money because turnaround is speeded up as the aircraft does not need to be cleaned and catered, galley space can be replaced with seats and cabin staff can be reduced in number to the safety minimum. If the same free sandwich is provided to everyone, then it is only necessary to load the requisite number and dash round the aircraft handing them out. Once passengers are given an option of purchasing items, cabin staff have to waste time going to and from the galley, collecting money and giving change in different currencies; and with a choice of items either some passengers will be disappointed or a lot of wastage will occur. The take-up will be variable from flight to flight making it difficult to plan efficiently.

The complications coupled with the negative image it conveys prompted Lufthansa to reinstate free catering on Swiss a few months after taking them over. This brought the Swiss product back into line with Lufthansa.

Among the airlines still offering free catering within Europe, BA has trimmed back provision on shorter routes to only cookies or nibbles after 10.00. On domestic routes, hot breakfast is still available until 10.00 (continental breakfast to Europe and Ireland). Hot paninis are favoured on longer routes. A full range of free drinks is offered from the bar. KLM and Lufthansa basically offer a sandwich and a drink (KLM did not offer alcoholic drinks even for payment in economy but has now reinstated these for consistency with Air France). Air France is generally a bit sparser on food, with only biscuits on domestic routes and between main meal times.

Bmi has moved to paid-for catering in economy class from Heathrow and axed business class except to Edinburgh, Glasgow, Belfast, Dublin and Brussels. Bmi regional flights are all economy class and continue to provide free refreshments, however (unless travelling to the Channel Islands or Ireland). The phrase 'dog's dinner' found some resonance with journalists, and (at least before the Gate Gourmet crisis) BA hoped to attract higher-yield passengers who became fed up with the uncertainties and inconsistencies that bmi were creating (Jamieson, 2005). The carrier that BA has tended to benchmark itself against over the years is Lufthansa and as long as they are still providing free catering, there is at least some pressure to maintain the status quo.

Abandoning business class

Whereas in long-haul markets there will always be some passengers willing to pay more for sleeper seats, it is difficult to offer passengers additional comfort features that add significant value on short-haul European routes. Business class significantly increases unit costs but for most of the major airlines there remain several rationales for continuing to offer it. First, it is necessary to provide passengers connecting to first and business class long-haul flights with a segregated product on the short-haul feeder routes. Otherwise they are likely to desert to rival carriers and these travellers are valuable for their long-haul revenue. Second, many of the European airlines still do not face low-cost competition on much of their short-haul network. Thus they can maintain traditional practices on pricing, forcing trips without a Saturday night stay into business class. Third, some passengers (or their employers) are still willing to pay for the highest level of service available and if the additional revenue received more than offsets the marginal costs of providing the premium cabin then it is sensible to do so.

Almost all European flag carriers still offer a two-class cabin on short-haul international routes with aircraft of Boeing 737 size or larger. Aer Lingus is the only exception to this rule. It now operates a single class in Europe but with all passengers able to purchase a range of hot and cold food.

Some airlines also offer business class on the 100-seater equipment such as the Avro RJ or Fokker 100. On aircraft in the 50-seat range there is typically only one class.

Many airlines only offer one class on their domestic network. These routes are usually short-sectors with either a semi-monopoly position (e.g. Alitalia) or a large proportion of business passengers (e.g. BA). SAS effectively offers a three class arrangement with free refreshments for full-fare economy passengers as well as a separate business class.

For independent European airlines without a long-haul network to support, business class is now effectively dead. Whereas the traditional flag carriers remain wedded to this concept, almost all the independent airlines have got out. Bmi was one of the last to maintain a two-cabin arrangement but this is now reduced to a handful of routes. Nevertheless, with the cost levels of the traditional airlines, the opportunity to obtain a few passengers paying £300 each way, for the sake of putting up a curtain and buying in a few hot meals, still seems attractive compared to taking dozens down the back at £30.

Reducing distribution costs

One area where the low-cost airlines have managed to reduce expenses with negligible impact on standards of service, as perceived by the passenger, is through axing commissions to travel agents. The view of traditional airlines was that travel agents were necessary to distribute their product as widely as possible, particularly in areas away from the home market. If one airline stepped out of line, then the agents would push all the business to their rivals, losing them much more than the 9 per cent commission. This assumption began to change for several reasons, however. By turning price into the major selling point – with fares 50 per cent or more below the traditional airlines – the low-cost airlines found passengers would book the low fares even if it meant using different distribution channels. Internet penetration was growing rapidly, providing the ability for customers to book their own flights using automated systems. A short-haul airline selling simple point-to-point flights didn't require complex GDS equipment or yield management.

The network airlines could no longer afford to pay commissions for a service the passenger didn't value. There was little incentive for passengers to book direct with the airline when the price was the same. Pass the money back to the passenger, however, and suddenly many more people will book direct. It was easiest to do this in the home markets where the airline typically has a dominant position through high frequencies/network coverage, FFP membership etc. Airlines also needed to incentivize passengers to book through their own website by offering the lowest total payment by that method. In overseas markets and for smaller airlines, however, there may be too low a level of awareness for airlines to generate much business direct. Many UK passengers, for example, will examine the websites of easyJet, Ryanair and BA but overlook carriers such as Air France or Lufthansa. This tends to reinforce the national bias among airline customers. Travel agents (including the online agencies such as Expedia) may still be the best option in these circumstances and even low-cost airlines have to spend heavily on advertising.

British Airways commission payments as a proportion of sales have fallen from 14 per cent in the financial year ended 1997 to 9 per cent in 2002 and 6 per cent in 2005. Travel agents (including internet intermediaries) have been forced to add service fees to maintain their income. This has the consequence of driving more customers to book direct and online. Another benefit of direct internet sales is the ability to automate associated aspects of the travel process such as check-in (*Aviation Strategy*, 2004a).

Increasing aircraft utilization

The constraints of hub operations do not make it easy to maximize aircraft utilization. Aircraft often have to be left on the ground for longer than the minimum time period in order to synchronize with other flights at the hub. Traditional airlines have also scheduled longer turnarounds to allow for catering and cleaning of the aircraft and provide a contingency allowance to improve the chance of on-time departure. Passengers find it less stressful to stroll onto the aircraft 20 minutes before departure and relax in their seats than to wait in the gate area for a last minute boarding call. The use of loading bridges provides a higher level of passenger service, particularly in inclement weather conditions and for disabled passengers. However, it also slows down boarding and alighting. This is primarily because only the front entrance/exit from the aircraft can be used whereas with steps onto the apron, passengers can board and alight through both the front and rear doors, potentially halving the time taken to load or unload. Allocated seats are another delaying factor in the boarding process. Passengers take longer to find their designated seat than simply going into the first one available. In the process they may block the aisle accessing the overhead bins. The pressure from passengers behind creating a scrum to secure the best seats is also removed. The trend among low-cost airlines to encouraging cabin baggage and minimizing the number of checked bags will, however, have a negative impact on turnaround times as passengers take longer trying to stow hand baggage. Indeed the UK Department of Transport was threatening to legislate on cabin baggage (*Travel Trade Gazette*, 2006) after security search points became bogged down by passengers taking as much as possible on board due to charges for checked-in bags (e.g. Ryanair or Flybe) or reduced restrictions on carry-on bags (e.g. easyJet). This saves the airline money on ground handling but simply moves the cost somewhere else. Traditional airlines are needless to say unhappy that their passengers should be delayed in queues at security behind these low-cost travellers.

The traditional European airlines have generally increased the aircraft utilization of their short-haul fleets in response to the low-cost threat (Table 7.8). This is particularly marked with BA, Lufthansa, Iberia and SAS, while

Table 7.8 *Changes in aircraft utilization 2000–2005 (selected short-haul aircraft)*

Airline	Aircraft type	Daily utilization 2000 (hours:min)	Daily utilization 2005 (hours:min)
British Airways	A319	6:56	8:45
	737-400	8:04	9:01
Lufthansa	A319	7:52	9:42
	737-500	7:22	7:55
Air France	A319	7:52	8:59
	A320	7:58	8:10
KLM	737-300	8:26	7:18
	737-400	8:11	7:36
Iberia	A319	6:10	8:59
	A320	7:05	8:10
SAS	737-800	7:06	8:09
	737-700	7:36	8:29
Swissair/Swiss	A319	8:18	8:34
	A320	8:48	9:40

Source: IATA World Air Transport Statistics

Table 7.9 *Changes in aircraft scheduling and utilization – an example*

2002 – old schedule				2005 – new schedule			
	depart		arrive		depart		arrive
Gatwick	07:00	Edinburgh	08:30	Gatwick	06:25	Edinburgh	07:50
Edinburgh	09:10	Gatwick	10:35	Edinburgh	08:25	Gatwick	09:50
Gatwick	11:30	Glasgow	13:00	Gatwick	10:25	Glasgow	11:55
Glasgow	13:45	Gatwick	15:15	Glasgow	12:25	Gatwick	13:50
Gatwick	16:05	Edinburgh	17:35	Gatwick	14:45	Manchester	15:45
Edinburgh	18:15	Gatwick	19:45	Manchester	16:15	Gatwick	17:15
Gatwick	20:25	Glasgow	21:50	Gatwick	17:50	Newcastle	19:00
				Newcastle	19:30	Gatwick	20:45
				Gatwick	21:20	Glasgow	22:40

10 hours 20 minutes aircraft utilization	11 hours 30 minutes aircraft utilization
7 sectors	9 sectors
14 hours 50 minutes start to finish of day	16 hours 15 minutes start to finish of day
Average turnaround 45 minutes	Average turnaround 35 minutes

KLM's utilization appears to have gone down. These figures must be treated with some caution, however, as fleet renewal and network changes mean aircraft types are not necessarily used on the same mix of routes as five years previously. British Airways has made some of the greatest strides at Gatwick to emulate the low-cost model with earlier starts, later finishes and tighter scheduled turnarounds (Table 7.9), but have retained features such as allocated seats, cleaning and catering and use of airbridges, which make it difficult to achieve a 30-minute turnaround, particularly with a full flight.

Anecdotal evidence suggests that BA often still take 35–40 minutes to turn the aircraft around so an on-time departure is only possible if the aircraft actually arrives early. There is some contingency in the en-route schedule which may permit an on-time arrival, although even this has been pared back by about 5 minutes per sector from the old timetable. Whether the yields on the first and last flights exceed the marginal cost of operating at these times is an interesting question. With higher fuel prices it must be more difficult. BA regularly have their lowest fare on sale for the very late evening flights, in many cases still bookable up until a week or so before departure.

Setting up a low-cost subsidiary

Numerous attempts have been made by traditional airlines in North America and Europe to set up subsidiary carriers on the low-cost/no-frills model as a competitive response to the growth of new entrants. The objectives of these carriers are somewhat varied and in many cases have not enjoyed great success (Morrell, 2005; Graham and Vowles, 2006).

British Airways set up Go to fly from Stansted and subsequently other airports such as Nottingham East Midlands and Bristol. They were eventually sold off to a consortium involving the management and subsequently taken over by easyJet.

Lufthansa has an interest in Germanwings through Eurowings. Research in Germany suggests this is an efficient approach to serving different market niches (Lindstadt and Fauser, 2004). SAS set up Snowflake to take over low-yield/leisure type routes. Snowflake suffered the worst of all worlds – with aircraft and crews seconded from the parent company it didn't achieve much cost saving but yields plummeted as feeder traffic to the SAS network disappeared and large numbers of seats had to be filled by stimulating the point-to-point markets. Snowflake is now merely a booking class on flights that are back within the SAS operation.

Another variation on this theme involves handing routes to franchise partners with lower cost levels. Most franchises are in the regional sector of the market where the use of smaller aircraft is the primary motivation. One notable exception however was GB Airways, the British Airways franchise that operated between Gatwick and holiday destinations in southern Europe until spring 2008. GB had cost levels (stage length adjusted) around 20 per cent below BA. This meant that it could operate viably on lower yields and compete more closely on price with the low-cost airlines. It nevertheless provided a full BA branded product with the network benefits of through fares, interlining and schedule coordination, and FFP participation. GB used A320 and A321 aircraft. This was manageable largely because it served destinations that were not in the BA network at all in recent times. Attempts to transfer routes from BA mainline to GB with similar size aircraft would have been likely to meet with union resistance.

Conclusions

Although some of the European flag carriers such as Alitalia and Olympic continue to rack up huge losses, the financial recovery of airlines such as BA, Lufthansa, KLM/Air France, Aer Lingus and Iberia provides some evidence that the traditional network carrier model can still work. Indeed, apart from Ryanair which has enjoyed very large and perhaps somewhat unrealistic profit margins in recent years, the majors are doing as well as anybody. EasyJet typically makes about a 5 per cent surplus, similar to BA. The other low-cost carriers are loss-making in many cases and in 2004, Virgin Express became the first to surrender to what is effectively a takeover by a traditional airline, SN Brussels.

The most successful strategy for the network carriers in the short-haul market involves concentrating on their major hub or hubs and off-loading peripheral routes. Cost reductions can be achieved in the first instance by increasing crew and aircraft productivity and outsourcing services. The passengers will usually notice little negative impact from such changes. Low-cost subsidiaries only appear to be a successful diversification in markets away from the main hub cities, although for some of the 'second tier' flag carriers with mainly point-to-point traffic this may effectively mean reinventing the whole airline – as in the case of Aer Lingus. In contrast, franchising could be more widely exploited throughout the short-haul network. A need to avoid damaging labour disputes may inhibit all these cost-reduction measures, however.

The most successful product specification appears to be based on retaining full-service business class and a more basic but still free-service economy class. This provides a differentiator to the low-cost airlines while being compatible with the long-haul product for connecting passengers. Paid-for food and drink is not a very efficient option as Lufthansa identified with Swiss. Pricing for local passengers needs to be brought in line with the terms and conditions of the low-cost carrier offering, although it should be possible to command a premium for a more convenient service (in terms of airports, schedules and 'frills'). It is becoming increasingly unfeasible to operate a differentiated pricing structure with unrestricted and quite possibly loss-making fares where there is competition from low-cost airlines, while retaining traditional controls on cheap fares in other markets. This also raises issues of unfair competition and abuse of monopoly power. Network pricing of connecting flights still remains an important competitive weapon for the hub operators, which in turn necessitates a GDS presence, although much short-haul traffic can be encouraged to book direct.

The European majors are generally in better shape than their US counterparts (the so-called 'legacy' carriers). They have more emphasis on long-haul travel which is a growing but currently less competitive part of the market. They also have a protected position at their major hub airports due to capacity constraints. Nevertheless, many of the mainland European airlines have not yet felt the full thrust of the low-cost carrier onslaught. There is little evidence that operators such as Air France have moved far enough to compete with these new entrants. Given the large number of aircraft that easyJet and Ryanair have on order and the increasing saturation of the UK and Ireland markets, the most interesting battles may be yet to come.

The difficult business conditions of recent years have led to some retrenchment of long-haul services from European airports. Certain low-frequency destinations have been discarded in favour of higher frequencies on the trunk routes. The four largest airlines have widened the gap with the rest by continuing to expand intercontinental services at their major hub airports. The greatest cutbacks have been by British Airways at London Gatwick – as part of the airline's 'future size and shape' review and Brussels where only part of Sabena's long-haul service has been replaced by other carriers. Overall, however, most of the smaller national carriers continue to stubbornly hang on in the long-haul market even though many of them are losing large amounts of money in doing so. Swiss has recreated much of the former Swissair network, although it has little unique coverage compared to the larger airlines. Iberia is perhaps the only carrier outside the big four that has a clear and defendable niche in long-haul operations with its extensive Latin American network.

Within Europe, most of the hubs have actually expanded in recent years. One of the few losers is KLM at Amsterdam, which has become isolated from many of its former feeder partners such as Eurowings, Braathens and Alitalia.

SN at Brussels is also a pale shadow of the former Sabena operation. Even airlines which have decided to reduce their long-haul presence have maintained their short-haul networks, such as BA at Gatwick and SAS at Copenhagen.

The low-cost airlines currently have only about 25 per cent of the intra-European market but this is rising rapidly. In the UK and Ireland they now carry almost half the short-haul scheduled traffic – higher than in the US domestic market where Southwest has been operating for 30 years. It seems likely that the natural market share of low-cost airlines operating point-to-point services, often from secondary airports may be around a third. Although some of this traffic is new growth, it means that the traditional airlines are going to have to review their short-haul strategies and withdraw from markets where they do not have a strong competitive position and do not require long-haul feed. The example of Belfast International shows how a medium-sized market can be dominated by the low-cost carriers, and other places where the majors are likely to be squeezed include Birmingham, London Gatwick, Brussels, Geneva, Paris Orly, Milan and Nice.

Hubs are not going to go away, however. Indeed, for the majors they remain crucial to maintain some competitive advantage over the low-cost new entrants and to feed the long-haul flights for which demand is much more dispersed. The main strategic response of the major airlines to changing industry conditions has been to group themselves into international alliances. This only brings efficiencies, however, if accompanied by some rationalization and identification of complementary roles. Europe continues to have too many airlines attempting to operate hubs in close proximity to each other and certain locations such as Vienna, Milan Malpensa and Barcelona add little to their relevant alliance and appear to be prime candidates for hub withdrawal.

For the cities which find their airport marginalized in terms of alliance strategy or de-hubbed as a result of airline industry consolidation, the economic consequences are potentially severe. As well as losing direct employment there is a penalty in terms of accessibility to the rest of Europe and the world. Brussels, for example, saw its level of air service collapse on the demise of Sabena. This then makes the city less attractive as a location for business, leading potentially to a spiral of decline. In the US, Boeing recently moved its corporate headquarters from Seattle to Chicago, citing the much better level of non-stop air service available there. Whereas once geographical patterns of demand determined the configuration of airline networks, now it is the network strategies of airlines that can have a profound effect on geographical patterns of industrial location and economic activity.

Although the current downturn has produced relatively few changes in the European airline industry, several significant developments lie around the corner. The EU is negotiating air services agreements with outside countries to replace the old bilaterals and there are strong signs that national ownership rules will disintegrate. The biggest restructuring may still be yet to come.

Note

1   This chapter is based on two articles originally published in the *Journal of Air Transport Management* (Dennis, 2005, 2007).

References

Aer Lingus (2005) Airline website, available at www.flyaerlingus.com/cgi-bin/ obel01im1/Services/bar_service.jsp?BV_SessionID=@@@@0731843617.1125500400 @@@@&BV_EngineID=cccjaddfihjkklgcefecfigdffgdfkk.0&P_OID= -8074&Category=3

Agusdinata, B. and de Klein, W. (2002) 'The dynamics of airline alliances', *Journal of Air Transport Management* 8(4): 201–211

Airline Business (2000) *Airports Special Report*, June, 55–66

Aviation Strategy (2004a) 'British Airways CeBA vision', *Aviation Strategy*, June, 17–18

Aviation Strategy (2004b) 'Aer Lingus: Boom instead of bust', *Aviation Strategy*, July/August, 1–3

Campbell, A. (2003) 'SAS questions its long-haul future', *Flight International*, 27 May–2 June, 26

Civil Aviation Authority (2006) *No-frills Carriers: Revolution or Evolution?*, a study by the Civil Aviation Authority, CAP 770, London: The Stationery Office

Dennis, N. (2005) 'Industry consolidation and future airline network structures in Europe', *Journal of Air Transport Management* 11: 175–183

Dennis, N. (2007) 'End of the free lunch? The responses of traditional European airlines to the low-cost carrier threat', *Journal of Air Transport Management* 13: 311–321

Denton, N. and Dennis, N. (2000) 'Airline franchising in Europe: Benefits and disbenefits to airlines and consumers', *Journal of Air Transport Management* 6(4): 179–190

Doganis, R. (2006) *The Airline Business*, 2nd edn, London: Routledge

Flottau, J. (2005) 'Dodging legacy bullets', *Aviation Week and Space Technology*, 15 August, 40–42

Franke, M. (2004) 'Competition between network carriers and low-cost carriers: Retreat, battle or breakthrough to a new level of efficiency?', *Journal of Air Transport Management* 10: 15–21

Graham, B. and Vowles, T. M. (2006) 'Carriers within carriers. A strategic response to low-cost airline competition', *Transport Reviews* 26(1): 105–126

Gudmundsson, S. V., Oum. T. H. and Unal, M. F. (eds) (2005) 'Special issue on Ninth Conference of the Air Transport Research Society, Istanbul, July 2004: Analysis of low cost airlines', *Journal of Air Transport Management* 11: 301–354

Halstead, J. (2001) 'Has downsizing worked?', *Aviation Strategy*, April, 6–9

Hanlon, P. (1999) *Global Airlines*, 2nd edn, Oxford: Butterworth-Heinemann

Jamieson, A. (2005) 'How bmi is struggling to cater for all', *The Scotsman*, 4 August, 49

Lawton, T. (2002) *Cleared for Take-Off: Structure and Strategy in the Low-Fare Airline Business*, Aldershot: Ashgate

Lindstadt, H. and Fauser, B. (2004) 'Separation or integration? Can network carriers create distinct business streams on one integrated production platform?', *Journal of Air Transport Management* 10: 23–31

Morrell, P. (2005) 'Airlines within airlines: An analysis of US network airline responses to low cost carriers', *Journal of Air Transport Management* 11: 303–312

Morrish, S. C. and Hamilton, R. T. (2002) 'Airline alliances – who benefits?', *Journal of Air Transport Management* 8(6): 401–407

Noakes, G. (2003) 'BMI/Virgin deal "unlikely"', *Travel Trade Gazette*, 2 June, 4

Ott, J. (2005) 'Market focus', *Aviation Week and Space Technology*, 22/29 August, 15

Pels, E. and Rietved, P. (2004) 'Airline pricing behaviour in the London-Paris market', *Journal of Air Transport Management* 10: 277–281

Small, N. O. (1997) 'Making the right connection: Airline deregulation, airline service and metropolitan economic development', unpublished doctoral dissertation, University of Reading

Stewart, D. and Michaels, K. (2003) 'LCC growth: Implications for the suppliers', *Aviation Strategy*, March, 17–19

Travel Trade Gazette (2003) 'Star Alliance welcomes US Airways', 9 June, 21

Travel Trade Gazette (2005) 'SAS offers one-way seat rates', 26 August, 6

Travel Trade Gazette (2006) 'Hand baggage jams "too much"', 7 April, 3

Tretheway, M. W. (2004) 'Distortions of airline revenues: Why the network airline business model is broken', *Journal of Air Transport Management* 10: 3–14

Part III
Socio-economics and Politics

8
Aeropolitics and Economics of Aviation Emissions Mitigation

David Timothy Duval

Introduction

The purpose of this chapter is to review and put forward some conceptual arguments relating to the global aeropolitical landscape and its influences on several factors relating to emissions and air transport. The chapter broadly adopts and incorporates various principles of policy analysis and political economy analysis to assess the significance of the positions held by various actors around the issue. A short case study on the European Union Emissions Trading Scheme (EU ETS) is offered. The chapter argues that aeropolitics, and the associated aspects of climate change versus green agendas, is deeply embedded within politics and shifts in political capital.

Aeropolitics: An introduction and review

As is commonly known, international aviation is situated within wider frameworks of politics and regulatory structures and environments, and these have substantial positive impacts on national and local economies (Button and Taylor, 2000). These structures govern access by aircraft from designated countries and are negotiated in a manner that is not unlike negotiations undertaken for trade in goods and services. In civil aviation (with cargo being not entirely dissimilar), negotiations of access are generally undertaken in a two-step procedure between two or more governments. The first is the establishment of a bilateral agreement which would set the tone for the agreement (i.e. unlimited access or otherwise, any restrictions etc.). The follow-up Memorandum of Agreement would set specific explicit operational guidelines.

For example, two countries may negotiate an air service agreement that has strict limits on the number of flights, the size of gauge (i.e. which type aircraft is to be used, and whether there is a maximum number of seats) and whether there are any intermediate or beyond rights (i.e. initial or subsequent stopovers). Air service agreements may be regularly reviewed or may be entirely left 'as is' for decades.

This framework of air service negotiations can broadly be characterized as the aeropolitical operating environment of international civil aviation. Thus while aeropolitics is concerned with the regulatory environment within which international air transport (particularly commercial) operates, it can more specifically relate to government oversight of accessibility, operations, and ownership and control (e.g. Chang et al, 2004). For example, the level of accessibility granted by one government to airlines designated by another can be almost entirely relaxed and unfettered. A good example of this is Europe, which acts largely on the basis of one substantial market and with few constraints over access. Operations of aircraft range from security matters (i.e. whether one government allows airlines of another country to transport armed air marshals) to safety issues (particularly with respect to maintenance and overhaul provisions as carried out by a particular carrier that has been given rights to access a particular country). Operations can largely be covered by international organizations such as ICAO, and form part of the agreed-upon fundamentals associated with membership. Ownership and control is substantially politically driven and features consideration of (1) whether to allow foreign-owned or foreign-controlled carriers to operate within a country's domestic airspace, and (2) whether 'onward' flights to third-party countries allow for foreign ownership of carriers. The question of ownership and control is both a public policy issue with respect to national government policy leanings as well as a trade issue. Public policy may be explicit in terms of limiting ownership and control to foreign nationals or airlines to an assigned percentage. This is almost always balanced on the basis of existing bilateral agreements held by a country with other countries, where some bilaterals may make it explicit that access granted under the Agreement only applies to carriers wholly owned by non-foreigners.

Despite an increasing trend toward the liberalization of access with respect to air transport globally, there still exist several examples of regulatory structures imposed by governments or trading blocs that limit air transport movement or potential expansion. In essence, while on the one hand there is a steady increase of liberalization and globalization of the transfer of goods and services, the flow of international air transport generally continues along transnational and bilateral treaties that govern, and often restrict, flow, mode and networks.

Aeropolitics, as a policy analysis mechanism, attempts to extract and unravel the political basis for existing and revised operating environments (see, for example, Jönsson, 1981). Given consideration of the economic benefits of international (and national) civil aviation for trade in goods and services, an aeropolitical framework becomes a derivative of political economy analysis. From the perspective of tourism, aeropolitics as a framework is critical as it defines the conduits by which accessibility is afforded. It is also a useful framework when examining route structures, alliances, and trade and tariff agreements. It helps clarify government and industry negotiations over ownership, control and access within wider aspects of international trade. Most importantly, it sets the stage for understanding how carriers approach large externalities such as climate change when these very externalities challenge the public policy regimes of many national (and bloc) governments.

The economics of airline networks

Along with the global aeropolitical environment, it is critical to review the basic economics of airline operations and networks as these concepts help position the financial and economic basis for decision making. As is shown, airline operating costs are volatile and market penetration and access are critical for ensuring revenue exceeds cost on critical routes. One of the most useful overviews of airline economics is Holloway's (2003) publication, which provides an excellent overview. This section, then, draws largely from Holloway's (2003) work, which should be sought for further clarification and understanding.

As Holloway (2003) notes, airlines have strong incentives to track four main aspects of operations from an economic perspective:

1   the overall unit cost, measured as cost per available seat kilometre (CASK): this is a measure of the total cost per seat of transporting a certain seat (with the total number obviously fluctuating depending on the gauge of aircraft) across a certain stage length;
2   the unit revenue, measured as the revenue earned per available seat kilometre (RASK), which denotes, as is evident, the total revenue derived per seat along a particular stage length;
3   yield, which is generally a measure of the revenue earned per revenue-seat-kilometre, so not a total measure of the revenue earned across the entire flight but the revenue earned across the total number of potential revenue-earning seat kilometres; and
4   load factor, which is measure of performance in terms of seats sold in a particular aircraft (i.e. the number of occupied seats in an aircraft expressed as a percentage of the total number of seats in the same aircraft).

No single factor above takes a huge amount of precedence over another in terms of standard airline operational parameters, but it is generally recognized that a shift in one can have significant impacts on others. For example, higher unit costs (e.g. as a result of the increased price of kerosene) can mean pricing shifts which may have an ongoing impact on yield and load factors. Similarly, through revenue management (sometimes called yield management), an entire aircraft can achieve high load factors through deep discount pricing of fares. This would reduce RASK to the point where CASK can exceed RASK, thus rendering the operation a loss (although for strategic reasons, this may be desirable, depending on any potential revenue opportunities for interlining passengers (transferring passengers from one carrier to another using a single itinerary)).

What is critical in this discussion is the recognition that several externalities can have a significant impact on an airline's CASK. These can include, but are not limited to:

- increasing cost of kerosene/jet fuel or other direct (but variable) operating costs;
- increased indirect operating costs (e.g. airport fees and charges);
- regulatory compliance costs (e.g. safety and navigational upgrades or restandardization directives); and
- recapitalization costs (e.g. fleet renewal or upgrades).

As outlined in other chapters, airlines are increasingly being asked to account for their greenhouse gas emissions. This can have an impact on several of the areas above, including the cost of compliance, indirect operating costs associated with any additional charges, financing costs of equipment upgrades (perhaps in association with compliance measures introduced in some jurisdictions) and, depending on the point of obligation, increased fuel costs if fuel suppliers are required to account for emissions from their product.

For example, in the current framework brought on by the European Union with respect to the inclusion of aviation in the European Emissions Trading Scheme in 2012 (discussed later in the chapter), this may have several implications for added costs for airlines. For one, the added regulatory and compliance costs are, at present, unknown and it is difficult to predict whether they will be substantial or inconsequential. In addition, as a direct cost to the operation of aircraft for commercial passenger service, accounting for emissions raises the CASK. Unless the RASK can be lifted as well, margins will shrink. Of course, one way an airline may elect to ensure that RASK outpaces CASK is to pass on to the customer any additional costs as a result of entering the EU ETS. In this sense the traditional argument is that those of high net worth will bear the increase in fares. However, Brons et al (2002) argue that, if the share of air transport demand is positively correlated to demand from high net-worth individuals, then the resulting utility losses from increases in fares would be higher, even though a decreasing marginal utility of income could be recognized. Critically, Brons et al (2002) suggest that these higher net-worth segments might as a result actually become more price-sensitive.

The subsequent question to be explored at this juncture revolves around the strategic implications of decreases in RASK, increases in CASK, declining yields and problematic load factors as a result of any emissions-related regulatory edict, either globally or regionally. Airline networks as a whole are economic entities and sets which, when taken as a whole, define the financial and economic viability of an airline's operations (Lederer and Nambimadom, 1998). As such, increases in CASK on individual segments or city pairs can mean reductions in services and, consequently, alter the shape and profitability of the network.

With increases in CASK, several options for adjusting direct operating costs are available to carriers, including reductions in frequency, capacity and the elimination of routes. As well, several Australian carriers (e.g. Qantas and Jetstar) have been slowing the speed at which some domestic segments are run. At the time of writing (May 2008), there have already been alterations to the networks and operational contingencies as a result of increasing aviation fuel costs. Qantas, for example, has cut several domestic routes that have been performing poorly in the past (*The Australian*, 2008). Clearly, when RASK does not exceed CASK (or where margins are too thin to warrant continuation), it is simply uneconomic to operate a specific gauge of aircraft on a particular route and costs must be reduced. This is even more prevalent if markets will not bear the increase in direct operating costs (i.e. when yields and RASK can be improved). With oil having risen to over US$140 a barrel in June 2008, the global aviation sector is probably heading towards a period of instability and higher costs. Indeed, in April 2008 IATA argued for increased consolidation within the sector following the downgrade of profit forecasts for 2008 (*Air Transport World*, 2008a). By early July 2008, several significant carriers worldwide have reduced profit forecasts, shed routes (thus diminishing access) and staff. An IATA briefing note from June 2008 indicates that, if oil settles at prices around current levels (between US$135 and US$140 a barrel), net profits in the industry are forecast to decline by US$6.1 billion (IATA, 2008). Interestingly, IATA forecasts a net profit decline of US$2.3 billion even if the price of oil dips below US$100 (IATA, 2008).

Aviation and emissions

Ironically, with the increasing price of oil and, consequently, jet aviation fuel, it could be argued that reductions in emissions are already under way through voluntary operational adjustments such as those discussed above. While other chapters in this volume speak more coherently and substantively to the nature and extent of emissions from international aviation, a summary for perspective is useful here. Despite unequivocal evidence regarding the impact and volume of CO_2 emissions (although measures may not be entirely universal in agreement), the contribution from aviation remains disputed. *The Stern Report*, commissioned by the UK Treasury, argued that, based on 1990 levels, aviation contributes no more than 1.6 per cent of all emissions globally, although Intergovernmental Panel on Climate Change (IPCC) estimates suggest that, with additional radiative forcing, the true impact of GHG emissions from air transport could be anywhere from two to four times higher. As announced at a recent UNWTO conference in Davos, CO_2 emissions from transport, accommodation and other tourism activities account for roughly 4–6 per cent. We know from other work (e.g. Gössling et al, 2005) that the bulk of emissions from tourism, or its ecological footprint, largely comes from transport.

Problematic, however, is the range of unknown contributions made by air transport, such that CO_2 is but one element in the sector's contribution to global warming. Where this becomes an aeropolitical issue is the use of these data in the formulation of and contribution to government policy. A good example is the APD (air passenger duty) in place in the UK. A report from *The Daily Telegraph* (UK) in mid-October 2007 suggested that the Government had been incorporating the per-passenger duty into the general tax pool (*The Daily Telegraph*, 2007). Mayor and Tol (2007) argue that the doubling of the APD (announced November 2006) has resulted in a slight increase in emissions because the APD levy may be spread across longer-sector flights by passengers consciously opting to fly longer distances rather than short-haul sectors.

From an aeropolitical perspective, the lack of agreement on the true impact of air transport renders appropriate policy generation problematic and economically risky. Recent attention directed at air transport's contribution to climate change carries significant implications:

- the obvious impact on the environment: although the actual extent of the damage caused by aircraft is perhaps not fully known (see Kim et al, 2007, Lee et al, 2007), there is irrefutable evidence that emissions from aircraft are increasing due to global increases in traffic brought through profitable business models (including not only 'traditional' low-cost carriers, but the emulation of their practices by 'legacy' or more established carriers) that address increasing demand;
- the potential for route networks to be impacted through mitigation efforts, thus potentially leading to a reduction in supply offered due to increased CASK;
- the potential for existing services to face increased costs, which can have consequential flow-on effects for passengers and, by extension, quantity demand.

These three implications form the basis of the range of unknowns facing the commercial air transport sector worldwide as governments face increasing pressure to regulate emissions in one form or another. It is argued here, then, that an aeropolitical framework is a useful and suitable means by which these implications can be situated and debated in terms of urgency and potential economic impacts. Quite often, decisions by governments to pursue aggressive sustainable development and management policies are couched within political realities that may not always be obvious or transparent.

Politics, public policy and aviation emissions: The EU ETS

The recent push by the European Union to include aviation in the Emissions Trading Scheme (as an amendment to Directive 2003/87/EC, which forms the basis of the EU ETS) highlights the growing importance that trading blocs and individual governments have ascribed to the issue of the growth in aviation emissions. Intriguingly, the manner in which aviation was to be included in the ETS shifted during the calendar year 2007 and entailed disagreements among Parliamentary Committees over the details and timing of its implementation.

A first reading in Parliament was held in November 2007, where it was argued that airlines should reduce emissions by 10 per cent of 2004–2006 averages and that all carriers should join the ETS by 2011 (where the Commission's original proposal called for a tiered approach to entry, with international flights joining in 2012 with domestic/European-only flights coming into the ETS in 2011). The first reading in Parliament also called for airlines to be subjected to the auctioning of 25 per cent of permits. The European Council, in a December 2007 decision, recommended that all airlines flying into or out of the EU join the ETS by 2012, with emission levels to be set at 2004–2006 averages and 90 per cent of permits to be allocated free. The push to include aviation in the EU ETS follows on the proposed revisions to Directive 2003/87/EC (as COM [2008]30, i.e. the EU ETS itself) which, in addition to general improvements in monitoring and measurement, includes provision for an expansion of the Scheme itself to cover industrial sectors not considered in the original Directive, including aviation. An agreement was reached in late June 2008 by European Union MEPs and member states. The agreement included the following parameters:

- All flights, including both European and non-European, are to be included in the EU ETS beginning in 2012.
- The total number of permits allocated to air transport operators is to be capped at 97 per cent of the average GHG emissions from 2004–2006 (noting that MEPs had recommended 90 per cent, while national govern-ments had requested 100 per cent). This is effectively a requirement for the air transport sector to reduce emissions by 3 per cent in 2012. The cap is scheduled to be lowered to 95 per cent from 2013 to 2020.
- Of the total number of permits allocated based on historical emissions, 85 per cent will be allocated freely, with the remainder to be sold at auction (a figure which may be reduced following general reviews of the ETS Directive).

Not surprisingly, the reaction from the aviation industry has been strong. IATA released a statement (available at www.iata.org/pressroom/pr/ 2008–07–08–01.htm) immediately after the agreement between Council and Parliament was reached, criticizing the decision on several fronts:

- Legal: IATA questions the legal ability of the EU to impose emissions charges on aircraft flying into Europe, suggesting that it contravenes Article 2 of the Kyoto Protocol which states that (1) air transport in particular is to work through ICAO in emissions reduction, and (2) 'policies and measures' should be implemented 'in such a way as to minimize adverse effects' such as international trade.
- Timing: given the current cost of fuel faced by air transport operators, IATA argues that many are already striving to reduce fuel burn, suggesting that the formal agreement over the Single European Sky (SES) (effectively replacing almost 30 traffic control zones across Europe) would result in savings of up to 16 million tonnes of CO_2. The European Commission, in late June 2008, urged the rapid deployment of the SES.

Overall, the agreement to the EU's Directive 2003/87/EC for including aviation is one example of a regional 'solution' to emissions generated from air transport, albeit with the potential for recognition of bilateral emissions reduction targets between the EU and third countries. Indeed, the final agreement contained a strong recommendation that the EU pursue global measures, including the possibility of alterations to existing bilateral agreements. However, regional approaches are at odds with the perspectives taken by the International Civil Aviation Organization (ICAO; the UN body largely tasked with tackling emissions as per Article 2 of the Kyoto Protocol) and the International Air Transport Association (IATA). Both, with support from various airlines, have called for measures to be introduced that revolve around addressing inefficiencies ahead of cap-and-trade systems which may favour some operators over others (although as discussed below, ICAO recognizes the validity of emissions trading, but only when contracting states are in agreement). The Association of European Airlines' chairman Peter Hartman has called for a thorough rethink of how aviation is to be included within the EU ETS rather than the current 'clumsy political compromise which will generate huge costs that neither airlines nor their passengers can afford, and consequently will extinguish airline businesses, large and small, across the length and breadth of Europe' (*Air Transport World*, 2008b). Some environmental organizations and European governments have, however, criticized ICAO for dragging its feet over the very environmental responsibilities granted to it as part of Kyoto. Through Resolution 36-22 (adopted in September 2007), ICAO has recognized that many contracting states to the original Chicago Convention (IASTA, as discussed below) support emissions trading on the basis of mutual agreement and such that actions taken by states are non-discriminatory. In adopting a revised Directive for the EU ETS, EC member states 'placed a reservation on this resolution and reserved the right under the Chicago Convention to enact and... [applied] market-based measures on a non-discriminatory basis to all aircraft operators of all States providing services to, from or within their territory' (European Parliament, 2008).

From an international trade law perspective, incorporating aviation into the EU ETS has, according to the US, treaty implications for the enforcement of emissions trading schemes, particularly in relation to Article II of the International Air Services Transit Agreement signed at Chicago in 1944 (currently ratified by over 120 member states worldwide). The US has threatened legal challenges on the basis of Articles 15 and 24 of the Chicago Convention. Article 15 states:

> No fees, dues or other charges shall be imposed by any contracting State in respect solely of the right of transit over or entry into or exit from its territory of any aircraft of a contracting State or persons or property thereon.

Furthermore, Article 24 states:

> Fuel, lubricating oils, spare parts, regular equipment and aircraft stores on board an aircraft of a contracting State, on arrival in the territory of another contracting State and retained on board on leaving the territory of that State shall be exempt from customs duty, inspection fees or similar national or local duties and charges.

The lack of the word 'tax' in the Convention could be interpreted in such a manner as to allow a tax to be implemented. ICAO considers a tax as a levy which is 'designed to raise national or local government revenues which are generally not applied to civil aviation in their entirety or on a cost-specific basis' (ICAO, 2007). To this end, and despite the recent signing of the first round of a EU-US Open Skies Agreement (with the second round destined to be more horizontal in terms of ownership and control as well as address environmental issues), the US, at the time of writing, continues to argue that Article 15 of the Chicago Convention prevents aviation bunker fuel from being exposed to additional charges, unless both parties (each of whom would be signatories to ICAO) agree. Further, under the amended Directive (European Parliament, 2008), flights from the US to Europe would be liable for all emissions, even those emitted over non-EU airspace. Article 25A in the revised Directive (European Parliament, 2008), however, allows for amendment to be made if emissions mitigation measures for air transport are adopted in so-called 'third countries' (such as the US). The same Article also provides for outright negotiations should these be necessary:

> Where necessary, the Commission may adopt amendments to provide for flights arriving from the third country concerned to be excluded from the aviation activities listed in Annex I or to provide for any other amendments to the aviation activities listed in Annex I which are required by an agreement pursuant to the

fourth subparagraph. Those measures, designed to amend non-essential elements of this Directive, shall be adopted in accordance with the regulatory procedure with scrutiny referred to in Article 23(3). (European Parliament, 2008)

Disputes between the EU and the US with respect to ICAO (and the Chicago Convention) are not new. In 1999, the EU introduced legislation designed to force airlines operating aircraft into the EU to utilize quieter aircraft. As Murphy (2002) notes, noise guidelines fall under the Convention on International Civil Aviation and any amendments authorized through ICAO (with agreement, and thus pursuant to the original Convention). As Murphy (2002) notes, the EU were keen to establish their own guidelines due to the lack of meaningful progress by ICAO in this area. Using Article 84 of the Chicago Convention, which outlines the process by which disputes may be brought to ICAO, the US argued that aircraft operated by its designated airlines were most affected as the regulation as proposed by the EU targeted specific technologies and airframes rather than specific noise levels. The US therefore argued that certain carriers operating within the EU were exempt; thus the proposed legislation was contrary to anti-discrimination clauses within the original Chicago Convention that prohibited states from favouring airlines of one state over another state. Critically, ICAO adopted a more 'balanced' approach to international noise level monitoring and regulation, allowing for specific airports to be identified and measures to be taken to explore reduction strategies (ICAO, 2001).

Notwithstanding the 2008 elections in the US, where it remains unclear at the time of writing just what kind of support any new US Federal Government may have for having US airlines included within the EU ETS, emissions reductions (along with ownership and effective control provisions) will undoubtedly be a critical feature of the second round of EU-US Open Skies discussions in the second quarter of 2008. Of interest here is whether the current dispute between the US and the EU with respect to aviation emissions will follow a similar path. The crux of the dispute is the allocation of emissions from aircraft, with the US arguing that it should not be liable for emissions generated over non-European airspace. Indeed, one of the more vexing economic issues with respect to including aviation in a regional emissions trading scheme is the question of allocation of fuels from outside the region itself (see e.g. Morrell, 2007). The allocation and control of bunker fuels continues to be a critical shortcoming in addressing aviation emissions at a wider global level, and may even complicate the inclusion of aviation into the EU ETS in 2012. This is an issue that the UNFCCC Subsidiary Body for Scientific and Technological Advice (SBSTA) has been investigating since 1995. Recalling that international aviation was excluded from the Kyoto Protocol, the third SBSTA session at Geneva in 1996 identified eight options for the allocation and control of emissions bunker fuels from the first Conference of the Parties:

Option 1:   no allocation, as in the current situation;

Option 2:   allocation of global bunker sales and associated emissions to Parties in proportion to their national emissions;

Option 3:   allocation to Parties according to the country where the bunker fuel is sold;

Option 4:   allocation to Parties according to the nationality of the transporting company, or to the country where a ship or aircraft is registered, or to the country of the operator;

Option 5:   allocation to Parties according to the country of departure or destination of an aircraft or vessel; alternatively, the emissions related to the journey of an aircraft or vessel could be shared by the country of departure and the country of arrival;

Option 6:   allocation to Parties according to the country of departure or destination of passenger or cargo; alternatively, the emissions related to the journey of passengers or cargo could be shared by the country of departure and the country of arrival;

Option 7:   allocation to Parties according to the country of origin of passengers or owner of cargo;

Option 8:   allocation to the Party of all emissions generated in its national space (UNFCCC, 1997).

The EU ETS, and the inclusion of air transport by 2012, is an example of popular means of mitigating aviation emissions, including incentive-based systems such as cap-and-trade systems (of which the EU ETS is an example) or the use of absolute charges or taxes based on emissions (Schipper et al, 2001; Carlsson and Hammar, 2002). The former can often carry favour with regulators and many carbon-intensive industries as there is incentive to reduce emissions and thus reduce dependency on emissions permits; permits not needed can therefore be sold in an open market. Critics of cap-and-trade schemes point to the cost of implementation and monitoring and the need to strike a logical balance between the number of permits and the total amount of emissions (the failure of which can lead to a reduction in economic scarcity of permits if their number exceeds total emission units, thus driving down value). Critics of emissions taxes argue that such methods do little to encourage more efficient production.

Critical within this is the level ascribed to aviation services. The exact measure of aviation's current contribution to global or even regional economic well-being is complex, sometimes unrefined and not always universally accepted. If an agreed-upon value of aviation services can be identified, an argument could be made for negotiated levels of emissions between two parties, not unlike the structure afforded to property rights through principles adapted from Coasian economics (Duval, 2006).

Conclusion

At present, Europe represents the only regional bloc where aviation emissions are being considered for application and consideration of control and accountability (although New Zealand's Emissions Trading Scheme, due for a second reading in the New Zealand Parliament in August 2008, will include liquid fuels, and thus domestic aviation emissions, beginning January 2011). Notwithstanding the specific examples from Europe, several conclusions can be drawn from the above with respect to the power of an aeropolitical framework in assessing the link between emissions and international air transport (particularly of the commercial variety):

- Aeropolitics emerges from a political economy perspective in that it attempts to trace the position of economic and political actors and factors within a system. From this, it is clear that actors are driven by both ideological (in the case of groups such as www.enoughsenough.org) and commercial (in the case of ICAO, IATA) interests, yet the factors involved include the economic impact of accessibility through air transport.
- Aeropolitics incorporates various theories from international studies, particularly international law and policy (e.g. Richards, 1999), and as such the ability of regional or national governments to affix tariffs, levies or taxes on inbound international aircraft is unclear given existing bilateral/multilateral agreements and conventions.
- Finally, the link between air transport and climate change has given rise to conflict and vested interests within the current aeropolitical landscape. Several examples can be identified: between some governments (e.g. British) and the industry, within the air transport industry itself (e.g. between carriers), between external organizations (such as AirportWatch) and the air transport industry, and between the air transport industry and other affiliated sectors (e.g. airports).

Market conditions in 2008 and onwards may actually serve to reduce emissions, rather than government regulatory fiat. As indicated previously, oil above even US$120 a barrel (although it has been over US$140 in the first half of 2008) has forced several airlines to carefully evaluate the associated rising cost of fuel. As a variable but direct cost, fuel can be anything from 20 per cent to 30 per cent of overall operating costs, thus increases can have a serious impact on CASK. Faced with increased costs, many airlines face significant losses. In a standard supply/demand model, two scenarios can be envisioned. In the first, increased prices force the quantity demanded along a demand curve to shift. Second, extraneous macroeconomic variables (e.g. the global credit crisis, a slump in housing values in the US, risk of recession) can cause a demand curve to shift, thus resulting in a significant gap between what a market is willing to pay versus what an airline must charge to spread in the long run costs across shrinking output due to shrinking demand. In both scenarios, emissions may be reduced 'naturally' through reductions in quantity demanded of airline products.

At present, it is unlikely that the process for inclusion of global civil aviation within any emissions reduction scheme (whether global itself or a patchwork of national or regional efforts) will be smooth. Critically, however, there is consensus between the aviation sector and governments that aviation contributes to emissions, although the level and extent of disagreement generally rests on the means by which aviation should be limited, given its economic benefits. Without question, there exists a policy balance between operational responsibilities and aeropolitical realities. This chapter has attempted to demonstrate that these aeropolitical realities (both in a political and a regulatory sense) are useful for exploring policy directives.

References

Air Transport World (2008a) 'IATA again lowers full-year forecast, says industry has "no secure long-term future"', *Air Transport World* (online) 2 April, available at www.atwonline.com/news/story.html?storyID=12254, accessed 3 April 2008

Air Transport World (2008b) 'AEA: European ETS "ill-considered"', *Air Transport World* (online), 30 May, available at www.atwonline.com/news/story.html?storyID=12868, accessed 31 May 2008

The Australian (2008) 'Spike in oil forces Qantas cutbacks', 29 May, available at www.theaustralian.news.com.au/story/0,,23775561-23349,00.html, accessed 29 May 2008

Brons, M., Pels, E., Nijkamp, P. and Rietveld, P. (2002) 'Price elasticities of demand for passenger air travel: A meta-analysis', *Journal of Air Transport Management* 8: 165–175

Button, K. and Taylor, S. (2000) 'International air transport and economic development', *Journal of Air Transport Management* 6: 209–222

Carlsson, F. and Hammar, F. (2002) 'Incentive-based regulation of CO_2 emissions from international aviation', *Journal of Air Transport Management* 8: 365–372

Chang, Y.-C., Williams, G. and Hsu, C.-J. (2004) 'The evolution of airline ownership and control provisions', *Journal of Air Transport Management* 10: 161–172

The Daily Telegraph (2007) 'Airlines ask how "green" APD taxes are spent', 13 October, available at www.telegraph.co.uk/travel/main.jhtml?xml=/travel/ 2007/10/13/et-apd-113.xml, accessed 26 October 2007

Duval, D. T. (2006) 'Coasian economics and the management of international aviation emissions', *International Journal of Innovation and Sustainable Development* 1(3): 201–213

European Parliament (2008) European Parliament legislative resolution of 8 July 2008 on the Council common position for adopting a directive of the European Parliament and of the Council amending Directive 2003/87/EC so as to include aviation activities in the scheme for greenhouse gas emission allowance trading within the Community (5058/2008 – C6–0177/2008 – 2006/0304(COD)), available at www.europarl.europa.eu/sides/getDoc.do?pubRef=-//EP//TEXT+TA+ P6-TA-2008–0333+0+DOC+XML+V0//EN&language=EN

Gössling, S., Peeters, P., Ceron, J.-P., Dubios, G., Patterson, T. and Richardson, R. R. (2005) 'The eco-efficiency of tourism', *Ecological Economics* 54: 417–434

Holloway, S. (2003) *Straight and Level: Practical Airline Economics,* Aldershot: Ashgate

IATA (International Air Transport Association) (2008) 'Financial forecast, June 2008', *IATA Economics,* available at www.iata.org/whatwedo/economics/, accessed 29 July 2008

ICAO (International Civil Aviation Organization) (2001) *Assembly resolutions in force,* A 35-5, available at www.icao.int/icao/en/env/a35-5.pdf, (Doc 9848)

ICAO (2007) *Resolution 36–22,* available at www.icao.int/icao/en/env/ A36_Res22_Prov.pdf

Jönsson, C. (1981) 'Sphere of flying: the politics of international aviation', *International Organization* 35(2): 273–302

Kim, B. Y., Fleming, G. G., Lee, J. J., Waitz, I. A., Clarke, J-P., Balasubramanian, S., Malwitz, A., Klima, K., Locke M., Holsclaw, C. A., Maurice, L. Q. and Gupta, M. L. (2007) 'System for assessing Aviation's Global Emissions (SAGE): Model description and inventory results', *Transportation Research Part D* 12: 325–346

Lederer, P. J. and Nambimadom, R. S. (1998) 'Airline network design', *Operations Research* 46(6): 785–804

Lee, J. J., Waitz, I. A., Kim, B. Y., Fleming, G. G., Maurice, L. Q. and Holsclaw, C. A. (2007) 'System for assessing Aviation's Global Emissions (SAGE): Uncertainty assessment', *Transportation Research Part D* 12: 381–395

Mayor, K. and Tol, R. S. J. (2007) 'The impact of the UK aviation tax on carbon dioxide emissions and visitor numbers', *Transport Policy* 14: 507–513

Morrell, P. (2007) 'An evaluation of possible EU air transport emissions trading scheme allocation methods', *Energy Policy* 35: 5562–5570

Murphy, S. D. (2002) *United States Practice in International Law: Volume 1: 1999–2001,* Cambridge: Cambridge University Press

Richards, J. E. (1999) 'Toward a positive theory of international institutions: Regulating international aviation markets', *International Organization* 53(1): 1–37

Schipper, Y., Rietveld, P. and Nijkamp, P. (2001) 'Environmental externalities in air transport markets', *Journal of Air Transport Management* 7: 169–179

UNFCCC (SBSTA) (1997) *Report of the Subsidiary Body for Scientific and Technological Advice on the Work of its Fourth Session,* Geneva, 16–18 December 1996 (FCCC/SBSTA/1996/20/27)

9
Aviation and Economic Development: The Implications of Environmental Costs on Different Airline Business Models and Flight Networks

Cherie Lu

Introduction

Over the years, increasing attention has been paid to the sustainable development of the aviation sector (e.g. Caves, 1994a, b; Fawcett, 2000). Environmental and social concerns are gradually posing limitations on the growth of the air transport industry. Although the global economic downturn and political turmoil of increased global security have caused a decline in the number of flights and passengers over the past years, the air traffic has picked up momentum and is foreseen to grow even more rapidly than before, especially in the emerging markets. Therefore, these environmental concerns have attracted more attention from government bodies and international aviation organizations. Nevertheless, based on the polluter pays principle, it is widely recognized now that the costs of these externalities must be internalized (European Commission, 1999). For this reason, the sustainable development of the air transport industry is a significant issue that should be incorporated into all activities concerned.

Two of the most important externalities generated from commercial flights are noise nuisance and aircraft engine emissions. Of these two, noise nuisance has the largest impact on the communities surrounding airports, and causes both annoyance (nuisance) and health effects, for instance sleep deprivation, stress and hypertension (Franssen et al, 2004; Black et al, 2007; Jarup et al, 2008). Engine emissions have both local and global impacts on air quality and greenhouse gases, respectively, which have long and lasting effects on the environment and pose a great threat to human beings.

More and more airports, often forced by governments or public pressure, are applying different types of noise management measures that range from noise abatement procedures to limits on the total noise allowed (Lu and Morrell, 2006). Following the ICAO (International Civil Aviation Organization) 'balanced approach', among these measures are night flight restrictions and curfews, night quotas, and noise charges and penalties (Hullah, 2007). In 1999, only 14 countries in the world had some form of noise charges; by 2007, 24 countries, including 18 European, 2 Asian and 2 North American countries, had applied noise-related charges (Boeing website, 2007).

Aircraft engine emissions have extensive impact on human health, vegetation, materials, ecosystems and the climate. Aircraft exhaust pollutants are emitted during landing and take-off (LTO), ground stages and during the cruise mode of flights. Damage is incurred from these pollutants at all flight stages and aircraft are the only source that injects pollutants into the upper troposphere and lower stratosphere, resulting in a higher level of global warming than is the case for similar ground-level emissions. Compared to the introduction of noise management measures, there are fewer airports applying engine emissions mitigation measures. Some airports have restrictions on the use of aircraft engines, ancillary power units and ground power units; or improvement of air traffic management; or measures applied to ground vehicles and energy uses of terminal buildings. Regarding economic instruments, so far engine emissions charges are in place only at airports in four countries, namely Switzerland, Sweden, the United Kingdom and Germany.

At a global or international level, emissions trading[1] or voluntary agreements might be a feasible approach in controlling the total amount of pollutants from aviation activities. As regards economic measures which could be applied at airports, environmental charges are seen as one of the most effective ways of mitigating the impacts from aircraft operations. Any environmental charge does not stand alone. In fact, it should be established as a system or mechanism which takes into account the actual environmental costs, their subsequent impacts on airline operations and passenger behaviour, as well as the use of the collected revenues in order to achieve the maximum social welfare objectives (OECD, 1997). Hence, the implications of various environmental charge scenarios on different kinds of airline business models, airline costs and passenger demand need to be estimated before they are put into practice (Brueckner and Girvin, 2008).

The section headed 'Engine emission charges at airports' compares the engine emissions charges which have been applied at airports. A systematic generic approach to setting up environmental charge mechanisms and charge levels is then proposed in the section headed 'Environmental charge mechanism: A generic systematic approach', with the consideration of environmental social costs, the cost of noise mitigation measures, airport user charges, and related parties involved.

The section headed 'Methods for estimating engine emissions and noise social costs' presents the evaluation techniques used for estimating the social costs of both aircraft noise and engine emissions. Noise nuisance incurs social costs; while aircraft engine emissions generate socio-environmental costs; for simplicity, this chapter has used social costs or environmental costs to imply the external impacts on society and environment. The environmental costs here are defined as the aggregation of both aircraft engine emissions and noise social costs. To better illustrate the impacts of environmental costs on airline economics, three sets of numerical and analytical analysis based on real case studies are presented in the sections on 'The impacts of environmental costs on air-passenger demand for different airline business models', 'The environmental costs of two patterns of airline service, hub-to-hub and hub bypass' and 'The implications of aircraft engine emissions costs on the operating costs of Asian airlines'.

The cases chosen cover a wide range of airlines, airline business models, flight routes and markets. The conclusions are given in the last section.

Engine emission charges at airports

So far only some airports in Switzerland[2] and Sweden, as well as London-Heathrow, London Gatwick and Frankfurt airports, have aircraft engine emissions-related surcharges. Swiss and Swedish airports have the longest history of implementing such charges, both since the late 1990s. No other airports joined the move until BAA's (British Airports Authority) London Heathrow Airport introduced emissions charges in 2004, followed by London Gatwick in 2005 and Frankfurt airports in early 2008 (Fleuti, 2007).

All these airports have different ways of charging for aircraft engine emissions. However, NO_x is the only pollutant on which emission charges are based at all of these airports. London and Frankfurt airports apply unit rates per kilogram of NO_x during LTO. Swiss and Swedish airports have more complicated ways of calculating emissions, based on formulas taking into account VOCs (volatile organic compounds) and HCs (hydrocarbons) respectively, in addition to NO_x. Figure 9.1 shows the emissions charges on three aircraft types (B747–400, A330–300 and B737–800) at four airports. Stockholm Arlanda has the highest charges for all aircraft types with around €350 for a B747–400, €175 for a A330–300 and €50 for a B737–800. Zurich and Frankfurt have similar charge levels, with London Heathrow having the lowest charges.

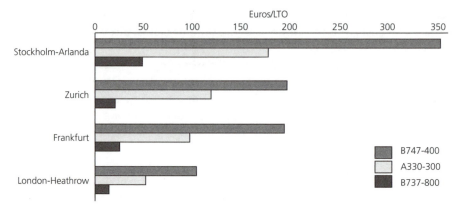

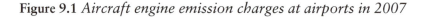

Note: the calculation is based on assumptions on maximum take-off weights (MTOWs), engine types and operating procedures.

Figure 9.1 *Aircraft engine emission charges at airports in 2007*

Environmental charge mechanism: A generic systematic approach

Based on the findings of theoretical research and the review of the current emission charge schemes, a generic approach to setting up environmental charge mechanisms is proposed here, as illustrated in Figure 9.2. The application of environmental charges involves airports, government authorities, the surrounding neighbourhood, airlines and even passengers. The theoretical basis behind environmental charges is for internalizing this externality. Hence, the social costs of the externality concerned should first be estimated in order to have a clearer understanding about the true costs of the impacts.

In practical terms, the actual environmental charge levels should be then related to the total costs/investment of related mitigating measures. Meanwhile, the charge schemes and levels as well as the equity of the scheme should be accepted by all the actual payers concerned, namely airlines. As the environmental charge is part of the airport user charges, the competitiveness of an airport in terms of airport user charge levels should also be investigated while determining the proper charge level for different types/categories of aircraft.

Theoretically, it is possible to estimate the percentage of charges, based on the increase in operating costs, that an airline would pass on to passengers through higher air fares, depending mainly on passenger's price elasticity as well as on the characteristics of the market in which airlines are operating. Within the competitive operating environment, airlines might try to reduce their costs through various strategic measures, which would result in only a certain percentage of environmental charges being passed on to passengers (Lu and Morrell, 2001).

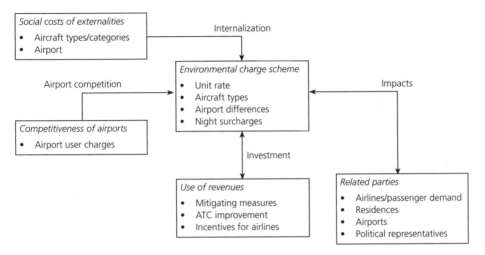

Figure 9.2 *The structure of environmental charge mechanism*

In addition to the charging methods and charge level, a further vital step of establishing an environmental charge mechanism is the use and the implications of revenues, which have been collected from environmental charges. The ICAO Council (1996) identified key policy issues regarding environmental charges and taxes on aviation, and strongly recommended that any environmental levies on air transport should be in the form of charges rather than taxes. In addition, the revenues collected should be applied in the first instance to mitigating the adverse environmental impacts of aircraft emissions.

As this chapter focuses on the environmental charges imposed by individual airport authorities instead of worldwide or region-wide, the use of charges to supplement government income is eliminated from the consideration. Therefore, revenues can be applied in the following ways:

- To compensate for damages from emission impacts and noise nuisance: the mitigation options include various noise insulation schemes, real monetary compensation for both noise and emission issues etc.
- To cover the cost of mitigation measures for environmental reasons: such as air quality measuring equipment, aircraft noise monitoring system, etc.
- To invest in air traffic control (ATC) improvement or increase fuel efficiency in air traffic management (ATM) operations: this can reduce flight delays due to inefficient ATC systems and heavy traffic demand, and results in the reduction of aircraft engine emissions.
- To invest in more environmentally friendly aircraft and engines: this could be done in two ways: by sponsoring research by aircraft manufacturers and by creating financial incentives for airlines' purchase of greener engines or aircraft types.

However, the overall use of charges should be based on the cost–benefit analysis for each implementation option in order to make the most use of the revenues, which in turn would lead to a better correction of the market failure due to the existing externalities (Lu and Morrell, 2001).

Methods for estimating engine emissions and noise social costs

Before applying any aircraft engine emission mitigating measures, it is vital to estimate the social costs of these externalities in monetary terms, to better understand the extent and scope of the impacts and to determine cost-effectiveness. A cost–benefit analysis of particular measures may also be conducted. This section presents the methods commonly used for estimating aircraft engine emission and noise social costs.

Engine emission social costs

Differences in aircraft operations, engine types, emission rates and airport congestion are considered important parameters influencing the damage level of pollutants. Air pollution at ground level resulting from the LTO phase of flights is distinguished from the cruise-level impact, and therefore should be analysed separately, as the damage pattern and magnitude is different for these two phases of flights. As far as one flight is concerned, the LTO emissions result in local air pollution; however, the emissions during the cruise stage contribute to climate change, global warming, the depletion of ozone layer and the formation of contrails etc, all of which have a global rather than a local scale of effects.

The study results from Pearce and Markandya (1989) show that the dose-response technique is, comparatively, the most comprehensive method for valuing the damages resulting from the aircraft engine exhaust pollutants. This method is also categorized as the direct valuation method, which traces the links between air emissions and adverse consequences, considered as the best developed method for evaluating the social cost of emissions (Small and Kazimi, 1995). This is done by estimating the environmental costs of damage to human health, vegetation, buildings and climate change as well as global warming, based on the dose-response relationships between pollution and effects, and then summing the individually derived monetary results.

There have been some applications of this method to measuring the external costs of various exhaust pollutants both on the local level and on the global level (ExternE, 1999; Pearce, 2003; Green, 2003). Furthermore, results have been applied by several researchers for assessing the environmental costs of the aviation industry (Pearce and Pearce, 2000; UK DfT, 2003; Dings et al, 2003; Schipper, 2004). Table 9.1 lists the range of results found in various literature and the average value for the pollutants considered in this research. As the monetary evaluation of the damage is still uncertain (reflected in the wide range of monetary impacts), the unit social cost estimates for each pollu-

Table 9.1 *Social costs of each exhaust pollutant*

Pollutant	Average (2005 €/kg)[a]	Rural	Urban
HC	4.5	2.8–5.2	2.8–9.0
CO	0.1	0.02–0.20	
NO_x	10.1	4.2–13.3	7.2–25.3
PM	167.8	18.2–202.0	85.5–2005.0
SO_2	6.8	3.2–8.8	3.5–52.0
CO_2	0.03[b]	0.01–0.04	

Notes: a The figures are inflated to 2005 values by applying the Euro area inflation rates.
b The figure of 0.038, used in the calculation, has been rounded to two decimal places.

Source: Pearce and Pearce (2000), Dings et al (2003), Lu and Morrell (2006)

tant have been averaged across all the studies for use in the later empirical analysis.

The listed pollutants are considered as the main ones emitted by aircraft movements. Some pollutants, especially PM, SO_2, NO_x and HC, although accounting for a lower weight of emissions, have higher unit social costs. On the other hand, CO_2 has lower unit social cost, but the total amount emitted is far larger than the others. As shown in Table 9.1, the social costs evaluated from the previous research for each pollutant vary significantly. The population density in the research area considered was clearly one of the main factors in determining the impacts of pollutants. Moreover, this was also due to the differences in their fundamental assumptions on the types of damage included, such as the effects on health, vegetation, materials, aquatic ecosystem, as well as on the climate change and the area considered (i.e. local, regional or global).

Concerning the pollutants emitted during cruise as well as the subsequent damage, the scientific research results have not so far come to any definitive conclusion (IPCC, 1999). However, the impacts of the greenhouse gas, CO_2, have been evaluated in more recent studies and have also been addressed in government policies. There is considerable uncertainty in quantifying the impacts of contrails and other pollutants, such as NO_x and H_2O (IPCC, 1999). This impact is measured in terms of 'radiative forcing', which is intended to capture the change in average net radiation at the top of the troposphere that results from a change in greenhouse gas concentrations. The radiative forcing index (RFI) measures the importance of aviation-induced climate change relative to CO_2 effects only. The range of estimates of these impacts is given as a multiplier of between 1.2 and 4.2 (IPCC, 1999, pp211–212), capturing CO_2, NO_x and other emissions and their effect on global warming. For this reason, no RFI multiplier has been included in the analysis that follows, but the reader can easily apply whichever estimate they prefer (Morrell and Lu, 2007).[3]

Six exhaust pollutants (HC, CO, NO_x, PM, SO_2 and CO_2) for LTO stages have been shown to have significant impacts from aircraft operations (Figure 9.3). There might be some other pollutants, such as VOCs, but the impacts of those have not been clearly studied and assessed. However, with more research

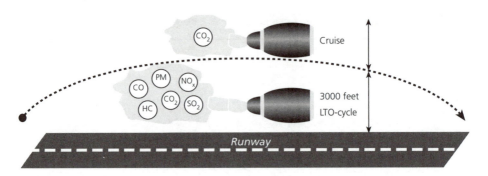

Note: all of the above pollutants and other gases (notably water vapour) are emitted during both LTO and cruise flight stages; however, the ICAO engine databank shows the above range of pollutants only for the LTO cycle.

Figure 9.3 *Diagram of the pollutants emitted during LTO and cruise flight stages*

results in the future, the figures in Table 9.1 could be updated and more pollutants could also be included. As far as the cruise stage is concerned, the most well-known greenhouse gas, CO_2, is included throughout the case studies in this chapter. With regard to non-carbon pollutants, note that NO_x is now getting more attention internationally, but its real impact on a global scale is yet to be characterized scientifically.

The calculation of engine emission social costs uses a so-called bottom-up approach. The main inputs for estimating aircraft engine emission social costs are listed as follows (Figure 9.4):

- Time (minutes) for different flight modes: according to the ICAO standard setting for engine testing, these are take-off (0.7 minutes), climb-out (2.2 minutes), approach (4.0 minutes), idle (26 minutes). The cruise stage would depend on the flight distance and aircraft speed.
- Fuel flow (kg/s) for different flight modes: according to the ICAO standard setting.
- Emission index (g/kg fuel) for different flight modes: HC, CO and NO_x are included in the ICAO engine emissions databank; SO_2, PM and CO_2 will be based on other scientific findings.
- Unit social costs (€/kg pollutant): based on scientific findings to date (Table 9.1).

With various parameters and unit social costs for different pollutants, as well as aircraft operation characteristics, the aircraft engine emission social costs could be estimated for different aircraft and engine combinations (Figure 9.5).

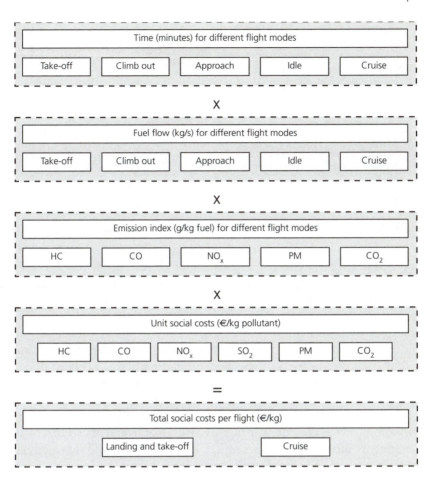

Figure 9.4 *Procedures to estimate engine emissions social costs*

Noise social costs

The hedonic price method (HPM) is the most commonly used technique for estimating noise damage costs (Lu, 2008). This method extracts the implicit prices of certain characteristics that determine property values, such as location, attributes of the neighbourhood and environmental quality. By applying the HPM, the annual total noise social cost at an airport could be derived by having the following inputs (Figure 9.6):

- The noise depreciation index (NDI): the percentage reduction of house price per dB(A)[4] above background noise. The average NDI from literature review is generally assumed to be 0.6 per cent.
- The number of residences within each zone of the noise contour.
- The annual average house rent in the vicinity of the airport: could be derived from the average house value in the area.

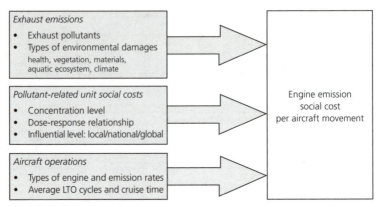

Figure 9.5 *Inputs for estimating aircraft engine emissions social costs*

As opposed to the estimation of aircraft engine emissions, the noise social costs are calculated using the top-down approach. After deriving the aggregate noise social cost, it is necessary to decide how to allocate this total external cost to individual flights. The principle of this process should be based on the real impact of noise nuisance generated dynamically from each specific flight. A simplified approach to deriving the marginal noise nuisance (noise index), caused by each specific aircraft/engine combination flight, has been developed (Lu and Morrell, 2006). The calculation of noise index is based on the average of three ICAO-certified noise levels, namely the effective perceived noise level (EPNdB) for take-off, sideline and approach, for different aircraft/engine combinations. With the composition of aircraft movements by aircraft type and engine combinations, the annual noise index could be aggregated. Considering the noise index for different aircraft types and engine combinations, the noise social cost per aircraft movement could then be derived.

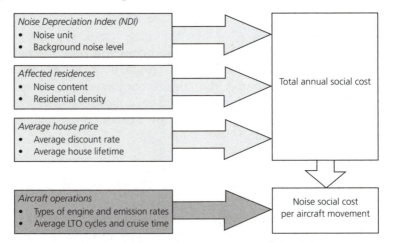

Figure 9.6 *Methodology of hedonic price method for estimating noise social costs*

The impacts of environmental costs on air-passenger demand for different airline business models

This analysis has chosen two European city pairs, which have flight services both from full-service carriers and low-cost carriers. The analysis focuses on the potential passenger demand reduction for these two types of airline business model, if environmental charges are added to air fares (Lu, 2008). However, the extent to which airlines might adapt their pricing strategies will not be explored.

Market selection

Considering the current existing routes which are operated both by low-cost carriers and full-service carriers, as well as the availability of the data, this section selected two city pairs for empirical analysis, namely London–Amsterdam and London–Paris, with a total of six flight routes operated by three airlines (British Airways, Air France-KLM, and easyJet), out of five airports (London Heathrow, London Stansted, London Luton, Amsterdam Schiphol and Paris Charles de Gaulle). The combination of flight routes and airlines are shown in Table 9.2.

Table 9.2 *Flight routes and airlines selected*

Routes from London to Amsterdam			
Business model	Airline	Origin in London	Destination in Amsterdam
Full-service carriers	British Airways	Heathrow	Schiphol
		Gatwick	
Low-cost carriers	easyJet	Gatwick	Schiphol
		Stansted	
		Luton	
Routes from London to Paris			
Business model	Airline	Origin in London	Destination in Paris
Full-service carriers	Air France	Heathrow	Charles de Gaulle
	British Airways	Heathrow	Charles de Gaulle
Low-cost carriers	easyJet	Luton	Charles de Gaulle

Source: British Airways (2005), easyJet (2005), Air France-KLM Group (2005)

Aircraft engine emissions and noise social costs for the cases

With regard to engine emissions, the social costs estimates for these aircraft types are listed in Table 9.3, assuming the impacts of engine emissions are related to engine types and fuel efficiency, disregarding their flight origin or destinations.[5] The aircraft types used by these airlines are either A320 series or B737 families, which are typical Chapter 3[6] short-haul narrow-bodied jets. The figures in Table 9.3 show the social costs at the ground level resulting from the standard LTO procedures, including take-off, climb-out, approach and taxi-idle modes, as well as the cruise stage. The costs of the emissions from the cruise stage depend on the engine fuel efficiency and the actual distance flown.

Table 9.3 *Engine emission social costs by airline, flight route, aircraft/engine combination and flight stage*

Airline	Route	Aircraft type*	LTO (€/flight)	Cruise (€/flight)	Total (€/flight)
British Airways	LHR-AMS	A319	217	108	325
		A321-200	327	128	455
	LGW-AMS	B737-300	187	106	293
		B737-400	187	113	300
		B737-500	187	117	305
	LHR-CDG	A319	217	101	318
		A321-200	327	119	446
		A320-211	209	108	317
		A320	239	108	347
Air France-KLM	LHR-CDG	A319	188	101	289
		A320	227	108	335
easyJet	STN-AMS	A319	190	92	282
		B737-700	203	88	291
	LTN-AMS	A319	190	103	293
		B737-700	203	99	390
	LTN-CDG	A319	190	110	300
		B737-700	203	105	308

Note: * The same aircraft type with different engines will result in different engine emissions.

The engine emission social costs for LTO range from €187 to €327 depending on aircraft/engine combinations. Adding the costs of the cruise stage, the total engine emissions social costs would vary from €291 to €446.

Based on the research results from Lu and Morrell (2006), the estimates of noise social costs for these aircraft types applied in this empirical analysis are shown in Table 9.4. The assumptions are mainly based on the concept that the noise social costs are in proportion to the residences within certain noise contours and the house price in the vicinity of the airports.

Table 9.4 *Noise social costs estimates for different airports*

Social costs (€/LTO)	London Heathrow	Amsterdam Schiphol	London Gatwick	London Stansted	London Luton	Paris CDG
Noise	510	265	19	11	11	265

Source: Lu and Morrell (2006)

Air fares and demand elasticities

The air fares range greatly in these selected markets, depending on days of travelling, time of day, time of booking prior to departure, fare restrictions and promotions etc. This research had continuously observed the fare changes for a period of one month in 2006, marking the highest and lowest fares for different airlines, seating classes (if applicable) and routes. The range of fares is divided into four quarters. The value at the lowest quarter is selected as the air fare for leisure passengers and the highest quarter is used for business passengers (Lu and Chen, 2007).

Regarding demand elasticities, the figures vary widely depending on trip purpose (business or leisure), flight distance (long haul or short haul), seating class (economy, business or first class), market sector and time. This research adapted the values, listed in Table 9.5, from Gillen et al (2004), as it summarizes the demand elasticity results from many countries and categorizes them into six markets according to flight distance, trip purpose, international and domestic flight. It is worth noting that, based on the research from BAA, 28 per cent of passengers originating from UK airports between 2004 and 2005 were on business, with 72 per cent of passengers on leisure trips (2nd Annual Aviation Forecasting Conference in Vienna, 2006).

Table 9.5 *The air demand elasticity of business and leisure passengers used in the empirical analysis*

| Type | Length | | Elasticity | |
		Average	Lowest	Highest
Business	Short haul	−0.70	−0.78	−0.59
Leisure	Short haul	−1.52	−1.74	−1.29

Source: Gillen et al (2004)

Empirical results
Leisure passengers
Assuming the environmental costs are added on top of air fares (through airport environmental charges), Table 9.6 shows the fares, social costs per passenger, social costs as a percentage of fares and the potential demand reduction for different airlines running on different routes. With the consideration of the number of seats and load factors of different aircraft configurations by airlines, the results reveal that the average social costs per passenger are higher for those flying with British Airways and Air France-KLM than those with easyJet. Substituting the average elasticity value of 1.52 listed in Table 9.5, the potential demand reduction for the London–Amsterdam route varies from 4.5 per cent to 7.8 per cent; for the London–Paris route, the range is between 5.5 per cent and 7.1 per cent. EasyJet's markets are shown to have the highest percentage of demand reduction in both city pairs.

Business passengers
For passengers on business, the social cost per passenger clearly remains the same as for leisure passengers. Assuming the elasticity value of 0.7 for business passengers, the potential demand reduction for the London–Amsterdam route varies from 0.9 per cent to 1.9 per cent; for the London–Paris route, the range is between 1.1 per cent and 1.7 per cent (Table 9.7). Because of the price inelasticity of the business market, the impacts of environmental costs/charges are clearly less significant than for the leisure markets. Similarly, easyJet's markets

Table 9.6 *The potential demand reduction of leisure passengers*

Route		Airline	Distance	Fare	Social cost/pax	Social cost/fare	Potential demand reduction
			km	€	€	%	%
London–Amsterdam							
Case 1	LHR-AMS	British Airways	372	164.98	6.68	4.1	6.2
Case 2	LGW-AMS	British Airways	367	158.19	4.69	3.0	4.5
	LGW-AMS	easyJet	367	68.97	3.53	5.1	7.8
Case 3	STN-AMS	easyJet	315	67.15	3.38	5.0	7.6
Case 4	LTN-AMS	easyJet	356	68.97	3.47	5.0	7.6
London–Paris							
Case 5	LHR-CDG	British Airways	346	180.31	6.55	3.6	5.5
	LHR-CDG	Air France-KLM	346	179.95	7.58	4.2	6.4
Case 6	LTN-CDG	easyJet	378	75.18	3.52	4.7	7.1

Source: Lu (2008)

are shown to have the highest percentages of demand reduction in both city pairs, the reason being their lower air fares.

Sensitivity analysis

A range of price elasticities is further conducted for sensitivity analysis. Based on results from the literature review, elasticities between 1.3 and 1.8 are used for leisure markets; for business markets, they range from 0.5 to 0.8. The sensitivity results are further summarized in Table 9.8. With the range of price elasticity, the potential demand reduction would be around 7.1–7.8 per cent for easyJet's leisure passengers and approximately 1.7–1.9 per cent for business passengers. The figures are higher than those for full-service carriers (British Airways and Air France-KLM), being 4.5–6.4 per cent and 0.9–1.3 per cent, respectively.

Table 9.7 *The potential demand reduction of business passengers*

Route		Airline	Distance	Fare	Social cost/pax	Social cost/fare	Potential demand reduction
			km	€	€	%	%
London–Amsterdam							
Case 1	LHR-AMS	British Airways	372	365.00	6.68	1.8	1.3
Case 2	LGW-AMS	British Airways	367	357.48	4.69	1.3	0.9
	LGW-AMS	easyJet	367	145.62	3.53	2.4	1.7
Case 3	STN-AMS	easyJet	315	125.55	3.38	2.7	1.9
Case 4	LTN-AMS	easyJet	356	145.62	3.47	2.4	1.7
London–Paris							
Case 5	LHR-CDG	British Airways	346	410.99	6.55	1.6	1.1
	LHR-CDG	Air France-KLM	346	411.36	7.58	1.8	1.3
Case 6	LTN-CDG	easyJet	378	148.18	3.52	2.4	1.7

Source: Lu (2008)

Table 9.8 *The potential demand reduction for different airline business models with the range of price elasticity*

Type	Full-service carriers	Low-cost carriers
Airlines	British Airways and Air France-KLM	easyJet
Leisure	4.5~6.4%	7.1~7.8%
Business	0.9~1.3%	1.7~1.9%

Source: Lu (2008)

Summary

Facing competitive air transport markets and more stringent environmental measures applied at airports, airlines with different business models are bound to find a balance among costs, fares and demand for growth. This section has selected the well-developed intra-European short-haul routes for the case studies. The results have shown the impacts of environmental costs on passenger demand if the environmental costs are passed on to consumers through environmental charges on airlines. The results show that the potential percentage of demand reduction would be higher for easyJet's markets. As British Airways and Air France-KLM operate from large hub airports with a high population density around them, they incur higher noise social costs than does easyJet, which generally operates from secondary airports in less-populated areas (Lu and Morrell, 2006). Moreover, easyJet's fleet tends to produce better fuel efficiency due to more recent aircraft/engine combinations. However, with lower environmental costs per passenger, easyJet is estimated to suffer more from environmental charges because of their lower fares than those of full-service carriers. While implementing environmental charges or any measure which internalizes the external costs, policy makers should wisely find a balance between economic growth and environmental impacts.

The environmental costs of two patterns of airline service, hub-to-hub and hub bypass

Hub-and-spoke versus direct flight

Origin/destination (O/D) passenger markets can be carried on non-stop flights, or routed via intermediate points. At these points, they either stay on the same aircraft and continue to their destination after a stopover (transiting), or transfer from one aircraft to another. The latter is the more common way that hub carriers use to combine a number of O/D markets across their network. This gives considerable potential for scale economies both on the feeder flights (spokes) and on the hub–hub flights. Network carriers use this hub-and-spoke network structure to build up traffic volumes (Morrell and Lu, 2007).

Most long-haul markets are low volume, and thus the hub-and-spoke model is still the most appropriate one to provide adequate frequency and economic sized aircraft. However, with the growth of air traffic over the years and in the future, there will be more city pairs which have built up their volume

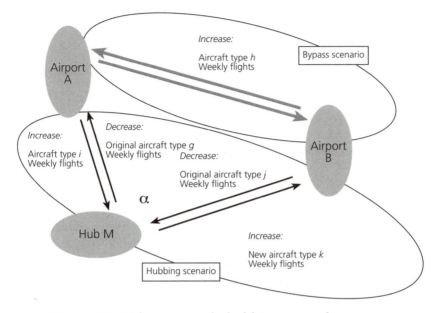

Figure 9.7 *Airline network: hubbing versus bypass scenarios*

and where it would be economical for network airlines to operate direct flights. This section explores the environmental implications of serving long-haul markets by stopping over at one hub airport, or by using hub bypass routes.

The economic rationale for a change in the global network structure away from hub-to-hub operations to hub bypass is growing congestion at the hubs and improved economics for hub bypass. The latter could come from a new long-haul aircraft type or from the application of low-cost carrier (LCC) techniques to these sectors. Another driver could be the internalization of environmental costs, and the valuation of the likely future extent of this is the focus of this section.

The model is designed to evaluate the environmental implications of carry-ing a given number of passengers between city pair A/B, either via hub airport M or on a non-stop routing using: (a) a hubbing scenario or (b) a hub bypass scenario. Figure 9.7 illustrates the structure of the network.

Scenario (a) is most likely to be accommodated by moving to a large aircraft type for both feeder and hub-to-hub sectors. This is because slots are likely to be scarce at many major hubs, especially at times when the feeder flights arrive and depart to connect with long-haul flights. Scenario (b) is dependent on an economic and smaller seat capacity aircraft, as well as a suffi-ciently good mix of high- and low-yield traffic. Any stimulation of demand from the reduced trip time will not be considered at this stage of the modelling process, since it is the per passenger impact that will be estimated for the two scenarios.

Market selection

Two UK airports (London Heathrow and Glasgow Abbotsinch), two German airports (Frankfurt and Hamburg), three US airports (Chicago O'Hare, San Diego and Dallas) and one Japanese airport (Tokyo Narita) are taken as the case studies for the empirical analysis. These include airports in the three major air transport regions, as well as a mix of major hubs and cities that are not hubs but have potential for their own long-haul scheduled air services. Based on the aircraft size and noise certificated levels, all aircraft types at these airports are categorized into eight categories, with a representative aircraft type being selected for each of the categories, as shown in Table 9.9.

Table 9.9 *Aircraft categorization*

Category	Aircraft	Representative aircraft
1	Propeller aircraft	Jetstream 31
2	Regional jets	CRJ
3	Chapter 3 jets: short haul, network small	B737-700
4	Chapter 3 jets: short haul, network large	A321
5	Chapter 3 jets: wide-body twins	B767/B777
6	Large Chapter 3 jets: 2nd generation wide-body multi-engines	B747-400
7	Large Chapter 3 jets: 1st generation wide-body	B747-100/200/300
8	Hush kitted jets: 1st/2nd generation narrow body	B727Q

Aircraft engine emission and noise social costs for the cases

The social cost of engine emissions for different aircraft has been calculated on the basis of different engine types and emission rates. The average social costs during LTO and cruise stages for jet aircraft categories are shown in Table 9.10. As the impacts of engine emissions are less airport-specific (or at least little is known about their subsequent dispersion around the airport), the social costs for individual aircraft types are assumed to be the same for all eight airports.

Table 9.10 *Engine emissions social cost by jet aircraft category (2004 €/flight)*

Jet aircraft category	Aircraft type	LTO	30-minute cruise	LTO+cruise	Fuel burn during 30-minute cruise (kg)
2	CRJ	79	61	140	576
3	B737-700	224	130	354	1230
4	A321	323	160	483	1518
5	B767-300	620	263	883	2493
5	B777-300	838	335	1173	3174
6	B747-400	1283	503	1785	4764
7	B747-100/300	1455	541	1996	5121
8	B727Q	220	234	454	2220

Note: Midpoint between the worst and best engine/aircraft combination for each aircraft type.
Source: Morrell and Lu (2007)

The data in Table 9.10 include not only the social cost at the ground level resulting from the standard LTO procedures, including take-off, climb-out, approach and taxi-idle modes, but also the costs of the emissions from 30 minutes of cruise[7] either prior to landing or following take-off. The engine emission social costs range from €140 to €1996 depending on aircraft types for LTO and cruise stages. For the cruise stages, only the environmental cost of CO_2 emissions has been included in the table.

The noise social costs by aircraft category at different airports are listed in Table 9.11. The noise social costs for different aircraft categories at Heathrow vary from €2 per landing for the Jetstream to €2778 for the B747–100/200/300, with the weighted average of €523 per landing and take-off (or €262 per movement). Heathrow has the largest number of houses within the critical contour, as well as having the second highest average house price (after San Diego). The average noise social cost at Chicago O'Hare, in contrast, is very low, because there are few dwellings within the noisier contours, relatively low house prices, and a favourable aircraft mix. Chicago has many more small regional jet movements and few movements in the heavier, noisier categories, especially compared with both Heathrow and Narita. These figures are based on the certificated noise levels for each aircraft type, rather than the actual measured noise. This means that more favourable operating procedures at some airports might reduce the figures shown.

Table 9.11 *Noise social cost by aircraft category (2004 €/LTO)*

Category	Aircraft type	London Heathrow	Glasgow	San Diego	Hamburg	Frankfurt	Tokyo Narita	Chicago O'Hare	Dallas
1	Jetstream 31	2	2	1	1	2	0	0	0
2	CRJ	77	70	44	46	49	3	8	1
3	B737-300	242	219	139	145	153	11	24	2
4	A321	341	309	196	205	215	15	33	3
5	B767/B777	607	550	349	365	383	27	60	5
6	B747-400	1713	1552	984	1028	1081	77	168	15
7	B747-100/200/300	2778	2516	1595	1667	1753	124	273	25
8	B727Q	1009	914	579	606	637	45	99	9
Weighted average		523	165	142	111	89	59	37	2

Note: Ranked by weighted average noise social cost.
Source: Morrell and Lu (2007)

Empirical results

Five cases have been included for the evaluation of these costs for the two scenarios, (a) and (b), described above. The first case examines the impact of passengers who wish to travel between Glasgow and Chicago, either on a non-stop flight or via the hub, Heathrow. The second case has two airports in the US and only one in the UK. Passengers wishing to travel between London and San Diego are routed non-stop or via the Chicago hub. Case 3 is from Hamburg to Tokyo Narita, via Frankfurt for the hubbing scenario. Both cases 4 and 5 have Dallas at one end with Glasgow and Hamburg at the other end, respectively.

Table 9.12 summarizes the results for the five cases. The non-stop flight from Glasgow to Chicago and back shows a marked advantage over the routing via Heathrow in terms of noise. This is because of the use of noisier aircraft (especially the B747-400), as well as the location of housing around Heathrow. The non-stop flight also incurs fewer LTO emissions costs, although the difference is smaller. The indirect flight via Heathrow incurs a distance penalty of just over 1000km and so has a greater CO_2 environmental cost of €2866 per day. Together the incremental environmental impact of the non-stop flight is only €59 versus €101 for the multi-sector routing (which is thus 71 per cent higher). All five scenarios appear to have similar results. The full incremental environmental costs for the indirect routing have been attributed to the additional 150 passengers. Without these extra passengers, the existing market could be carried on the smaller aircraft at the same frequency. Conversely, the additional environmental costs could be avoided by carrying the 150 passengers on the non-stop service.

Table 9.12 *Environmental costs for five cases*

	Noise cost A (€/day)*	LTO Emissions cost B (€/day)	Sector cruise CO_2 emissions cost C (€/day)	Environmental cost (€/day) A+B+C	Environmental cost (€/passenger)
1 Glasgow to/from Chicago (via Heathrow for hubbing)					
Hubbing	2996	2370	9866	15,232	101
Bypass	610	1240	7000	8850	59
2 Heathrow to/from San Diego (via Chicago for hubbing)					
Hubbing	2629	2370	10,766	15,765	105
Bypass	956	1240	10,456	12,653	84
3 Hamburg to/from Tokyo Narita (via Frankfurt for hubbing)					
Hubbing	1861	2370	14,329	18,560	124
Bypass	392	1240	10,651	12,283	82
4 Glasgow to/from Dallas (via Heathrow for hubbing)					
Hubbing	2799	2370	11,808	16,977	113
Bypass	556	1240	8534	10,330	69
5 Hamburg to/from Dallas (via Frankfurt for hubbing)					
Hubbing	1782	2370	12,676	16,827	112
Bypass	370	1240	9642	11,253	75

Note: * Assume two or three daily flights for different flight stages, substituting existing smaller aircraft with larger aircraft in order to accommodate new demand of 150 passengers per day for hub scenarios.

Source: Summarized from Morrell and Lu (2007)

Summary

Based on the networks analysed, each of the hub bypass routes generates considerable saving in both noise and engine emissions costs. The networks analysed have incorporated realistic assumptions on likely future airline operations, with the hub bypass routes more likely to be operated by airlines in the country that is not the location of the hubs considered. It should be noted that the end point of the long-haul flight was also a hub airport, and that this

Table 9.13 *Flight distance, airlines, aircraft and engine types, seat numbers and weekly flights of the selected intra-Asian flights, originating from Taipei – as of March 2007*

Destination	Distance	Airline	Aircraft type	Engine type	Seats per flight	Weekly frequency
Hong Kong	803	Cathay Pacific	B747-400	RB211-524G/H	383	28
		Cathay Pacific	A340-300	CFM56-5C4	287	7
		Cathay Pacific	B777-300	Trent 892	385	28
		Cathay Pacific	A330-300	Trent 772-60	311	42
		EVA Air	B747-400	CF6-80C2B1F	272	28
		EVA Air	B777-300	GE90-115B	316	7
		Thai Airways	A330-300	PW4164	305	7
		China Airlines	B747-400	PW4056	408	49
Seoul	1480	Cathay Pacific	A330-300	Trent 772-60	311	7
		EVA Air	A330-200	CF6-80E1A3	252	9
		Thai Airways	B777-300	Trent 892	388	7
		China Airlines	A330-300	CF6-80E1A4	313	7
		Korean Air	A300-600	PW4158	276	7
		Korean Air	B737-800	CFM56-7B24/26	164	2
Tokyo Narita	2158	Cathay Pacific	B747-400	PW4056	383	7
		China Airlines	B747-400	PW4056	408	23
		EVA Air	A330-200	CF6-80E1A3	252	14
		All Nippon	B767-300	CF6-80C2B2	216	12
		Japan Airlines	B767-300	CF6-80A	232	7
		Japan Airlines	B747-400	CF6-80	454	21
Bangkok	2531	China Airlines	B340-300	CFM56-5C4	265	10
		China Airlines	B747-400	PW4056	408	14
		Thai Airways	B777-300	Trent 892	388	7
		Thai Airways	A330-300	PW4164	305	7
		EVA Air	B777-300	GE90-115B	316	12
		EVA Air	B747-400	CF6-80C2B1F	386	5
		EVA Air	A330-200	CF6-80E1A3	252	3
Singapore	3247	China Airlines	A330-300	CF6-80E1A4	313	7
		EVA Air	B747-400	CF6-80C2B1F	386	7
		Singapore Airlines	B777-200	Trent 884	306	14
		Singapore Airlines	B777-300	Trent 892	332	7
		Jetstar Asia	A320-200	V2500 IAE	180	7

airport would also have had the potential to collect from and distribute to other cities in that region. The key characteristic, however, is that the long-haul sector includes at least one non-hub city (e.g. Glasgow and Hamburg). Further analysis could be done on routes where both cities are non-hubs, but it would then be less likely that the route would have sufficient traffic potential. The difference in environmental costs ranged between 25 and 71 per cent, depending on the concentration of population around the airports and the degree to which the hub routing involved extra mileage.

The implications of aircraft engine emissions costs on the operating costs of Asian airlines

Market selection

Originating from Taipei Taoyuan International Airport, five routes representing various distances of intra-Asian flights are chosen for this analysis, with nine Asian airlines included. These routes are from Taipei to Hong Kong, Seoul, Tokyo Narita, Bangkok and Singapore. Table 9.13 lists the main information for these flights.

Aircraft engine emission social costs for the cases

Table 9.14 lists the lowest and highest aircraft engine emissions social costs for different routes. The results are also shown graphically in Figures 9.8 and 9.9. Airlines operating bigger aircraft, such as wide-bodied aircraft, generate more engine emissions social costs per flight and also per seat. Long-range wide-bodied aircraft are generally designed for long-haul intercontinental flights. For these intra-Asian flights, which are under 3500km, these aircraft types do not perform well with regard to engine emissions social costs. If these costs were actually internalized, either through emissions trading schemes or emissions charges, airlines might have to re-evaluate their selection of aircraft or engine types for different routes (Lu and Lin, 2007).

Table 9.14 *Aircraft engine emissions social costs for different flight routes*

Originating from Taipei Destination		Aircraft type	€/flight			€/seat		
			LTO	Cruise	LTO + Cruise	LTO	Cruise	LTO + Cruise
Hong Kong	Lowest	A330-300	574	479	1053	1.8	1.5	3.3
	Highest	B747-400	1442	806	2247	3.8	2.1	5.9
Seoul	Lowest	B737-800	219	492	711	1.3	3.0	4.3
	Highest	B777-300	905	1210	2115	2.3	3.1	5.4
Tokyo	Lowest	B767-300	443	1287	1730	1.9	5.5	7.4
	Highest	B747-400	1000	2140	3140	2.6	5.6	8.2
Bangkok	Lowest	A330-300	574	1509	2083	1.9	4.9	6.8
	Highest	B747-400	1000	2481	3481	2.5	6.1	8.6
Singapore	Lowest	A320-200	284	888	1172	1.6	4.9	6.5
	Highest	B747-400	951	3182	4133	2.5	8.2	10.7

Implications for airline operating costs

Figure 9.10 shows the engine emissions social cost as a percentage of airline operating costs for all the selected routes and airlines concerned. The percentage varies from a high of around 12 per cent to a low of around 5 per cent as the flight distance increases. This is due to the fact that the social costs during the LTO stages have been spread as the distance grows. Based on the data

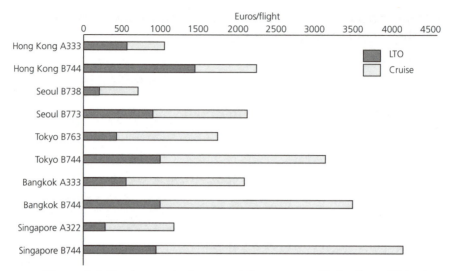

Figure 9.8 *Engine emissions social costs per flight from Taipei to various Asian cities*

analysis, the impact on low-cost carriers is clearly higher than that on traditional carriers.

With the consideration of the actual airline load factors, Figure 9.11 shows the engine emissions social costs per passenger by flight distance. Each passenger has to bear the social cost of around €6 for the Taipei–Hong Kong route, compared with around €12 for a Taipei–Singapore flight.

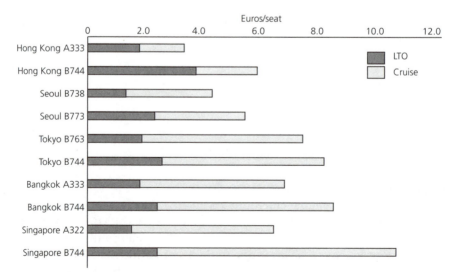

Figure 9.9 *Engine emissions social costs per seat from Taipei to various Asian cities*

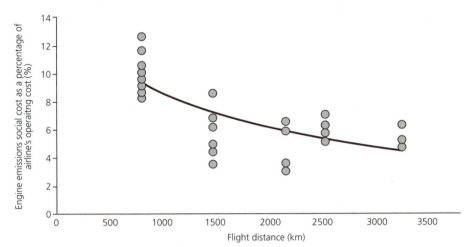

Figure 9.10 *Engine emissions social cost as a percentage of airline operating cost by flight distance*

Summary

Asian airlines tend to operate larger aircraft than the rest of the world. Even just for intra-Asian routes, there are aircraft types such as B747–400 or B777–300 being used by airlines. For the selected Asian airlines and routes, the engine emissions social costs as a percentage of airline operating costs range from 8 to 12 per cent for shorter routes, and from 4 to 8 per cent for longer routes. Clearly, the percentage is higher for low-cost carriers due to their lower operating costs. Considering the actual load factors of these airlines which are around 70–80 per cent, the engine emissions social costs would then vary from €4 to €13 per passenger. This is also equivalent to €3–€13 per seat, or €600–€4000 per flight.

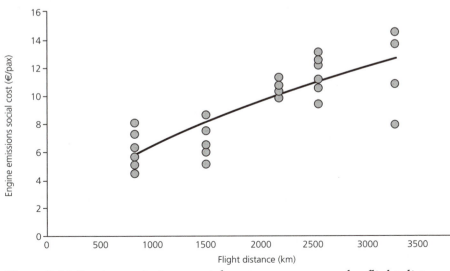

Figure 9.11 *Engine emissions social cost per passenger by flight distance*

Conclusions

The research results have shown that, besides the internationally agreed environmental restrictions through ICAO, there have been a growing number of airports worldwide introducing specific environmental regulations and charges. Among these, European airports tend to have stricter environmental measures than others, and environmental charges are being implemented more widely, tackling not only noise nuisance but also emissions issues. Combining the theoretical research results with practical considerations, the proposed systematic generic approach to setting up environmental charge mechanisms and charge levels could be applied to any airport that wishes to revise its current charge schemes or set up a new one.

After reviewing approaches to measuring externalities, this chapter described the methods of estimating aircraft engine emissions and noise social costs in practical terms, underpinning the main parameters and inputs for the calculation. The three sets of empirical results investigate the social cost estimates for different cases, illustrating LTO emissions, cruise emissions and, in some cases, noise nuisance. If internalizing these externalities through charges or some other measures, the implications for airline business models, network scenarios, operating costs and passenger demand are further evaluated and discussed.

The annual average growth of air traffic for the next 20 years is forecast to be around 5–6 per cent according to various forecasts (Boeing, 2007; Airbus, 2007). Is this really the rate of sustainable development for the industry? The measures taken by some airports and airlines to control emissions certainly help in mitigating the impacts, but are so far limited to certain parts of the world. What if all the air travellers bore the full costs of these externalities, as should be the case, through more stringent environmental measures worldwide? Airline business models, the selection of aircraft types, passenger travel patterns and the cost of flying would certainly have undergone a fundamental restructuring.

Notes

1   Some countries, such as the UK and New Zealand, have already implemented emissions trading schemes with several industries included.
2   Basel/Mulhouse Airport, a Swiss/French airport, introduced emission-related landing charges in 2003.
3   Note that unqualified use of a multiplier is problematic. For a technical discussion of metrics, see Peeters et al, 2007.
4   The decibel unit (dB) is a measure, on a logarithmic scale, of the magnitude of a particular sound relative to the intensity that represents the threshold of hearing. The 'A-weighted' decibel scale (dB(A)), which takes into account the sensitivity of the human ear to a given frequency, is most commonly used as it gives the best indication of the perception of a sound by humans.
5   Based on the estimation of social costs for different pollutants listed in Table 9.1, where the airport is situated might result in different impacts as the population

density varies. However, since there is no definite consensus on this area yet, the research results throughout this chapter do not differentiate LTO emissions social costs according to the location of an airport.

6 ICAO's Annex 16 defines noise standards for jet aircraft. These aircraft are subdivided into different 'Chapters' according to their noise certification values. Chapter 3 applies to all aircraft with a type licence issued after 1978.

7 CO_2 is the only pollutant included for the calculation of social costs during the 30-minute cruise stage. Its social cost is obtained by multiplying the unit social cost of CO_2 with its emission index (Dings et al, 2003) and fuel burn at different flight altitudes (EUROCONTROL, 2004).

References

2nd Annual Aviation Forecasting Conference (2006) *The Impact on Airports of Changing Passenger Demographics,* 14 February, Vienna

Airbus (2007) *Global Market Forecast,* available at www.airbus.com/en/corporate/gmf/

Air France-KLM Group (2005) *Annual Report 2005,* available at www.airfranceklm-finance.com/financial-publications.html

Black, D. A., Black, J. A., Issarayangyun, T. and Samuels, S. E. (2007) 'Aircraft noise exposure and resident's stress and hypertension: A public health perspective for airport environmental management', *Journal of Air Transport Management* 13: 264–276

Boeing (2007) *Current Market Outlook,* available at www.boeing.com/commercial/cmo/

Boeing website (2007) www.boeing.com, accessed 15 June 2007

British Airways (2005) *Annual Report 2005,* available at www.bashares.com/phoenix.zhtml?c=69499&p=irol-reportsannual

Brueckner, J. K. and Girvin, R. (2008) 'Airport noise regulation, airline service quality, and social welfare', *Transportation Research Part B* 42: 19–37

Caves, R. E. (1994a) 'Aviation and society – redrawing the balance (I)', *Transportation Planning and Technology* 18: 3–19

Caves, R. E. (1994b) 'Aviation and society – redrawing the balance (II)', *Transportation Planning and Technology:* 18: 21–36

Dings, J. M. W., Wit, R. C. N., Leurs, B. A. and Davidson, M. D. (2003) *External Costs of Aviation,* environmental research of the Federal Ministry of the Environment, Nature Conservation and Nuclear Safety, Research Report 299 96 106, UBA-FB 000411

easyJet (2005) *Annual Report 2005,* available at www.easyjet.com/EN/Investor/investorrelations_financialreports.html

EUROCONTROL (European Organisation for the Safety of Air Navigation) (2004) *Aircraft Performance Summary Tables for the Base of Aircraft Data,* Revision 3.6, EEC Note No. 12/04, EUROCONTROL Experimental Centre

European Commission (1999) *Air Transport and the Environment: Towards Meeting the Challenges of Sustainable Development,* communication from the Commission to the Council, the European Parliament, the Economic and Social Committee and the Committee of the Regions, COM, Brussels: Commission of the European Communities

ExternE (1999) *Externalities of Energy,* Luxembourg: Office for Official Publications of the European Commission

Fawcett, A. (2000) 'The sustainability of airports and aviation: Depicturing air travel, impacts and opportunities for sustainable change', *Transport Engineering in Australia* 6: 33–39

Fleuti, E. (2007) *Local Emission Charges in Europe,* presented at ICAO Colloquium on Aviation Emissions with Exhibition, May, Montreal

Franssen, E. A., van Wiechen, C. M., Nagelkerke, N. J. and Lebret, E. (2004) 'Aircraft noise around a large international airport and its impact on general health and medication use', *Journal of Occupational and Environmental Medicine* 61: 405–413

Gillen, D., Morrison, W. G. and Stewart, M. A. (2004) *Air Travel Demand Elasticities: Concepts, Issues and Measurement,* a study commissioned by the Department of Finance, Canada

Green, J. E. (2003) 'Civil aviation and the environmental challenge', *The Aeronautical Journal* 107: 281–299

Hullah, P. (2007) *MIME Noise Trading for Aircraft Noise Mitigation,* paper presented at Air Transport Research Society Conference, June, San Francisco

ICAO (1996) *Environmental Charges and Taxes on International Civil Aviation,* paper presented by the Secretariat to the 14th Session of the Council, AT-WP/1794, October, Montreal: International Civil Aviation Organization

IPCC (1999) *Aviation and the Global Atmosphere,* Intergovernmental Panel on Climate Change, Cambridge: Cambridge University Press

Jarup, L., Dudley, M.-L., Babisch, W., Houthuijs, D., Swart, W., Pershagen, G., Bluhm, G., Katsouyanni, K., Velonakis, M., Cadum, E. and Vigna-Tagliant, F. (2008) 'Hypertension and exposure to noise near airports (HYENA)', *Environmental Health Perspectives* 116: 329–333

Lu, C. (2008) 'The implications of environmental costs on air passenger demand for different airline business models', *Journal of Air Transport Management* (in press)

Lu, C. and Chen, B. L. (2007) *The Impacts of Environmental Charges on Air Passenger Demand,* paper presented at the Air Transport Research Society Conference, June, San Francisco

Lu, C. and Lin, Y. C. (2007) *The Implications of Aircraft Engine Emissions Costs on the Operating Costs of Asian Airlines,* paper presented at the European Transport Conference, October, Leiden, the Netherlands

Lu, C. and Morrell, P. (2001) 'Evaluation and implication of environmental charges on commercial flights', *Transportation Reviews* 21: 377–395

Lu, C. and Morrell, P. (2006) 'Determination and applications of environmental costs at different sized airports – aircraft noise and engine emissions', *Transportation* 33: 45–61

Morrell, P. and Lu, C. (2007) 'The environmental cost implication of hub–hub versus hub–bypass flight networks', *Transportation Research Part D* 12: 143–157

OECD (1997) *Evaluating Economic Instruments for Environmental Policy,* Paris: Organisation for Economic Co-operation and Development

Pearce, B. and Pearce, D. (2000) *Setting Environmental Taxes for Aircraft: A Case Study of the UK,* CSERGE working paper, GEC 2000-26

Pearce, D. (2003) 'The social cost of carbon and its policy implications', *Oxford Review of Economic Policy* 19: 362–384

Pearce, D. W. and Markandya, R. (1989) *Environmental Policy Benefits: Monetary Valuation,* Paris: Organisation for Economic Co-operation and Development

Peeters, P., Williams, V. and Gössling, S. (2007) 'Air transport greenhouse gas emissions', in Peeters, P. M. (ed) *Tourism and Climate Change Mitigation,* Breda: NHTV, pp29–50

Schipper, Y. (2004) 'Environmental costs in European aviation', *Transport Policy* 11: 141–154

Small, K. A. and Kazimi, C. (1995) 'On the costs of air pollution from motor vehicles', *Journal of Transport Economics and Policy* 29: 7–32

UK DfT (Department for Transport) (2003) *Aviation and the Environment – Using Economic Instruments,* March, available at www.dft.gov.uk/pgr/aviation/environmentalissues/uei/

10
Air Freight: Trends and Issues

Cordula Neiberger

Introduction: The increased importance of air freight

For many years the air freight sector has been a growing market worldwide. The total air freight volume more than tripled from 5.1 million metric tonnes in 1986 to 17.9 million tonnes in 2000 (Lufthansa, 1994, 2001). This development can be traced to the increased globalization of the economy, the growth in worldwide production and the resulting interconnection of delivery systems. 'Worldwide', however, mostly implies North America, Europe and Asia, with an increased flow of information, finance and trade currents between these continents. Figure 10.1 clearly depicts this trend based on the flow of goods between the continents from 1980 until 2005. Current studies project an increased annual growth of air freight volume by approximately 5.8 per cent (Airbus, 2008) and 6.2 per cent (Boeing, 2008) respectively until 2026. This means that the volume of air freight will triple within the next 20 years. Trade between the countries of the above triad can be expected to grow at rates of more than 8 per cent and the growth of air freight volume will also increase within Asia at above average rates (Airbus, 2008). It is expected that 26 per cent of the entire global air freight volume will be transported within Asia as early as 2011. Another 31 per cent of the air freight volume will be transported along the lines Asia/Pacific–Europe–Asia/Pacific and Asia/Pacific–North America–Asia/Pacific (Logistics Management, 2008).

The largest volume of intercontinental transport services are provided by shipping. Air freight accounts for a mere 1 per cent of all intercontinental freight services by volume. However, the proportion of the value of the transported goods is much higher and is rated at 40 per cent. This is related to the time-sensitive nature of air freight. In particular, products in the IT industry are

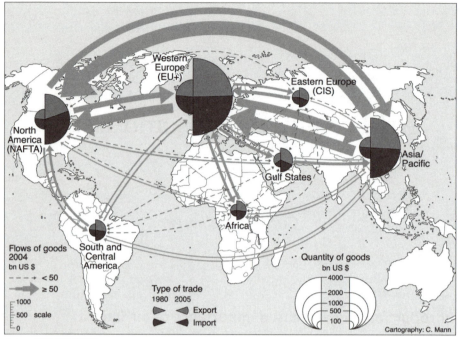

Source: UNCTAD (2007)

Figure 10.1 *Structure of world trade and flows of goods*

transported, whose main revenues fall into the months immediately following their release. Likewise, products from the (literally) fast-moving fashion industry travel this way. Furthermore there are fast-spoiling products such as tropical fruit, fish, meats and particularly cut flowers, and also unscheduled shipments are substantial. The latter become necessary, for example, because of problems in production runs or the construction of new manufacturing sites. Also bottleneck situations with sea freight capacities can lead to use of air freight because of time restrictions (see Leinbach and Bowen, 2004).

The following is an analysis of the development of air freight based on the concept of a 'value chain'. After presenting this concept in outline, subsequent sections further explore its dimensions and a further section focuses on and describes a case study of the trends discussed above.

The global value chain of air freight

The processes by which air freight delivery is being reorganized are best examined via the concept of a value chain. A value chain is defined by the path a consumer good travels from its stage as raw material to its consumption as a finished good and on to its disposal. This is defined as a chain because a concise order governs each step of production, at which value is added. As an economic concept, the question arises as to which production steps should be considered internal or external to a company's production (input–output dimension). A further dimension of such a chain is related to the physical locality of individual production steps.

A third dimension concerns the coordination of the work-sharing processes among varying locations, i.e. controlling such a value chain, so that the individual links in this chain work together with regard to the final product. This includes the question of how single links in the chain, i.e. businesses, can control the entire value chain for their own interests. This is the question at the heart of empirical research in recent years. However, the chains operate in concrete regulatory systems, i.e. laws in specific countries, politics, institutions and social processes. The individual links in a chain are therefore subject to different political, social and cultural influences. This is the fourth dimension, known as institutional embedding (see Gereffi et al, 2005).

Below, the concept of the value chain of production is applied to the air freight service sector. Here each progressive 'station' of a transported good is defined as a 'production step'. At the same time a distinction is made between the flow of information and the flow of goods, in order to clarify the second dimension of value chains: the control mechanism. The input–output structure of the air freight service chain is represented in Figure 10.2a. The commissioned air freight expeditor controls the organization of the transportation of goods. The expeditor organizes and controls the entire chain, i.e. the company engages a number of businesses to handle and carry goods from the dispatcher to the airport, warehousing them, packaging them, getting them on palettes and loading them onto the aeroplane. An air freight company is also contacted abroad, which will then handle the organization at the destination point.

In traditional air freight services, all the previously mentioned services are performed by specialized businesses, whose relationships with one another can be defined as market negotiated. Up to 15 different service companies can be involved in a traditional air freight shipment. The organizational expense of communication, coordination and inspection is correspondingly high. This is expressed by a particularly high number of necessary arrangements, documents and information interfaces, from which a corresponding number of errors may arise and much time be consumed. This means high costs and also translates into a long total transit time, usually five to six days. Based on this traditional organization of the air freight chain, as depicted in Figure 10.2a, the following section will more closely investigate the structure, as well as the current restructuring processes of the air freight industry, by means of the four dimensions of value chains. However, before focusing more closely on the single participants in the chain and their control, the general conditions in the industry will be discussed.

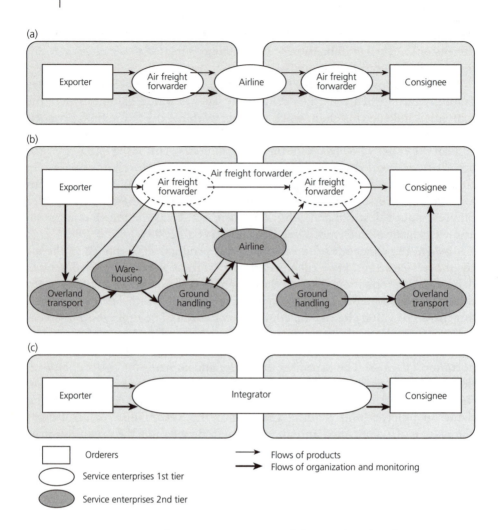

(a)

(b)

(c)

Orderers

Service enterprises 1st tier

Service enterprises 2nd tier

Flows of products

Flows of organization and monitoring

Figure 10.2 *The reorganization of the air freight chain*

Changing general conditions: Customer requirements, new technologies and deregulation

The increase in air freight volume reflects the economic changes caused by globalization. As well as the international division of labour by multinational corporations, this also includes an increasing degree of fragmentation of production processes, where steps of value appreciation are outsourced from traditional production chains. The automobile industry is an example of this, where manufacturers most often only assemble premanufactured parts. This way a number of legally independent companies become interconnected over a series of value appreciation steps in worldwide locations. Producing companies are thereby given the opportunity of using such global networks, but they also face the increased demands of a complex global organization (see Arndt and Kierzkowski, 2001; Gereffi and Korzeniewitz, 1994).

It is increasingly difficult to make a profit with standardized mass products; rather, new demographic structures and the development towards a post-industrial society mean that more individual goods with a higher level of service are required, and it is becoming ever more difficult to forecast demand. Thus business success is increasingly dependent on the ability to adapt to rapidly changing customer requirements. Also, product cycles are becoming shorter, so that it is important for businesses to bring new technologies and products onto the market as quickly as possible. As early as 1988, Stalk diagnosed a shift from competition based on costs and prices to 'time-based competition' (Stalk, 1988).

This means new requirements as to the speed of product development and the processing of commissions, as well as the optimization of the entire logistical information and goods flows – not just within individual companies but within entire global production networks. These concepts have to be developed by modern logistics, which thus have an extremely important task, namely the organizational and technical integration and networking of the global economy (see Hesse and Rodrigue, 2004).

This development was made possible by tremendous technological advances. The most significant are developments in the IT sector, such as data transmission between companies and parts of companies (EDI: electronic data interchange), EAN-codes (European article number) to identify goods during transport and storage, the internet as a medium for communication and data transfer, as well as new software for disposition, route planning, consignment tracking and customs processing. The newest technology is RFID (radio frequency identification), a means of goods identification using chips which transmit data up to a distance of 30m, by means of which goods flow processes can be simplified. Likewise, the development of new types of aircraft, such as the A380 with its larger volume, will bring change to logistical processing, because their increased storage capacities allow for larger groupings and larger distances, which, in turn, allow for new flight routes.

The growing significance of logistics companies has been reinforced by worldwide deregulation and privatization measures, as these enable the firms to expand and redefine their field of activity. Although a comprehensive deregulation process had taken place in the US in the 1970s, the European states only initiated similar measures in the mid-1980s. The EU foundation treaty of 1958 allowed for the development of a common transport policy, but this had been blocked for decades by individual member states, especially Germany, France and Italy. The deregulation of the European transport sector only began after a judgment from the European Court of Justice in 1985 after the European Parliament had sued the European Council for its failure to act on the issue. State regulatory measures were abandoned in favour of a uniform EU market in the areas of air transport (three liberalization packages from 1987 to 1997), inland navigation (liberalization of cabotage, i.e. transport between two points in the same country, from 1995), rail transport (rail regulations since 1991) and road transport (abolition of state tariff regulation in 1994, liberalization of market access and cabotage since 1998) (see Goetz and Sutton, 1997; Hanlon, 2001; Leinbach and Bowen, 2007).

Landing rights and rights to fly over territory granted to each other by the states involved ('transit rights') play an important role in international air traffic. Thus within the European Economic Area (EEA) the fifth right applies (the right to transport passengers and goods between two countries, as long as the starting or finishing point of the flight is within the operator's country of origin), but it does not apply between EEA countries and third parties, with the exception of some EU members and the US (open skies agreements). Therefore these airlines have to fly via hubs (see Graham, 1998).

Freight forwarders, airlines and integrators: Participants in the goods chain

As explained in the previous section, the general conditions for air freight service companies have changed considerably over the past years. Global production, in particular, has not only caused the volume of air freight transport to continually increase, but has, at the same time, increased the demand for expediency, flexibility and service. In order to achieve the performance of a global, highly complex and very capital-intensive transport organization, the service companies of the logistics industry themselves have to be strong performers and globally organized. Worldwide liberalization of air traffic markets combined with deregulation of the air traffic markets in Europe will give service providers in the air freight industry new opportunities. The companies in the air freight industry are reacting to these general changes by developing new strategies to maintain their competitiveness. This is particularly the case in the shipping sector, where many international corporations have been established and global freight operations developed.

Deregulating the traffic markets has made it possible for shipping companies to develop more efficient organizational structures and to provide more services. Companies, originally only plain transportation providers, have developed into logistical service corporations with complex services for organizing and controlling the flow of materials and information among businesses. Today's logistical service provider has to 'collect and implement the knowledge and the methods of optimized flow structures and processes, and their fair control and mobilization for both market and customer' (Klaus, 2003, p26).

In the 1980s, shipping companies were still primarily transporting between individual locations. Ever since deregulating measures took effect, the percentage of special logistics services has been growing. These services provide for the distribution of consumer goods and consumer goods contract logistics, as well as industrial contract logistics, which include the services of connecting to and provision with industrial materials, for production in specialized and customer specific systems (see Klaus, 2003). In the recent past the service range of freight providers has been extended by so-called value added services, including packaging, labelling, and also the assembly of product modules (Bowen and Leinbach, 2003, 2004).

As logistic services providers focus on the tasks of organizing and controlling logistical processes, certain services are themselves outsourced from within the logistics industry. So-called asset-based services, i.e. services that are bound by warehouse locations or by vehicles, are outsourced to specialized service providers, who, in turn, themselves subcontract out simpler services, such as point-to-point transportation. This practice leads to a hierarchical system within the industry.

Because of the multifaceted demands on logistics services providers, the phase of concentration described above has gone hand in hand with a phase of dissolving traditional modal and product-specific industry segments. Modern forwarders need a wide range of competences in order to cope with the multitude of their new tasks. This is often achieved by taking over competitors. Mergers and acquisitions, however, do not often take place within a national framework. Instead, the sector is experiencing a process of becoming ever more international. Companies operating mostly in the national arena in the 1990s are now integrated into extensive international transport markets by logistic services providers. This is where the big shipping (maritime) companies operate, achieving service diversification through direct investments and additional acquisitions, so as to cover the range from carrier-specific provider to multi-infrastructure company, with an entire range of logistical services. Table 10.1 lists the largest air freight companies worldwide (see Lamoine and Dagnas, 2003).

This is how organizational changes have developed along the air freight service chain over the last decade and a half. In summary, strong fragmentation of the chain has been reduced by the creation of international shipping companies that take charge of worldwide organization. Figure 10.2b clarifies the hierarchy within the chain.

The rise in demand for freight transport has of course affected not only shipping companies, but airlines as well. Freight-carrying airlines can be split into different groups (Figure 10.3). First passenger airlines, who only operate passenger aircraft, but also transport 'belly' freight. These airlines, who had originally focused on passenger travel only, hardly realized what potential freight goods had for their businesses until the 1990s. Additional 'belly' freight is stored below the passenger cabins. This way further revenue can be generated on top of the passenger revenue and at very low additional cost. These airlines can again be separated into those (second) who deliberately focus on carrying air freight, creating a hub system for transportation and those (third) who only transport limited amounts of freight on a point-to-point basis. Fourth, next to these airlines in terms of classification, there are others, so-called 'combined airlines', which have expanded so heavily into air freight, that, next to a passenger fleet, they operate a fleet of convertible aircraft,

Table 10.1 *Air freight contractors worldwide, 2005*

	Germany	The Netherlands	GB	USA	Australia
1	Schenker	DHL	DHL	DHL Danzas Air & Ocean	DHL Danzas Air & Ocean
2	Kuehne + Nagel	TMI	Exel	BAX Global	Airtrade Int'l
3	DHL Danzas Air & Ocean	Panalpina	Nippon Express	Expeditors	C.T. Freight
4	Exel	Kuehne + Nagel	Kuehne + Nagel	EGL Eagle Global Logistics	Hellmann Worldwide
5	Panalpina	UPS	Air Menzies Int'l.	Menlo Worldwide	Link Logistics Int'l
6	UTI	TNT	Geologistics	Exel	Exel
7	Dachser	Expeditors	EGL Eagle Global Logistics	UPS	Schenker
8	K.H. Dietrich	EGL Eagle Global Logistics	BAX Global	Nippon Express	DHL
9	Menlo Worldwide	Blue Sky	Panalpina	Panalpina	BAX Global
10	ABX Logistics	UTI	Schenker	Kuehne + Nagel	Vision Int'l.

Source: Aircargo Asia-Pacific (2006)

quick-change planes, combination planes or dedicated freight aircraft. Many of these companies have made such headway in this market that they now operate under a trademark name (i.e. Air France Cargo) or as a subsidiary company (i.e. Lufthansa Cargo) (Bjelicic, 2001, p11).

Fifth, there are airlines that engage in air freight only. These are primarily cargo airlines that operate dedicated freight aircraft as charter services or as regular line services. The Luxembourg-based Cargolux is such a company. Another group (sixth) operates either as a contract carrier for other airlines or

	Passenger airline		Combination airline	Cargo airline		
	non-cargo focused	cargo focused		Cargo airline	Contract carrier	Integrator
Fleet structure	Passenger aircraft		Passenger aircraft Convertible aircraft Quick-change aircraft Combis Dedicated freighter	Freighter		
Commitment to air cargo business	weak	middle	middle	strong		
Examples	• Luxair • Miskov • British Midland	• American • Air Canada • Finnair	• Air France • British Airways • Emirates	• Air Hong-kong • Cargolux • Nippon Cargo Airlines	• Asian Express Airlines • Atlas Airlines	• European Air Transport • FedEx • TNT Airways

Figure 10.3 *Types of airlines involved in air cargo transportation*

as an integrated subcontractor or as a freight forwarder. This service may be provided for one client exclusively or to many customers. Here the boundaries between contract carrier and cargo airline begin to blur. Special flights, for instance, are handled by Cargolux for the Swiss forwarding company Panalpina. Also to be mentioned (seventh) are airlines that own integrators. These are operated as an integral component of the company or as a subsidiary, such as European Air Transport, located in Belgium, as a subsidiary of DHL.

Approximately 50–60 per cent of all current air freight is transported by passenger planes ('belly freight'). This is due to the available freight capacities and the cost-effectiveness of using passenger aircraft. Most forecasts assume a stronger growth of freight traffic compared to passenger travel. It can therefore be expected that more freight aircraft will be in operation in the future.

In 2007, 1696 freighters operated worldwide, of these 49 were 'quick-change' aircraft (convertible from all-passenger to all-cargo within minutes) and 61 were combined aircraft, which carry both passengers and freight on the main deck. The role of combined aircraft will diminish over time, as these aircraft types are gradually converted into full freighters. Freighters are withdrawn from use after 35–37 years. Consequently, it is estimated that 83 per cent of all currently operating freighters will be exchanged within the next 20 years. These are likely to be replaced with aircraft with greater operational range. In the next 20 years, the global freighter fleet will grow by 150 per cent (Airbus, 2008, p121).

Figure 10.4 shows the airline companies with the largest volumes of air freight traffic. Also shown is an alliance of airline companies that carry freight (SkyTeam Cargo). This is a collaborative operation between airlines, much like the existing alliances between passenger carriers. The reason for these alliances is the airlines' endeavour to offer their customers worldwide connections, although these are practically impossible, because of complex, international bilateral sets of regulations[1] (see Doganis, 2002; Kleymann and Seristö, 2004).

Areas of cooperation within these freight business alliances include the coordination of ground services, joint usage of ground services, coordinating customer rebates, code-sharing, block-space agreements, coordination of flight plans and joint development of systems and software. It is also important to look at the cooperation between airlines and integrators. For example, in 2007 DHL Express and Lufthansa Cargo founded a joint venture to transport air freight and express goods to Asia (see Agustdinata and de Klein, 2002; DPWN, 2008).

Also among airlines, we have seen the emergence of new, mostly regional enterprises, as well as an increase in mergers and acquisitions, following the recent liberalization of air markets. Frequently national or regional airlines are acquired by larger airlines in the same country (Wiezorek, 1998, p335), although foreign regional airlines are also targets for the merger and acquisition activities of large airline companies. The difficult economic situation of many airlines has also occasioned a recent trend to acquire or merge with flag

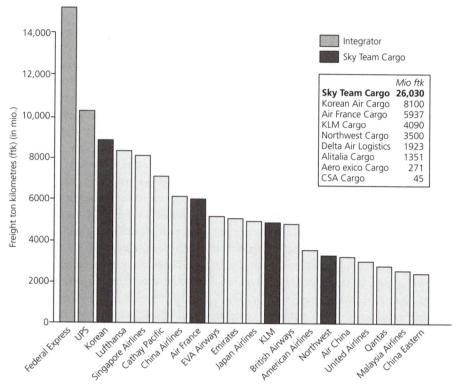

Source: Lufthansa (2008)

Figure 10.4 *The 20 largest airlines in terms of freight volume, 2006*

carriers, such as the takeover of Sabena by Swissair and the merger of KLM and Air France (see Iatrou and Oretti, 2007).

Notable in Figure 10.4 is the domination of the big integrators. This new way of organizing air freight was introduced by the American courier, express and parcel services after the deregulation of the American air traffic market in 1977. It is very successful to this day. These integrated carriers (called integrators) combine the entire air freight chain in one hand (ownership), in order to transport packages. In so doing, the transaction fees for high coordination efforts as incurred in traditional air freight are avoided. At the same time a high degree of cost and time efficiency can be achieved by streamlining the entire logistical chain and by introducing processing innovations, such as automatic processing facilities located at airports, hub-and-spoke systems for air transportation, as well as tracing systems in order to coordinate and control the flow of goods. By integrating the entire service chain, it has been possible to cut both transaction and production costs. This, in combination with such product innovations as a fast door-to-door service with expedited delivery times (overnight) and high reliability (guaranteed delivery), explains the success of the integrators (see Taylor and Hallsworth, 2000; Campbell, 2001; Sage, 2001).

Figure 10.2c shows the air freight service chain as regards the productivity of the integrators. So far their field of operation is limited to the tightly regulated parcel business. Through their standardized practices, they can offer a cost-efficient, reliable and very quick door-to-door service. This makes them big competitors of the air freight companies and the airlines, with both trying to achieve a higher degree of integration within their own air freight chains. Simultaneously, integrators are currently trying to expand beyond the delivery of parcels, leading to increased competition between expeditors/airlines and integrators.

Tendencies for structural change can be seen all along the service chain. Due to increased competition, the high cost of transactions between the market players has become a priority for active companies. To lower these costs the participants have several alternatives. The first option is service standardization, so as to maximize the potential for rationalization. This underpins the pairing of freight loading companies' increased demands for high speed with reliable and predictable procedures. This is why a number of airlines in recent years have begun to clearly differentiate their cargo into general and special cargo categories. The latter category can be classified as relating to time-defined products with fixed processing schedules (express goods), or as product-specific service packages, i.e. for perishable goods, specifically goods of high value or hazardous goods (Clausen, 2001, p11). Special goods are predicted to have a higher growth potential than standard freight. As a result of provider and service expansion, international express has grown at more than twice the rate of total worldwide air cargo traffic, averaging 12.9 per cent annually over the past decade, as measured in revenue tonne kilometres (RTK). As a proportion of total international air cargo traffic, international express cargo expanded from 4.1 per cent in 1992 to nearly 11.4 per cent in 2005 (Boeing, 2008).

By differentiating between freight groups, standardizing the corresponding services and developing a clear price structure, potential expenses can be better isolated and controlled, while operations with airline clients and shipping companies can be standardized.

The airlines' expense-reducing strategies are not limited to optimizing processes. Airlines are also trying to expand their status as carriers, as service providers to shipping companies with limited airport-to-airport transportation tasks, and the necessary route and surface management. They achieve this by either approaching shipping companies directly or founding their own shipping subsidiaries. Their goal is to reach the client directly with a 'one-stop option', similar to the integrators. So far this strategy has had very limited success with clients. There has also been vehement opposition from established independent air freight companies, causing several closures of airline-owned shipping companies.

A small number of the very large air freight corporations with internationally settled networks are also pursuing strategies of vertical integration along the value chain. Only these have the organizational skills and the financial means to make headway into the business territory of the airlines. They are likewise aiming for the seamless door-to-door transaction, made possible by the uninterrupted transport chain from one single provider. They work with their own fleet or permanently chartered aircraft and their own surface crew. This business is, however, endangered by the high price of purchasing and maintaining aircraft, the cost of personnel and the fluctuation of orders. This is why, in recent years, we have seen shipping companies withdraw from this market or reduce their work to self-maintaining operations in times of low orders.

Simultaneously, discount charter companies have become increasingly popular. They profit from registering their fleets in African countries, by being awarded advantageous routes, by tax advantages and lower personnel costs. Traditional air freight companies, such as Lufthansa Cargo and others, are therefore increasingly under competitive pressure (DVZ, 2004, p7).

It can be assumed that the processes of structural change outlined here have not finished. In the market segment of forwarders and airline companies, mergers and acquisitions will continue to take place. It is also possible that cooperative ventures will be created along the value chain. It can be assumed that freight will increasingly be concentrated in the hands of a limited number of global players.

World traffic junctions: Airports

Another dimension of value chains is the interconnectedness of locations. Analysis of the air freight service chain makes it apparent that both big actors, the freight forwarders and the airlines, and the other essential, the transport companies, are mostly located at airports.[2] Thus in a global air freight chain the locations for producing and processing world traffic, namely the airports, are linked with one another.

Today these junctions themselves are also subject to increased competition, causing pressure to become ever more efficient and requiring more capital. The public owners often cannot, or do not wish to, provide this funding, which is why a trend started in the 1980s to privatize former publicly owned airports (see Starkie, 2002; Graham, 2003).

Reasons for the growth in competitive pressures on airports include the deregulation of traffic markets and the corresponding competition by regional airports, many of which were once operated by the military and today are locations for successful low-cost airlines, as well as the liberalized ground service industry (see Barrett, 2000).

The customers of the airport operators are airlines, whose choice of location depends on their organization of air traffic. Nowadays, airlines use so-called hub-and-spoke systems to process their flights. This means that passengers, or freight respectively, usually leave from regional airports and are brought along 'spoke'-like routes to a continental hub, from where they transfer to intercontinental routes. This system was introduced by American airline companies and is now in use all over the world (see Goetz and Sutton, 1997;

Source: ACI-Europe (2007)

Figure 10.5 *Freight at European airports, 2005*

Barla and Constantatos, 2000; Rodrigue et al, 2006:48). Advantages primarily arise from economy of scale.

This principle is also evident in the European airport system. Figure 10.5 shows the volume of freight processed at each airport. Frankfurt, London, Paris and Amsterdam are the intercontinental nodes (major hubs) of European air freight traffic, each with more than 1 million tonnes of air freight per annum. This is largely due to their hub function for airlines with a high freight turnover, the countries' so-called flag carriers, such as Lufthansa, British Airways, Air France and KLM, who had already established their home bases here and started their intercontinental flights from these airports before the emergence of the hub system (see Frenken et al, 2004).

A second category consists of airports with a freight volume between about 200,000 and 600,000 tonnes. This includes airports such as Cologne/Bonn, Brussels, Liege and East Midlands, which play a lesser role in passenger transport but have a remarkably high freight turnover because they have specialized in large freight aircraft and/or are home to an integrator. Also included in this group are airports such as Copenhagen, Zürich, Milan and Munich, which are also flag-carrier hubs or are used as subhubs by large airlines. Thus Munich airport increasingly plays a role as a second hub for Lufthansa because of the growing amount of air freight in south-eastern Europe. The third category consists of airports which merely feed into hubs or have a low number of international connections.

The hub system works on the principle of collecting loads from regional bases (spokes) in a central location (hub), where they are consolidated, transferred to pallets and loaded. It is not economical to pack freight onto pallets in the regional locations because of the different aircraft types used between the supply airports and the hubs, and between the hubs and intercontinental destinations, as they would have to be unpacked and transferred to new, larger pallets in the hub. As a result a large proportion of freight from the regional airports is not flown to the hub but transported by road ('trucked'). Thus, for example, only about 11 per cent of freight from Nuremberg airport is flown to its next destination, while 89 per cent left the airport by road in 2007 (Airport Nuremberg, 2008; ADV, 2008). As well as these road feeder services run by the airlines or on their behalf, the air freight contractors also transport goods to the hub by road in order to optimally consolidate the freight. This system is not tied to state boundaries as all airlines within the EU provide flights. High levels of road traffic arise from the acquisition of air freight abroad, as the freight is transported by road to the respective hubs.

The implementation of the hub principle has led to the development of hierarchies within the European airport system. However, the restructuring of this system is not yet complete; instead a further selective process at the upper levels is to be expected, with the reasons for this including the growing number of mergers and acquisitions in the airline sector, e.g. the merger of Air France and KLM or the takeover of Swiss by Lufthansa, so that a loss of significance for the affected airports of Amsterdam and Zürich seems likely.

Second, recent innovations, such as the Airbus A380F with a 150-tonne capacity, mean a large increase in potential transport volumes. This has increased the flight range to about 15,000km, i.e. 2000km more than the hitherto most frequently used cargo aeroplane (747–400F). This implies new concentration potential for airlines as well as new options for the organization of worldwide transport, as the greater range means that completely new routes are possible. Also, these developments mean that the airports have to fulfil new requirements, as special equipment is necessary for loading and unloading. At Frankfurt airport alone, €50 million must be invested to facilitate the loading, unloading and servicing of the A380.

Third, the development of global networks among logistical service providers exerts direct and indirect competitive pressure (via airlines and other logistical service providers) on the airports. Global networks can only be competitive if the actors within the network are efficient and capable of meeting requirements relating to speed, punctuality, reliability and the availability of storage space. Therefore more efficient structures for the handling of goods and corresponding technical systems are necessary. Only airports with optimal conditions for the provision of services will guarantee the competitiveness of service providers located there and thus participation in the global networks. The construction of new runways in Amsterdam Schiphol (2005) and Frankfurt (planned for 2009) must be seen in this context (see Gardiner et al, 2005).

If airports are to meet increased requirements they will need to occupy larger spaces and will also make a greater impact on the environment, especially through growing road traffic and night flights. This implies a high degree of potential for local conflict, because in Europe company activities are limited by rigid laws and strong civil movements. In Frankfurt alone there have been more than 40,000 complaints concerning the new maintenance hangar for the A380 (Zukunft-Rhein-Main, 2008). A mediation process was carried out for the construction of the new runway in order to find a solution in accordance with the wishes of all interest groups. To compensate for the new runway a ban on night flights was put in place, which can be seen as a competitive disadvantage for the airport and the freight sector in particular.

As airport expansions are contending with a rise in protests, there is a discussion about decoupling passenger and freight traffic and using airports outside densely settled areas. However, there are limitations to this concept, because it is passenger airlines that carry 'belly' freight, i.e. the use of passenger aircraft is necessary. Also up to 60 per cent of freight is carried by combined airlines. Moving freight flights to remote locations is only practical to a limited extent, because of freight transfers (using the hub system). In recent years, Frankfurt has been trying to offer airlines alternatives and the former military airbase Hahn (Hunsrück) is being expanded. At the same time, integrators look for new locations when conditions in existing locations are not favourable enough. Thus DHL completed its move from Brussels to Leipzig in 2007 because a ban on night flights in Brussels limited its transport possibilities.

In general, the performance of the global airport system is volatile (or, at least, dynamic) in terms of freight carriage trends. Figure 10.6a depicts the world's 30 largest airports in terms of cargo volumes in 1991. Figure 10.6b shows the same airports in 2007. One can clearly see the general increase in freight volume that is handled by these airports, as well as the shift in focal points. Following the shift of production in the direction of Asia, specifically China, Asian airports show significant growth.

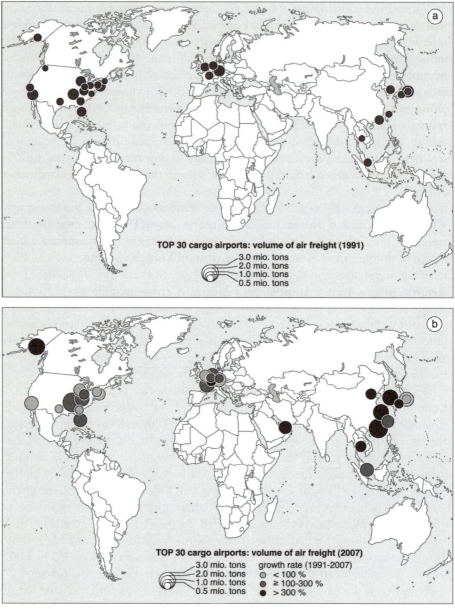

Source: ACI (2008)

Figure 10.6 *Top 30 cargo airports*

Of course, new airports are created not only in China (e.g. Shanghai), and many of the airlines and their hub airports are profiting from the boom in air freight. Notably, Emirates, with their hub airport Dubai, has been able to boost their freight volume significantly in recent years. This is due to the strategy of the ruling family in Dubai to make their Emirate less economically dependent on oil in the future: Dubai has oil reserves for another estimated 20 years, which is why new economic focal points are being sought today, including tourism and logistics. Next to a new seaport, the Dubai international airport is being expanded and an additional airport (Shebel Ali) with six runways is being built. Next to these a free-trade zone and a 'logistical city' are being created. Figure 10.6b shows the evident success of these efforts. Whereas Dubai was not included among the 30 largest airports in 1991 (144,086t), it is ranked as number 13 of the world's freight airports today (1,668,506t) (ACI, 2008).

The continued development of concentrating airport systems will be marked by the corresponding tendencies of concentrating shipping and airline industries. It may be that in 20 years there will be no more than nine mega-hubs worldwide. This is supported by the introduction of large freighters with a higher capacity to bundle goods and passengers. The total increase in air freight will make it possible to have more direct flights, a circumstance from which additional international airports would be able to profit.

Air freight, reorganizing and traffic: A case study

The processes of reorganization in the air freight industry and the possible implications for traffic can be explored by looking at an example, the global cut-flower industry.

Prior to the Industrial Revolution, cut-flower cultivation was distributed regionally on a local scale. In the 18th century, centres of cultivation began to develop, such as Aalsmeer in Holland. Here tulips and especially their bulbs were cultivated and distributed, also beyond the region. Following the increase in demand for flowers at the beginning of the 19th century, growers in Aaalsmeer and other Dutch cultivation regions founded joint auctions to sell their products. From here traders transported these goods to distant markets. Not until the development of chilled transportation in the 1940s, however, was it possible to distribute flowers all over Europe by truck. To this day, the flower auctioneers in the Dutch cultivation centres are the leading flower merchants in Europe, making the Netherlands the largest flower exporter in Europe (Figure 10.7a).

Not only has the distribution of cut flowers become international, but the locations of production have also moved further away from the consumer. Since the 1970s an ever increasing number of flowers are produced in favourable climates, and low-labour-cost countries, for markets in Europe, North America, and Japan/Australia. In particular, the higher locations of the Andes in Columbia and Ecuador are ideally suited for flower cultivation, due to the amount of sunshine and moderate temperatures. Primarily the North American market, but also Europe, is supplied from here. Thailand produces flowers mostly for Japanese and Australian markets. Even by the 1950s, the European market was supplied from flower farms in Israel. Since the 1980s, supplies have increasingly come from African countries, such as Kenya,

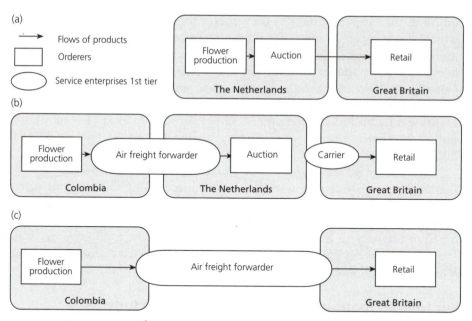

Figure 10.7 *The reorganization of the cut-flower chain*

Tanzania and Uganda. Auctioneers in Holland have kept their role as inter-mediaries: flowers from overseas are traded in Holland, making the Netherlands not only the largest European flower exporter, but also importer (Figures 10.7b, 10.8).

The global development of the flower trade was only possible because of the development of air traffic, as fast-spoiling cut flowers can only be trans-ported to the international markets in this way. In order to transport them with speed and reliability, a number of logistic services companies are needed, i.e. freight forwarders, perishable centres and airlines with the necessary know-how, in order to meet the high standards of an unbroken cooling chain.[3]

However, the supremacy of the Dutch auctions has been shaken in the last decade. Now many large European retail companies buy cut flowers directly from the farms in producing countries. This allows them to have greater influ-ence on production and costs by circumventing the auctions and allowing for long-term contracts with producers (Figure 10.7c). This change in the organi-zation of the value chain also changes the flow of transportation. Flowers are not necessarily brought to Amsterdam anymore: instead they can be distrib-uted via other points of transfer.

In Dubai, where a global logistics location is to be established by the will of the royal family, a perishable centre (Dubai Flower and Perishable Center) has been built at the international airport. This building, which opened in 2006, measures 20,000m^2 and 180,000t of fresh produce can be transferred each year, which corresponds to the size of the perishable centre at Frankfurt a.M. airport. Cut flowers chiefly from producing countries are to be commissioned

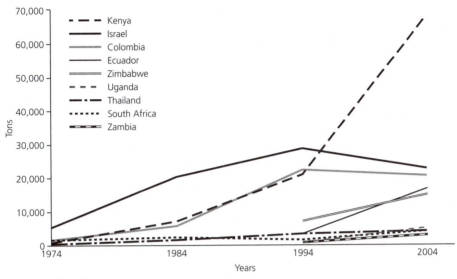

Source: AIPH (2006)

Figure 10.8 *Growth of export by country of production*

here. The operators of this centre, as well as the airline Emirates, see this as a focus of interest not only for the Gulf region but also for European and Asian markets (Government of Dubai, 2004).

The following calculation illustrates the consequences of the emergence of this new actor for air freight traffic in the future. Traffic volumes for the years 2015 and 2025 have to be estimated. This means that certain assumptions have to be made. The possible consumption of cut flowers was estimated by assuming a linear correlation between income and purchase of cut flowers, i.e. based on a regression function. By using this assumption and the data about the development of population and income, a forecast for the consumption of cut flowers for Europe, including Russia, and the Middle and Far East was made for the years 2015 and 2025. These forecast consumer values (in billions of US$) were then transformed into units of weight, based on the flower import statistics in terms of US$ and quantities for the years 2000, 2002 and 2004. Cut-flower production was estimated based on current trends. It is assumed that the production in African countries for the European market will continue to rise, whereas production rates in Europe will continue to drop. Also Columbia and Ecuador, as leading exporters in Latin America, and Thailand will increase their share. Emerging producers, such as India and China, are likely to greatly increase their rate of production. They will not be considered in this estimate, however, because their production is assumed to mostly supply their own domestic markets. All European countries, countries in the Middle and Far East and Russia are treated as importers in this scenario, with their entire demand supplied by imports from foreign-grown flowers.

The expected traffic volumes (in FTK=freight ton kilometres) for the years 2015 and 2025 have been calculated for two scenarios. Scenario 1 assumes a continued supremacy of Dutch auctioneers. Therefore it is assumed that all flowers destined for the European markets are flown to Amsterdam. From there they are brought to their destinations by truck. Goods destined for the Middle East are flown directly from the production companies to the Dubai Flower and Perishable Center, from where they are distributed on surface roads.

The second scenario assumes that all flower imports for all regions are shipped via Dubai. A distinction is made between scenario 2a, where shipments leave Dubai for various importing countries by air and are further distributed by truck, and scenario 2b, which assumes that all commissioned flowers are flown to Frankfurt, from where they are again further distributed in Europe by truck.

Table 10.2 lists the calculated traffic volumes for the years 2015 and 2025. It can clearly be seen that scenario 1, the distribution via Amsterdam, requires the least traffic performance. If the Dubai Flower Center rises to the position of a global player and transports the same amount of flowers to their destinations via Dubai, as assumed in scenario 2a and 2b, much more traffic is generated (i.e. the same freight is carried much further). Most traffic is generated in scenario 2b, where final distribution takes place in Frankfurt a.M. via Dubai.

Table 10.2 *Transport (in RPKs) by scenarios*

	Means of Transport	Transport (RPKs) 2015	Transport (RPKs) 2025
Scenario 1			
Production Countries to Amsterdam	Airplane	26,169,271,842	54,927,233,496
Amsterdam to Europe	Truck	4,216,984,914	8,564,822,906
Production Countries to Dubai	Airplane	1,280,909,028	3,260,553,960
Dubai to Gulf States	Truck	251,759,881	736,496,661
Total		31,918,925,665	67,489,107,023
Scenario 2a			
Production Countries to Dubai	Airplane	21,883,430,831	46,420,235,668
Dubai to Europe	Airplane	22,058,557,371	46,522,360,660
Dubai to Gulf States	Truck	251,759,881	735,396,661
European Airports to Europe	Truck	1,053,247,900	2,080,233,224
Total		45,246,995,983	95,759,326,213
Scenario 2b			
Production Countries to Dubai	Airplane	21,883,430,831	46,420,235,668
Dubai to Frankfurt	Airplane	23,270,261,294	49,290,417,762
Frankfurt to Europe	Truck	4,336,382,848	8,971,779,383
Total		49,490,074,973	104,682,432,813

The proximity of Dubai's facilities to the production locations cannot compensate for the proximity of Amsterdam to its consumers. Economically, increasing freight transport distance does not seem viable. Viewed from the position of a single company, however, this distribution can be of advantage. As explained in detail above, the transportation of goods is organized by the air freight companies. They decide which airline carries the goods. Decisions are based on cost, speed and reliability. If the airline Emirates can be competitive within these parameters, then cut flowers will also reach the European market via Dubai.

Conclusions: Air freight and climate change

This chapter has provided a discussion of the ongoing reorganization of the global air freight sector. Based on the concept of value chains for air freight, the chapter has sought to demonstrate how air freight has been traditionally organized and under which new conditions the sector is currently operating. It can be expected that value chains will be increasingly fragmented, while competition will increase, particularly with regard to fast delivery times. Observed developments indicate that the globalization of the economy will lead to a growing demand for air freight transport, with anticipated annual growth rates of 5.8–6.2 per cent per year. However, transport growth in terms of aircraft movements will not match volume growth, because a higher process optimization and thus efficiency in transport chains can be expected, which will lead to a focus on fewer and larger hubs, while new freighters will be larger and simultaneously have higher load factors. Because of increasing transport volumes, there will also be more direct flights.

The situation for climate change is thus that the efficiency of freighters will substantially increase, leading to lower energy use and greenhouse gas emissions per unit of freight transported, while overall, absolute emissions from the sector will continue to grow, as technical efficiency gains will be outpaced by transport growth in this sector. Given transport volume growth of 6 per cent per year and efficiency gains in the order of about 1–2 per cent per year, net growth in emissions may, for a rough estimate, be in the order of 4 per cent per year. Consequently, the growth in this sector is thus in contrast to global emission reduction goals, and, in terms of growth, possibly even more relevant than passenger transport.

Acknowledgement

The author would like to thank Eva Wagner for providing some insights obtained from her diploma thesis. The author is also grateful to Cordula Mann and Eva Wagner for their helpful support with the figures.

Notes

1   With international air traffic, the different fly-over and landing rights that states grant one another play an important part ('traffic liberties'). Within the European Economic Area (EEA), liberty is granted (the right to transport passengers and freight between two foreign countries as long as the initial and terminal location of a flight route are in the country of origin), not, however, between EEA countries and third countries, with the exception of certain EU countries and the US (open skies agreement) (Rodrigue et al, 2006, pp109–110; Graham, 1998, p316).

2   At Frankfurt am Main airport (Germany) alone there are 54 airlines, 13 sales agents, 153 air freight expeditors, 3 integrators, 101 service companies, 1 customs office, the German Federal Office for Quality Control, veterinarian and phyto-sanitary control posts and various infrastructural arrangements for processing special cargo, such as a freshness centre, animal station etc. (Fraport, 2006).

3   I.e. air-conditioned transport by truck to an airport, into an air-conditioned aircraft, on by air-conditioned truck to the auction hall and from there to the retail outlet, again by air-conditioned truck.

References

ACI (2008) *World Airport Traffic Report 2007*, Geneva

ACI-Europe (2007) 'Traffic info', available at www.aci-europe.org, accessed 15 October 2007

ADV (2008) *Monatsstatistik Dezember 2007*, available at www.adv.aero/download/presse/MS-Dezember_207.pdf, accessed 18 July 2008)

Agustdinata, B. and de Klein, W. (2002) 'The dynamics of airline alliances', *Journal of Air Transport Management* 8: 201–211

AIPH (2006) *International Statistics Flowers and Plants*, Zoetermeer, the Netherlands: International Association of Horticultural Producers and Union Fleurs

Aircargo Asia-Pacific (2006) 'Top CASS/IATA forwarders', available at www.aircargo-ap.com.au/ac/ac-news.htm, accessed 10 March 2006

Airbus (2008) *World Traffic Forecast*, www.airbus.com/en/corporate/gmf/summary-data/freight-traffic-forecast/, accessed 18 July 2008

Airport Nuremberg (2008) *Airport Website*, available at www.airport-nuernberg.de/unternehmen/konzern/zahlenfakten

Arndt, S. and Kierzowski, H. (eds) (2001) *Fragmentation. New Production Patterns in the World Economy*, Oxford and New York: Oxford University Press

Barla, P. and Constantatos, C. (2000) 'Airline network structure under demand uncertainty', *Transportation Research Part E* 36: 173–180

Barrett, S. D. (2000) 'Airport competition in the deregulated European aviation market', *Journal of Air Transport Management*, 6: 13–27

Bjelicic, B. (2001) *Industrial Research: The Global Air Cargo Industry*, Frankfurt a.M.: DVB Group

Boeing (2008) *World Air Cargo Forecast*, available at www.boeing.com/commercial/cargo/, accessed 18 July 2008

Bowen, J. T. and Leinbach, T. R. (2003) 'Air cargo services in Asian industrializing economies: Electronics manufacturers and the strategic use of advanced producer services', *Papers in Regional Science* 82: 309–332

Bowen, J. T. and Leinbach, T. R. (2004) 'Market concentration in the air freight forwarding industry', *Tijdschrift voor Economische en Sociale Geografie* 95: 174–188

Campbell, J. (2001) *The Rise of Global Delivery Services,* Washington: Campbell Press

Clausen, U. (2001) 'Frachtleistungen der Zukunft' in VDI (ed) 6. Jahrestagung *Airport Logistics – Air Cargo 2001.* VDI-Reports 1634: 11–33

Doganis, R. (2002) *Flying off Course: The Economics of International Airlines,* London and New York: Routledge

DPWN (2008) 'Lufthansa Cargo and DHL Express launch cargo carrier', *Deutsche Post World Net,* 20 September 2007, www.dpwn.de

DVZ (2004) *Seriencharter sind auf dem Vormarsch.* Deutsche Logistik Zeitung, available at www.dvz.de, accessed 14 March 2008

Fraport (2006) Unternehmensverzeichnis (list of companies), Frankfurt a.M.

Frenken, K., Terwisga, S. and Verburg, T. (2004). 'Airline competition at European airports', *Tijdschrift voor Economische en Sociale Geografie* 95: 233–242

Gardiner, J., Ison, S. and Humphreys, I. (2005) 'Factors influencing cargo airlines' choice of airport: An international survey' *Journal of Air Transport Management* 11: 393–399

Gereffi, G. and Korzeniewicz, M. (eds) (1994) *Commodity Chains and Global Capitalism,* Westport, CT: Praeger

Gereffi, G., Humphrey, J. and Sturgeon, T. (2005) 'The governance of global value chains', *Review of International Political Economy* 12: 78–104

Goetz, A. R. and Sutton, C. J. (1997) 'The geography of deregulation in the U.S. airline industry', *Annals of the Association of American Geographers* 87: 238–263

Government of Dubai (2004) 'Actual and future projects of the Ministry for Civil Aircraft of the Government of Dubai', available at www.dfm.ae/dfm/statments/Profiles/prospectus.pdf, accessed 25 October 2007

Graham, A. (2003) *Managing Airports: An International Perspective,* Amsterdam: Elsevier

Graham, B. (1998) 'International air transport', in Hoyle, B. and Knowles, R. (eds) *Modern Transport Geography,* Chichester: Wiley, pp311–336

Hanlon, P. (2001) *Global Airlines: Competition in a Transnational Industry,* Oxford: Butterworth-Heinemann

Hesse, M. and Rodrigue, J.-P. (2004) 'The transport geography of logistics and freight distribution', *Journal of Transport Geography* 12: 171–184

Iatrou, K. and Oretti, M. (2007) *From Alliances to Mergers,* Aldershot: Ashgate Publishing

Klaus, P. (2003) *Die Top 100 der Logistik: Marktgrößen, Marktsegment und Marktführer in der Logistik-Dienstleistungswirtschaft. Deutschland und Europa,* Hamburg: Deutscher Verkehrs Verlag

Kleymann, B. and Seristö, H. (2004) *Managing Strategic Airline Alliances,* Aldershot: Ashgate

Lamoine, W. and Dagnas, L. (2003) 'Globalisation strategies and business organization of a network of logistics service providers', *International Journal of Physical Distribution & Logistics Management* 33: 209–228

Leinbach, T. R. and Bowen, J. T. (2004) 'Air cargo services and the electronics industry in Southeast Asia', *Journal of Economic Geography* 4: 299–321

Leinbach, T. R. and Bowen, J. T. (2007) 'Transport services and the global economy: Towards a seamless market', in Bryson, J. R. and Daniels, P. W. (eds) *The Handbook of Service Industries,* Northampton: Edward Elgar

Logistics Management (2008): *2008 Annual Report – Air Freight: Carriers Alter Course,* available at www.logisticsmgmt.com, accessed 7 January 2008

Lufthansa (various years) *Weltluftverkehr* [world air traffic], available at www.konzern.lufthansa.com

Rodrigue, R., Comtois, C. and Slack, B. (2006) *The Geography of Transportation Systems,* London and New York: Routledge

Sage, D. (2001) 'Express delivery', in *Handbook of Logistics and Supply-Chain Management,* Oxford: Elsevier Science

Stalk, Jr, G. (1988) 'Time – the next source of competitive advantage', *Harvard Business Review* 80, 41–49

Starkie, D. (2002) 'Airport regulation and competition', *Journal of Air Transport Management* 8: 63–72

Taylor, M. and Hallsworth, A. (2000) 'Power relations and market transformation in the transport sector: The example of the courier services industry', *Journal of Transport Geography* 8: 237–247

UNCTAD (2007) *Handbook of Statistics,* available at www.unctad.org, accessed 18 June 2007

Wiezorek, B. (1998) *Strategien europäischer Fluggesellschaften in einem liberalisierten Weltluftverkehr*, Frankfurt a.M.: Harry Deutsch

Zukunft-Rhein-Main (2008) Website at www.zukunft-rhein-main.de, accessed 1 July 2008

11
Practice(s) and Ratchet(s): A Sociological Examination of Frequent Flying

Sally Randles and Sarah Mander

Introduction

At Tyndall Manchester we have developed a framework for the study of aviation as a complex production–consumption system. For this chapter we focus on the consumption side of the story. Specifically, we are interested in flying for leisure, with a particular focus on *frequent* flying. We have talked to people in considerable detail about the *doing* of flying from the perspective of the wide range of activities, events and occasions which, we find, now involve flying as a constitutive part. We find that for certain identified groups in society, flying now forms an integral part of celebrating a birthday, anniversary or retirement, taking a city break, relaxing and getting away from it all, visiting friends and family, or pursuing a special interest such as golfing or climbing. Importantly, we conclude that to understand why frequent flying – measured as the number of flights per person per year – has grown considerably in the UK, we need to understand how the norms and standards of the *occasion* to fly have themselves changed. This shifts attention away from the actual flight, and away from simply counting the number of journeys involving flying, to the wider context of the practices into which flying now inserts. We thus highlight the extent to which flying has become a normalized and taken for granted part of many types of occasion, event, activity or celebration, whereas previously it was not.

The overall project takes an interdisciplinary, multi-method approach. Our key conclusion and thesis from the overall project is that the growth of aviation can be understood as an outcome of two coupled and co-evolving processes. These are: (a) the expansionary tendencies of air service provision in the UK (and perhaps internationally, though we haven't yet undertaken international comparative case studies), in part fuelled by coalitions of regional economic agents, including airports, airlines and publicly funded regional development agencies (reported in chapter 12 of this volume); and (b) the growth of flying in general, and frequent flying in particular, which we argue can be partially explained by the transformation and normalization of the conventions of occasion, which now routinely incorporate flying whereas previously they did not, or did not to the same degree. Together, we argue, these coupled tendencies are producing 'upward ratchets' on flying which lead us to quite pessimistic conclusions regarding the scope for emissions reduction, even taking account of technology and efficiency improvements discursively promoted by the industry as the primary solution to the aviation emissions problem.

Although falling air ticket costs relative to disposable income is arguably a key driver in this proliferation of flights, our focus here is on the subsequent and iteratively related processes of consumption: that is, the ways in which frequent flight has become 'ordinary' (Grenow and Warde, 2001). Understanding this has implications for reversing the trend; for once an activity becomes integrated into everyday practices, the political stakes for a government wanting to change the situation for reasons of climate policy are raised. In this context, perhaps rising oil prices and economic recession will do what governments dare not do, but that is another story.

We are interested in the whole flying event, from the decision to go away, to talking about the trip and organizing it with others, to the journey itself – including negotiating airports, travelling in the plane, arriving at the destination, participating in the occasion; returning home and effectively continuing to participate in the activity by talking about it with others. (Although interestingly, some interviewees said they intentionally *avoided* talking about their trip with others on their return home. To engage in what they deemed inappropriately excessive post-holiday descriptions was considered 'showing-off'. In Bourdieu's terms it perhaps represents a breach of unspoken rules governing 'good taste' (Bourdieu, 1984).)

Our entry point for this chapter is practice theory, developed by Alan Warde and colleagues in the context of understanding why contemporary practices, taking various substantive examples such as cleanliness and washing, food and food preparation, or dealing with household waste, are difficult to reconcile with a policy aim of 'sustainable consumption'. Similar conclusions are drawn in our study which switches the context to transport, specifically flying. Additionally we identify 'ratchets' in the system, a notion introduced by Elizabeth Shove (Shove, 2003a, 2003b; Shove et al, 2008). These system ratchets appear to be driving upwards the tendency to fly for leisure.

Flying for business was explicitly excluded from the study. Though in fact we found the leisure/business distinction to be conceptually problematic and methodologically troublesome. For example, a number of the trips described in interviews combined work and leisure in ways that we had not anticipated. In several examples, touring, visiting and cultural activities were 'piggybacked' onto trips taken primarily for work. Indeed some conference/work events were attended *because of* their leisure potential rather than as an imperative for work. In other examples, relatives accompanied the main traveller on a business trip in order to enjoy the leisure amenities or other attractions of a destination. In a third type of example, flying to a new location for work heightened the likelihood of a return visit taken explicitly for leisure. In this case, the second or subsequent trip was taken with friends and family, thus multiplying the number of passengers flying. This shows that an initial visit has the potential to both trigger future visits and multiply the number of flying passengers on future visits. It seems that flying for business and flying for leisure iteratively co-construct each other.

So in the case of frequent flying a work/leisure ratchet is identified. That is, where there is a growth trend in the former, then this will amplify the tendency for growth in the latter. A dynamic is therefore established which supports Shove's (2003a, 2003b, 2008) 'ratchet' theory of transformation. As she demonstrates, this has a number of implications for policy aimed at transitioning to more sustainable pathways. In Shove's examples 'sustainability' is discussed in the context of the consumption of energy resources. In the case of aviation, sustainability is framed by a notion of containing the growth of aviation emissions. In our chapter 'upward' ratchets are identified which suggest that reversing the growth of frequent flying as a contribution to climate policy targets will be difficult to achieve. However, there is, as we discuss and illustrate with interview material, evidence that frequent flying has its limits and even that 'downward ratchets' on frequent flying are not inconceivable.

Shove's ratchet theory is outlined from the perspective of her case examples (heating/cooling in buildings and doing household laundry). The theory is found to be broadly robust when extended to the case of flying. However, some development and refinement of her concepts are suggested in this chapter to take account of *mobility*, that is John Urry's thesis of proximity and co-presence developed to address the question of why people *physically travel* (Urry, 2002).

The chapter draws upon qualitative interviews with frequent flyers, defined as people who took two or more return trips by air for leisure in the preceding year and on secondary data and reports on leisure, tourism and flying trends. The chapter concludes by reflecting upon the policy implications of our findings, particularly prospects for containing and reversing the current growth in journeys by plane and thence levels of CO_2 emissions.

The context of UK emissions reduction targets and aviation growth

The sociological account of the phenomenon of frequent flying reported in this chapter situates within a broader project at Tyndall Manchester, which aims to understand the context, dynamics and constituent elements of aviation growth in the UK. We focus on aviation because earlier analysis has suggested that if current rates of growth in terms of air passenger km continue, the absence of short-term radical efficiency improvements will probably result in this sector taking up the entire carbon budget available for the UK economy (Bows et al, 2006). The budget is formulated as that level consistent with the UK Government's own climate change target of not exceeding a global temperature increase of 2°C (DEFRA, 2006).

Aviation has also recently come under intensified EU regulatory pressure with the publication in 2006 of the European Commission's draft legislative proposal for the inclusion of aviation in the European Union's Emissions Trading Scheme (EU ETS). The proposal provides for aviation to be brought into the Scheme in two steps. From the start of 2011, emissions from all domestic and international flights between EU airports will be covered. One year later, at the start of 2012, the scope will be expanded to cover emissions from all international flights – from or to anywhere in the world – that arrive at or depart from an EU airport. At both the national and EU regulatory scales therefore, aviation is coming under increasing regulatory pressure to 'clean up' its greenhouse gas emissions, particularly but not exclusively CO_2. We can put this into context by comparing aviation with the emissions reduction perfor-mance of other sectors. For example while the EU's total greenhouse gas emissions fell by 3 per cent from 1990 to 2002, emissions from EU inter-national aviation increased by almost 70 per cent (Europa, 2008) (though, the aviation industry argues, this is from a low base when compared to the total for all sectors).

But it is not only the regulatory cordon that is tightening around aviation. Influential, indeed iconic voices, from of all places within tourism journalism, are mounting a significant critique against flying and the aviation industry. This critique is particularly acute against the perceived excesses of frequent flying, which has attracted the derogatory term 'binge flying'. Mark Ellingham is founder of the Rough Guides, a publication series more readily associated with encouraging and *facilitating* travel on a low budget to less-explored desti-nations (see O'Reilly (2006) on how 'backpacker travel' has become a 'mainstream' activity). He is attributed with initiating a particularly damning critique, referring to flying as 'the new tobacco':

> *The development he regrets most is the public's appetite for what*
> *he calls binge flying. 'The tobacco industry fouled up the world*
> *while denying [it] as much as possible for as long as they could,'*
> *said Ellingham. 'If the travel industry rosily goes ahead as it is*

> *doing, ignoring the effect that carbon emissions from flying are*
> *having on climate change, we are putting ourselves in a very*
> *similar position to the tobacco industry.'* (Hill, 2007)

We now turn to a necessarily abridged discussion of practice theory in order to
frame its application and transfer to the context of flying.

Practice theory and (un)sustainable consumption

Contemporary practice theory sheds a specifically sociological light on that
most elusive of objects: sustainable consumption. It is mainly associated with
the work of British sociologists Alan Warde, Elizabeth Shove and Dale
Southerton, who build upon the work, for example, of Bourdieu, Schatzki and
Reckwitz, where Reckwitz proposes a definition:

> *A 'practice' [Praktik] is a routinized type of behaviour which*
> *consists of several elements, interconnected to one another: forms*
> *of bodily activities, forms of mental activities, 'things' and their*
> *use, a background knowledge in the form of understanding,*
> *know-how, states of emotion and motivational knowledge. A*
> *practice – a way of cooking, of consuming, or working, of inves-*
> *tigating, of taking care of oneself or others, etc. – forms so to*
> *speak a 'block' whose existence necessarily depends on the*
> *existence and specific interconnectedness of these elements, and*
> *which cannot be reduced to any of those single elements.*
> (Reckwitz, 2002, pp249–250)

A practice is a coordinated entity that is reproduced and transformed through
its performance. It has understandings, rules and purposes that constitute it as
what Schatzki (1996) calls an 'integrative practice'.

The growing corpus of theoretical and empirical sociology of *practice*
stresses the 'stickiness' of practice which is considered relatively unreflexive
(i.e. we 'do' practice but don't much 'think' about it). The 'stickiness' of
practice – in other words its resilience – has two dimensions. First because in
the general conduct of practice we don't much think about it; rather to borrow
another of Bourdieu's key concepts, it becomes part of our *habitus* (Bourdieu,
1977). Second as indicated by Reckwitz above, because practice comprises a
number of interconnected parts – institutions, discourses, activities and personnel – the constitutive parts of practice together confer structural rigidities.
Practice is theorized as 'preceding' individuals in the sense that people are seen
as 'the sum of their practices' rather than as autonomous, separate and discon-
nected actors. Although of course within a given practice there is latitude to
accommodate different decisions concerning choosing between one course of
action and another, the more central point, and therefore the object of analyses, are the norms, standards and routines of a particular practice, including

developing a shared notion of what constitutes the 'competent conduct' of it (Schatzki, 1996; Reckwitz, 2002).

Yet the resilience of practice, *sui generis*, does not imply that there is no room for change or internal differentiation of any given practice. Indeed both of these are important concerns. For example Shove (2003a, 2003b) presents four models depicting the transformative potential of practice, illustrated by descriptions of how conventions of comfort, cleanliness and convenience have changed in the everyday domains of living and working. She finds that new conventions of comfort (for those who can afford access to it) have become standardized within a very narrow temperature spectrum. Indeed temperature regulation, involving intensive energy consumption in order to artificially heat/cool buildings is delivered – and standardized – by the building and maintaining of the building infrastructure itself, i.e. by those responsible for the specification, installation and maintenance of air conditioning and central heating systems.

Shove also finds this temperature band to have become globally standardized, influenced by a globally concentrated industry responsible for the setting of what constitutes indoor comfort in terms of temperature. This places upward pressure on energy use because it requires air conditioning to artificially cool buildings (even to chilly levels, which paradoxically require occupants to wear more clothing indoors than out). And it requires central heating to raise temperatures, so that shirt-sleeve attire becomes the norm within buildings even as temperatures outside fall. In essence it takes the onus of responsibility for personal comfort away from building occupants who previously took responsibility for controlling their own personal comfort by changing their clothing: putting on a jumper when temperatures fall outside for example.

This means also that in order to understand the conventions of temperature comfort we must draw back from focusing on individual building occupants (especially their propensity to change their own behaviours, i.e. behaving as a consciously green consumer). It also highlights the hazards of relying on individual self-referencing accounts of behaviour as something over which individuals exercise reflexive autonomy. Instead the focus for practice theorists becomes the routines and conventions that shape practice and thus, indirectly but fundamentally, shape behaviours.

Turning to conventions of cleanliness, Shove finds this to be socially constructed and historically contingent, currently involving twice daily showering rather than the previously dominant one weekly bath, according to research conducted in the UK (Hand et al, 2005). Bodily cleansing, which has in contemporary practice become wrapped up in the idea of refreshment by taking a shower (in the morning, after sport and before going out in the evening) is also linked to new conventions of laundering, involving refreshing clothes at low temperatures rather than sanitizing them at high temperatures. The practice of doing the laundry also involves new conventions of prewash sorting of garments according to colour-fastness and the fragility of garment, a convention encouraged by manufacturers and the intensive marketing of washing powders, differentiating washing events into those that produce outcomes that are whiter than white, those that work on the hardest stains and those that protect delicates for example. Here again we find changing practice intertwined and co-constructed with changing sociotechnical infra-structures (Southerton et al, 2004) and promoted by washing machine and washing powder producers; but in this case some of the pressures involve a reduction in energy resource use (washing at lower temperatures) while others have implications for raising energy consumption (washing garments more frequently).

Similarly anthropological studies have demonstrated that what constitutes waste is socially constructed and wrapped up in taboos about the body, pollu-tion and cleanliness (Douglas, 2002 [1966]). Practices concerning the household management of domestic waste are further informed by a surround-ing infrastructure which influences practice, concerning the organizing and storing of domestic waste, and making it ready for collection and recycling. But space is needed to sort and temporarily store waste, that is artefacts deemed surplus to requirements. This is itself a changing notion which has a bearing on what to discard and what to keep. Nevertheless, once that decision is made, the need to set aside space in which to sort and temporarily hold waste needs to marry up with an externally organized and dictated set of rules and institutions concerning what to sort and store, and when and how it will be collected. Thus a *coordinated* system of domestic waste practice and external institutions is needed for the whole process of waste management and recycling to operate (Southerton et al, 2004). A sociology of waste has emerged which provides a very different understanding of the problem of waste in a resource-constrained world, than does, for example, a more engineering systems account of the waste problem (Randles and Warde, 2006).

The corpus of theory and case study in the sociology of practice literature provides us with a wealth of examples within which to study and understand the phenomenon of frequent flying. For example, one part of our explanation of the growth of flying concerns the changing norms, conventions and standards of celebrating (birthdays, anniversaries, retirements, stag and hen parties), which increasingly involves flying abroad, as part of group celebra-tion. The flying part of this event is therefore rather incidental – a means of achieving the celebration, not an end in itself. This suggests that it is the changing rationales and activities involved in the practice of *celebrating* that should be the focus of analysis, not simply the flying part of it. Flying is merely a way of achieving the celebration; it is not an activity pursued for its own sake. This is important for deciding how to study the phenomenon of flying – that is we have to situate it within the various practices which now involve flying as part of their competent performance. What turns out to be a common context to these practices – that is their *internationalization* – changes the standards, activities, discourse and rationales of what comprises and consti-tutes their appropriate or preferred execution.

A further point highlighted in all the examples above, and reconfirmed in our study of flying, is that practice co-evolves and indeed requires a surrounding physical and institutional infrastructure which co-constitutes and shapes the practice. Thus, the context in which flying takes place and co-evolves requires a booking system, airports, air traffic control and flights to certain locations. The practice and its surrounding physical and institutional structures are intertwined and need to be understood together (Shove, 2003a, 2003b; Southerton et al, 2004; Randles and Warde, 2006; Shove et al, 2008).

We can also note that an explicit turn (or turn away) was made by the practice theorists who reminded us that much consumption, especially that which has significant resource-use implications, is intrinsically about the consumption of services and is set within contexts which are quite simply an invisible part of everyday life. The empirical focus of these researchers became the taken for granted settings of the daily routines of the household, such as washing and grooming, which though invisible to date in terms of the sociologist's lens nevertheless are highly significant when considered in terms of their implications for water and energy use.

This line of research became associated with the term 'ordinary consumption' and it made a significant contribution by turning attention away from the more visible 'display' settings which remain the more dominant objects of analysis within cultural studies of consumption (Grenow and Warde, 2001). In cultural studies, for example, the prime focus is on conspicuous consumption (which has a lineage tracing back to Veblen (1925 [1899]), concerned with how notions of fashion and taste in clothes, accessories, cars and home décor develop and contribute to processes and outcomes of social stratification (Bourdieu, 1984). The focus is on artefacts, which by virtue of their visibility act as material carriers of prestige and social distinction. In sharp contrast, ordinary consumption shines a spotlight on the large and largely ignored but paradoxically resource-intensive arenas of consumption which are about the much more mundane settings of washing, doing the laundry, showering, eating in the home (and outside the home), using kitchens and domestic appliances, sorting domestic waste etc. (Grenow and Warde, 2001; Southerton et al, 2004; Shove, 2003a, 2003b; Randles and Warde, 2006; Shove et al, 2008).

Applying, extending, developing practice theory: The specific case of frequent flying

In moving on, we must now highlight the specificity of the context of flying, which in fact in important ways differentiates it from other case studies of the practice sociologists, and requires that we also call upon additional theoretical tools in the sociology literature to help us understand frequent flying.

Part of this exercise involves re-invoking and revisiting cultural sociology with its emphases on the symbolic meaning of artefacts, goods and services mobilized and displayed to indicate cultural capital, a process which contributes to the creation and reproduction of social class and its attendant structures. So the practice of travelling and holidaying, particularly in exotic locations, notably off the tourist trail or indeed away from tourists accumulates cultural capital:

> ...[C]ultural capital, defined by Bourdieu as legitimate knowledge, is accrued through the legitimating force of experience that travel is thought to provide. Knowledge of the world and oneself gained through this experience are valuable, and being acknowledged as such more widely in almost all social contexts... As Harrison points out, travel is a way of expressing particular tastes that reinforce middle class status and help guard against falling down the social ladder, even when income levels are not, for the time being at least, commensurate with the social status a person wishes to demonstrate. (O'Reilly, 2006, p1013)

Others, notably John Urry (invoking Putnam), say that physical travel can be understood by appreciating its role in the formation and maintenance of social capital. Simply, it is understandable, and indeed highly likely that where people have a wide (and increasingly international) network of friends and family, they will travel to see them, and this has positive outcomes in terms of well-being. He links mobility with a notion of the 'good life'. He posits a link between a society which enables and facilitates mobility for its subjects, and its characterization as a 'good society', that is one which recognizes the social and mental health returns to society of enabling corporeal travel (that is co-presence, involving physically being in a place, as opposed to virtual presence, mediated by information and other technologies). In a number of contexts, from spending time in the physical presence of friends and family, to bodily experiencing place and landscape, he suggests it makes a difference as to whether the travel is corporeal or virtual. In this sense he is doubtful whether IT-enabled co-presence will ever fully substitute for corporeal co-presence.

Moreover, all other things being equal, then we could imagine that a good society would not limit, prohibit or redirect the desire for such co-presence. The good society would seek to extend possibilities of co-presence to every social group and regard infringements of this as involving undesirable social exclusion. This is partly because co-presence is desirable in its own right, but also, according to Putnam's research, there are other desirable consequences. It is, he says, 'good to talk' face-to-face since this minimizes privatization, expands highly desirable social capital, and promotes economic activity, in mutually self-sustaining ways (Urry, 2002, p270).

Our analysis supports this thesis. Furthermore this process of extending the 'farawayness' of holiday destinations was raised in a number of the qualitative interviews, with examples given such as holidaying in more exotic 'undiscovered' locations, playing golf at more distant, often newly constructed golf resorts, climbing in previously inaccessible terrain, celebrating main life events in faraway 'special' places etc.

Trophy tourism

Moreover, our analysis supported the phenomenon of trophy tourism (e.g. Barkham, 2008), that is, a tendency to mentally 'tick off' destinations which have been visited or experienced in a process of 'infilling' visited destinations, even if for only a couple of days, in order to add that destination to one's mental list of places visited during one's lifetime, no matter how superficial or 'surface' the experience. In our interviews Louis provides an illustrative example. He and his friend have organized an extensive Pacific, North America and Latin America tour for the following summer. The tour will take five weeks and in that time they will visit Thailand, Mexico, Cuba, Chile, El Salvador and Belize. They will spend just four days in Thailand, describing this length of time as: 'just enough to have a look at the place' (Louis, young male). When discussing the city breaks to be taken within the package of destinations he suggested that four days, three nights is 'about right for a city itinerary, it gives you just enough of a "a bitesize package"'.

Last-chance tourism

Louis' comments also provided an illustrative example of what might be termed *last chance tourism*, that is being able to say that you have witnessed a destination before a particular, significant and widely known characteristic of it disappears for ever. Referring to a previous trip to Cuba, Louis commented, 'Cuba was terrifying, but I wanted to take a look at the place – Fidel will die soon.'

Referring to the rise in visits to the Antarctic continent, now estimated at around 50,000 per year (officially, a rise during the summer season from 7413 in 1996–1997 to 29,530 visitors ten years later), Barkham reports on one visitor who says: 'It gives you a much better perspective about what people are talking about when you hear about global warming' (Collins, reported in Barkham, 2008). For Collins, as for many others, the irony of rising numbers of tourists to the Antarctic is that it provides a chance to witness shrinking glaciers at first hand, while contributing in emissions terms to the processes which are causing those same glaciers to melt.

When the exotic becomes everyday, and flying becomes routine, we come full circle to ordinary consumption

Flying, in contrast to the ordinary, everyday settings on which practice theorists have recently alighted to investigate the relationship between sustainability and consumption, remains a highly visible, conspicuous form of consumption. It provides a vehicle by which cultural, economic and social capital can be accrued as a marker of social class (*pace* Veblen and Bourdieu):

> *Long weekends will come up. A group of us might just fancy Prague. I would avoid Spain; I don't want to go to Spain. I'd like somewhere more different than Barcelona. Spain is too close. I'd*

rather go somewhere not close... I think you should see as many countries as you can. South America – Chile, Peru, Honduras, Nicaragua, Costa Rica. (male)

However, the recent empirical trend to *frequent flying* requires us to revise the notion that flying contributes to the production and reproduction of relations of class, based simply on a single variable of holiday *location*. We find on closer inspection that frequent flying is an activity indulged in disproportionately by wealthier groups (see below). We suggest therefore that cultural capital has become more difficult to secure and protect singularly through the *criterion* of location, because even flying to exotic locations has taken on characteristics of the mass market. Thus we can suggest that frequency of flying has replaced location as the key indicator of cultural, social and indeed economic capital in terms of outbound tourism. Frequent flying signifies an ability to fly *routinely* to carry out a multiplicity of wide-ranging trips abroad involving flight. Statistics to support this hypothesis are given below.

Furthermore, frequent flying requires a great deal of investment in organizing and coordinating multiple trips, since the trips need to be inserted into already crowded annual, weekly and daily schedules. Mary provides just one of many examples of how organizing multiple trips which involve flight, within a short space of time (a year), brings with it a corresponding need for competence and effort on the part of the traveller to successfully organize and coordinate the trips, on time and *to* time.

Mary and her husband are retired. In the previous year she undertook eight return holidays and short breaks involving flight from Manchester. In January she flew to Faro for a week to celebrate New Year. In March she went golfing with friends for two weeks. In July she spent a weekend in Paris with three people to celebrate a birthday. In the summer she spent a further week in Faro. For her fifth trip she spent a week in Prague with a group of six friends. Fitting in a further trip to Algarve in the summer, she then had her main holiday of six weeks comprising a multi-country tour from Manchester to Singapore, Melbourne, Auckland and Sydney (including a cruise as part of the Australian leg). Recounting these trips she nearly forgot to mention a week in a time-share apartment with her husband in Madeira in November, 'because we do it every year I forgot all about it'.

In this example we see how trips involving flying may be becoming so routine and taken for a granted for frequent flyers that a week-long holiday in Madeira – a luxury for many if not most people – easily slips the memory.

An interesting additional observation for travel patterns like this is that the overseas trips did not substitute for domestic UK trips. Rather, UK trips were taken as a matter of routine and were valued as much as overseas breaks. Yet all these travelling events have implications for coordination and time scheduling because they all need to be timetabled to fit between and around each other. Southerton and colleagues write about time scheduling, indeed 'time-squeeze' as a specific attribute that both accompanies and contributes to the experience of leading 'busy lives', since in part it can be understood as the result of an increasing proliferation of additional practices in which any particular person or family now engages. Furthermore, this tendency to add on new practices is skewed, in terms of its distribution across the social spectrum, towards middle and higher classes (Southerton, 2003; Southerton and Tomlinson, 2005). Our research supports the time-squeeze thesis. Interviewees described processes of planning and organizing their trips:

> We sort our holidays out at the beginning of the year. We have to resolve work first. Our business is small and we are it, it is about our personalities. We are closely involved with our customers every day. It is individual, so it's difficult to find cover. We are in our fifth year; it gets easier but there is always an issue for us around time, trying to manage our time. We are at work from 8am till 6pm, it is a long day. And it's been two evenings till 9pm this week. It's nice to have some holidays planned. And we don't want to spend time travelling to airports, so we would also go from Manchester, Liverpool, easyJet. A regional airport cuts time. It's expensive getting to further ones, and we are not going to stay the night, so we wouldn't go to Luton due to the time. (Adam)

However in contrast to the consequential dimension described by Southerton et al (2001) of feeling 'hurried and harried', many interviewees in our research considered the planning and scheduling of trips to be an enjoyable experience – an integral part of the leisure activity itself and a means of temporarily suspending everyday pressures; that is holiday planning and organizing provides a preview of the holiday: anticipation and enjoyment ahead of the holiday proper.

It is interesting to illustrate how this time scheduling process is described by interviewees. Indeed so many interviewees gave similar accounts of the time scheduling activity in the context of the routine taking of holiday breaks, that it appears to have become an integral part of trip preparation and planning. That is, it appears to have become an institutionalized part of the practice.

So long summer holidays were given priority in terms of securing and agreeing dates. The main summer break is planned with the greatest lead time (six to nine months), while winter skiing trips were described as having around four months lead time. One respondent, who flew to Miami three times per year to visit a son and daughter-in-law, described making plans and booking for the next trip as soon as she returned home from the previous one. Booking was often described in and of itself as a pleasurable activity, shared with a friend over a glass of beer for example, or undertaken as part of 'cheering oneself up' by imagining sunnier climes during dull autumn and winter months in the UK. The planning of trips was therefore an integral part of scheduling them. Indeed spontaneous short trips were reported as themselves providing a means to escape for a short 'burst' of sun:

I just go in to Joanne at ABC Travel, I go back to her every time because it's local to home. I just pop in every time whether it's Madeira or Prague. I go in and say: 'Want some sunshine Joanne, just want a bit of sunshine Joanne'. (Mary),

When we are planning a trip I get together with the friends who are going. We get together and the planning starts 3 weeks before. We meet up to get prepared, talk about it, packing, shopping... We talk about holidays every teatime. (Heather)

Finally, essential trips such as a funeral abroad were given priority in a perceived hierarchy of trips, albeit they were organized at very short notice. As well as these main events, local trips within the UK are also organized. There was no sense of hierarchy between overseas and local breaks; indeed sometimes the local breaks are more a necessity to visit core family members, perhaps because they are elderly or poorly or simply are due a visit. Over a period of months the perceived more important trips (e.g. the long summer break) are organized first. Other trips are gradually infilled until the whole year is punctuated with a mix of short and long, very important and more spontaneous, and home and overseas holidays and breaks.

So, to complete Mary's year in terms of UK trips, she, her niece and her sister who are all flower-show enthusiasts (as well as keen golfers), took UK trips to flower shows in Malvern, Harrogate, Chester and Southport. She described these as 'very different' to the (primarily overseas) trips she took with her husband. Indeed, many respondents described how multiple trips can be differentiated in terms of the composition of the 'group' with which they are taken. Some trips are taken with 'core' family, others seem to be intentionally taken as an opportunity to holiday without core family members. Many of these are taken with same-sex companions, whether all male, or all female: a weekend away 'with the girls' or 'with the lads'. Multiple trips therefore coincide with the expectation that different companions provide a qualitatively different experience. Separate experiences with differently constituted groups are explicitly and intentionally taken, again requiring a high degree of coordination: trips with exclusively female friends, trips with exclusively male friends, and trips with core family members need to be fitted in alongside the mixed-group celebrations:

My wife belongs to the gym. She and her girlfriends went for a weekend to Alicante around September or October for the first time. They are just planning the next one now. They are in the process of planning the next. To the beach. 10 girls are going to a villa to relax. Her friend from gym made all the decisions. She would go again if someone organized it, yes. (male)

Furthermore, a dominant view was held by respondents who prefer to travel by plane that the successful execution of the organization of multiple trip taking coincides with the view that flying (rather than taking the train for example) takes less time and is therefore the mode of choice when inserting multiholi-daying into already time-pressed busy lives. That is, flying was considered the fastest and easiest mode of transport when planning and executing the door-to-door organization of transport by which to get to and from home and an overseas destination, despite detailed accounts of long time delays and long periods spent waiting at various stages of check-in, security, lounges etc. A further ratchet therefore becomes evident – the more practices people take on, the more they will be time-squeezed and the more they will privilege flying, and flying from an airport as close as possible to home, as a coping strategy:

> *You can just cram more in now. You can sit in departure lounge and think, 'in three hours' time I will be sat in Milan'. You used to think, 'this time tomorrow I'll be nearly there'. It's just a quicker journey – you've done it and found out, and now expect it.* (Toby)

Paradoxically then, the taking of ever more long and short, but more impor-tantly *frequent* holidays at home and abroad, provides opportunities to 'take a break' or take time out from the mundane routines of daily life. This finding takes our explanatory account right back to where we started: flying has now become an *integral* part of occasions and events which themselves have become a normalized part of everyday life – no longer special or exotic. At the same time, the increasing accessibility of exotic locations renews and revises the level and scope of cultural capital needed to maintain cultural difference.

The combination of this search for new and alternative 'special' locations (Barkham, 2008), at the same time as the increased frequency of flying moves flying from the context of a special event to the realm of the everyday, gives rise, we suggest, to a new dynamic and set of simultaneous processes where everyday life is punctuated *on a regular basis* with trips abroad and in the UK involving flying, including both trips to popular destinations and more exotic (distant) locations.

Indeed, leisure flying can now be understood as intrinsically bound up with taking a break from mundane daily routines. The notion of temporarily suspending everyday routines: of explicitly not doing the laundry or eating in, or at least not doing them in the usual way, in the usual setting, seems central to the objective of the practice that was frequently referred to in interviews as 'getting away', associated with travelling for a short break to a better (sunnier) climate.

Groups on the move

A final dimension of the frequent flying phenomenon appears to capture not only the *frequency* in frequent flying, but also the *number of people flying* within a single party. Thus we encountered many examples of groups travelling together. We have labelled this phenomenon 'groups on the move'. It can be situated within the general idea and thesis that the group does abroad things which previously it would have been done locally: celebrations, short breaks, families holidaying in groups comprising several families together etc:

> *I went to Alicante in November, it was with Monarch. My brother retired from the police and decided he would like a weekend away. There were about 30 people. Someone else arranged it. I haven't done weekends away before; when we all got there we just played it by ear, there were no fixed rules. We'd meet up in evening for a meal. And on the second night we all went for meal to celebrate. Best deal with Monarch. He'd been on two previous retirement functions, one was to Riga in Latvia, but he wanted to go somewhere warmer than Latvia. Benidorm was just half an hour's drive. It felt like a warm summer day. We'd just sit in the sun and drink. In fact we did much too much drinking! There's a different clientele there in the winter. You can see it, in October to March; there are groups, older, celebrations, weddings, functions. It's families in the summer.* (Stuart)

Three things fascinated us about this type of holidaying where large groups of friends are mobilized to fly in a group in ways that do not seem to have been previously the case. The first is the size and constitution of the group and the logic around which this was formulated (groups were mobilized around different types of trip, for different reasons, and at different times of the year). The second is that such events take a very high degree of organization, including coming to a decision as to where to go, when, and who or how the party of travelling companions should be organized. The third provides evidence supporting the existence of another ratchet. That is, increasing the size of the group increases the likelihood that new flyers, 'newbies' in the group, will once initiated to the routines of flying be more ready (and readied) to be frequent flyers in future. At the same time, experienced flyers in the group are readied for return visits to the location with a differently constituted group (with friends first and then returning with family, for example).

Coming home – to talk or not to talk?

Finally we were interested in the extent to which the practice and experience of holidaying is extended in temporal terms, as it were, by talking about the trip with others afterwards. Several interviewees, particularly women, described feeling down or a bit low in spirits, on return from holiday: 'You feel depressed for a couple of days' (Mary).

For some, this feeling was a trigger to beginning to think and plan for the next trip, supporting the notion that the taking of holidays has become associated with an expectation of taking breaks on a regular basis to escape daily domestic and work contexts associated with being at home. For others (a young group of friends for example), post-holiday discussion was in fact a way of extending the trip metaphorically by reminiscing about it during social get-togethers *after* the trip:

> *Went to Prague with friends. I went back to enjoy it. I booked for all eleven on internet. Sorted out hostel and taxis – we headed to the hotel bar to have a meal – then some of us decided to go for a walk and explore. It was very flexible. I'd been before so the second time was able to help others… I was thinking of Prague from the beginning. I wanted to go in January – I hate January and wanted something to look forward to. I wanted to get back for a weekend cheaply. I started looking at the end of October and November and sent an email out saying that I was thinking about it – who wants to go? I found out the approximate costs (hostel, plus flights, plus spending). I found Jet2.com. I found and chose the hostel. I emailed all my friends over a couple of weeks – they came from Leeds, Bradford, Blackpool – I didn't book for most people – I sent link to flight saying 'book now'. The first priority – it had to be cheap – next it had to be from the north, anywhere in the north with convenient flights… When we got back we chatted about it, what we'd liked about it, through emails and in the pub.* (Hatty)

Travel bores?

Conversely there were mixed reactions and some debate in one group about the value of engaging in post-holiday reminiscences. One lady said she doesn't talk about holidays much on return, but she was contradicted by others – her friends and golfing companions – who said that on the contrary, she did. She found a compromise:

> Liz: *I don't talk about it much – people think its silly.*
> Mary: *Yes, you do!…*
> Liz: *Well, a little if asked. But I had a friend who went to Vietnam and Cambodia, she brought 6 packs of photos to look at.*

This ambiguity as to the appropriateness of post-holiday conversation adds further to the thesis that trips to exotic locations are becoming the norm. As a consequence, perceived excessive post-holiday conversation now should, in the normative sense, be removed from post-holiday public reminiscing. Activities that would place a trip in the category of special and exotic are now no longer deemed to be so. Since everyone else in the social group already has access to the exotic, engaging in post-holiday extension by describing the trip in fine and long descriptive detail is deemed somehow distasteful and showing-off.

The rising norms and standards of occasion and celebration

We can provide illustrative support and further elaboration of our thesis that flying now forms a constituent part of *other* practices: celebrations, occasions, and specialist interests and hobbies, in ways that it did not previously, with the effect that the norms and standards of what it is to 'do' those practices is ratcheting upwards.

Perhaps our most stark illustration is the case of a family taking a 24-hour package tour to Lapland at Christmas, organized by an airline to visit 'Santa'. Here we see the rising norms, standards and expectation of what has become an extended, and in consumption terms enlarged, arena constituting the doing of 'Family Christmas'. It is no longer sufficient, for example, to hurry along to a nearby garden centre or department store to visit Santa. Rather, this integral part of traditional Christmas now includes a 24-hour return visit to Lapland to experience the Santa Claus story surrounded by the usual, traditional visual cues of reindeer and elves, but now in the 'better' – described as more 'authentic' – setting of the 'north pole', as Helen explains:

> It was a trip to Lapland on 16 December, just one day; we went on a sleigh ride to see Santa. We flew out at 10am and returned late at night. It was just a spur of the moment thing but it was something I'd always wanted to do for the children. We booked by internet five weeks before – it was a particular excursion – it cost £1800 through British Airways. The flight is part of the holiday, it was so exciting – going to see Father Christmas singing on the plane – it only takes an hour. My mum treated her nephews 20 years ago – it was similar but in that case Santa came on the plane – the plane went up and then came down. Actually going there was so much better; the kids thought it was wonderful. We noticed how the elves ears were so real. (Helen)

At the other end of the spectrum, but also illustrating the proliferation of (very) short breaks, which now incorporate flying as part of celebration, are stag and hen parties, now routinely incorporating partying in an overseas destination:

> You see them in the departure lounge at Gatwick or Stansted. They have no luggage, only what they are dressed in – going for a night out in Barcelona or Milan. Literally going for a night out, back the next morning. The bride in fancy dress, just a night out. I have spoken to people who have done it too. (Trevor)

But perhaps the ultimate combination of the separate strands described above (of 'groups on the move', organization, scale, planning and exotic location) is the wedding celebration, wherein the changing expectations of a wedding occasion includes a wedding party in an exotic location which might be considered the ultimate show in terms of cultural, social and economic capital. In Liz's case the wedding of a family member involved participants 'sharing out' the associated activities – Liz made the bridesmaid dresses – for a wedding celebration which involved organizing 30 people travelling to the Caribbean.

Our final example is that of amateur and semi-professional outdoor sports, such as climbing. Here the group proclaimed that they 'Fly to climb!' (Tom). This, in its stark simplicity, shows how practice shapes the flying and not vice versa. For climbers, the primary reason for flying is to access good quality climbing terrain. A secondary reason was reported as providing an opportunity to visit friends and family, as an add-on to the climbing. The choice of which location to visit is a combination of the right price combined with a 'good' climbing venue. What surprised us about the climbing group was that despite being self-reported environmentalists, keen geographers and admirers of landscape, their willingness to fly in order to access ever better climbing locations appears to easily outweigh any conscious thought about the relationship between flying, aviation emissions and climate change. Indeed when climbers were asked, the irony is that climate change may in some instances bring forth new, better or drier climbing conditions.

The primary rationale for flying came from within the practice itself, from the unspoken norms and understandings which climbers share. The climb was described as the opportunity to participate in a very individual competition which pits the climber against nature. The objective is to succeed against the climb (indoor or outdoor). Climbing was also described as an opportunity for the climber to improve, and demonstrate to others, his competence in an activity which was described as combining competition, gymnastics and sport. One climber described it as 'a discipline, just a self-discipline' (Tom).

Surprisingly to us, climbing was not undertaken in the general sense as an opportunity to appreciate nature. Just the opposite, in fact. Climbing was not about appreciating the environment in its natural sense, rather about fixing the conditions and topography that the landscape and microclimate need in order to provide a good 'sport climb'. This predominantly means dry conditions. It is somewhat paradoxical that in some locations a new climate-change-induced microclimate and set of climate conditions may even be *improving* the climbing conditions and therefore attracting more climbers to fly in by air. We witness another ratchet therefore. What you need for good rock climbing is rocks; and regardless of whether the terrain is created by climate change or not, dry, cold, rocky conditions will attract more climbers.

Furthermore we can see explicitly in the case of climbing how the sport is becoming international. International climbing competitions have only been in existence for the last 20 years. The first 'world cup' was held in the UK in 1989. International sports climbing is embedded in and facilitated by a plethora of surrounding institutions, set up explicitly to facilitate climbing, not to help address climate change. This institutional structure connects regional clubs, national and international institutions. There are now a half dozen international competitions per year. In addition, certain faraway places may invest considerable effort into attracting climbers in order to generate economic development resources for their own, very local, benefit. For example, the tiny territory of La Réunion promotes itself to the climbing community and will benefit economically from decisions to send large groups of climbers to the location. Indeed an international politics of climbing is instituted which ensures that scarce climbing spaces are shared out between the participants, all seeking to attract the large fraternity of circulating international climbers. So, attracted by dry climates, climbers will come as climbing tourists. French, Italians, Austrians, that is wealthy European nations, lead the trend. Russians and Ukrainians also play an important but less visible role. Finally it is worth noting that international climbing as a sport is Eurocentric and concentrated among wealthier people, although there is significant growth in Asia.

Flying trends: Exotic and mundane, but still the preserve of the rich

Secondary data supports the thesis that flying in general (and frequent flying in particular) is differentiated according to social class. Simply put, wealthier people, and those in higher social class bands, are more likely to fly frequently, and indeed have contributed disproportionately to the growth of the number of journeys taken by air.

This contradicts a familiar discourse from airlines about low-cost flying. Falling ticket prices, especially as offered by so-called budget airlines, they argue, have made flying more accessible to lower income groups, thus producing a more equitable distribution of flying across social class. We might call this a trickle-down thesis of flying. The secondary data does not support this claim in relative terms, however, though it does in terms of absolute numbers, as we can now demonstrate in the UK context.

The travel and tourism sector can be divided into three categories: domestic tourism by UK residents within the UK; outbound tourism by UK residents travelling abroad; and inbound tourism by oversees residents travelling to the UK. In 2004, total expenditure across the three categories was £70.08 billion, a rise of 4.8 per cent on 2003 levels across the three categories, rising in 2004 to a total of 239.8 million visits and 1.35 billion overnight stays. But the best performing sector between 2000 and 2004 was outbound tourism, which experienced a 12.9 per cent growth in the number of trips, compared to domestic tourism which *declined* by 15.6 per cent, and inbound tourism which grew at the slower rate of 9.9 per cent. Expenditure saw an even more dramatic increase, with a 24.9 per cent increase in the value of outbound tourism during the period 2000–2004 and only a 1.7 per cent increase in inbound tourist expenditure.

The profile of those holidaying abroad demonstrates that they are more likely than others to be young and in social group AB. In 2004, 31 per cent of all adults aged 20–24 years who took one holiday in the previous year took their holiday abroad, while 19 per cent of this age group holidayed in Great Britain.

In terms of social group, 31 per cent of all adults who were social grade A (and a further 27 per cent of social grade B) took their single holiday abroad in 2004 (the equivalent percentages for these social grades A and B staying in Great Britain were 25 per cent). For social grade E the situation reverses, with 17 per cent holidaying in Great Britain and 12 per cent holidaying abroad. The predominant mode of transport for all the outbound trips was by air, with 27 per cent taking scheduled and 18 per cent taking chartered flights (Gower, 2005).

Frequent holidaying

The group most likely to take multiple oversees holidays is, in fact, an early retirement group with 9 per cent of 45–54-year-olds and 10 per cent of 55–65-year-olds taking three or more holidays abroad in the previous twelve months (2004), compared to 5 per cent of 20–34-year-olds. Income data supports this, with the highest penetration of those taking three or more holidays in the previous year being those with an annual income over £50,000 (Gower, 2005). This finding was supported in our qualitative interviews where the group of lady golfers, most of whom described themselves as early retired, recorded the highest levels of frequent holidaying abroad, reaching ten and twelve overseas holidays in the previous twelve months.

Short breaks

The number of short breaks (defined as holidays of one to three nights' duration) taken in any of the years 1999–2003 from the UK exceeds the UK population, so that the average number of short breaks taken by a UK resident is more than one a year, although 15 per cent of UK adults have never taken a short break.

Quantitative secondary surveys confirm that household tenure (which we take as a proxy for income and social class) differentiates those taking short breaks. In the UK in 2003, homeowners with a mortgage had a greater propensity to take a short break than those in rented council accommodation (40 per cent and 12 per cent, respectively) and of those who took a historical or cultural break, homeowners were relatively more likely to do so than those in rented council accommodation (46 per cent, 8 per cent), while short breaks to the beach were relatively more likely to be taken by those from rented council accommodation than homeowners with a mortgage (36 per cent, 12 per cent) (Graham, 2004, p62; Gower, 2006).

A particularly notable trend (again supported and illuminated in our qualitative interviews) is for so-called long-haul mini-breaks, dubbed 'speed breaks' or 'break-neck breaks' (Halifax plc, 2008). A survey commissioned by Halifax General Insurance finds that 3.7 million Britons flew on long-haul mini-breaks during the twelve months to March 2008. They endured a flight of at least seven hours for a holiday lasting less than seven days. Britons from south-east England were most likely to take a long-haul mini-break with the most popular destinations being New York and Los Angeles (for shopping purposes, incentivized by the strong pound:dollar exchange rate), while so-called cultural trips to the Far East were the second most popular destination, and India the third.

Activity holidays

Activity holidays can be defined as holidays that involve some form of physical, sporting or related activity as their main purpose. Once again we see strong growth in overseas markets. Between 2001 and 2005 activity holidays taken abroad by UK residents increased by 8.2 per cent to 7.4 million trips in 2005, while domestic holidays rose by 4.0 per cent. The profile of respondents who have taken an activity holiday abroad in the last five years (survey dated 2005) is male (58.4 per cent), female (41.6 per cent), young (46.6 per cent of 16–19 year olds), and more likely to be social grade A or B (40.9 per cent of the 8.1 per cent all grade A, 35 per cent of the 25.1 per cent of all grade B).

Considering individual activity areas, and assuming walking or trekking as analogous to climbing, the profile of people who took at least one overseas golfing and/or walking/trekking holiday abroad in the last five years was male (79.9 per cent of all men compared to 49.9 per cent of the full sample profile); aged 25–44 (28.9 per cent of all 25–34-year-olds compared to 22.9 per cent of the population), even more so 35–44 (24.9 per cent compared to 14.7 per cent of the population as a whole), and social grade B (29.0 per cent compared to the population 16.6 per cent) (2005 figures).

Ratchets

Elizabeth Shove offers 'ratchet' as a simple metaphor for capturing the idea that practices do change, but that a particular triple characteristic is noted in the dynamic of change:

1   Once a practice has shifted to a different ratchet 'notch', then a new configuration of practice – that is a new level of standardized norms comprising conventions of behaviours, knowledge and meaning – and a surrounding sociotechnical infrastructure, is visible. A high level of sociotechnical and institutional lock-in therefore exists.
2   This means that there is a high level of historical path dependency.
3   The distinctive architecture of institutionalized practice (convention) and their surrounding sociotechnical infrastructures are difficult to reverse.

The definition of a ratchet she offers is 'a set of teeth on the edge of a bar or wheel in which a device engages to ensure motion in one direction only' (Allen, 1990 in Shove, 2003a, p399); and while warning against excessively stretching the metaphor, Shove nevertheless finds it a helpful heuristic to capture the above properties of the dynamics of practice. In the case of the temperature regulation of buildings, she sees the increase in standardization of temperatures to be an example of this, creating an upward ratchet on consumption (and therefore resource use) that is difficult to reverse.

She does, however, refine her basic model. In some cases – notably the formation of new conventions for doing the household laundry – she notes new conventions that move the consumption ratchet simultaneously in opposite directions, with corresponding different implications for resource and energy use. She notes, in the case of domestic laundry, on the one hand new conventions for wash temperatures, that lower the water temperatures in washing machines, and therefore reduce energy use, while on the other new conventions for sorting clothes (into smaller categories) coupled with tendencies to wash clothes more often, where both have implications for increasing energy use. She therefore refines the basic ratchet model and suggests new variants of it. In the latter, the ratchet model would resemble a number of cogs, on an axle, with the cogs moving in different directions.

We will complete our analysis by briefly presenting six processes, each of which is evident in the conventions for flying and their surrounded institutional infrastructures, where three (there may be more) of the characteristics witnessed might be said to be 'ratcheting up' the tendency to fly, while three (there may be more) provide at least the possibility and potential to ratchet down flying.

Ratcheting up?

First fly

We note that there are initiation rites and processes involved in flying for the first time. Flyers are at first anxious, and it may have taken a considerable effort on the part of the person and their friends and family to overcome their anxiety about the first flight. In essence there appear to be certain rites of passage, a sense of being inducted into flying and 'learning to fly'. But the barriers to flying appear from that point to have been lowered and after that flying is much easier to perform. Sarah first flew quite recently, in 2004. Although she had never flown before, she 'felt she should' and took an ambitious trip to New Zealand via Los Angeles, as part of an organized tour. Although she recalls, 'the flight nearly killed me – it was not pleasant', she has subsequently flown several times (twice in the last year alone) and anticipates flying at this level for the foreseeable future. The implication is that as more people fly for the first time, this drives future flying upwards as first-flyers, often encouraged by the mechanism of 'groups on the move', overcome their fears and rapidly gain confidence, potentially becoming the frequent flyers of the future. One interviewee described this as 'letting the genie out of the bottle'.

Budget airlines and penny flights

Another example of using the term 'letting the genie out of the bottle' was in descriptions of the activities of budget airlines. Susan described her experience of Australian low-cost airlines. The growth of budget airlines in Australia triggered rapid domestic air-travel growth. Susan used to visit her niece on the other side of Australia every two or three years. Now since Quantas introduced a low-cost domestic route, she does two or three domestic flights per annum during her annual visit to family in Australia. She says, 'Flights got cheaper so Australians got used to flying domestically.'

Low-cost flying has undoubtedly raised expectations around the norms of the price of flying. Flyers expect, and indeed seek out, bargains and are either taken aback at, or expect as a new convention of flying, flight promotions which bring prices down to what was described as 'ridiculous' levels, including the 1p flight. This phenomenon is enabled, indeed is fostered and encouraged, by new procedures and practices of scheduling booking through the internet.

Trevor described how he 'checked out' availability and price for his annual spring trip to Italy to attend a series of Italian league football games. Flights to Milan were available for £120 return. He knew he could get cheaper ones if he waited. He therefore decided to wait and keep 'checking out' the situation. He checked two or three times more and by January the cost was £75 return. He was happy with that so left it a few days until he had the opportunity to book. When he came to book in February, the price was £45 return. He made the booking online, and found that it showed up as 1p return. Surprised, he booked, not expecting it to be that price. Sure enough, the cost came up as taxes plus 1p. The total flying cost of flying was £45 per person. He was happy to commit immediately on behalf of himself and his friends, even though they didn't at that point know what the football fixtures would be. He would have been happy to pay much more for the flight. He also noted that this experience 'raises the bar' on expectations of flight prices: 'Having paid £40, next time you want to match that – you have a figure in your head' (Trevor).

This example also highlights the role of internet technology in changing the procedures and process of securing a flight.

Schools standards and curricula

An unexpected link can be made between changing conventions in unlikely places – such as in education curricula – and their consequences for flying. Trevor, a secondary school teacher, described how the school curriculum for less able pupils now includes the opportunity to participate in an overseas trip (to France) in order to gain confidence and improve relationships with teachers and peers, by experiencing a different cultural context and asking pupils to undertake activities requiring a high level of self-organization and cooperation with others in an unfamiliar context. But in fact last year two return journeys were needed in order to execute this new curricular objective. The first was a fact-finding trip; the second was the trip proper involving around 30 pupils and adults. A colleague booked and paid (securing the cheapest flight). The trip was described as 'a bit of both work and pleasure' for staff and pupils. The trip abroad was part of the 'drive for excellence' in the school curriculum, that is for pupils who traditionally engage little in the education process to develop skills in self-sufficiency, organization and improved relationships. Trevor noted improvements in relations with peers and teachers, a reduction in negative attitudes and less disruptive behaviour after the trip. This example draws attention to how changing standards and conventions of practice in one domain of practice, indeed 'good practice', here in education, have iterative impacts on another domain area, frequent flying.

Ratcheting down?

Although far from a dominant feature of our account of frequent flying, we note some evidence – just a drop within an ocean of upward-ratchets – of tendencies and potential which may exert a downward pressure on frequent flying. These 'limits' to the growth of frequent flying can be grouped under three headings: the (dis)comfort of the flying experience; upper limits to the number of trips that can be taken in a year; and concern for the environment. Each of these has implications for overall levels of corporeal travel, and for modal substitution away from flying.

(Dis)comfort and the flying experience

Much of the account of paradoxical (dis)comfort experienced on journeys taken by air, involve the discomfort of the airports and the flight itself:

> *There's no pleasure in the journey (train is hugely more enjoyable). Feel can enjoy the trip once cleared customs. Not at all comfortable in lounges, don't like shopping. People are twitched when they are flying, people like to be in control, when you're flying you have no control – when you're cycling or driving you are in control. On the train you have more personal space, more freedom to move about. People are more likely to engage in conversation. ... I'm happy to initiate a conversation but I'm less likely to initiate a conversation (on a plane). Can just tell, people don't want to ...* (Trevor)

Almost unanimously our interviewees reported being extremely uncomfortable in the aircraft. This included both physical discomfort, related to physical conditions of lack of leg room and 'cramped' conditions; and social discomfort related to the 'unusualness' in social terms of being in such physical proximity to strangers, for an extended period of time:

> *I'm uncomfortable, there's no leg room ... sitting is uncomfortable. It's hassle and tiring getting to the airport... I find myself sweating when there's turbulence. I listen to my iPod, sleep, read a book, I don't talk to people no, I don't like talking to people in planes.* (Stephen)

> *I hardly ever eat – I read magazines, watch TV, talk to friends, do puzzles – I never talk to people I don't know – its just the situation I'm not bothered... On the way to Prague it was really*

> *stressful we were delayed on the airplane and sat for an hour, I*
> *hated it and we hadn't even taken off. I was on that plane so*
> *long, I was really stressed, in the end it was a total of four hours*
> *on the plane. I had bought sandwich and drink at Boots and*
> *taken on – the food on the plane 'overpriced and rubbish'... I*
> *never would like to go further by plane because I have a bad back*
> ... (Heather)

Upper limits

A number of factors involving upper limits to time scheduling and fitting multiple trips into daily life, and limits to the level of acceptance of extreme security appear to have the potential, at least, to exert a downward tendency on the propensity to fly:

> *I'll probably do the same pattern as last year in the next few years*
> *– but feel as if I've got too many (trips) – it is a pressure, all that*
> *packing, just settling down then you are away again... I have*
> *family in Miami, otherwise I wouldn't go... There's a limit, last*
> *year I was out of the country each month of the year. Limit*
> *before it becomes uncomfortable to be preparing & getting back*
> *all time.* (Gail)

> *I swore I would never go through Washington again – the*
> *American security – Americans stupidly reactive – my plastic*
> *forks were taken away.* (Gail)

Discourses of environmental concern

Environmental concern did feature in what people said they would do in the future. Whether this translates into action, will be another matter, since we have insisted that the propensity to fly does not reside within the flying itself, but within the practices and sociotechnical infrastructures that induce flying. Still it is interesting to witness a high level of dissonance between frequent flying and how frequent flying is beginning to be perceived as socially unacceptable.

Sometimes interviewees made an explicit statement concerning the uncomfortable trade-off between having an environmental conscience and still flying:

> *I will have a conscience, but I won't not go to Miami.* (Gail)

We did get the impression that concerns about how to reconcile frequent flying with a sense that flying is damaging the climate through carbon emissions were emerging, but were not (yet? ever?) acted upon:

> *It seems that climate change will be more extreme than at first*
> *thought. It's the observations of the scientists, it matters, doesn't*

it, when you think about what flying might be doing to the environment? (Andrew)

At the moment, we appear to be on a cusp between the ratcheting standards inducing frequent flying on the one hand and a 'tipping' of popular discourse against flying for environmental and climate change concerns on the other. We see this playing out as feelings of discomfort and dissonance on the part of our interviewees at least, as they seek to reconcile multiple notions of what it is to be a 'good' citizen, and how this sits alongside the now deeply embedded tendencies to fly.

Conclusions and implications for theory and climate policy

Our conclusion, in line with the growing corpus of practice sociology written from within the context of (un)sustainable consumption, is that it will be difficult to curtail/reverse/influence practice – in our case the conventions of celebration which sit behind flying, and specifically which induce frequent flying – through voluntary means.

Often referred to as 'the demand side' by climate policy and actors seeking to reduce aviation and other sources of greenhouse gas emissions, this conclusion paints a pessimistic picture of the likelihood of achieving aviation emissions reductions without deep interventions to reduce frequent flying through formal regulation and fiscal means.

We also need to bear in mind the puzzling juxtaposition of the 'societal good' provided by and through mobility, and the tendency for frequent flying to be, in actual terms, the disproportional domain of the wealthy. John Urry theorizes that the encouragement of mobility and co-presence brought about by corporeal as opposed to virtual travel, is the mark of a 'good society' and, conversely, that a 'good society' would take care not to curtail corporeal mobility. But we see that frequent flying is disproportionately the domain of wealthier groups, it is not evenly distributed across social groups, and this pattern may itself be considered inequitable in terms of providing access to the 'well-being' of mobility. This clearly has policy implications, going forward, as to who should bear the cost for the impact on the environment of activities disproportionately concentrated within wealthier groups, whilst maintaining and encouraging mobility as a 'social good'.

Through the 'ratchets' metaphor we suggest that although the predominant ratchet on consumption that sits behind the phenomenon of frequent flying is upward, there are some indications that this has its limits, and there are flickerings of downward ratchets.

References

Barkham, P. (2008) 'How far will you go?', *The Guardian*, 9 July

Bourdieu, P. (1977) *Outline of a Theory of Practice*, Cambridge: Cambridge University Press

Bourdieu, P (1984) *Distinction: A Social Critique of the Judgement of Taste,* London: Routledge

Bows, A., Anderson, K. and Upham, P. (2006) *Contraction and Convergence: UK Carbon Emissions and the Implications for UK Air Traffic,* Tyndall Centre Technical Report, No 40

DEFRA (2006) *Climate Change: The UK Programme 2006,* UK Government Publication, Department of Food and Rural Affairs, London, HMSO, Norwich

Douglas, M. (2002 [1966]) *Purity and Danger: An Analysis of Concepts of Pollution and Taboo,* 2nd edn, London: Routledge

Gower, I. (ed) (2005) *Travel and Tourism Market Review 2005,* Key Note, October

Gower, I. (ed) (2006) *Activity Holidays: Market Assessment 2006,* Key Note, February

Graham, H. (ed) (2004) *Short Breaks: Market Assessment 2004,* Key Note, January

Grenow, J. and Warde, A. (2001) *Ordinary Consumption,* London: Routledge

Halifax plc (2008) *Long Haul, Mini Breaks Take Off,* 10 March, Halifax Press Office

Hand, M., Shove, E. and Southerton, D. (2005) 'Explaining showering: A discussion of the material conventions and temporal dimensions of practice', *Sociological Review On-line,* 10(2), June

Hill, A. (2007) 'Travel: The new tobacco', *The Observer,* 6 May

O'Reilly, C. (2006) 'From drifter to gap year tourist: Mainstreaming backpacker travel', *Annals of Tourism Research* 33(4): 998–1017

Randles, S. and Warde, A (2006) 'Consumption: The view from theories of practice', in Green, K. and Randles, S. (eds) *Industrial Ecology and Spaces of Innovation,* Cheltenham: Edward Elgar, Chapter 10

Reckwitz, A. (2002) 'Toward a theory of social practices: A development in culturalist theorizing', *European Journal of Social Theory* 5(2): 243–263

Schatzki, T. R. (1996) *Social Practices: A Wittgensteinian Approach to Human Activity and the Social,* Cambridge: Cambridge University Press

Shove, E. (2003a) 'Converging conventions of comfort, cleanliness and convenience', *Journal of Consumer Policy* 26: 395–418

Shove, E. (2003b) *Comfort, Cleanliness and Convenience: The Social Organisation of Normality,* Oxford: Berg

Shove, E., Watson, M., Hand, M. and Ingram, T. (2008) *The Design of Everyday Life,* Oxford: Berg

Southerton, D. (2003) '"Squeezing Time": Allocating practices, coordinating networks and scheduling society', *Time and Society* 12(1): 5–25

Southerton, D. and Tomlinson, M. (2005) '"Pressed for time" – the differential impacts of "time squeeze"', *The Sociological Review* 53: 215–239

Southerton, D., Shove, E. and Warde, A. (2001) 'Harried and hurried: Time shortage and coordination of everyday life', CRIC Discussion Paper No 47: University of Manchester

Southerton, D., Chappells, H. and van Vliet, B. (eds) (2004) *Sustainable Consumption: The Implications of Changing Infrastructures of Provision,* Cheltenham: Edward Elgar

Urry, J. (2002) 'Mobility and proximity', *Sociology* 36(2): 255–277

Veblen, T. (1925 [1899]) *The Theory of the Leisure Class: An Economic Study of Institutions,* London: Allen and Unwin

12
Aviation Coalitions: Drivers of Growth and Implications for Carbon Dioxide Emissions Reduction

Sarah Mander and Sally Randles

Introduction

Using a mixture of interview and historical analysis, this chapter considers the growth of aviation as partly arising from coalitions of actors working together to sustain that growth. Particular attention is paid to the coalition that has driven the UK Aviation White Paper, as this provides the policy support for decades of air traffic growth, with a corresponding impact on emissions. The research is one element of broader research undertaken at Tyndall Manchester that has explored the context, dynamics and drivers for aviation growth in the UK. The work concludes that aviation growth is fuelled by two coupled processes. The first, described in Chapter 11, consists of the way in which common practices, such as the celebration of an event, are coupled with the availability of cheap flights. This combination acts as a ratchet, increasing the number of flights taken. The second process is the expansion of the aviation industry, where coalitions of actors are working to achieve the expansion agenda set out by the UK Government in the Aviation White Paper (AWP). Together, these two processes combine to achieve rates of growth which will seriously undermine the UK's climate change and carbon targets (Bows and Anderson, 2007).

Prior to liberalization, the European aviation industry was dominated by state-owned national 'flag carriers' who enjoyed considerable power and control over policy, with the interest of the carrier becoming aligned with the national interest of the country itself. The provision of air travel was not seen as the sole purpose of the carrier, but instead on an equal footing with other benefits such as employment, national pride and the promotion of tourism (Barrett, 2006). Competition was highly restricted and as a result, many flag carriers were perceived as offering poor standards of service for a high price and via an inefficient carrier that required periodic injections of state capital to support it (Kangis and O'Reilly, 2003).

The aviation industry was revolutionized by the liberalization of the EU air industry and the subsequent emergence of new airlines into the marketplace in the shape of low-cost or volume carriers. Driven in part by capacity constraints at large hub airports, but also by the regionalization of economic policy, aviation growth has rippled outwards from the large airports of the capital, and volume carriers have supported the expansion of capacity at regional airports. A competitive airport, serving a comprehensive network of routes, is seen as important not only for bringing tourists to a region, but is also seen as key to attracting inward investment, and increasingly as a service sector centre in its own right. This changing economic landscape has not only brought new voices adding strength to the drive for expansion, but also different agendas, tensions and alliances, and with growth in point-to-point traffic from regional airports promoted by volume carriers and their allies as an alternative to the hub-and-spoke model favoured by legacy carriers and hub airports.

This chapter uses the notion of a 'coalition', namely a collection of organizations working together for a common purpose, to explore the expansion of the aviation industry; the chapter begins with an introduction to the concept of growth coalitions. Common agendas, partnerships, discourse and conflict are identified, and are, it is argued, the glue that binds the coalition together; each of these are discussed in turn. Membership of the aviation growth coalition consists of airlines, airports, manufacturers as well as government actors at a variety of scales. In the concluding section we demonstrate that environmental objectives are secondary to aviation expansion, with technology seen as the primary mechanism for meeting those environmental goals.

Growth coalitions: Governance for aviation expansion

The past decade has seen a decentralization of the UK's political system, with the creation of new structures for urban and regional governance. In England, regional development agencies were founded in 1999, with primary responsibility for driving regional regeneration, integrating the work of national, regional and local partners in economic development (DETR, 1998). Proximity and intimate knowledge of a region's problems and resources, and more intimate engagement with business, should arguably lead to better targeting of spending than by a central department, and hence more effective policies for economic development (DTLR, 2002). This rescaling of government functions, and re-emergence of the region, results in more complex, less institutionalized policy delivery, emphasizing governance as opposed to government. Government has relied on diverse, non-state actors to implement policy, and from an economic perspective, this approach assumes that ties must be forged with business interests to mobilize resources and promote economic growth (Pierre and Stoker, 2002).

From an aviation perspective, the AWP sets out a clear mandate for expansion, based on an economic argument. Airports are required to develop master plans that meet a specified level of passenger demand, with regional development agencies able to fund route development, working with airports and airlines to facilitate growth and meet the demands of the AWP. Airports are not owned by the UK Government, but are privately owned; therefore central government is not able to expand capacity in line with the AWP itself, but necessarily downscales policy implementation to the regional and local scales, with other actors relied upon to achieve policy objectives. This typifies the move from government to governance, due to 'an emphasis on national competitiveness', with a 'recognition of the role of sub-national production complexes' (Harding, 2005, p69).

Underpinning implementation of the AWP is therefore the need for actors to act collectively, and we argue that the notion of 'coalitions' provides a useful framework for exploring aviation growth in this context. A coalition can be thought of as a collection of organizations, state and non-state, working together for a common purpose. Given the economic drivers for the expansion of aviation, we loosely use a notion of a 'growth coalition', principally associated with the work of Logan and Molotch in the US (Molotch and Logan, 1984; Logan and Molotch, 1987). Logan and Molotch argue that local economic development is driven by landlords who seek to mobilize the powers of local government to attract inward investment and create a business environment conducive to economic growth. Membership of the 'urban growth coalition' would include local elites, land interests, local political leaders and other local actors such as local media or educational establishments. The growth coalition discussed here is not focused on a specific locality, or even a spatial scale, but is instead focused on an economic sector, namely the aviation sector, where diverse actors join forces to achieve government-sponsored growth.

Economic changes over the past two decades or so, such as growing competition between areas for inward investment, changing frameworks for urban governance and the emergence of partnerships between the public and private sectors for delivering development activities, have seen the UK's systems for local development activities converge with those in the US (Wood, 1996). Thus, while the growth coalition concept originated in the US, a number of studies have sought to apply the model to understanding UK case studies (see for example, Axford and Pinch, 1994; Strange, 1997; or Ward, 2000) with some deeming the framework to offer useful insights in an UK context (e.g. Harding et al, 2000). That said, the usefulness of the concept applied within the UK is contested, with Wood (2004) offering a comprehensive review of this debate. To summarize the limitations, the emphasis on local economic development within the model does not fully explain the patterns of involvement of interests within development activities, and suggests wider motivations. Moreover, differences in UK and US political systems may restrict the applicability.

When considering aviation growth, however, the dominant agenda for aviation in the UK is firmly focused on growth, and while the regional scale is in many ways more important than the local, activities are geographically grounded. Two of the major themes of the US model are the mobilization of local government to attract investment, and competition between regions (Wood, 1996), which as we will demonstrate are important features of coalition activities. With these points in mind, we deem the approach to offer a useful framework within which to explore aviation growth.

A coalition can be thought of as a group of competing, sometimes even conflicting actors, using their resources and working together for a common purpose, in this case the expansion of aviation. The features of a coalition emphasized within the literature are (see Sabbatier, 1988; Marsh and Rhodes, 1992; Hajer, 1995):

- the use of resources in working together to towards a common agenda;
- partnerships;
- a shared discourse;
- a combination of cooperation and conflict, with different members of the coalition having different motivations.

Using a combination of interview and written material, each of these features are explored as we identify the members of the aviation growth coalition.

A national aviation growth agenda

The strategic framework for the future development of the UK's airports is set out within the Aviation White Paper (AWP), published in 2003. The AWP makes the economic case for the expansion of UK airports and forecasts future passenger numbers, rising from some 200 million passengers passing through UK airports in 2003 to between 400 and 600 million passengers by 2030 (DfT, 2003). These figures are based on 'unconstrained' (demand-led) capacity assumptions in the sense that no deliberate demand reduction policies are included, with the AWP cautioning that lack of sufficient capacity at airports will constrain growth, and impact on future economic growth and competitiveness. The original forecasts were further updated in 2006, based on new assumptions, e.g. in relation to changing market structure, and although actual passenger numbers in 2005 were in line with the 2003 forecasts, unconstrained demand projections were lower at between 440 and 530 million passengers (DfT, 2006). The additional development of airports as outlined within the AWP is deemed insufficient to support the projected growth, and a constrained level of demand of 465 million passengers is forecast for the medium case scenario (DfT, 2006).

Commissioning an economic case for expansion

The economic case for the AWP, that is the provision of knowledge and evidence to support a pro-growth policy, was not produced independently of those who will benefit from policy. In the update to the AWP, the economic case for development of UK airports is made based on a study by Oxford Economic Forecasting (OEF) assessing the economic benefit of aviation to the UK. The work was commissioned not only by the Department for Transport (DfT), but also by organizations with a stake in the UK aviation industry (OEF, 2006, p9). The impartiality of OEF is not questioned, instead the intention is to highlight that the motivation for the generation of this knowledge was not neutral intellectual interest. It is often the case in policy studies and environmental campaigns that NGOs themselves commission studies to inform and support their causes. Our point is not that this should not happen, but to emphasize the way in which this knowledge generation can substantially shape government policy processes when the commissioning actors are aligned with government interests.

In the OEF study, aviation is deemed to be a substantial industry, contributing 1.1 per cent of GDP in 2004, and supporting 186,000 direct, and 520,000 indirect (along the supply chain and intermediaries) and induced (as a result of the income of those employed in the industry) jobs (OEF, 2006). Estimates of indirect and induced jobs are, however, estimated using a multiplier from the number of direct jobs created, an aspect of methodology particularly susceptible to critique and illustrating succinctly how alternative assumptions may be used by supporters and opponents of aviation expansion (SACTRA, 1999; Whitelegg, 2003).

OEF (2006) state that the key benefits to the UK economy from aviation result from tourism and trade, with air links considered a crucial factor in attracting inward investment, particularly in growth sectors such as the knowledge economy and increasing the efficiency of business – by, for example, increasing the size of the available market. The report also looks to downplay the impact of UK carbon emissions from aviation upon the climate, stating that at present UK aviation 'is a fairly minor contributor to total UK CO_2 emissions' (OEF, 2006, p84). Taking a value of £70 per tonne of carbon, and using an uplift factor for the non-CO_2 impacts of aviation, the cost of CO_2 emissions from UK aviation in 2002 are estimated to be £1.4 billion, rising to £4 billion by 2030 for the central AWP passenger projections. Comparing the CO_2 emission costs of elements of airport development set out in the AWP with estimates of the economic benefit arising from the expansion, OEF make the case that these CO_2 emissions amount to 5 per cent of the economic benefit accrued (OEF, 2006).

The AWP adds to the economic case for expansion by comparing the constraints of London airports, particularly Heathrow, with the expansion of hub capacity in other EU countries, namely the Netherlands (Amsterdam Schiphol), France (Paris Charles de Gaulle) and Germany (Frankfurt). Heathrow currently has the highest number of passengers of any European airport, but with demand in excess of runway capacity, demand is rising more slowly than at other UK airports, and the route network is largely static. Consequently DfT have cautioned, as a justification for expansion, that its role may diminish compared to other EU airports, particularly with the advent of open skies agreements, with a knock-on effect for the UK economy.

Beyond making the case for the expansion of the aviation industry, the AWP puts into place a framework for its implementation, through the use of airport master plans and route development funds. Each of these is discussed in turn below.

Strategic use of airport master plans

The AWP mandates airport operators to produce an 'airport master plan' setting out how the airport intends to take forward the strategic framework for aviation as set out in the White Paper. The master plan should contain forecasts of traffic, and outline how an airport intends to make best use of existing capacity as well as proposals for increasing capacity. Plans should contain block layouts for land use plans up to 2015–2016, but less detailed land use layout with text description for up to, and beyond 2030. Access infrastructure requirements, integration with adjacent development, and environmental and social impacts should be considered. In addition to ensuring strategic thinking about future development, the master plan is intended to inform local and regional planners of the airport's plans and to facilitate communication with stakeholders. The plan must therefore be written in the context of relevant regional spatial strategies (RSSs) and local development frameworks (LDFs), which in turn have to take into account the master plan when they are updated. Given the importance attached to the role of airports as drivers of economic regeneration at the regional scale, regional development agencies are also expected to take the conclusion of the AWP into account in their investment plans.

A master plan is not a statutory document;[1] therefore while it will be subject to a process of consultation and review, this is unlikely to be as representative and rigorous as required for RSS and LDF planning documents. Given, however, that master plans have to be taken into account within the development of statutory plans, over time, they are likely to achieve a level of legitimacy through this inclusion in broader policies. In this way, the DfT is setting the agenda for the expansion of aviation, and its passenger forecasts will become enshrined within the policy framework at all scales, without other scales having to prepare specific, and statutory plans as for other areas of national need, such as minerals.

Air traffic forecasts and other data contained within master plans are also included in the forecasting processes of the UK's air traffic control service operator to enable the management of airspace. Individual master plans allow a breakdown of growth projections to the regional scale to enable bottlenecks in capacity to be identified. Given that one of the statutory responsibilities of air traffic control is to provide the airspace capacity to meet predicted growth (in AWP and master plans), this is another manner in which the AWP projections are becoming normalized.

Assistance from local authorities and agencies

The AWP also allows for regional governments to set up 'route development funds' to support routes to a regional airport that may be desirable from the perspective of economic benefit to the region, but less attractive to an airline, due to, for example, slot constraints. Such funds have been established by the Scottish Executive, the Northern Irish office and the North East Development Agency which has helped establish three new routes from the region to the EU (DfT, 2006). The Scottish Executive fund, for example, provided £6.8 million, with 35 routes operating in January 2008 (Scottish Executive, 2008). Geographically peripheral local authorities may, at the extreme, even purchase an airline if this is perceived to be in their vital economic interest: in May 2003 British Airways announced that it was planning to end its Gatwick–Guernsey route, which is important for business links, particularly for the offshore finance sector. Aurigny Air Services, an airline based in the Channel Islands, were prepared to take over the route, but only on the condition that no additional financial risk was accrued by shareholders. Faced with this situation, the States of Guernsey (the local authority) took Aurigny into public ownership to safeguard the island's link with both the UK mainland and France.[2]

More commonly, incentives may be offered by airports, regional development agencies and chambers of commerce to encourage a carrier to land locally, though subject to EU State Aid rules. Following an EU Commission ruling in relation to payments received by Ryanair to support services to Charleroi airport in Belgium and Strasbourg airport in France, a distinction is made between publicly and privately owned airports (Europa, 2004). A privately owned airport is able to offer incentives to encourage an airline to land there, for example a reduction in landing rates. By contrast a publicly owned airport is only able to offer airlines support with the costs of marketing flights to that airport; other payments, such as reduced landing rates or payments for opening new routes, are deemed to be discriminatory and anti-competitive, supporting one airline over another, thus contravening State Aid rules. There may also be penalties if a promised level of demand is not met: budget airline Flybe advertised for actors to fill seats on a route from Norwich to Dublin to avoid a £280,000 penalty charge for not carrying 15,000 passengers on the route before 31 March 2008 (BBC, 2008).

One of the key drivers of agreements between airports and airlines is the desire to increase the throughput of people with money to spend in the airport itself. In many ways, the modern airport is as much a shopping and entertainment centre as a transport hub, with revenue from these activities (and car parking) being an important element of the balance sheet. In 2006/2007, for example, BAA had retail revenue of £726 million compared to revenue from aircraft landing charges of £820 million (BAA, 2008). Over and above the importance of tourists and the money that they spend, local economies, regional and local development organizations are also looking to attract inward investment and associated jobs so the proximity of an airport with a good network of routes is a key source of competitive advantage.

In short, it is clear that actors at a variety of scales are working together towards an agenda of aviation expansion in the UK, within the strategic framework set out within the AWP. Aviation expansion is seen as an important driver of economic development at national, regional and local scales. For a specific airport, master plans set out the strategic framework to meet a given level of capacity, and these become normalized through inclusion in statutory plans at other scales. Regional administrations are able to incentivize the development of new routes, as are local authorities and other economic actors such as chambers of commerce. The role of joint working through partnerships will now be considered.

Sectoral partnerships

Within the aviation sector, partnerships are primarily focused on reducing the environmental impact of aviation through new technology. Some of the partnerships can be considered formal, in that they operate through a constituted and funded organization, such as Greener by Design or ACARE. Others are looser examples of organizations working jointly together to achieve a specific aim, for example mixed-mode operation at Heathrow (BAA and NATS) or biofuel innovation (Virgin Atlantic, General Electric, Boeing and Imperium Renewables). Examples of different types of partnership initiatives in the aviation sector are outlined below.

Industry-wide environmental performance

ACARE, the Advisory Council for Aeronautics Research in Europe, was established in 2001 to develop and maintain a strategic research agenda (SRA) for aeronautics in Europe. Membership comprises member states, the EU Commission and stakeholders, including manufacturers, airlines, airports, service providers, regulators, research establishments and academia. ACARE has developed a SRA that sets out a vision for aviation in 2020 and how these goals may be achieved. Focusing on quality and convenience, safety and environment, the SRA sets out specific targets in all these areas, with the environmental targets consisting of:

- reducing CO_2 emissions by 50 per cent per passenger kilometre;
- reducing NO_x emissions by 80 per cent;
- reducing perceived aircraft noise by 50 per cent (ACARE, 2001).

The ACARE targets have been adopted at the national scale in the UK by the Department of Trade and Industry's (DTI's) Aerospace Innovation and Growth Team, and Greener by Design who describe them as 'challenging, but the laws of physics do not ... make them unattainable' (Greener by Design, 2005, p2).

Greener by Design is itself described as a coalition 'dedicated to sustainable aviation'. It was formed in 1999 by the Airport Operators Association, the British Air Transport Association, the Royal Aeronautical Society and the

Society of British Aerospace Companies (SBAC). The coalition brings together experts from every part of the aviation industry with government bodies and research institutions to 'seek practical and environmentally and economically sustainable solutions to the challenge posed by aviation's impact on the environment'. Solutions are not confined to technology, with operational, economic and regulatory options also considered. The work is funded by the Department for Business, Enterprise and Regulatory Reform and numerous companies in the aviation sector. The coalition is pro-growth, with speed essential to counter the 'threat to the growth in air travel that arises from its environmental impact' (Greener by Design, 2005, p2).

Capacity constraint relief projects

A further example of a national-scale partnership is that involved in the planned switch to mixed-mode operation at Heathrow, where the airport operator, BAA, and National Air Traffic Control (NATS) are working together. Heathrow's two runways currently operate alternately, with planes taking off from one, and landing on the other; under mixed-mode operation, planes would take off and land on the same runway. Mixed-mode operation was identified in the UK AWP (DfT, 2003) as a means of increasing the capacity of Heathrow, and initial technical studies have been performed by NATS. Such changes to operating practices are the subject of public consultations, with a response (at the time of writing) awaited for the 'Adding capacity at Heathrow' consultation that closed in February 2008. The primary mandate for air traffic control is safety, and measures to reduce congestion at airports address this mandate. Mixed mode also has the potential to reduce either per-aircraft and/or per-passenger emissions by reducing the time that planes are in the air (though of course additional flights would in time negate these efficiency gains in emissions terms). From DfT's point of view, however, as stated within the UK AWP and in Heathrow mixed-mode consultation documents, mixed mode is seen as essential to increase capacity, either overall, or at peak times, as constraints at Heathrow are 'damaging UK interests, not only in aviation but more widely across the economy' (DfT, 2007, p6).

Single technology innovations

Technological innovation may also be the focus of less institutionalized and more bilateral partnerships than the ACARE or Greener by Design examples. An example at the international scale: Virgin Atlantic, General Electric, Boeing and Imperium Renewables are working together to drive and test innovation in biofuels, with a passenger jet flying between London and Amsterdam on 24 February 2008 (Boeing, 2008) with one of the four engines biofuelled. This flight is seen as a breakthrough, given that until this initiative was launched, it was considered to be highly unlikely that biofuels would break through as an aviation fuel within 30 years (RCEP, 2002; Saynor et al, 2003; Bows et al, 2006). It also demonstrates that partnerships can drive innovation once the industry has the will to do this.

This section has identified a number of examples of aviation organizations working in partnership, with a focus on technological developments to reduce the impacts on the environment. A common theme across these examples, to be returned to later, is the role of technology in addressing the environmental impacts of an expanding aviation industry.

Evidence of coalitions in aviation discourse

Further evidence for the presence of a coalition of organizations working to promote the expansion of aviation can be found by considering the discourse of key actors within the aviation industry. Hajer (1995, p60) defines discourse as 'a specific ensemble of ideas, concepts and categorizations that is produced, reproduced and transformed in a particular set of practices and through which meaning is given to physical and social realities'. Communication and argument are therefore of crucial importance for a coalition seeking to further its position by making the case for aviation expansion. The AWP is only the starting point for the case for expansion; the argument has to be won more widely, with the case for expansion being seen to win the debate with those seeking to curb growth. In previous sections, analysis of the AWP and the role of partnerships identified the following main themes:

- Aviation is important for the UK economy, and capacity must be increased to allow aviation expansion.
- Technology is the key to reducing the environmental impact of an expanding aviation industry.

On this theme, consensus around the role of environmental legislation, particularly EU ETS and air passenger duty (APD), has also emerged from interviews conducted with industry members. Each of these three themes of discourse (the economic case, technology and legislation) will be discussed in turn.

Aviation growth equals economic growth

The economic case for the expansion of aviation has been made in the AWP as outlined previously, with the following comments typical of support for this viewpoint:

> There is an unquestioned link between airport development and the economic activity that generates in the area as well. (Airport, interview)

The UK's position as a leading aviation nation is seen as threatened by capacity constraints, particularly at Heathrow, and there is a widespread view in the industry that these must be addressed (there is less agreement on which airports should grow to accommodate 'latent' demand – hence the AWP included four growth scenarios, one of which was the 'South-east

Constrained', in which regional airports grew at the expense of those in the south-east of England).

The advent of open skies agreements between the US and the EU and the increased range of modern aircraft are seen as a further threat to Heathrow, as these potentially enable other hub airports in the EU and Far East to capture a greater proportion of the US market. Outside London and the south-east, if capacity constraints are not reduced at Heathrow, feeder flights from regional airports to hubs outside the UK are expected to be a profitable alternative for those airports and countries, to the detriment of the UK:

> *Capacity has always been behind the curve for a long time so an airport like Heathrow is grotesquely overcrowded and it takes a lot of imagination and initiative, engineering genius to re-carve so that it works.* (Airport, interview)

> *Ideally Heathrow would be the hub airport, but that isn't going to happen... But, it could equally be done via Amsterdam. Doesn't have to be a UK airport.* (Airport, interview)

Overall, across the industry, support was expressed for the framework for growth outlined in the AWP, and this support was reasoned in economic terms.

Technological innovation equals reduced climate change impacts
In the light of the policy push behind the growth in aviation, it is unsurprising that technology, not demand reduction, is widely perceived as the key to reducing the environmental impact of an expanding industry. At the EU scale, ACARE and its fuel consumption targets are supported by airport operators, airlines and manufacturers alike:

> *The ACARE targets have accelerated the rates of progress.* (Manufacturer, interview)

> *The ACARE targets have tried to orient the industry.* (Manufacturer, interview)

> *Major gains are from technology.* (Technology developer, interview)

Similarly, support is evident for initiatives that accelerate the pace of innovation, both in terms of technology generally and alternative fuels:

> *We would love to change things every day, but we don't have enough money. If the government really wants green innovation it needs to fund it.* (Manufacturer, interview)

> *Technology breakthrough could deliver a 25 per cent reduction in carbon intensity by 2035.* (Manufacturer, stakeholder workshop)

> *Support is needed to develop third generation of biofuels. Sunlight and flash distilling of biofuels are key technologies.* (Airline, stakeholder workshop)

'EU ETS good (if properly designed), APD bad'

Overall, the inclusion of aviation in the EU ETS is seen by the pro-growth coalition as the right mechanism for achieving environmental objectives, because it impacts on the whole aviation system including airlines, airports, manufacturers, air traffic control and passengers, with the following comments typical:

> *It is an international regulation, treats all carriers the same way (legacy and volume), drives innovation.* (Trade organization, interview)

> *Certainty over environmental outcomes if linked to a cap.* (NGO, interview)

> *Push–pull effect so will drive innovation, and reduce demand... Cost of ticket will reflect the carbon price.* (Airport, interview)

However, concerns are expressed over the design of EU ETS and the fact that it is not global:

> *But because in practice it is not global, volume carriers will be penalized more than legacy.* (Trade organization, interview)

> *Will not have much effect as it is not global so you miss out a high proportion of the market.* (Manufacturer, interview)

Air passenger duty (APD) is an excise on the carriage of passengers from UK airports. APD has been levied since 1984, but was controversially doubled from the 1 February 2007. Although tabled by the Government as an environmental tax (HM Treasury, 2006), APD is almost universally (both within and without the pro-growth coalition) seen as a poor piece of legislation:

> *Poor as considers climate change at the national level.* (Airline, interview)

> *A blunt instrument.* (NGO, interview)

Not an environmental tax but to raise revenue, it has cost the industry £50 million. (Trade organization, interview)

Cooperation and conflict in the coalition

Analysis of the discourse surrounding aviation growth has highlighted the consensus among coalition members regarding the importance of aviation to the economy, the role of technology and the support for EU ETS over other environmental economic instruments. However, there are also tensions between actors, as expected, given that the coalition literature stresses that within a coalition power is not distributed uniformly. While actors may share an understanding of a policy problem, in this case the need for the expansion of aviation, and choose to cooperate to further this agenda, there will probably be conflict over other issues within the coalition (Hajer, 1996).

Indeed, within the pro-growth coalition, power is not distributed uniformly and there are tensions between the different agendas of groupings of stakeholders with different interests (airlines, airports, local economic development agencies, manufacturers and passengers). The interests of airports and airlines, clearly key components of the aviation system, have always been different but aligned and intertwined. The emergence of the low-cost airlines alongside the traditional charter airlines has caused a fragmentation within the expansion coalition, and a clear distinction can be made between groups of actors favouring a point-to-point model and those following a hub-and-spoke model. Within these two paradigms, volume carriers (the characteristics of which are discussed below) and hub airports hold power over other coalition members.

Volume carriers rely on maximizing revenue per flight, with secondary sales important to supplement the ticket price. Operating costs are minimized with low wages; low air fees; extensive use of external contracts for check-in and maintenance provision, which leads to lower costs; a homogeneous fleet to allow greater flexibility for standby crews and reduced training costs; and high resource productivity: short ground waits due to simple boarding processes, no air freight, no hub services, short cleaning times with cabin crew often carrying out cleaning operations. Point-to-point flights are favoured, and are aligned with regional airport growth, facilitated by local economic development alliances. Carriers provide a steady supply of flow-through customers for secondary sales within airports. Routes are fluid and flexible; new routes are opened and old ones closed. This is a continual process that may have implications for a location and airport if flights are abandoned. Carriers maintain tight control of their cost base, and are able to drive down costs due to asymmetric power over other actors (and employees). The technological strategy is to drive innovations and standardization by tightening performance specifications, for example on engine types. Mergers and acquisitions are used to increase route complementarity and the number of routes offered. Volume carriers have therefore influence and power over regional airports, their own members of staff, manufacturers, and even over air traffic control with respect to reducing delays and allowing ground and airspace for point-to-point operations.

Volume carriers do not aim to operate out of hub airports, which prioritize flights from the main regional airports that feed large planes and onward international connections. Given the capacity constraints at Heathrow, the UK's major hub airport, the supply of slots lags behind demand and slots are a highly valuable commodity. The scarcity of slots, combined with the premium that can be charged for seats from a hub airport, and the optimum positioning of Heathrow with respect to the jet stream gives the airport power over legacy carriers. For legacy carriers and hub airports, the air traffic control priority relates to ensuring that large aircraft can operate without delay.

The distinction between hub-and-spoke and point-to-point can also be seen in the future aircraft design planes of the two major manufacturers, Boeing and Airbus. With the A380, the world's largest passenger plane, capable of carrying 850 passengers, Airbus envisages a strong market for large planes to meet demand for long haul under constrained capacity. The latest Boeing design, the 'Dreamliner', has a smaller capacity of 210–330 passengers, and is catering for growth in medium haul. Little consensus emerged from our research as to whether future growth (and associated new technology) in point-to-point or hub-and-spoke would have the greatest impact on emissions.

Addressing the environmental agenda: Sustaining aviation, not sustainable aviation

In this chapter, we have applied the notion of growth coalitions to the UK aviation system to demonstrate that aviation expansion, as mandated in the AWP, is promoted by a coalition of actors. The AWP sets out a vision for the future of aviation, and a master plan framework through which airports will meet DfT growth projections. As master plans diffuse into statutory development plans at the local and regional scale, these demand-led assumptions will become normalized, and will achieve legitimacy without being subject to broader democratic debate.

The growth agenda is driven by regional and local scale development activities where regional development agencies and airports, keen to capture the perceived economic benefits from a competitive airport, offer inducements to entice airlines. The evidence for the existence of coalitions is provided by considering the joint activities engaged in by actors, the common agenda and the shared discourse. Tensions and conflict exist within the coalition, however, with competition between two business models, namely the point-to-point model of volume carriers and regional airports, and the hub-and-spoke model of legacy carriers and hub airports. Figure 12.1 is a schematic representation of the aviation growth coalition.

Given that the expansion agenda paradoxically coincides with the stated aim of the UK Government to be at the forefront of the fight against climate change, what are the implications for emissions reduction?

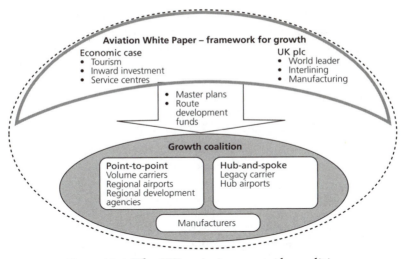

Figure 12.1 *The UK aviation growth coalition*

In terms of reducing the climate change impact of aviation, the agenda is clearly one of technology solutions as opposed to demand reduction. Although the scale of benefits of aviation to the UK economy is contested, the dominant discourse is one of a sector whose emissions are small in comparison to its climate impact. Reducing demand, the coalition discourse argues, will have impacts beyond airlines, given the importance of aviation to regional economic policy, and the revenue earned from airports themselves. The argument is also made that efforts to curb demand would impact disproportionately on poorer passengers, ignoring the evidence that higher- and middle-income passengers are flying more often as opposed to stronger growth in passengers from lower income groups (CAA, 2006).

In the coalition's thinking, although tempered by pro-environment rhetoric, climate change is perceived as a threat to the rate of aviation growth. Given that curbing growth is not considered, technology initiatives are focused on speeding up innovation in alternative fuels, improving air traffic management, engine technology to reduce fuel consumption, new materials etc. Within these boundaries, the industry argues that it is taking climate change seriously, and points to the innovations that have made considerable improvements in safety and noise impacts over the past decades as an example of what can be achieved when resources are focused on a problem. With the new climate change imperative, and given adequate resources, it is hoped that new aircraft technology will deliver a 50 per cent improvement in carbon emissions per passenger km by 2020. Moving beyond technology, competing business models claim to offer the optimum climate change solution. Volume carriers and regional airports argue that enabling passengers to fly point-to-point, in a new, fuel-efficient plane from their regional airport offers higher fuel efficiency than feeding a large plane at a hub airport. A similar claim for smaller climate impact is made by hub airports and legacy carriers.

The inclusion of aviation in the EU ETS has near universal support, although the scheme's structure is considered by volume carriers and their allies to favour legacy airlines. The design of the scheme, however, with aviation able to buy permits from other sectors, once again demonstrates that the aviation sector assumes a growth privilege over others in the economy. 'Government policy, supported by the industry, is that any such increases in emissions should be offset by lower emissions elsewhere through emissions trading covering the aviation sector' (OEF, 2006, p85). This is despite the fact that if the industry is allowed to trade emissions, EU ETS will have less of an impact on innovation than would have otherwise been the case.

Conclusion

To observers of the UK aviation industry, it is clear that UK aviation environmental policy is subordinate to the economic interests of a wide set of actors. Indeed, these are very definitely actors and not in any sense passive stakeholders. The AWP was explicitly researched and designed to support aviation growth in the UK for decades to come (in fact to 2030). It is intended to provide the policy support and ratification for the necessary physical infrastructure, and, at the time of writing (five years on from its publication), the AWP has resisted all attempts to prevent the realization of its vision. The AWP is the example par excellence of how a strong, multi-sector coalition can drive a public policy from inception to implementation, and be resistant to equally strong counter-arguments from environmental lobbyists, who lack the support of a similar coalition.

Acknowledgements

This work was funded by the Tyndall Centre for Climate Change research and we would like to thank them for this support. We would also like to thank Alice Bows who, as a member of the project team, carried out a number of the stakeholder interviews and helped develop the research. Thanks must also go to Paul Upham for editorial guidance and support and the industry interviewees without whom this work would not have been possible.

Notes

1   Unless the plan were to take the form of an area action plan for a given location or regeneration project.
2   See e.g. www.gov.gg/ccm/general/press-releases/2003/may/aurigny-purchase.en

References

ACARE (2001) 'European Aeronautics: A vision for 2020: Meeting society's needs and winning global leadership', report of the group of personalities
Axford, N. and Pinch, S. (1994) 'Growth coalitions and local economic development strategy in Southern England: A case study of the Hampshire Development

Association', *Political Geography* 13: 344–360

BAA (2008) available at www.baa.com/portal/page/Corporate%5EMedia+Centre%
5EFacts+and+figures/70c771e1c2d72010VgnVCM100000147e120a____/
448c6a4c7f1b0010VgnVCM200000357e120a____/, accessed 21 November 2008

Barrett, S. D. (2006) 'Commercialising a national airline: The Aer Lingus case study',
Journal of Air Transport Management 12: 159–168

BBC (2008) available at http://news.bbc.co.uk/1/hi/england/norfolk/7323212.stm,
accessed 12 August 2008

Boeing (2008) available at www.boeing.co.uk/ViewContent.do?id=34423&Year=2008,
accessed 21 November 2008

Bows, A. and Anderson, K. L. (2007) 'Policy clash: Can projected aviation growth be
reconciled with the UK Government's 60% carbon-reduction target?', *Transport
Policy* 14: 103–110

Bows, A., Anderson, K. and Upham, P. (2006) Contraction & Convergence: UK
carbon emissions and the implications for UK air traffic, Technical Report 40

CAA (Civil Aviation Authority) (2006) *No-Frills Carriers: Revolution or Evolution?*
CAP 770

DETR (Department of the Environment, Transport and the Regions) (1998)
Modernising Local Government: Local Democracy and Community Leadership,
London: Department of the Environment, Transport and the Regions

DfT (Department for Transport) (2003) *The Future of Air Transport*, CM 6046,
London: Department for Transport

DfT (2006) *Air Transport White Paper Progress Report 2006*, London: Department
for Transport

DfT (2007) *Adding Capacity at Heathrow Airport*, Consultation Document, London:
Department for Transport

DTLR (Department of Transport, Local Government and the Regions) (2002) *Your
Region, Your choice: Revitalising the English Regions*, London: Department of
Transport, Local Government and the Regions

Europa (2004) 'The Commission's decision on Charleroi airport promotes the activities
of low-cost airlines and regional development', available at
http://europa.eu/rapid/pressReleasesAction.do?reference=IP/04/157&format=HTM
L&aged=0&language=EN&guiLanguage=en, accessed 27 July 2008

Greener by Design (2005) *Mitigating the Environmental Impact of Aviation:
Opportunities and Priorities*, London: Royal Aeronautical Society

Hajer, M. (1995) *The Politics of Environmental Discourse: Ecological Modernisation
and the Policy Process*, Oxford: Clarendon Press

Hajer, M. (1996) 'Ecological modernisation as cultural politics', in Lash, S.,
Szerszynski, B. and Wynne, B. (eds) *Risk, Environment and Modernity: Towards a
New Ecology*, London: Sage, 246–268

Harding, A. (2005) 'Governance and socio-economic change in cities', in Buck, N.,
Gordon, I., Harding, A. and Turok, I. (eds) *Changing Cities*, Basingstoke: Palgrave,
pp62–77

Harding, A., Wilks-Heeg, S. and Hutchins, M. (2000) 'Business, government and the
business of urban governance', *Urban Studies* 37: 975–994

HM Treasury (2006) *Investing in Britain's Potential: Building Our Long-term Future*,
London: HM Treasury

Kangis, P. and O'Reilly, M. D. (2003) 'Strategies in a dynamic marketplace: A case
study of the aviation industry, *Journal of Business Research* 56: 105–112

Logan, J. and Molotch, H. (1987) *Urban Fortunes: The Political Economy of Place*,
Berkeley: University of California Press

Marsh, D. and Rhodes, R. A. W. (1992) *Policy Networks in British Government*, Oxford: Clarendon Press

Molotch, H. and Logan, J. (1984) 'Tensions in the growth machine: Overcoming resistance to value-free development', *Social Problems* 31: 483–499

OEF (Oxford Economic Forecasting) (2006) *The Economic Contribution of the Aviation Industry in the UK*, Oxford: Oxford Economic Forecasting

Pierre, J. and Stoker, G. (2002) 'Toward multi-level governance', in Dunleavy, P., Gambler, A., Heffernan, R., Holliday, I. and Peele, G. (eds) *Developments in British Politics*, 6, Basingstoke: Palgrave

RCEP (Royal Commission on Environmental Pollution) (2002) *The Environmental Effects of Civil Aviation in Flight*, Special Report, London: RCEP

Sabbatier, P. (1988) 'The advocacy coalition framework: Revisions and relevance for Europe', *Journal of European Public Policy* 5: 98–130

SACTRA (Standing Advisory Committee on Trunk Road Assessment) (1999) *Transport and the Economy*, London: Department of the Environment, Transport and the Regions

Saynor, B., Bauen, A. and Leach, M. (2003) *The Potential for Renewable Energy Sources in Aviation*, Imperial College Centre for Energy Policy and Technology

Scottish Executive (2008) available at www.scotexchange.net/partnership_working/tourism_initiatives/business_development_route_development_fund.htm#future, accessed 27 July 2008

Strange, I. (1997) 'Directing the show? Business leaders, local partnership, and economic regeneration in Sheffield', *Environment and Planning* 15: 1–17

Ward, K. W. (2000) 'From rentiers to "rantiers": "Active entrepreneurs", "structural speculators" and the politics of marketing the city', *Urban Studies* 37: 1093–1107

Whitelegg, J. (2003) *The Economics of Aviation: A North West England Perspective*, A report for CPRE

Wood, A. (1996) 'Analysing the politics of local economic development: Making sense of cross-national convergence', *Urban Studies* 33: 1281–1295

Wood, A. (2004) 'Domesticating urban theory? US concepts, British cities and the limits of cross-national applications', *Urban Studies* 41: 2103–2118

Part IV
Mitigation

13
Technical and Management Reduction Potentials

Paul Peeters, Victoria Williams and Alexander de Haan

Introduction

Most innovations in aviation were probably made in the first 50 years of its development (Kroo, 2004), with the difference between the Wright Flyer (first flight in 1903) and the Boeing 707 (first flight in 1954) being much larger than between the Boeing 707 and the Airbus A380 (first flight in 2005). Current technology on the market for the civil aviation sector is in effect mature. Furthermore, the strong increase of cost and risk involved with revolutionary innovative new aircraft programmes have become prohibitive factors (Kroo, 2004). Without financial or new regulatory or economic pressures to innovate, only incremental developments are likely in the near and medium future (Bows et al, 2006, p56).

This chapter describes what can be expected from technology and operational efficiency to reduce fuel consumption in air transport. First we will show how fuel efficiency developed during the jet age, and also before, and what prospects this gives for further improvements. Then we will assess several individual technologies that may increase fuel efficiency. The next section describes the options available to save fuel by improving the efficiency of flight operations and optimizing flight paths to avoid non-carbon impacts on the climate. Finally, we will briefly discuss the options open for further development of aviation within constraints set by the objective of avoiding dangerous climate change.

History and future of aviation fuel efficiency

Historical analysis of fuel efficiency

In 1999, the IPCC published a special report, *Aviation and the Global Atmosphere*, which contains a graph showing the development of the fuel efficiency of long-haul jet aircraft since their introduction in the 1950s (Penner et al, 1999, p298). Figure 13.1 reproduces the IPCC graph, but to complement the development of fuel efficiency, the energy intensity (E_I) of piston engine powered airliners such as the Lockheed Super Constellation L-1049, L1049H and L-1649G and the DC-7C has been added (see Peeters and Middel, 2007). It appears that the early jet aircraft had a much lower fuel efficiency than the last piston airliners. However, the new jets were faster, flew comfortably above the weather, and jet fuel was much cheaper than the high-grade fuels for pistons, so their replacement was fully rational from an economic point of view. Furthermore, the technology for jets developed fast, though it took until the 1980s before they became more fuel efficient than the early piston airliners.

The reduction of the energy intensity (EI), that is the energy consumption per available seat kilometre (ASK) measured as (MJ/ASK), to show the technological (transport) performance of individual aircraft or an aircraft fleet (Lee et al, 2001), is often modelled as:

$$E_I = E_{I_b} \cdot (1 - c_a)^{(Y - Y_{ref})} \qquad [1]$$

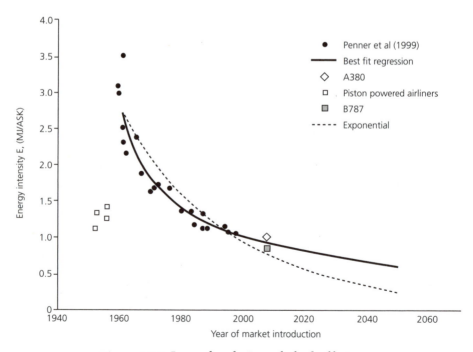

Figure 13.1 *Long-haul aircraft fuel efficiency*

where E_I is the energy intensity (unit MJ/ASK) and $(Y-Y_{ref})$ the number of years since a base year Y_{ref}. E_{I_b} is the energy intensity at the base year and c_a the annual (fractional) reduction of the energy intensity. The IPCC special report assumes values between 1.2 per cent and 2.2 per cent for c_a (Penner et al, 1999). However, as the line labelled 'Exponential' in Figure 13.1 – a 2.7 per cent average reduction over the period 1960–1990 – clearly shows, this model cannot represent the measured historical development. The annual gain of fuel efficiency declines year by year, because the technology matures. Therefore most authors assume that the constant decline is valid only for a shorter period and reduce the constant for the next period (e.g. 1.7 per cent between 2004 and 2010 and 1.2 per cent between 2010 and 2050 (Bows et al, 2006, p38); –0.87 per cent per year between 2010 and 2020 and then –0.5 per cent/year until 2050 (Fulton and Eads, 2004, p72); 2.0 per cent fuel efficiency per year improvement until 1992 and 1.5 per cent thereafter (Pulles et al, 2002, p53).

However, an advanced regression model could be developed using GraphFirst (Vasilyev, 2002) that fits all data with one set of parameters. The best fit was obtained with the 'sigmoidal (logistic 5)' regression developed by Gottschalk and Dunn (2005). As shown in Figure 13.1, the new Airbus A380 and the Boeing 787 Dreamliner (data taken from UNWTO, 2008) fit the sigmoidal regression.

This sigmoidal regression has the form:

$$E_I = E_{I_0} + \cfrac{C_{E_1}}{1 + \left(\cfrac{(Y - Y_{ref}) - C_1}{C_2} \right)^{\gamma}} \qquad [2]$$

where E_I is the energy intensity (MJ/ASK) and $(Y-Y_{ref})$ the number of years since a base year Y_{ref} (i.e. the year of introduction of a new technology or the starting year of the database), E_{I_0} is a theoretical minimum energy intensity and C_{E_1}, C_1, C_2 and γ are constants.

Fuel efficiency forecast

The sigmoidal model has been fitted for the long-haul only data from IPCC (Penner et al, 1999) and for a data set containing both long- and short-haul aircraft (Lee et al, 2001) (see Table 13.1).

Table 13.1 *Parameters as estimated with FindGraph (Vasilyev, 2002) for equation [2] and the two available time series*

Case	E_{I_0}	C_{E_1}	C_1	C_2	γ	Y_{ref}
IPCC individual long-haul aircraft data set (Albritton et al, 1997; Penner et al, 1999)	−0.2010	3.207	2.214	19.69	0.7183	1958
Lee individual long- and short-haul aircraft data set (Lee et al, 2001)	0.0446	2.855	2.213	19.69	0.7183	1958

Figure 13.1 shows that the common practice of a constant percentage reduction of energy consumption per year is less suitable for projections as it does not very well represent the economic and physical processes behind the development. In many studies this shortcoming is countered by using different 'constants' for different periods of time in the future. However, such a method leaves us with rather arbitrary choices. Therefore, one model able to represent the whole historical development with one set of parameters would help to reduce this uncertainty. The proposed sigmoidal model represents such a model. The IPCC data fit (long haul only) yields a 2040 EI of 0.658 MJ/ASK (35 per cent) reduction with respect to IPCC value in 2000), the Lee data (short and long haul) yields 0.810 MJ/ASK (28 per cent reduction with respect to the Lee value in 2000). These data are both lower than the constant reduction per year of 1.4 per cent proposed in some scenarios by Penner et al (1999), which would yield a reduction of 43 per cent in 40 years.

The presented data support the idea that most aviation technology developments are clearly driven by cost savings, productivity increases, safety improvements, increased range, and take-off and landing performance. Fuel burn is only one of the cost components. The transition from piston engines to gas turbines illustrates this clearly as it was made predominantly to increase aircraft speed and altitude and to some extent range. The transition increased transport efficiency in terms of revenue tonne kilometres per year as well as passenger appeal and comfort. As kerosene was much cheaper than the fuel used for piston-powered aircraft (avgas), the transition did not significantly raise fuel cost. However, the overall effect at the outset of this transition was higher energy intensity.

The pistons were at the end of their development cycle, so it would be wrong to suggest that a return to pistons would save any fuel over current jets. Nevertheless, high fuel prices will cause renewed attention for propeller-like propulsion systems such as ducted or unducted fans.

Limitations of aircraft technology

In determining the contribution of technology to the reduction of greenhouse gas emissions, it is not only the technology itself which is important. The development of total aviation-related emissions is also determined by the potential growth in air travel demand. The main issue is: can efficiency improvements keep up with the growth of air transport demand? First, several potential technologies are identified and their potential efficiency gains are described. Second, time frames are identified in which new technology can be developed, certified and implemented fleet-wide. Third, studies are identified that indicate air transport demand growth.

Identification of some promising technologies[1]

The aeronautical scientific literature was used to find options for reducing emissions. In addition interviews were held with technology researchers and developers. In this way, technologies were identified that within a certain time frame could be developed into real prototypes. The technologies are divided into categories. In random order these are: ultra high-capacity aircraft, high aspect ratio wings, composite materials, blended wing bodies, hydrogen fuel and propellers for high speed.

Ultra high-capacity aircraft aim to create economies of scale. The currently largest available aircraft, the Airbus A380, can host 550 passengers in a three-class configuration, and up to almost 800 passengers in an all-economy layout. A preliminary design study for an over-1000 passenger ultra high-capacity aircraft showed a reduction in fuel consumption (and thus CO_2 emissions) of roughly 10 per cent per seat kilometre (Blok et al, 2001). Disadvantages were also found, ranging from psychological resistance by both potential passengers and crew to fly with so many people together in one plane, to dimensional restrictions, as this aircraft would not fit the current 80 × 80m 'box' restriction for the largest aircraft that an airport can handle. A combination of this very large aircraft with high aspect ratio wings could give more fuel reduction (ideally up to an extra 10 per cent), although this would cause even more problems with the 80 × 80m box.

Another idea is to combine wing and fuselage in a configuration called blended wing body. This configuration leads to one construction responsible for both generating lift and containing the payload. Using new materials, this configuration could be lighter than a conventional aircraft with the same capacity and cause less drag. It may reduce CO_2 emissions per seat kilometre by 20 per cent (Bowers, 2000).

High by-pass ratio turbofan engines combine the power of the jet engine with the efficiency of the traditional propeller by putting a large fan on the engine shaft which, in addition to the high-speed jet stream, also accelerates cold air, but not up to such high speeds. By thinning the traditional propeller blades and curving them backwards, an efficiency increase of 20–25 per cent can be reached in comparison with current high-bypass turbofans (Jeracki and Mitchell, 1981). However, the development costs are enormous, and a serious economic incentive (like a very high oil price for a long period of time) will need to be present for a propeller to become reality at high flying speeds. Already with current oil prices there are indications that propeller-driven aircraft flying at lower altitudes at lower speed are economically attractive for the short haul (Dings et al, 2000).

New materials, such as composites, are lighter, but with comparable fatigue, strength, buckling and damage tolerance characteristics. Composites can consist of traditional aluminium in combination with fibres, but generally consist of fibres (e.g. carbon) and epoxy. Composites allow the construction of large panels and the omission therefore (to various extents) of classical riveted lap joints. The full-fibre materials can be wound and are expected to make possible the production of vessel-like shapes (such as fuselages) as a single component. Significant cost and weight reductions would then be possible.

Weight reductions of up to 30 per cent may result in fuel consumption reductions of 15 per cent per seat kilometre (Lee, 2003). Disadvantages are the increased complexity, cost of maintenance and repairs, and the difficulty of detecting potentially dangerous damage (Lee, 2003; Tempelman, 1998).

Development and fleet renewal

Aircraft reach a considerable age. Smaller aircraft that fly the shorter routes and feed the big hub airports are designed for typically around 100,000 flights (e.g. Fokker 50: 90,000 flights). Larger aircraft that fly long haul are designed for much fewer flight numbers. These 'designs in number of flights' combined with the usage of aircraft determines the lifespan of aircraft in years; 25 years is the minimum, 30 years is more common, but also many aircraft stay in service for more than 30 years.

New aircraft technology typically takes up to 10 years' development before the first aircraft is delivered to the customer. The new technology has to be operationalized into a preliminary design, a fully certified design, and a prototype must be built and extensively tested before a type certificate can be obtained. Then production can start and new aircraft can be delivered to the client. After that it will be at least another 25 years before the new technology will fully replace the old fleet and full benefit can be gained from the higher fuel efficiency.

Changes in renewal policies of the world aircraft fleet may reduce the average energy consumption per seat kilometre by up to 8 per cent for all aircraft with a design age older than 20 years (i.e. the age of a specific aircraft design as measured from its first year of introduction onto the market) (Pulles et al, 2002, p236). Due to the extra cost of this measure, an extra 4 per cent reduction of CO_2 emissions will be attained by reduction of demand, and the total cost will increase by about 1 per cent.

Growth in air travel demand

Each year, Airbus and Boeing present a report in which they forecast what the demand for air travel will be for the next 20 years (see, for instance, Airbus, 2007; Boeing, 2007). Typically air transport volumes are predicted to grow by 4–6 per cent per year. The latest forecasts up until 2026 do not encompass the time frame required for this new technology to fully replace an old aircraft fleet, as described earlier, because for that, forecasts up until 2050 are required.

There are several studies available for such forecasts, which of course differ in assumptions and outcomes. For a discussion of air travel demand growth, see for instance (Humphreys, 2003). The outcomes of the scenarios show demand growth (number of trips) by a factor ranging from 2.5 to approximately 10 times current aviation demand (Penner et al, 1999; Humpreys, 2003; de Haan, 2007). The lower growth scenarios assume, for instance, faster maturation of markets and increasing opposition to airport expansion. The question now is whether technologies can be found to keep up with the growth pace of aviation demand. The growth numbers above imply that an increase in fuel efficiency of at least 2.5 times is needed before 2050 to obtain technology that is capable of keeping up with growth, at least for the low-growth scenarios.

Obstacles and impediments

The fuel-saving technologies identified so far are all at least in the preliminary design phase and can thus potentially be further developed and implemented within the time frame of 2050. The word 'potential' is used because the aviation system is very resistant to revolutionary change and generally only adopts technologies that fit neatly into the current air transport system. Obstacles to implementation in general are caused by lock-in effects (de Haan, 2007): a certain technology could not be introduced without substantially changing the present main system elements (e.g. runways, fuel provisions, historically grown distributions of responsibilities and power etc.).

Many examples of such obstacles can be given. The introduction of ultra high-capacity aircraft is mainly hampered by the large airport investments required and by psychological resistance from both crew and passengers. Composite materials are still not mature technology; they require high development and certification costs. High aspect ratio wings also meet problems due to airport space limitations. Free flight (aircraft choosing their own optimal flight path instead of getting direction from ATC) requires complete redistribution of power. Reduced thrust take-off requires redistribution of power between crew and air traffic control. High-speed propellers suffer from a slightly lower speed that may disrupt current optimized schedules and lower comfort due to lower cruising altitudes and higher internal noise. However, current high fuel prices might induce renewed interest in propeller or ducted fan driven aircraft, as these are generally more fuel efficient. Hydrogen-fuelled aircraft face many caveats, such as the necessity of installing a completely new fuel system worldwide, the problem of carrying the very low-density fuel in a confined space, and the fact that the current aircraft performance paradigm – cruise speed, range etc. – are strongly based on high energy density kerosene. Blended wing bodies require completely new aircraft design, major redesign of airports, and face problems with evacuation requirements (everybody out within 90 seconds), given their wide bodies, their increased safety might not make that 90 seconds necessary.

An important obstacle is the investment risk. The market for new airliners is dominated by just two manufacturers and in such an oligopolistic situation it is not very likely one of them will take the full risk of developing a new aircraft model involving new, non-proven technology. Furthermore, safety requirements are very onerous, and the cost of testing completely new technologies is prohibitive.

Another important kind of obstacle looks to be psychological rather than rational. Re-introducing propeller aircraft might be considered old-fashioned, ultra high-capacity aircraft unsafe, and hydrogen fuel very dangerous (the so-called 'Hindenburg effect', referring to fear of burning hydrogen after media pictures of the burning Zeppelin *Hindenburg* in the 1930s). However, the reality is likely to be the opposite: modern ducted or unducted fans are high-tech, and opportunities to survive a crash may be increased in large aircraft. Hydrogen has been shown to be much less a hazard then kerosene, because it burns upwards and very rapidly, while kerosene flows burning all over the crash site and burns relatively slowly (see, e.g. Faass, 2001; Verfondern and Dienhart, 2007).

On the other hand there are also drivers for change. An obvious one is the invention of a new and fully commercially advantageous technology. An example was the invention of the jet engine. After launch of the first long-haul jets (mainly DC-8 and B707), the brand new piston engine aircraft were almost completely removed from passenger services within a decade. The pressures for this change were a combination of passenger appeal, lower cost and higher speeds. This illustrates that revolutions may happen, but only with an exogenous incentive, an external driving factor that strongly influences the development of the technology. Such incentives may be a very strong rise in oil prices, a tightly capped emissions trading system, or strict government regulation.

Finally we need a word on alternative fuels. Hydrogen has been discussed above. We may add to this that the impact of air transport on the climate shifts from the aircraft to hydrogen production facilities. Currently the cheapest way to produce hydrogen is from coal, but of course this method releases large amounts of CO_2. Biofuels theoretically have some potential to reduce overall emissions, but so far the first generation of biofuels has generated several environmental and economic problems, among them deforestation and undesirably high food prices. For an extensive discussion on biofuels see Chapter 14 of this volume. For all biofuels it seems that the enormous amount of space required is too great to cover the future increasing energy demands of air transport (let alone of all transport).

Operational measures to reduce radiative forcing

Operational measures can contribute to reducing radiative forcing by aviation in two ways. The first is by reducing the distance flown, by improving the systems for air traffic navigation and management. The second is by enabling optimized flight trajectories to minimize specific radiative impacts.

Improving fuel efficiency using air traffic management measures

Changes in the way air traffic is controlled will contribute to reducing emissions from aviation. Currently, aircraft fly significantly further than the direct route between the departure and arrival airports. Ground-based navigation systems mean flight plans are defined as a sequence of fixed points. These make use of predefined routes, designed to facilitate the work of controllers by limiting the number of entry and exit points to an air traffic control sector, and to reduce the complexity of the traffic. In Europe particularly the legacy of national sovereignty over airspace means that existing sectors and routes do not favour direct routing or fuel efficiency, resulting in a system that is inefficient and costly (Majumdar et al, 2004; Helios Economics Policy Services, 2006). Globally, addressing inefficiencies in air traffic management could reduce CO_2 emissions per flight by up to 12 per cent (Penner et al, 1999). Airport capacity constraints also increase flight distance and emissions, particularly when aircraft are forced to circle before landing.

Some forthcoming changes include interim steps to increase capacity while using existing systems. Others will radically change the relationship between pilots and controllers. Changes to communication, navigation and surveillance systems could deliver more direct routing, reduced taxi-out delay, and reduced arrival delay. These improvements are expected to deliver a 5 per cent reduction in CO_2 emissions by 2015 for the ECAC states (ICAO, 2000), with the largest contribution coming from improvements in en-route flight trajectories. A similar annual reduction is expected for the US, but with a greater reduction in emissions coming from surface movements (ICAO, 2000).

En-route airspace will be reorganized to improve the division of airspace and the design of routes. With improved navigation and surveillance systems, the required separation between aircraft could be reduced. Air traffic control sectors will also be redesigned to take better account of traffic flows. For example, a dedicated 'highway' could isolate traffic on a key route in a single tube-shaped sector, reducing both crossing points and the need to pass the control of the aircraft between controllers at each conventional sector boundary, which is a significant contributor to controller workload. The size of sectors could also be adjusted dynamically in response to changes in demand (European Commission, 2003).

Route network optimization allows the system to respond to changes in demand and in aircraft technology. In 2006, route optimization measures on 350 routes reduced CO_2 emissions by 6 million tonnes, 0.9 per cent of the global total in that year (IATA, 2007). As new communication, navigation and surveillance technologies are introduced, the existing route structure will eventually become redundant. Free routing will be the first step, with aircraft selecting preferred routes but remaining under air traffic control. Between 2015 and 2020, designated regions of free flight airspace are expected to be introduced, with pilots taking on responsibility for maintaining separation (EUROCONTROL, 2003).

These moves towards direct routing could provide greater fuel efficiency and so reduce emissions for a specific flight. However, increasing capacity and reducing journey times could reduce cost and induce demand, which would offset any environmental benefit. Non-CO_2 radiative impacts, discussed below and in more detail in Chapter 3, may also grow faster than CO_2 emissions.

Reducing radiative impacts of aviation through cruise altitude selection

New approaches to air traffic management can contribute to reducing non-CO_2 climate impacts. For both NO_x emissions and contrails, the radiative impact depends on the cruise altitude (Köhler et al, 2008; Rädel and Shine, 2008), so improving the flexibility of routing could, in the long term and provided the capacity of ATC is increased, facilitate the selection of lower impact routes.

At cruise altitudes, NO_x increases ozone but reduces methane, so it makes both a positive and a negative contribution to radiative forcing. Below 30,000ft an increase in globally averaged NO_x emission has a net negative (cooling) effect. For cruise altitudes above 30,000ft, the positive forcing effect of an injection of NO_x increases with altitude (Köhler et al, 2008). Cruise altitude also affects the emission factor (the amount of NO_x emitted per kg of fuel) and the fuel efficiency, so these three altitude responses must be considered together to identify the flight trajectory associated with the lowest NO_x impact.

The radiative effect of an increase in linear contrail increases with altitude up to 10.5km (Rädel and Shine, 2008). Contrail formation conditions are also altitude dependent. Even small changes in the flight trajectory can prevent a contrail forming. Persistent contrails form in regions where the air is supersaturated with respect to ice. These regions vary in size, but are typically thin layers with a mean thickness of 560m (Spichtinger et al, 2003), suggesting that a small change in the flight level would allow the layer to be avoided (Mannstein et al, 2005). The mean path length of an aircraft through an ice-supersaturated region has been estimated to be 150km (Gierens and Spichtinger, 2000), so avoidance strategies which use small altitude changes are likely to have a smaller fuel burn (and CO_2 emission) penalty than diverting around the contrail formation region.

There are some key barriers to delivering reductions in the climate impacts of aviation through operational means (Williams et al, 2007). One is the scientific challenge in comparing and prioritizing between impacts – radiative forcing is only one available metric and must be used with caution when considering impacts with different spatial and temporal patterns. For contrail avoidance, the prediction of supersaturated regions is a technological challenge. Another issue is the burden placed on controllers, particularly given existing capacity constraints (Williams et al, 2002). There is also no current economic incentive for airlines to consider climate impacts from NO_x or contrail in flight planning. These barriers would need to be overcome before changes in flight trajectory could contribute to reducing aviation's climate impacts.

Eco-efficiency and a strategy for air transport

Several metrics can be used to measure the efficiency of aviation. Common ones are emissions per passenger kilometre (kg/pkm) and emissions per seat kilometre (kg/skm). The first gives an operational efficiency as it includes the occupancy rate; the second gives a technical (potential) efficiency. However, eco-efficiency is defined as the economic gain per unit of environmental cost (Heijungs, 2007) or environmental pressure per € of revenue (Gössling et al, 2005). Eco-efficiency helps to discover how economic growth can be achieved with the lowest possible level of emissions. Theoretically, the former definition applied to CO_2 emissions and aviation would mean that eco-efficiency is defined in terms of € per $kgCO_2$ emissions, the latter one $kgCO_2$ emissions per €. The former is theoretically better as it is similar to the term efficiency as used in thermodynamics (work produced divided by work done). Also greater eco-efficiency (more € per $kgCO_2$) will indicate the preferable case. However, the second definition is preferable practically as it avoids the problem of dividing by zero in case of no environmental damage (i.e. the zero emissions case; in physics this problem never arises as it is not possible). Therefore we adopt the second definition.

The concept of eco-efficiency can be used for strategic decisions regarding air transport and climate change. The main objective of any company is to grow its turnover and make a reasonable profit. Growth can be obtained in several ways. Current growth of air transport is fuelled by reducing cost and increasing total transport demand. The low-cost carriers reduce costs by abolishing all free onboard services, selling only e-tickets online and offering only one-class high-density cabin layouts. Also these airlines reduce on-ground time to the very limits and they offer only point-to-point connections, without optimizing a network. Finally these airlines use strong variants of yield management, offering some tickets at very low prices to boost demand. The effect of this strategy has been a reduction of price perception of air transport by some 25–30 per cent below average prices (Nawijn et al, 2007).

The load factor and seat density of aircraft can significantly alter the fuel consumed per seat kilometre, and vary extensively between airlines. For example, Boeing offers the 777-300 with 368–500 seats; the Airbus A320 is fitted with 150 seats as standard, but carries 179 in a single-class layout. A fleet average comparison of airlines flying to Swedish airports gives energy consumption per seat kilometre ranging from 0.82MJ for Ryanair, up to 1.25MJ for British Airways (Peeters, 2007). Low-cost carriers typically use the highest densities in addition to having the highest load factors. Therefore LCCs fly at the highest fuel efficiency per passenger kilometre. However, this does not mean that these airlines have the best eco-efficiency. For easyJet we found emissions of 95.6g per passenger kilometre (easyJet plc, 2008, p24). The revenues per seat kilometre were £0.0413 at 83.7 per cent load factor (easyJet plc, 2008, p13) and thus £0.0493 per pkm. For BA we found a revenue of £0.064 per pkm in 2006/2007 (British Airways, 2007, p1), 30 per cent more than for easyJet. Total CO_2 emissions for BA in 2006 were 16.62 million tonnes (British Airways, 2007, p24). Total revenue tonne kilometres were 15,909 million of which 4929 were cargo (British Airways, 2007, p33). This would mean that 69 per cent of the emissions can be attributed to passenger transport. However, passengers normally require more space than cargo. Total passenger transport volume was 109.7 billion pkm, thus 105g/pkm. It is clear that the eco-efficiency of BA at 1.64kg/£ is 15 per cent more favourable than of easyJet at 1.94kg/£.

Furthermore, the overall impact of a change from the conventional airline business model to the LCC model is extra growth of total air transport emissions, because the overall reduction of costs compared to flag carriers is 30 per cent larger than the reduction of fuel consumption per pkm at 9 per cent. This means that – assuming an elasticity of about –1.0 (Brons et al, 2002) – demand grows faster than the fuel efficiency improves. It seems to us that a strategy focusing on high-quality air transport instead of high-volume transport will provide better opportunities for economic growth under conditions of strict restriction on CO_2 emissions, although equity and mobility issues should not be overlooked.

Conclusions

This chapter has reviewed the technical and management reduction potentials for reducing emissions from aviation. Aircraft and engine improvements have historically delivered emission reductions, but are reaching maturity. Technology can reduce the emissions of CO_2 from aviation when measured in $kgCO_2$ per seat kilometre. Up to 50 per cent reduction in CO_2 emissions per seat kilometre is technologically attainable with the current aircraft paradigm (i.e. tube-like fuselage, turbofan engines running on kerosene, and wings optimized for cruising speeds near the speed of sound). However, the technological-economical aviation system is not likely to attain much more than 35 per cent reduction within the next four decades. Advanced air traffic management may add 10–15 per cent extra reductions. Finally airlines may choose to operate with higher-density cabin layouts, which can potentially reduce emissions per seat kilometre by another 10–25 per cent.

However, only the total amount of CO_2 emitted is important for the issue of climate change. As aviation demand will increase by 150–800 per cent by 2050, even the most optimistic scenario of combined technology, air traffic management and operational high-density seating will not be able to keep current emissions constant, let alone reduce them by the 50–80 per cent needed to avoid dangerous climate change (see Schellnhuber et al, 2006). Add to this that the rapid introduction of new technology and advanced air traffic management systems is hampered by several obstacles. These have in common a problem with 'sunk costs', that is large investments in the present infrastructure that become obsolete with new technology. Finally, a new and different technology needs several decades to develop and be certified and another three decades to be introduced into the whole fleet.

Without a (revolutionary) change to new technologies – a change comparable to the introduction of jet engines – it is unlikely that past rates of emission reduction can be replicated in the coming decades. Thus, even the best case scenarios for aircraft and air traffic management technologies do not allow for aviation to grow at its predicted rate without a continued significant rise in emissions. If society wants an absolute reduction of CO_2 emissions from aviation activities, in addition to technological and operational developments, there is no alternative to discussing and developing control of lifestyles (see also Chapters 3 and 6, this volume).

Note

1   This section is based on de Haan (2007).

References

Airbus (2007) *Flying by Nature: Global Market Forecast 2007–2026,* France: Airbus S.A.S.

Albritton, D., Amanatidis, G., Angeletti, G., Crayston, J., Lister, D., McFarland, M., Miller, J., Ravishankara, A., Sabogal, N., Sundararaman, N. and Wesoky, H. (1997) *Global Atmospheric Effects of Aviation,* Report of the proceedings of the symposium held on 15–19 April 1996 in Virginia Beach, Virginia, US, NASA CP-3351, Washington DC: NASA

Blok, G., El Bouzidi, N., Bruijn, P. d., Coninx, K. M., Geelhoed, P. J. M., Hermens, T. J. A. M., Heijkant, R. A. J. v. d., Lemmen, H. J. K., Meulen, J. v. d. and Sadée, C. (2001) *A3XL.* Delft: Faculty of Aerospace Engineering, Delft University of Technology

Boeing (2007) *Current Market Outlook 2007: How will You Travel through Life?,* Seattle: Boeing Commercial Airplanes Marketing

Bowers, A. (2000) *Blended Wing Body: Design Challenges for the 21st Century,* NASA Dryden Flight Research Center, TWITT meeting, 16 September

Bows, A., Anderson, K. and Upham, P. (2006) *Contraction and Convergence: UK Carbon Emissions and the Implications for UK Air Traffic,* Report 40, Norwich: Tyndall Centre for Climate Change Research

British Airways (2007) *2006/2007 Annual Report and Accounts,* Harmondsworth: British Airways

Brons, M., Pels, E., Nijkamp, P. and Rietveld, P. (2002) 'Price elasticities of demand for air travel: A meta-analysis', *Journal of Air Transport Management* 8 (3): 165–175

de Haan, A. R. C. (2007) *Aircraft Technology's Contribution to Sustainable Development,* PhD, Delft: Delft University of Technology Faculty of Technology, Policy and Management

Dings, J., Peeters, P. M., Heijden, J. R. v. d. and Wijnen, R. A. A. (2000) *ESCAPE: Economic Screening of Aircraft Preventing Emissions: Main Report,* Pub. code: 00.4404.16, Delft: Centrum voor Energiebesparing en Schone Technologie

easyJet plc (2008) *We're Turning Europe Orange: Annual Report and Accounts 2007,* Luton: easyJet plc

EUROCONTROL (2003) *Air Traffic Management Strategy for the Years 2000+,* Vols 1 and 2: EUROCONTROL

European Commission (2003) *Study on the Implementation Rules of Economic Regulation within the Framework of the Implementation of the Single European Sky, Final Report,* TREN/f2/28–2002 Brussels

Faass, R. (2001) *Cryoplane: Flugzeuge mit Wasserstoffantrieb,* available at www.mp.haw-hamburg.de/pers/Scholz/dglr/hh/text_2001_12_06_Cryoplane.pdf, accessed 31 October 2003

Fulton, L. and Eads, G. (2004) *IEA/SMP Model Documentation and Reference Case Projection,* Paris: International Energy Agency

Gierens, K. and Spichtinger, P. (2000) 'On the size distribution of ice-supersaturated regions in the upper troposphere and lowermost stratosphere', *Annales Geophysicae-Atmospheres Hydrospheres and Space Sciences* 18(4): 499–504

Gössling, S., Peeters, P. M., Ceron, J.-P., Dubois, G., Patterson, T. and Richardson, R. B. (2005) 'The eco-efficiency of tourism', *Ecological Economics* 54(4): 417–434

Gottschalk, P. G. and Dunn, J. R. (2005) 'The five-parameter logistic: A characterization and comparison with the four-parameter logistic', *Analytical Biochemistry* 343: 54–65

Heijungs, R. (2007) 'From thermodynamic efficiency to eco-efficiency', in Huppes, G. and Ishikawa, M. (eds) *Quantified Eco-Efficiency: An Introduction with Applications,* Dordrecht: Springer, pp79–103

Helios Economics Policy Services (2006) *The Impact of Fragmentation in European ATM/CNS,* Performance Review Commission, EUROCONTROL

Humpreys, I. (2003) 'Organizational and growth trends in air transport', in Upham, P., Maughan, J., Raper, D. and Thomas, C. (eds) *Towards Sustainable Aviation,* London: Earthscan

IATA (2007) 'Key priorities for developing next generation ATM systems', Speech by Giovanni Bisignani to the Civil Air Navigation Service Organization (CANSO) Conference, Maastricht, Netherlands, 13 February, available at www.iata.org

ICAO (International Civil Aviation Organization) (2000) *Environmental Benefits Associated with CNS/ATM Initiatives: Model for Assessing Global Aviation Emissions and Potential Reduction from CNS/ATM Measures,* available at www.icao.int/

Jeracki, R. J. and Mitchell, G. A. (1981) *Low and High Speed Propellers for General Aviation: Performance Potential and Recent Wind Tunnel Test Results,* Cleveland: National Aeronautics and Space Administration

Köhler, M. O., Rädel, G., Dessens, O., Shine, K., Rogers, H. L., Wild, O. and Pyle, J. A. (2008) 'Impact of perturbations to nitrogen oxide emissions from global aviation', *Journal of Geophysical Research* 113, in press

Kroo, I. (2004) 'Innovations in aeronautics', 42nd AIAA Aerospace Sciences Meeting and Exhibit, 5–8 January, Reno: AIAA

Lee, J. (2003) 'The potential offered by aircraft and engine technologies', in Upham, P., Maughan, J., Raper, D. and Thomas, C. (eds) *Towards Sustainable Aviation,* London: Earthscan, pp162–78

Lee, J. J., Lukachko, S. P., Waitz, I. A. and Schafer, A. (2001) 'Historical and future trends in aircraft performance, cost and emissions', *Annual Review Energy Environment* 26: 167–200

Majumdar, A., Ochieng, W. Y., McAuley, G., Lenzi, J. M. and Lepadatu, C. (2004) 'The factors affecting airspace capacity in Europe: A cross-sectional time-series analysis using simulated controller workload data', *Journal of Navigation* 57(3): 385–405

Mannstein, H., Spichtinger, P. and Gierens, K. (2005) 'A note on how to avoid contrail cirrus', *Transportation Research Part D: Transport and Environment* 10: 421–426

Nawijn, J., Dams, E. and Peeters, P. (2007) 'Airline price perception and sustainability', 16th Nordic Symposium in Tourism Research, 27–30 September, Helsingborg

Peeters, P. M. (2007) *Report on the Environmental Performance Class of Airlines Flying at Swedish Airports,* Breda: NHTV CSTT

Peeters, P. M. and Middel, J. (2007) 'Historical and future development of air transport fuel efficiency', in Sausen, R., Blum, A., Lee, D. S. and Brüning, C. (eds)

Proceedings of an International Conference on Transport, Atmosphere and Climate (TAC), Oxford, United Kingdom, 26–29 June 2006, Oberpfaffenhoven: DLR Institut für Physic der Atmosphäre, pp42–47

Penner, J. E., Lister, D. H., Griggs, D. J., Dokken, D. J. and McFarland, M. (eds) (1999) *Aviation and the Global Atmosphere; A Special Report of IPCC Working Groups I and III*, Cambridge: Cambridge University Press

Pulles, J. W., Baarse, G., Hancox, R., Middel, J. and van Velthoven, P. F. J. (2002) *AERO Main Report. Aviation Emissions and Evaluation of Reduction Options*, The Haag: Ministerie van Verkeer and Waterstaat

Rädel, G. and Shine, K. (2008) 'Radiative forcing by persistent contrails and its dependence on cruise altitudes', *Journal of Geophysical Research* 113, in press

Schellnhuber, J., Cramer, W., Nakicenovic, N., Wigley, T. and Yohe, G. (eds) (2006) *Avoiding Dangerous Climate Change*, Cambridge: Cambridge University Press

Spichtinger, P., Gierens, K., Leiterer, U. and Dier, H. (2003) 'Ice supersaturation in the tropopause region over Lindenberg, Germany', *Meteorologische Zeitschrift* 12(3): 143–156

Tempelman, E. (1998) *Sustainable Transport and Advanced Materials*, Haarlem: Eburon

UNWTO (2008) *Climate Change and Tourism: Responding to Global Challenges*, Madrid: UNWTO

Vasilyev, S. (2002) *FindGraph*, version 1.491, Vancouver: Uniphiz Lab

Verfondern, K. and Dienhart, B. (2007) 'Pool spreading and vaporization of liquid hydrogen', *International Journal of Hydrogen Energy* 32(2): 256–267

Williams, V., Noland, R. B. and Toumi, R. (2002) 'Reducing the climate change impacts of aviation by restricting cruise altitudes', *Transportation Research Part D: Transport and Environment* 7(6): 451–464

Williams, V., Noland, R. B., Majumdar, A., Toumi, R., Ochieng, W. and Molloy, J. (2007) 'Reducing environmental impacts of aviation with innovative air traffic management technologies', *The Aeronautical Journal* 111(1125): 741–749

14
Biofuels, Aviation and Sustainability: Prospects and Limits

Paul Upham, Julia Tomei and Philip Boucher

Introduction

Use of biofuel as a substitute or extender for mineral jet fuel (Jet A1 kerosene) has rapidly moved from a relatively niche research topic to mainstream attention, with Virgin Atlantic in 2007 announcing plans for biofuel tests with one of its 747s and then making a test flight with a 747 in February 2008, using fuel derived from a mixture of Brazilian babassu palm oil and coconut oil, with one of the four engines connected to an independent biofuel tank that could provide 20 per cent of the engine's power (BBC, 2008).

This chapter provides a broad overview of the issues relating to the use of biofuel as a Jet A1 substitute or extender. It is intended to provide the reader with an awareness of the main issues involved, not to provide a definitive view. Unfortunately most of the issues are problematic, as much current biofuel feedstock production is considered far from being environmentally or socially sustainable. It is all very well to state that algae may be used in future (as Richard Branson does in the BBC article above[1]), but this will require substantial investment and time. Algae and other feedstocks are considered in greater detail below. In the case of climate change, time is short and demand management (often used as a euphemism for demand reduction) is – or ought to be – a very much simpler and quicker option than building vast algae or other biomass supply chains and conversion infrastructures.

The chapter summarizes the prospects for biofuel production and relates this to projected global air fleet fuel demand. In the most optimistic scenarios, bioenergy could provide over twice current global energy demand without competing with food production, forest-protection efforts and biodiversity. In the least favourable scenarios, however, bioenergy could supply only a fraction of current energy use. The range hinges on many assumptions, not least of which is the extent to which one believes that institutions, treaties and policy tools can be relied upon as a buffer against misaligned corporate and individual economic interest. Taking all these factors into account, we draw conclusions about the prospects and limits for biofuel use in aviation and make policy recommendations accordingly.

Climate change context

There is no need to labour the point here: we have very little time left to avoid breaching the EU climate change commitment not to exceed a 2°C rise in global mean surface temperature above the pre-industrial level (EC, 2007a). See Chapter 4, this volume, by Alice Bows and Kevin Anderson for more detail. The proposed Directive to include aviation in EU ETS (EC, 2006) is to be welcomed, but its benefits will be largely conditional on the proposed baseline and ways in which the wider EU ETS develops, particularly the level of the cap. To stand a modest chance of not exceeding the +2°C threshold, the EU has a window of only 10 years or so in which to begin substantial year-on-year reductions in greenhouse gas emissions. Remaining within this +2°C threshold requires a maximum global atmospheric CO_2 concentration of 450ppmv CO_2, and preferably 400ppmv CO_2. 450ppmv CO_2 requires 3.1–5.7 per cent annual reductions in total EU CO_2 emissions over the period 2012–2030 (implicit in Bows et al, 2007; the range reflects alternative climate models). Note that 450ppmv CO_2 is not a 'safe' concentration: only at levels of around 400ppmv CO_2 equivalent are the risks of overshooting a 2°C target low enough that its achievement can be termed 'likely' (Meinshausen, 2005).[2] CO_2 equivalent (CO_2-eq) is a wider measure than CO_2 alone. Its definition varies but may include tropospheric ozone and sulphur aerosols. CO_2-eq concentrations are measured in terms of the concentration of CO_2 that would achieve the equivalent climatic effect: 400ppmv CO_2-eq is roughly equivalent to 345ppmv CO_2.

The EC +2°C threshold thus allows industrialized nations only a brief period of growth in carbon emissions. Exploring 450ppmv CO_2 scenarios for the UK, Bows et al (2006) found it necessary to allocate the contracting carbon budget to those sectors with the fewest options for change, particularly aviation. Although they found that both static and high mobility scenarios are possible (the latter assuming that UK individuals' travel (in passenger km) increases threefold by air and twofold by road and rail in the period 2004–2050), both scenarios require rapid decarbonization by every other sector. Moreover, air passenger growth rates must fall from the current UK level of 7 per cent per annum to a maximum annual average of just over 2 per cent. In addition, the aviation industry must improve fuel efficiency, significantly increase its load factor and switch to 50 per cent biofuel by 2050 (Bows et al, 2006, p56) (in the latter study, biofuels are considered carbon neutral –

this is discussed further below). In other words, a low level of aviation growth is possible in the EC, within climate limits, but only if several stringent conditions are met.

Non-biofuel alternatives to mineral kerosene

Biofuel is not the only fuel alternative to mineral kerosene and there are, of course, management options that can be implemented aside from fuel changes. Published reviews of the fuel alternatives include RCEP (2002), Saynor et al (2003) and Daggett et al (2007). This section is intended as a non-exhaustive, brief overview: there will be a variety of possibilities that could be discussed in more detail. For example, Daggett et al (2007) suggest that it may be better to tap the substantial sub-ocean methane clathrate reserves rather than risk these venting as climate change progresses. Although left implicit by Dagget et al (2007), a zero-carbon use of these reserves would require removal and burial[3] of the carbon in the CH_4 molecule and use of the hydrogen as discussed below. Another option is synthetic hydrocarbon oil produced via the Fischer-Tropsch process from coal or natural gas, for which the methane clathrate reserves could again be a source. However, the carbon emissions from this would not be sustainable. Similarly, captured carbon from power stations (or biomass) can be combined with hydrogen obtained via wind-turbine electrolysis of seawater (Mann, 2007), but again this would release carbon to the atmosphere.

Hydrogen is generally considered a problematic and long-term proposition as a jet fuel replacement. The volume of cryogenic hydrogen (assuming this form) would be some 2.5 times that of the equivalent kerosene. The airframe would therefore need to be larger, and so would have a correspondingly larger drag. The combination of larger drag and lower weight would require flight at higher altitudes. Therefore, RCEP (2002) concluded that hydrogen would most likely be used in large long-haul, high-altitude aircraft. Moreover, the effects of NO_x would still be present, as would be the enhanced production of water vapour which, depending on the cruise altitude, could increase contrail formation and hence cirrus cloud. RCEP (2002) comment that a hydrogen-fuelled aircraft flying in the stratosphere to reduce drag would produce more water than a kerosene fuelled aircraft, and since the water vapour produced by the latter cruising at 17–20km gives a radiative forcing (change of energy within Earth's atmosphere) some 5 times that of a lower-flying subsonic aircraft, a hydrogen-fuelled supersonic aircraft flying at stratospheric levels would be expected to have a radiative forcing some 13 times larger than that for a standard kerosene-fuelled subsonic aircraft. On a life-cycle basis this effect would be magnified if the hydrogen was not generated using renewable energy. Other fuels considered and subsequently rejected to date include ethanol and methanol. Their very low heat content, in mass and volume terms, render them of little value as jet fuels. Moreover, from a safety standpoint, these alcohols have very low flash points, also rendering them unsuitable.

Biodiesel and biokerosene

Historically, the key problem with biodiesel as a kerosene extender has been that it solidifies to a wax when cold. Neat biodiesel that has not been treated can be problematic in cold weather, even in road vehicles. The problem can be ameliorated via 'winterizing', a process involving the use of additives, pre-chilling to induce the formation of solids and then filtration to remove those solids.[4] Biodiesel thus does potentially have a future as a mineral kerosene extender. Indeed the Virgin Atlantic trial referred to above appears to have involved a biodiesel blend rather than biokerosene, though this is not clear.

As an alternative to biodiesel, kerosene can be manufactured from biomass using the Fischer-Tropsch chemical conversion process, in which lignocellulosic feedstocks are gasified, and then converted into a mixture of diesel, kerosene and naphtha. Biokerosene is chemically and physically similar to mineral kerosene, and therefore broadly compatible with current fuel storage and engines. However, its lack of aromatic molecules and the fact that it is virtually sulphur-free gives it poor lubricity (Saynor et al, 2003). It also has a lower energy density than mineral kerosene, which would impact on long-haul flights. A few modifications could, on the other hand, improve its lubricity, making it fit for use (Saynor et al, 2003). This type of kerosene is a potential medium-term option for the aviation industry.

Is there enough land?

In principle – and we will see later in this chapter that there are major practical obstacles to the realization of the principle – bioenergy can play two key roles in climate policy. First, biomass can substitute for fossil fuel (we discuss the carbon and energy balance issues of this below). Second, if the biomass is processed as fuel and the carbon removed and buried before or after combustion, then providing the biofuel is used as a substitute for fossil fuel, there may be net removal of CO_2 from the atmosphere. Read and Lermitt (2005) have been strong advocates of such bioenergy coupled with carbon sequestration, though they do not explain in detail how the sequestration should take place. Storage as biochar and as CO_2 in old oil extraction sites are possibilities, but this raises a host of issues in itself, not least of which is the requirement for transport to suitable sites, particularly in the case of CO_2 storage. It is also important to know that unless and until there is some technological innovation that allows capture of CO_2 from mobile sources (i.e. individual vehicles), the carbon would need to be removed before combustion to stand a chance of obtaining net reductions in atmospheric CO_2. This means the fuel will be hydrogen, the feasibility of which for surface transport will depend upon either a technological breakthrough in solid state storage, or installation of a distribution network for the hydrogen plus public acceptance of hydrogen's various foibles (not least of which are its tendency to leak through its storage tank and cryogenic temperatures). The problems of hydrogen for aviation have been summarized above.

To return to the land question: if we are aiming at a virtuous circle for aviation via biofuels, we need a biofuel production system that leads to net GHG emission savings and that possibly even reduces atmospheric CO_2 via removal of the carbon and use of the hydrogen. By 'net GHG emission savings' we mean that the biofuel production system should, when examined on a life-cycle basis, lead to the emission of a lower level of GHGs than would the supply and use of fossil kerosene. Considered from an exhaust perspective, therefore, we need some means of sequestering the same volume of atmospheric carbon emissions from aviation in the biofuel production process. Of course this is a corollary of producing sufficient biofuel to fuel the aircraft, but it is worth making the conceptual link in order to emphasize the possibility of a closed cycle. Note also that the warming effects of aviation emissions at high altitude are perhaps some three times higher than CO_2 alone, so one could argue that the sequestered volume of CO_2 should be three times that of emitted CO_2.

Land for carbon sequestration

Anyway, at least on the basis of a rough calculation, there does appear to be sufficient land for biological sequestration of global aviation emissions in the medium term, even within the territories of some the main emitters, and even focusing on forestry alone. However, note that this would preclude the use of the biological options discussed below to sequester carbon emissions from other sectors. Eyers et al (2004), as part of research for the AERO2K global inventory of aviation fuel usage and emissions (see below), estimate business as usual global aviation emissions in 2025 as $1029MtCO_2$, which is 280.38MtC. In the IPCC *Third Assessment Report*, Nabuurs et al (2000, in IPCC, 2001) estimate the carbon sequestration potential of forest-related activities (including protection from natural disturbance, improved silviculture, savannah thickening, restoration of degraded lands, and management of forest products) at 0.6GtC per year (600MtC per year) over six regions in the temperate and boreal zone (Canada, USA, Australia, Iceland, Japan and EU) alone. This value entails using only 10 per cent of the forest area. We can see that the projected 2025 aviation emissions can be accommodated by the annual sequestration potential of the main aviation-emitting territories, though if we multiply the emissions value by three to account for additional warming, we do exceed that (narrowly scoped) potential.

Nabuurs et al (2007), in Section 9.1 of Chapter 9 (Forestry) in the Working Group III report *Mitigation of Climate Change* (part of the IPCC (2007a) *Fourth Assessment Report*), state that IPCC (2007a) reports the latest estimates for the global terrestrial sink for the decade 1993–2003 at $3300MtCO_2$ per year, ignoring emissions from land-use change (Denman et al, 2007: Table 7.1). They state that the most likely estimate of these emissions for the 1990s is $5800MtCO_2$ per year, which is partly being sequestered on land as well (IPCC, 2007a) – that is there is substantial sink potential but we are experiencing net emissions due to deforestation and other land-use change. The IPCC *Third Assessment Report*

(TAR) (Kauppi et al, 2001) concluded that the forest sector as whole has a biophysical mitigation potential of $5380MtCO_2$ per year on average up until 2050, whereas the SR LULUCF (IPCC, 2000) presented a biophysical mitigation potential on all lands of $11,670MtCO_2$ per year in 2010 (copied in IPCC, 2001, p110). Forest mitigation options include reducing emissions from deforestation and forest degradation, enhancing the sequestration rate in existing and new forests, providing wood fuels as a substitute for fossil fuels, and providing wood products for more energy-intensive materials.

Summarizing, even if we assume 2025 global aviation emissions are the equivalent of roughly $3000MtCO_2$ (having approximately multiplied by three to account for additional warming), then this could in principle be sequestered via global forestry alone. Note, however, that if we increase that $3000MtCO_2$ at the expected 2002–2025 value of 3.3 per cent (AERO2K's assumption) for a further 25 years to 2050, then we do somewhat exceed the annual global forest mitigation potential estimated in the TAR ($6755MtCO_2$ in 2050 compared to $5380MtCO_2$ per year). Note that we could have expanded global terrestrial sequestration potential by referring to values that include non-forest soils and grasses, that we have completely ignored sequestration by crops that might be used for food directly or indirectly (e.g. via livestock), and that we have also ignored sequestration by algae, be these terrestrially based in specially built infrastructure or macro-algae at sea (seaweeds).

For information, the AERO2K study, commissioned by the EC, is the most recent global emissions inventory for the world's aircraft fleet, projecting from 2002 forward to 2025. In 2002, civil aviation used 156Gt of fuel, producing 492Gt of CO_2. The 2025 projections use Airbus and UK Departent of Trade and Industry (DTI) assumptions of demand growth and efficiency improvements. Global air passenger demand is expected to increase 2.6 times over the period 2002–2025. Global aircraft fuel burn is expected to grow by 2.1 times over the same period.

Global aircraft CO_2 is projected to grow at about 3.3 per cent per annum during the period 2002–2025. This is despite assumptions about increasing the average size of aircraft, continuing success in introducing fuel savings and emissions reduction technology. Fleet rollover timescales and demand growth are identified as key problems in holding back emissions growth.

Land for biofuel production

In the section above, we showed, fairly summarily, that in principle 'business as usual' global aviation emissions could be sequestered in global forests nearly up until 2050 (2043 on the basis of the above assumptions and estimates). In this section we start from the other end of the fuel cycle and ask whether there is enough land to produce biofuel for aviation until 2050 (a relatively arbitrary date, it should be noted, but one classically used in scenario studies).

First we need to establish our target fuel requirement. *The Digest of UK Energy Statistics* (Table A.1: Estimated Average Gross Calorific Values of Fuels) states that in 2006 aviation turbine fuel had an average gross calorific value of 46.2GJ/tonne. AERO2K estimates that in 2025 global civil aviation will use 327Tg of fuel, which is 327,000,000 tonnes. The calorific value of this is $327\times10^6\times46.2$GJ = 15,107,400,000GJ or 15.1EJ per year. If we assume that 3.3 per cent annual growth continues to 2050, that gives us a global 2050 fuel requirement for aviation of 34EJ per year in 2050. Of course the actual growth rate might be higher or lower.

For an estimate of how much land might be available to deliver biofuel, we will use Doornbosch and Steenblik (2007), as they have reviewed many such studies and are relatively conservative (or realistic) in their assumptions. Doornbosch and Steenblik (2007) argue that, globally, 0.44Gha should be seen as the technical upper limit to the land area that could be made available for dedicated bioenergy crop production in 2050. This is for all bioenergy, not just for transport fuels. They see the potential for expansion as mainly concentrated in Africa and South and Central America, as more than 80 per cent of additional cultivable land is located in these two regions. About half of this land would be concentrated in just seven countries – Angola, Democratic Republic of Congo, Sudan, Argentina, Bolivia, Brazil and Colombia (Fischer et al, 2006, in Doornbosch and Steenblik, 2007). However, African biofuel development is viewed as uncertain: unutilized land in sub-Saharan Africa faces a number of obstacles before it can be profitably brought into production, including poor infrastructure, underdeveloped financial markets, and a hostile investment climate on account of government policies (Kojima et al, 2007). In other global regions, the potential is either very limited or negative (i.e. it is likely to be dependent on biomass imports).

Doornbosch and Steenblik (2007) rightly observe that land-use availability estimates should be viewed with caution. As the FAO (2000, in Doornbosch and Steenblik, 2007) warns, the models used to calculate land availability have tended to overestimate the amount of land that could be used for agriculture and underestimate the area of land that is already in use by 10–20 per cent. Moreover, in practice it is often difficult to make land that is technically available for agriculture actually available. Other competing demands put constraints on future changes in land use. Reductions in land availability may be expected due to increasing demand for natural fibres and other materials, for foods grown less intensively or using organic production methods, for conservation of ecosystems and biodiversity, and for carbon sequestration (Doornbosch and Steenblik, 2007, p14). In short, competition for arable land among food, fibre, biomaterials and energy production cannot be avoided (Doornbosch and Steenblik, 2007, p14).

Doornbosch and Steenblik (2007) also critique the plausibility of assuming that high-quality arable land might be reserved for food production, with energy crops cultivated on land of lower quality, including set-aside land in, for example, Europe and poorly managed and degraded land elsewhere. They argue that this option will in practice be limited by the shortage of water resources in some regions and the increase of land degradation and desertification. They point out that water supply is already under stress (Brown, 2006, in

Doornbosch and Steenblik, 2007) and that there is a limited potential for the expansion of irrigation onto land unsuited for rainfall cultivation, as large volumes of water are needed and many regions in the dry zones are already experiencing water shortages. It should be noted that this runs counter to claims by BP and D1 Oils that Jatropha will be grown on marginal, arid land (BP, 2007). The practicality of giving priority to food production on high-quality land should also be questioned, as land will be allocated largely in a way that maximizes net private benefits to the land users/owners (WWF, 2006, in Doornbosch and Steenblik, 2007).

Taking all that into account, Doornbosch and Steenblik (2007) observe that their estimate of potential additional land still compares reasonably well with the average of 0.59Gha calculated from 11 studies (out of a total of 17) reviewed in Berndes et al (2003), some of which are very optimistic. Doornbosch and Steenblik (2007) describe their further assumptions as follows. In Europe, annual yields of 20–30 oven-dry tonnes per hectare (odt/ha) are the limit that sunlight, rainfall and climate permit, with adequate water and nutrients. In tropical regions, yields of up to 50odt/ha can be achieved. Given the large areas of moderately productive land included in the above additional land estimates, and following the IEA, they assume an average actual yield of 10odt per hectare with an energy content of 19GJ/odt – that is 190GJ per year of primary energy per hectare. Applying these assumptions to world regions provides a global estimate of approximately 110EJ per year in 2050 that could potentially be produced from the 0.44Gha that is judged to be available for dedicated bioenergy crop production.

In addition, Doornbosch and Steenblik (2007, p16) suggest a possible, technical potential of marginal and degraded land – for which they say there are no reliable estimates – in the order of 29–39EJ per year in 2050. However, they exclude this for reasons of uncertainty – a notable, highly conservative assumption. Regarding residues and 'wastes', they state that numerous studies have shown that only a fraction – typically 25–33 per cent of the technically available crop residues from grasses or corn (maize) – can be harvested from the land in a sustainable manner (e.g. Wallace et al, 2007, in Doornbosch and Steenblik, 2007). Using yields calculated by Fischer and Schrattenholzer (2001) for crop residues by world region provides a global total of 34.8EJ per year in 2050. Even this value is debatable, however: minerals removed in the plant sections used for fuel must be replaced somehow and using another source such as human sewage or imported manure means that some other location cannot be fertilized from the same source. We discuss this lack of materials loop closure a little more below – it runs counter to mainstream environmental thinking and is not given enough attention.

Continuing in this vein, Doornbosch and Steenblik (2007) state that where forests are managed sustainably, much of the forest residues are left on the ground – to protect the soil from erosion, to enrich the soil, and to provide habitat for wildlife. Furthermore, on land the energy potential of wood is restricted to distances of less than 200km between production and consumption (i.e. there is no point conveying wood further, though such calculations will of course make a variety of assumptions about vehicle and fuel type). Fischer and Schrattenholzer (2001) take these factors into account when estimating the potential from wood residues to provide an additional 90.6EJ per year by 2050 globally. Finally, the cost of collecting animal and organic waste is the most important cost element for these types of feedstocks and the global potential in this analysis is therefore judged as the lower estimate of the global technical potential in other studies summarized in Hoogwijk et al (2003), that is a further 10EJ per year by 2050. Note that the residues of this need to be returned to the land.

All things considered, Doornbosch and Steenblik (2007, p16) estimate that the primary energy supply for heat, electricity and transport that could technically be produced from global biomass, per year by 2050, is roughly 245EJ. They report that this is at the lower end of the wide range of 125–760EJ per year reported in the IPCC (2007a) *Fourth Assessment Report* and in other studies that they review. Doornbosch and Steenblik (2007) assume that half of the available surplus biomass will be used for electricity and heat, and half for the production of liquid biofuels. This is of course a completely arbitrary assumption. Finally, Doornbosch and Steenblik (2007) also assume that the conversion efficiency of biofuel technologies has the high efficiency of ethanol from sugarcane and therefore use 35 per cent as a conversion factor (i.e. 35 per cent of 245/2EJ is available in the resulting biofuel). In this way an upper limit for the potential of biofuel in 2050 is calculated, giving a figure of some 43EJ per year in 2050. This would mean biofuels could provide roughly 23 per cent of the 190EJ demand for liquid (transport) fuels in 2050, as foreseen in the IEA's baseline scenario (IEA, 2006a, in Doornbosch and Steenblik, 2007), or – the estimate we have been working towards – 126 per cent of the calorific value required of aviation biofuel in 2050 (34EJ). Alternatively if it is assumed that only the first 'core' yield of biomass was available (110EJ per year), arbitrarily half this, sufficient fuel for projected 2050 aviation demand would still be provided, but not for any other use!

Should we produce biofuel on this scale?

We have shown, albeit somewhat cursorily, that we can in principle use forestry to sequester business as usual global aviation emissions into the 2040s and also provide enough biofuel for this purpose from forestry alone, with other sources providing a surplus for other sectors. For comparison, Saynor et al (2003) estimate a global Fischer-Tropsch potential of 19.4EJ, using short rotation willow coppice as feedstock, which is a little less than half of the available calorific value estimated by Doornbosch and Steenblik (2007).

Of course there is no necessary requirement to link specific sources to specific sectors. Woody species are very frequently touted by biofuel advocates as being preferable to using potential food crops and would be amenable to biokerosene production via the Fischer-Tropsch (FT) method, but (as mentioned) Virgin Atlantic's trial in early 2008 used babassu palm and coconut oils and in associated press coverage Richard Branson suggested algae as a possible future source; however, whether or not biodiesel production from micro-algae is commercially viable on a large scale is contested and uncertain (Carlsson et al, 2007). A further point to make is that when relating 2050 aviation fuel consumption to potential biofuel production quantities, we have assumed complete replacement of fossil kerosene rather than a blend, which would certainly be more likely in the short and medium term.

The environmental performance of biofuels

The first issue to consider, given that the main advantage of biofuels is their supposed environmental benefits, is their overall environmental performance.

Energy balance

When assessing the energy balance of biofuel, that is the ratio of fossil energy input to renewable energy output, critical aspects of the life-cycle analysis (LCA) are the system boundary and – especially – the treatment of co-products. The system boundary defines what is included or excluded from the study (e.g. the manufacture of the harvesting equipment or even rabbit fencing). Co-products are valued by-products produced at the same time that can substitute for equivalent things produced at another time, such that those things no longer need to be produced (discussed below).

ICCEPT (2003) show, for example, that some pathways to biodiesel and bioethanol have a negative or small positive energy ratio, as shown in the DfT (2003) Table 14.1 below, *if co-products are ignored*. ICCEPT (Woods et al, 2003, piii) argue that allocation can be properly made only once actual plant and systems are in operation, and hence uncertainties and lack of data are resolved. An energy ratio of less than 1.0 indicates that more non-renewably sourced energy is put into the process than is embodied in the biofuel product.

The ICCEPT report concludes that biodiesel and bioethanol routes are generally energy-intensive and that significantly favourable energy balances are only achieved when renewable fuels – mainly residues from the biomass resource used – are used to produce energy for the process, and when energy and avoided emissions are allocated to co-products. In the case of corn (maize), these are principally animal feed, including pulp pellets and distiller's dry/wet grains

Table 14.1 *Carbon balances for illustrative biofuel*

Process	Energy ratio
Biodiesel from oil seeds	0.7–4.4
Biodiesel from FT processing of wood	18.1–44.3
Bioethanol from grain	0.9–2.6
Bioethanol from straw	0.8–2.4
Bioethanol from sugar beet	0.7–1.8

Source: DfT (2003): Table 7.1, from ICCEPT (2003)

Table 14.2 *Carbon balances for illustrative biofuel*

Process	Energy ratio
Biodiesel from oil seeds	2.3
Bioethanol from acid hydrolysis of straw	5.6
Bioethanol from wheat	2.2
Bioethanol from sugar beet	2.0

Source: DfT (2003), Table 7.2, from Elsayed et al (2003)

(DDGS or DWS). Regarding the FT kerosene from wood, the range in the energy ratio arises from variations in energy input requirements for feedstock production and feedstock transport, which jointly account for more than 80 per cent of input energy requirements. In contrast, a report for DTI by Sheffield Hallam University, examining carbon and energy balances for a range of alternative UK biofuel production routes, shows positive energy balances (DfT, 2003, Table 7.2, in Elsayed et al, 2003). They did not study ethanol from corn (maize), but did include ethanol from wheat. Study of the latter allocated energy inputs and GHG outputs between wheat straw and wheat grain, bran and coarse powder flour, animal feed and ethanol (Elsayed et al, 2003, Section 4.3.15).

Demonstrating a positive energy balance for particular types of biofuel is far from the end of the debate, even in narrowly defined energy terms. We need also to ask what we want to achieve with that positive energy return and whether this end use is an energy-efficient means of achieving it. Using the biofuel in a vehicle to travel to a business meeting, the purposes of which could have been served by a telephone or video call, is in relative terms inefficient and wasteful. We could then layer a further, normative aspect on the energetic issue, asking whether we have a right to incur this inefficiency, given competing demands on the fuel, wood, land, water etc. by humans and non-humans. In short, a positive energy balance is a good thing, but this is an insufficient justification for the use of the underpinning technological system.

Environmental impacts

In the section above, we saw that the energy balance of the two biofuels most suitable for aviation (biodiesel and FT kerosene) differ considerably and, in the case of biodiesel, can be negative if co-products are not accounted for. FT kerosene from wood was found to have a very good energy balance, by contrast. Note that while the consensus among LCA practitioners is probably that co-products should be accounted for, if they exist, this is still a debatable practice. Patzek (2004), for example, argues that co-products should be returned to the soil to avoid gradually depleting the humus, and certainly soil quality does need to be protected.

At the time of writing, Zah et al (2007) is the most recent, wide-ranging LCA of biofuels, undertaken as a basis for granting an exemption from the excise duty on fossil fuels in Switzerland. In addition, the impacts of biofuel use are compared with other bioenergy applications, such as the generation of

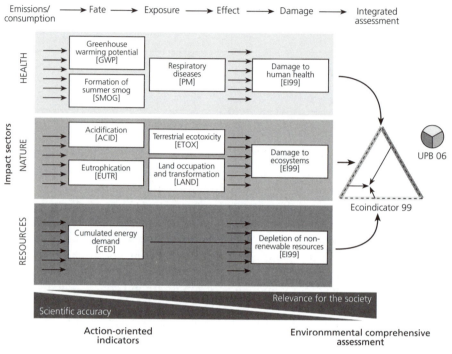

Source: Methods used by Zah et al (2007)

Figure 14.1 *Overview of the LCA methods*

electricity and heat. The study uses the Swiss life-cycle inventory database Ecoinvent, relating to Switzerland and western Europe. The study goes beyond the LCA inventory stage to the level of impact indication, which adds normative dimensions via impact weighting and choice of indication method (in addition to earlier decisions regarding system boundary, which is a normative stage of all applications of LCA).

The LCA impact assessment of Zah et al (2007) used two methods, summarily described in Figure 14.1. The first is the Swiss method of ecological scarcity (Environmental Impact Points, UBP 06), which evaluates the difference between environmental impacts and legal limits (Frischknecht et al, 2006); that is the impacts of the life-cycle inventory items are characterized in terms of their contribution towards a breach in regulated limits, for example for air and water quality. The second method is the European Eco-indicator 99 method commissioned by the Dutch Ministry of Housing, Spatial Planning and the Environment (PRé Consultants B.V., 2000), which quantifies the damage done to human health and ecosystems (i.e. it is not limited only to environmental indication of impacts regulated by law).

Both methods show similar results; Figure 14.2 shows the results of the more recent UBP method. In the case of tropical agriculture it is primarily the clear-cutting and burning of rainforests that releases the largest quantities of

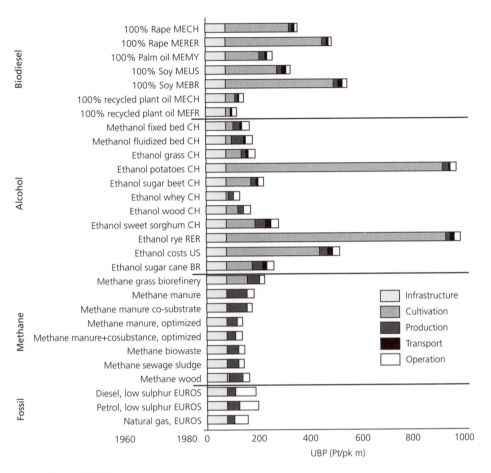

Source: Zah et al (2007)

Figure 14.2 *Aggregated environmental impact (method of ecological scarcity, UBP 06) of biofuels in comparison with fossil fuels*

CO$_2$, causes an increase in air pollution and has 'massive' impacts on biodiversity. In the moderate latitudes it is partly the lower crop yields, partly the intensive fertilizer use and mechanical tilling of the soil, that are the causes of a poor environmental evaluation. The study shows in sensitivity analysis how, for instance, a prohibition of clear-cutting would affect the LCA of biodiesel made from palm oil.

Zah et al (2007) find that most of the environmental impacts of biofuels can be attributed to the agricultural cultivation of the feedstocks (dark grey in Figure 14.2). The environmental impact from fuel processing is usually much lower, the environmental impact from the transport from the production site to Swiss filling stations is even less, even when the biofuels are produced overseas. The study shows that with most biofuels there is a trade-off between minimizing greenhouse gases (GHG emissions) and lower total environmental impacts. Thus while GHG emissions can be reduced by more than 30 per cent with several biofuels, most of the supply paths show greater impacts than petrol for various other environmental indicators. Zah et al (2007) conclude that it is particularly the use of biogenic wastes, grasses and wood that brings a reduction in environmental impact as compared with petrol.

Figure 14.2 also enables comparison of the greenhouse gas emissions by biofuels and fossil fuels (petrol and diesel, EURO3) on a $kgCO_2$-eq per passenger km basis. The study didn't consider biokerosene as the focus was on options for Swiss road vehicles, but ethanol from (Swiss) wood is shown and does perform relatively well. In general, although the environmental impacts of vehicle operation are much higher when fossil fuel is used, this is outweighed by the high environmental impacts of agricultural production. The causes of this are soil acidification and excessive fertilizer use in European and Swiss agriculture (Zah et al, 2007). In the case of tropical agriculture, the environmental impact arises from biodiversity loss, air pollution caused by clear-cutting, and the toxicity of pesticides. The very high impact of Swiss potatoes can be explained by the high weighting placed on nutrient leaching. The very high values for rye taken from European production are explained by the low harvest yield of rye in Europe (Zah et al, 2007). On the positive side, the lower impacts of waste vegetable oils, wood-ethanol and methane relative to the fossil transport fuels are notable.

The tropically sourced biofuels have high smog impacts because the cultivation areas are often accessed by means of clear-cutting or – in the case of bioethanol from sugar cane – the dry leaves are burned off before the harvest. Excessive fertilizer use was higher by several factors in the cases of agricultural processes compared to fossil fuels, though in the cases of Brazilian sugar cane and Malaysian palm oil, these values can be low. Ecotoxicity peaks with cultivation on clear-cut areas, due to the high toxicological evaluation of acetone emissions. The only biofuels that performed better than petrol across all environmental impacts were methyl ester made from waste cooking oil and methane from sewage and bio-waste.

The role of sustainability certification

So far we have established that we can sequester aviation emissions through global forestry and can produce enough biofuel for aviation up to 2050. We have established that not all biofuels are equal in terms of energy balance, GHG emissions or overall environmental impact. We have found that wood performs relatively well as a feedstock for Fischer-Tropsch kerosene in terms of energy balance and that it performs relatively well as an ethanol feedstock. We haven't looked at the specific case of babassu and coconut, which are used by Virgin Atlantic, but providing these don't encroach or cause encroachment onto uncultivated lands, they are likely to perform moderately well relative to other biofuels.

Should we, therefore, support the large-scale production of only specific types of feedstock, and establish regulations that incentivize those types and not others, leaving 'the market' to decide into which types of biofuel these are processed, and in what sectors the fuels are used? This is essentially the approach supported by the EC, with particular member states being more active than others on sustainability certification (see COM 2006a, 2006b and 2007; and Matthews, 2007). Unfortunately, there are many problems with sustainability certification as a regulatory option. Sustainability certification is widely considered unlikely or unable to capture the indirect, macro, cumulative and systemic effects on land use, which Gnansounou et al (2007) summarize as: effects on land prices, food prices, property rights, the availability of food, relocation of food production and cattle feeding, deforestation, and change in type of vegetation. As Gnansounou et al (2007) observe, in general, initiatives on biofuel certification recommend monitoring of these indirect effects without directly including them in the certification scheme (Gnansounou et al, 2007, p15). Moreover, there are also substantial shortcomings in some of the precedent certification schemes, such as those for palm oil, soya and Forest Stewardship Council wood (see Doornbosch and Steenblik, 2007; and Verdonk et al, 2007) for a review of emergent issues).

Making a decision on biofuels

As oil prices rise, the decision on whether to undertake large-scale biofuel production may not be one made by fuel suppliers to airlines, let alone hypothetical, environmentally discerning air travellers. All countries and governments have an interest in energy security. Although it is difficult to imagine global biofuel supply declining in the short or medium term, except as a result of climate change or some other major fuel source coming on-stream (such as the methane clathrate reserves referred to above), prioritizing national use of limited biofuel resources ahead of export for foreign exchange would not be an unreasonable scenario. There may be an ethanol surplus for export from Brazil, but ethanol is not an option for aviation. In other words, aviation will probably need to compete for a biofuel supply that is substantially more limited than that estimated above. On the other hand, use of biofuel as a mineral kerosene extender may redress the balance of competing demands.

Nevertheless, let us assume that individual citizens do have some influence over these processes. Should we support large-scale biofuel production for global aviation? Should we support this production only under certain conditions, most obviously of stringent sustainability certification? Perhaps limit production to particular locations and feedstocks that are relatively controllable in terms of sustainability standards? Our view is this: stringently certified biofuels may have a role to play in surface and air transport, but this should only be in parallel with strong demand-side reduction policies, particularly in developed countries, where this can be afforded. This means first developing and implementing the range of technologies available to improve the fuel efficiency of road vehicles, and promoting the reduced use of private cars, before expanding agricultural production and further displacing biodiversity, be this in tropical countries or on marginal European land. Similarly it means first instituting capacity constraints on air travel or raising the price of air travel so as to reduce air-traffic growth to at least match the rate of fuel efficiency gains. Using price rises as a demand reduction tool may introduce social tensions as aviation becomes a resource limited, once again, to those with sufficient income.

We are aware that there is still not a sufficient political mandate for this. The necessary changes could be stimulated by a largely closed EU Emissions Trading System (EU ETS) with a tight and downward-moving cap, but instead EU ETS is likely to be left open, allowing overseas investments via the Clean Development Mechanism instead of domestic emissions reductions. Until there is a real willingness among developed nation populaces to reduce domestic GHG emissions substantially, demand for biofuels will be substantially higher than it need be, a clearly problematic situation that should be avoided.

Conclusions

Globally we have sufficient land to biologically sequester global aviation emissions in the long term and to supply sufficient biofuel. Biofuels vary substantially in their environmental performance; woody species used for Fischer-Tropsch kerosene are probably the most suitable for aviation in terms of environmental and other criteria, but the information with which to make this judgement is limited. Large-scale biofuel production may legitimately have a role in sustainable development pathways, but we have not adequately assessed this here – again the available evidence is limited and currently we are reluctant to commit to that position when much of the evidence to date points to environmental harm and poor social conditions. Moreover, even if large-scale production of biofuels can be reconciled with environmental and social benefits, this should be pursued only after the vigorous implementation of demand-side reduction policies. In short, using biofuels to benefit people and planet is not going to be straightforward, and those who ignore this complexity do so because their interests are either narrow or short term. Biofuels may have a future in the aviation world but they need to be treated very cautiously.

Notes

1   It's not only Virgin Atlantic who are interested in biofuels as a mineral kerosene replacement or extender. See, for example, http://news.bbc.co.uk/1/hi/sci/tech/7817849.stm.
2   Global CO_2 equivalent concentration is currently 425ppmv and rising by 2–3ppmv (parts per million by volume) CO_2-eq per year (EC, 2007b).
3   Carbon capture and storage is itself contentious, of course. For further information from a relatively neutral perspective, see www.accsept.org/publications.htm.
4   See, for example, www.ars.usda.gov/is/AR/archive/jul01/jet0701.htm.

References

BBC (2008) 'Airline in first biofuel flight', BBC News Website, BBC, London, 24 February 2008, http://news.bbc.co.uk/1/hi/UK/7261214.stm, accessed 10 November 2008

Berndes, G., Hoogwijk, M. and van den Broek, R. (2003) 'The contribution of biomass in the future global energy supply: A review of 17 studies', *Biomass and Bioenergy* 25(1): 1–28

Bows, A., Mander, S., Starkey, R., Bleda, M. and Anderson, K. (2006) *Living Within A Carbon Budget,* report commissioned by Friends of the Earth and the Co-operative Bank, available at www.foe.co.uk/resource/reports/living_carbon_budget.pdf, accessed 11 November 2008

Bows, A., Anderson, K. and Peeters, P. (2007) 'Technology, scenarios and uncertainties', working paper, Tyndall Centre Manchester, The University of Manchester, available at www.tyndall.web.man.ac.uk/publications/ Technology %20Scenarios%20and%20Uncertainties%202007.pdf, accessed 11 November 2008

BP (2007) 'BP and D1 oils form joint venture to develop Jatropha biodiesel feedstock', BP press release, 29 June, available at www.bp.com/genericarticle.do?categoryId= 2012968&contentId=7034453, accessed 11 November 2008

Brown, L. R. (2006) *Emerging Water Shortages, Plan B 2.0: Rescuing a Planet Under Stress and a Civilization in Trouble,* New York: W. W. Norton

Carlsson, A. S., van Beilen, J. B., Möller, R., Clayton, D. and Bowles, D. (eds) (2007) *Micro- and Macro-Algae: Utility for Industrial Applications,* outputs from the EPOBIO project, CNAP, University of York: CPL Press, UK, available at www.epobio.net/pdfs/0709AquaticReport.pdf, accessed 11 November 2008

COM (2006a) *An EU Strategy for Biofuels,* Brussels: Communication from the Commission 8.2.2006, available at http://ec.europa.eu/agriculture/biomass/biofuel/ com2006_34_en.pdf, accessed 11 November 2008

COM (2006b) *Renewable Energy Road Map. Renewable Energies in the 21st Century: Building a More Sustainable Future,* Communication from the Commission to the European Council and the European Parliament, Brussels: CEC Commission of The European Communities 10.1.2007, available at http://ec.europa.eu/energy/energy_ policy/doc/03_renewable_energy_roadmap_en.pdf, accessed 11 November 2008

COM (2007) *An Energy Policy for Europe {SEC(2007) 12},* Communication from the Commission to the European Council and the European Parliament, Brussels: CEC Commission of The European Communities 10.1.2007, available at http://ec.europa.eu/energy/energy_policy/doc/01_energy_policy_for_europe_en.pdf, accessed 11 November 2008

Daggett, D. L., Hendricks, R. C., Walther, R. and Corporan, E. (2007) *Alternate Fuels for Use in Commercial Aircraft,* Seattle: Boeing, available at www.boeing.com/ commercial/environment/pdf/alt_fuels.pdf, accessed 11 November 2008

Denman, K. L., Brasseur, G., Chidthaisong, A., Ciais, P., Cox, P., Dickinson, R. E., Hauglustaine, D., Heinze, C., Holland, E., Jacob, D., Lohmann, U., Ramachandran, S., da Silva Dias, P. L., Wofsy, S. C., Zhang, X. (2007) 'Couplings between changes in the climate system and biogeochemistry', in *Climate Change 2007: The Physical Science Basis, The IPCC Fourth Assessment Report,* Intergovernmental Panel on Climate Change, Cambridge: Cambridge University Press

DfT (Department for Transport) (2003) 'International resource costs of biodiesel and bioethanol', DfT, London, www.dft.gov.uk/pgr/roads/environment/research/ cqvcf/internationalresourcecostsof3833?page=11, accessed 10 November 2008

Doornbosch, R. and Steenblik, R. (2007) *Biofuels: Is the Cure Worse Than the Disease?*, Paris: OECD, available at http://media.ft.com/cms/fb8b5078–5fdb-11dc-b0fe-0000779fd2ac.pdf, accessed 11 November 2008

EC (2006) 'Proposal for a Directive of the European Parliament and of the Council amending Directive 2003/87/EC so as to include aviation activities in the scheme for greenhouse gas emission allowance trading within the Community {SEC(2006) 1684} {SEC(2006) 1685}', Brussels: European Commission, http://ec.europa.eu/environment/climat/aviation_en.htm and http://eurlex.europa.eu/LexUriServ/LexUriServ.do?uri=CELEX:52006PC0818: EN:NOT, accessed 10th November 2008

EC (2007a) *Limiting Global Climate Change to 2 Degrees Celsius: The Way Ahead for 2020 and Beyond*, Communication from the Commission to the Council, the European Parliament, the European Economic and Social Committee and the Committee of the Regions, available at http://eur-lex.europa.eu/LexUriServ/ site/en/com/2007/com2007_0002en01.pdf, accessed 11 November 2008

EC (2007b) *Questions and Answers on the Commission Communication Limiting Global Climate Change to 2°C*, MEMO/07/17, Brussels, 10 January, available at http://europa.eu/rapid/pressReleasesAction.do?reference=MEMO/07/17&format= PDF&aged=0&language=EN&guiLanguage=en, accessed 11 November 2008

Elsayed, M. A., Matthews, R. and Mortimer, N. D. (2003) *Carbon and Energy Balances for a Range of Biofuel Options*, Sheffield: Resources Research Institute, Sheffield Hallam University

Eyers, C. J., Norman, P., Middel, J., Plohr, M., Michot, S., Atkinson, K. and Christou, R.A. (2004) *AERO2K Global Aviation Emissions Inventories for 2002 and 2025*, Farnborough: QinetiQ Ltd, available at www.cate.mmu.ac.uk/aero2k.asp

Fischer, G. and Schrattenholzer, L. (2001) 'Global bioenergy potentials through 2050', *Biomass and Bioenergy* 20(3): 151–159, reprinted as RR-01–009, Laxenburg: International Institute for Applied Systems Analysis

Fischer, G., Shah, M., van Velthuizen, H. and Nachtergaele, F. (2006) *Agro-Ecological Zones Assessment*, RP-06–003, Laxenburg: International Institute for Applied Systems Analysis, April

Frischknecht, R., Steiner, R., Braunschweig, A., Norbert, E. and Hildesheimer, G. (2006) *Swiss Ecological Scarcity Method: The New Version 2006*, Bern: Swiss Federal Office for the Environment, available at www.esu-services.ch/download/Frischknecht-2006-EcologicalScarcity-Paper.pdf, accessed 11 November 2008

Gnansounou, E., Panichelli, L. and Villegas, J. D. (2007) *Sustainable Liquid Biofuels Development for Transport: Frequently Asked Questions and Review of Initiatives*, Lausanne: LASEN, available at www.bioenergywiki.net/images/1/10/2007_ LASEN%27s_Review_of_Biofuels_sustainability_initiatives_Final_draft.pdf, accessed 11 November 2008

Hoogwijk, M., Faaij, A., van den Broek, R., Berndes, G., Gielen, D. and Turkenburg, W. (2003) 'Exploration of the ranges of the global potential of biomass for energy', *Biomass and Bioenergy* 25(2): 119–133

ICCEPT (2003) *Technology Status Review and Carbon Abatement Potential of Renewable Transport Fuels*, Imperial College, London, available at www.berr.gov.uk/files/file15003.pdf, accessed 11 November 2008

IPCC (2000) *Land Use, Land-use Change and Forestry*, Special report of the Intergovernmental Panel on Climate Change (IPCC), Cambridge: Cambridge University Press

IPCC (2001) *Climate Change 2001: The Scientific Basis*, contribution of Working Group I to the Third Assessment Report of the Intergovernmental Panel on Climate

Change, Cambridge, UK and New York, USA: Cambridge University Press

IPCC (Intergovernmental Panel on Climate Change) (2007a), *Climate Change, Mitigation*, Contribution of Working Group III to the Fourth Assessment Report, available at www.mnp.nl/ipcc/pages_media/AR4-chapters.html, accessed 11 November 2008

IPCC (2007b) *Climate Change 2007: The Physical Science Basis*, Contribution of Working Group I to the Fourth Assessment Report of the Intergovernmental Panel on Climate Change, Cambridge, UK and New York, USA: Cambridge University Press

Kauppi, P., Sedjo, R. J., Apps, M. C., Cerri, C., Fujimori, T., Janzen, H., Krankina, O., Makundi, W., Marland, G., Masera, O., Nabuurs, G. J., Razali, W. and Ravindranath, N. H. (2001) 'Technical and economic potential of options to enhance, maintain and manage biological carbon reservoirs and geo-engineering', in Metz, B. et al (eds) *Mitigation 2001. The IPCC Third Assessment Report*, Cambridge: Cambridge University Press

Kojima, M., Mitchell, D. and Ward, W. (2007) *Considering Trade Policies for Liquid Biofuels*, Washington DC: The International Bank for Reconstruction and Development/The World Bank

Mann, R. (2007) *Carbon-neutral Flying for Conventional Aircraft*, Tyndall Centre Seminar, The University of Manchester, available at https://lists.rbgi.net/pipermail/netnews-action/2007-December/002749.html, accessed 11 November 2008

Matthews, J. A. (2007) 'Biofuels: What a biopact between North and South could achieve', *Energy Policy* 35: 3550–3570

Meinshausen, M. (2005) 'On the risk of overshooting 2°C: Avoiding dangerous climate change', *International Symposium on the Stabilisation of Greenhouse Gas Concentrations*, Exeter, UK: Hadley Centre, UK Meteorological Office, 1–3 February, available at www.stabilisation2005.com/14_Malte_Meinshausen.pdf, accessed 11 November 2008

Nabuurs, G. J., Dolman, A. V., Verkaik, E., Kuikman, P. J., van Diepen, C. A., Whitmore, A., Daamen, W., Oenema, O., Kabat, P. and Mohren, G. M. J. (2000) 'Article 3.3 and 3.4 of the Kyoto Protocol – consequences for industrialised countries' commitment, the monitoring needs and possible side effect', *Environmental Science and Policy* 3(2/3): 123–134

Nabuurs, G. J., Andrasko, K. Benitez-Ponce, P. Boer, R., Dutschke, M., Elsiddig, E., Ford-Robertson, J., Frumhoff, P., Karjalainen, T., Krankina, O., Kurz, W. A., Matsumoto, M., Oyhantcabal, W., Ravindranath, N. H., Sanchez, M. J. S. and Xiaquan, Z. (2007) 'Forestry', in IPCC Working Group III report *Mitigation of Climate Change*, Intergovernmental Panel on Climate Change, Geneva, available at www.ipcc.ch/pdf/assessment-report/ar4/wg3/ar4-wg3-chapter9.pdf, accessed 11 November 2008

Patzek, T. W. (2004) 'Thermodynamics of the corn-ethanol biofuel cycle', *Critical Reviews in Plant Sciences* 23(6): 519–567, updated web version at University of California, Berkeley, available at http://petroleum.berkeley.edu/papers/patzek/CRPS416-Patzek-Web.pdf, accessed 11 November 2008

PRé Consultants B.V. (2000) *Eco-Indicator 99 Methodology Report*, PRé Consultants B. V., Amersfoort, available at www.pre.nl/download/EI99_methodology_v3.pdf, accessed 11 November 2008

RCEP (Royal Commission on Environmental Pollution) (2002) *The Environmental Effects of Civil Aircraft in Flight*, special report of the Royal Commission on Environmental Pollution, available at www.rcep.org.uk/avreport.htm, accessed 11 November 2008

Read, P. and Lermitt, J. (2005) 'Bio-energy with carbon storage (BECS): A sequential decision approach to the threat of abrupt climate change', *Energy* 30(14): 2654–2671

Saynor, B., Bauen, A. and Leach, M. (2003) *The Potential for Renewable Energy Sources*, Imperial College Centre for Energy Policy and Technology, available at www3.imperial.ac.uk/pls/portallive/docs/1/7294712.PDF, accessed 11 November 2008

Verdonk, M., Dieperink, C. and Faaij, A. P. C. (2007) 'Governance of the emerging bio-energy markets.' *Energy Policy* 35(7): 3909–3924

Woods, J., Bauen, A., Rosillo-Calle, F., Anderson, D., Saynor, B. and Howes, J. (2003) *Technology Status Review and Carbon Abatement Potential of Renewable Transport Fuels in the UK*, ICCEPT, Imperial College London, London, www.berr.gov.uk/Files/File15003.pdf, accessed 10 November 2008

Zah, R., Böni, H., Gauch, M., Hischier, R., Lehmann, M. and Wäger, P. (2007) *Life Cycle Assessment of Energy Products: Environmental Assessment of Biofuels*, Berne: EMPA, available at www.empa.ch/plugin/template/empa/3/60542/–l=2, english language summary available at www.theoildrum.com/node/2976, accessed 11 November 2008

15
Voluntary Carbon Offsetting for Air Travel

John Broderick

Introduction

The rapid growth in emissions from the aviation industry presents a number of challenges if we are to avoid climate change greater than 2°C above pre-industrial levels. As discussed elsewhere in this volume, absolute volumes of emissions from aviation will be significant under constrained, cumulative emissions budgets and opportunities for technological improvements are limited. Rather than internal abatement, carbon trading and voluntary carbon offsetting have been presented as alternative mitigation strategies and aroused much controversy in the process. This chapter focuses on voluntary carbon offsetting which in its simplest terms is an economic exchange between two participants: a transaction with money moving in one direction and emissions rights, quantified in tonnes of CO_2 equivalent (tCO_2-eq), in the other. The rationale is that rather than reduce emissions at source, a polluter may pay for reductions to be made elsewhere, usually at lower cost, on the assumption that both the initial party's emissions and the secondary party's reductions can be calculated and made equivalent. An example might be an airline passenger flying New York–Amsterdam paying a contribution towards the installation of a new hydroelectric dam in China that displaces coal-generated electricity from the local grid. Tree-planting schemes that are intended to sequester CO_2 from the atmosphere and store it biologically are also commonly developed.

The market is voluntary because transactions occur without or in addition to legislative requirements as a result of corporate social responsibility policy, efforts to improve brand image or individual ethical motivations. In addition to the emissions reductions, the credit-generating project might also result in ancillary sustainable development benefits such as local employment or reduced local air pollution. Voluntary trading as a whole has grown rapidly, with an estimated US$258 million worth of transactions in 2007, up from US$58.5 million in 2006 (Hamilton et al, 2008), demand for the service coming from both individuals and corporations. These are global developments with new emissions trading schemes developing in the US, Australia and New Zealand and international transactions in credits linking polluters in rich nations to project developers in Asia and Latin America. However, accusations of fraud and allusions to 'indulgences for climate sins' (Smith, 2007), have sat alongside celebrity endorsements and reports of much needed investment in developing country energy infrastructure. With the pressing need to tackle climate change and limited technological potential for decarbonization of air transport in the short term, it is easy to see why offsetting is an attractive solution, although it is far from clear what its implications are in the long term.

This chapter aims to summarize recent developments in the voluntary carbon markets and provide an introduction to a complex, dynamic and controversial topic. It is not a consumer guide to buying the 'best offsets' but will hopefully help the reader to assess different credit types and provide useful references to further resources. The first section will anatomize the process of offsetting, the production of carbon commodities and the development of proprietary and third-party standards that provide some degree of stability, transparency and rigour. This will necessarily involve some discussion of the regulated, compliance carbon markets. The next part will discuss the scale and direction of the voluntary market. Finally, this chapter will outline general criticisms of offsetting and then look at some specific issues raised by its use in relation to air travel.

Outline of voluntary carbon markets

First, it is useful to clarify a number of terms that have entered common use:

- 'A carbon offset' is loosely defined but is typically used to denote an emissions reduction credit produced by investment in a defined project.
- 'Offsetting' is the act of buying emissions reduction credits or permits to retire (cancel) them in lieu of direct reductions.
- 'Carbon neutrality' is a status where the quantity 'offset' is equal to total emissions attributed to an organization over a given time period.
- 'The voluntary market' is the sum of retailers, brokers, developers and consumers buying and selling emissions credits for retirement without a regulatory requirement.

Permits and credits are quite different things, the former being defined as a share of an emissions limit in a 'cap and trade' system while the latter is an award from a recognized body for undertaking actions to reduce emissions. Tackling greenhouse gas (GHG) emissions is ostensibly the central activity of carbon markets and as such, the central organizing feature is the commodity 'tonnes of CO_2 equivalent' (tCO_2-eq). It is in these units that emission output and reductions are measured and transacted, and while obvious, it is worth noting that neither permits nor credits are natural, pre-existing physical entities. Although there are tangible physical processes going on behind the carbon markets, the traded entities themselves are characterized by the institutions in which they are produced, exchanged and consumed, and as such it is important to understand the terms and structures of such institutions. In the case of the voluntary carbon market this is not straightforward.

Producing carbon commodities

Voluntary carbon trading requires no defined, single, central authority that structures and coordinates the institution. If a participant is not mandated by law to offset their emissions then it is their prerogative to decide who to interact with and the terms of the exchange. This is in contrast to the regulated markets organized by, for example, the United Nations Framework Convention on Climate Change (UNFCCC) and the EU, which strictly detail the parties to be regulated, their emissions liabilities and the terms of their settlement, calculation methods and legally recognized exchanges between parties. As a result, there are a range of commodities retired for voluntary purposes, including those produced within compliance regimes, but predominantly credits produced outside these and generically termed VERs (Verified, or Voluntary, Emissions Reductions). Recent estimates suggest that this admittedly broad classification represents 66 per cent of the volume of trade on the worldwide voluntary market (Hamilton et al, 2008).

In cap and trade systems, a central authority awards or auctions a finite quantity of permits to participants who are able to trade among themselves but must then surrender an amount equivalent to their emissions in a given period. Permits, such as EUAs from the EU Emissions Trading Scheme (EU ETS), can be retired voluntarily, reducing the quantities available for regulated participants. This action is only worthwhile if there is a shortfall in the quantity of permits at the outset, otherwise the purchase is simply of 'hot air'. If the permits have been given away freely to participants, such transactions might also be seen as transferring wealth to incumbent polluters. Both criticisms pertain to Phase 1 of the EU ETS, and as a result represent a small proportion of transactions in the voluntary market (Hamilton et al, 2008). Rather than purchasing emissions permits, a more effective approach to aggregate emissions reduction may have been to lobby elected representatives for stricter emissions limits.

Credits, rather than permits, are most frequently used for voluntary offsetting and are not restricted in quantity. In general terms, credits are recognized for interventions which are an improvement on existing practices and are in some way amenable to quantification. Subject to the terms and norms of the institution, they can be created by submitting a claim from a wide variety of project types: for example, planting trees to store carbon in maintained forestry, fuelling a power station with a mixture of biomass and coal rather than simply coal, collecting methane which would otherwise escape from agricultural slurry pits. Many credit institutions and credit consumers contend that there are supplementary 'sustainable development' benefits arising from the project. However, the definition, scope and interpretation of this term is vexed in this field and others. Credits are quantified as the reduction from a 'business as usual' baseline, an estimate of GHG emissions without the intervention of the project. These activities typically bear an upfront capital cost that may be raised from investors against the future sale of credits arising from the completed project. Credits are therefore a commodity form, a type of property right, that encourages investment in emissions-reducing practices by providing an opportunity for profit. In order for this to be possible, buyers need to be able to recognize the legitimacy of the property right for sale, which is not without its difficulties, and systems of standards and registries are key to negotiating this. They are also important for the environmental integrity of the trade; if credits have been awarded wrongly then there may be a net increase in emissions if they are used to justify ongoing pollution by their consumer. When credits are awarded project-by-project additionality, the idea that a project would not have gone ahead without intervention from the carbon markets is central to the validity of the credit but is difficult, if not impossible, to objectively define. Revenue from the sale of credits is usually not the only source of capital involved in implementing a project, nor is it necessarily the sole motivation. For example, improvements in industrial process efficiency lead to long-term cost savings for the operator and so may be worthwhile without credit revenue; forest plantations may be initiated to improve local amenities or achieve ecological objectives. Different approaches and stringency accepted by existent standards institutions mean that projects that meet additionality criteria in one may not in another.

At present, compliance and voluntary markets have the same essential structure for credit creation from emissions reduction projects, usually based on the UNFCCC's Clean Development Mechanism (CDM) project cycle. The CDM was initially proposed during the Kyoto Protocol negotiations as a means of distributing funds arising from punitive fines for non-compliance with the national emissions caps (Grubb et al, 1999). However, pressure from the US, which ultimately withdrew from the protocol, resulted in the proposals becoming a means of creating more pollution capacity for developed countries via offsetting projects in developing nations without emissions caps. The result is now an US$8.2 billion annual trade in CDM credits (Capoor and Ambroisi, 2008), which may be used by nation states to fulfil their 2008–2012 Kyoto commitments and regulated installations to meet their liabilities in the EU ETS. The creation of CDM credits, Certified Emissions Reductions (CERs), is regulated by a centralized administration, predominantly paid for by fees levied for the registration of projects, and supervised by an Executive Board (EB) which authorizes project methodologies and issuance of credits. Project audit itself is undertaken by certified external agencies.

The project cycle begins with a formal proposal, documenting parties to the development and detailing location, relevant national authorities, the period for credits to be claimed, and a justification case that the project is additional and requires support from the carbon market to proceed. A quantification methodology is defined which illustrates an alternative future emissions profile under 'business as usual' conditions, the savings to be claimed by the project, and the monitoring and auditing procedures to be used. The proposal is then validated by a certified third party against the project types, locations and methods acceptable to the standard. There may also be a period of public consultation where comments are invited on the project documents, usually posted to the standard's website. Once approved, the project is registered with the standards body and monitoring commences. As the project operates, further verification audits, conducted by certified third parties, check monitoring data as specified in the registered project documentation. The final stage is the creation of the credit within the standard's registry, an independent database of uniquely numbered credits, and issuance of the credits to the project developer. Ownership may then be transferred between market participants and credits ultimately retired by changing details in the registry. As such, a registry system reduces the likelihood that buyers may be defrauded by the 'double selling' of emissions reductions from a given project.

Emissions credit standards

Initially, credits transacted in the voluntary market were guaranteed only by the reputation of the retailer or developer, or their own proprietary standards with substantial variation found in retailers providing offsets services for air travel (Gössling et al, 2007). Retailers typically claimed that emissions reductions were 'real, verifiable, permanent and additional' but credit production lacked transparency. Even if consumers were able to judge procedures and scrutinize claims themselves, accessing information was difficult. In essence, the transaction was one way; the consumer paid for a service without receiving anything in return or being able to verify its execution. Auditing was not always carried out by independent organizations, nor were audit reports necessarily made publicly available. These issues and questions over the permanence and long-run responsibilities of offset retailers led to high-profile criticism in the news media (Muir, 2004; Dhillon and Harnden, 2006; Chapman, 2006; Elgin, 2007; Faris, 2007; Clarke, 2007; Harvey, 2007; Harvey and Fidler, 2007; Johnston, 2007; Davies, 2007). In the UK, the government responded by issuing a Code of Best Practice for voluntary offsetting, its most controversial aspect being the exclusive endorsement of the compliance regimes (Clean Development Mechanism, Joint Implementation and EU Emissions Trading Scheme) for the delivery of commodities for offsetting. The proposals appear to have been taken seriously by a number of UK airlines, easyJet, British Airways, Flybe and Virgin Atlantic programmes complying. Furthermore, the Code also specifies how credits are to be managed by a retailer and cancelled within a specific timescale. This effectively excludes *ex-ante* systems whereby a credit is claimed, and sold, 'up front' on the expectation of a successful reduction in the future. For example, energy-efficient light bulbs may only save an appreciable quantity of carbon over a 10-year period. However, an offset transaction may be arranged to supply the capital to fund a distribution project on the expectation of those savings, a precarious situation, although one which project developers contend facilitates the implementation of projects that would otherwise be unable to raise initial capital and thus be more clearly seen to be additional.

Independently of the UK Government proposals, a variety of market actors have developed autonomous quality assurance standards, formalizing different parts of the credit creation process and with varying degrees of rigour. The most prominent complete offset standards are outlined below; however readers are referred to the SEI/Tricorona report *Making Sense of the Voluntary Carbon Market* for fuller analysis (Kollmuss et al, 2008).

- Gold Standard (GS, www.cdmgoldstandard.org/). A not-for-profit organization initiated by the World Wide Fund for Nature (WWF), the Gold Standard was initially intended to supplement the CDM and promote local benefits from the emissions reduction projects, reduce risk of wrongful award of credits and stimulate innovation in clean technology rather than simply provide least-cost emissions abatement. To achieve GS certification, projects must be based on renewable energy or energy efficiency methods, undergo more detailed environmental impact assessment and local stakeholder consultation and meet stricter additionality tests. Other accounting and registration procedures are as for the CDM. There is also a GS VER standard with an independent registry, external audit procedures similar to but less onerous than the CDM, simplified procedures for 'micro-scale' projects generating less than 5000 tonnes of reductions per annum, less stringent requirements for host country approval and a wider variety of approved project implementation and monitoring methods.
- Voluntary Carbon Standard (VCS, www.v-c-s.org/). This system is operational but periodically reviewed, initially developed as a collaboration between NGOs The Climate Group, International Emissions Trading Association (IETA), the World Economic Forum Greenhouse Register and the World Business Council for Sustainable Development. The VCS has complete carbon accounting procedures similar to CDM but relies more heavily on auditors and consultants to perform quality assurance and adopts ISO standards (14064-1:2006, 14064-2:2006, 14064-3:2006) as the basis of emissions calculation, validation, monitoring and verification. The standard has no specific requirement for supplementary social or environmental beneficial outcomes from projects and accepts large hydro, nuclear, forestry and industrial gas destruction. There is the possibility of alignment of interests between auditor and developer given that the same company can validate and verify a single project and there is no further independent approval (Kollmuss et al, 2008).

- VER+ (www.netinform.de/KE/Beratung/Service_Ver.aspx). This standard and registry are offered by a prominent audit company, TÜV SÜD. VER+ credits are generated using calculation methods and audit procedures from the CDM but with more relaxed crediting periods and wider geographic scope. Like the VCS it offers no more of a guarantee of social or environmental benefits arising from project implementation than the emissions reduction credits, although industrial gas destruction, nuclear and hydro-electricity (>80MW) are not eligible.
- Chicago Climate Exchange (CCX, www.chicagoclimatex.com/). This is a hybrid system in two senses: first, it is 'cap and trade' with credit generating projects and second, membership is voluntary but commitments are legally binding. There are currently 130 full members representing a wide variety of organizations including electricity generators, primary and secondary industry, municipalities, states and educational institutions. Other organizations can qualify for offset credits for a variety of project types including forestry and agricultural practices. Additionality is assessed on a group basis rather than project by project and there have been question marks raised over projects rejected by the CDM subsequently entering the CCX (*Carbon Finance*, 2008).

Project types, sizes and locations

While the market for voluntary offsets was initially dominated by forestry projects, both afforestation in 'carbon plantations' and avoided deforestation in conservation concessions, there is now much more diversity. Neither the type of project eligible for credits nor the identities of project developers are exclusively defined by the standard regimes in advance, so there is the possibility for a wide variety of interventions, subject to the acceptance of their calculation methodologies and additionality justifications. The bulk of projects can broadly be categorized as being forestry and land use, fuel switching, renewable energy, energy efficiency, methane capture, or fugitive industrial gas destruction. Transportation projects have yet to be realized in large numbers because of the substantial practical and theoretical difficulties in quantifying emissions reductions. Projects do not solely reduce CO_2 emissions from fossil fuel consumption as other greenhouse gases are made equivalent by defining their global warming potential (GWP), a comparative metric that estimates additional warming effect over a stated time period, usually 100 years, of a unit mass of gas released into the atmosphere relative to CO_2. Different gases have different radiation absorption properties and different fates in the atmosphere, but by assuming that they are well mixed and relatively long lived, a set of simple multipliers for methane, nitrous oxide and a series of fluorinated hydrocarbons has facilitated a further variety of credit-generating projects. GWPs are contentious within the climate science community, retaining substantial error boundaries. It has been argued that a degree of ambiguity in their definition resulted from an interplay of scientific uncertainty and political expedience (Shackley and Wynne, 1997) with the subsequent 'black-boxing' of the process having profound effects. Although CO_2 remains the gas responsible for the bulk of anthropogenic climate forcing, the convention of using a GWP of 11,700 for trifluoromethane (HFC-23) and 296 for nitrous oxide has meant that $110MtCO_2$-eq credits, representing 72 per cent of the volume issued by the CDM to date (UNEP Risø CDM Pipeline, June 2008) have come from industrial gas destruction projects. It is estimated that the €100 million investment in pollution control made by these projects will yield €4.7 billion in credits on the compliance market (Wara, 2007). While these particular projects will not be able to reap credits indefinitely, the case highlights the social contingency and importance of calculation processes in market arrangements (MacKenzie, 2008).

Recent surveys have shown a rapid increase in renewable energy projects to 31 per cent of the voluntary market, $8.8MtCO_2$-eq traded in 2007 (Hamilton et al, 2008), the majority being wind and hydroelectricity developments in China and India. This may be a result of consumer preference for projects that promote decarbonization of energy systems or developers claiming voluntary compliant credits from projects prior to their acceptance by the CDM. Whether this is a positive outcome, the voluntary markets assisting worthwhile projects to reach the compliance market, or alternatively of questionable merit (if the revenue stream from the CDM is the primary motivation for project development, are the pre-compliance credits really additional?) is not clear. Methane destruction projects, capturing emissions from livestock waste, landfill sites or coal mines, made up 16 per cent of trades in 2007, such projects being relatively cheap to deliver and high yielding because of the 23 times GWP multiplier for methane. They may also be promoted by high demand from US consumers seeking 'home-sourced' offset credits (Hamilton et al, 2008). The relatively flexible nature of the voluntary markets means that consumer preference beyond price minimization may be important. However, online retailers often sell from a portfolio of offsets and there is no empirical evidence to demonstrate offset purchasers 'shopping around'.

Projects also vary substantially in size, the largest, typically industrial gas destruction and methane biogas plants delivering over $500,000tCO_2$-eq per annum, trading alongside household fuel efficiency projects generating savings a thousand times less. This has implications for the price of credits, given the transaction costs involved in registering, validating, operating and verifying a project; 49 per cent of credits traded in the voluntary markets in 2007 originated from projects over $100,000tCO_2$-eq per annum (Hamilton et al, 2008). There is an even more pronounced effect in the CDM which has led to criticism from commentators as one reason for the low sustainable development benefits of projects implemented thus far (Cosbey et al, 2006; Olsen, 2007). Costs related to documentation, validation and registration for the CDM can be between US$38,000 and US$610,000 depending upon project type, scale, novelty and complexity, in addition to the project implementation capital and operational costs (CD4CDM and EcoSecurities, 2007). While there are simplified regulations and procedures for approval of small-scale projects (those generating less than 60,000 CERs per annum), employing auditors for validation and verification is still costly. A recent Delphi study of experts in the field estimated average total transaction costs of a small-scale project is in the order of US$45,000, which by extension represents US$0.70 per tCO_2-eq generated, in comparison to US$0.05 for large scale, and a minimum viable size of between 20,000 and 50,000tCO_2-eq per annum (Cames et al, 2007). Voluntary market developers have endorsed 'light touch' auditing procedures as necessary to realize projects with local community benefits; however, the trend towards formalization of standards and competition for supply contracts may put pressure on retailers to commission cheaper reductions from larger projects.

The crediting institution also influences project locations. Projects are only eligible under the CDM if they occur in nation states that have ratified the Kyoto Protocol and do not have their own emissions reduction targets. The host nation must also have its own internal bureaucracy for the approval of projects, a Designated National Authority. As such, European national projects are not eligible and neither are those in the US. Some voluntary market standards do allow credits to originate in developed country economies although they may stipulate that equivalent quantities are removed from the relevant UNFCCC account to avoid double-counting of reductions. This marks a substantial distinction between compliance and voluntary carbon markets; 90 per cent of issued CDM credits originate from China, India, South Korea or Brazil (UNEP Risø CDM Pipeline, June 2008) while 47 per cent of credits transacted in the voluntary market originate from North America, Europe, Australia or New Zealand (Hamilton et al, 2008). The growth in voluntary emissions projects in the US may be seen as an opportunity created by the absence of leadership on climate change from the Bush administration. Legislated federal action, of the type surely needed to seriously tackle greenhouse gas emissions in the US, would probably render many projects non-additional in future. Market participants may or may not be supportive of such intervention, but voluntary action is not driving substantial investment in low-carbon technology in OECD nations at present.

Consuming carbon credits

The creation of credits is ultimately driven by a market for their cancellation against an increase in emissions elsewhere. In compliance markets this is a failure to meet national or corporate liabilities that are well defined, but this is not the case in the voluntary market. Air transport has become associated with voluntary carbon offsetting as it is not readily amenable to substitution with low-emission alternatives. Historically, greenhouse gas emissions from the aviation sector have also been overlooked at a range of political scales. In the international arena they are presently absent from the EU Emissions Trading Scheme and the Annex B targets set by the Kyoto Protocol, along with emissions from international shipping, and in the UK they are not included in the Government's greenhouse gas summary statistics. The combination of conspicuous growth and regulatory omission has presented an obvious target for voluntary measures although this may soon change. A substantial lobby, including some airlines, airports and trade associations (Sustainable Aviation, 2005), has argued for the expansion of the EU Emissions Trading Scheme to encompass aviation. In December 2006 the European Commission adopted a proposal to include intra-EU flights within open trading in the ETS. This was subsequently strengthened by the European Parliament's provisional amendments and adopted in July 2008, such that emissions from all flights entering or leaving European airports will be regulated by the EU ETS from the start of 2012. Annual emissions allocations will be capped at 97 per cent of mean 2004–2006 levels in the first year, and 95 per cent from 2013 to 2020. With just 15 per cent auctioning and the remainder a free allocation of emissions permits, the proposals appear to be an accommodation of aviation within the ETS rather than a purposeful attempt to limit growth rates. It is clear that in the short term at least, airlines will be substantial net buyers of permits as the price rises on individual air tickets are unlikely to substantially affect demand. Even if the cost of permits was to rise to €50–100 per tonne CO_2-eq, significantly higher than current EUA Phase II forward prices which are in the order of €20–30, analysis suggests a typical short-haul flight price increase of just €2–9 per passenger in 2012 or €3–10 in 2016 (Anderson et al, 2007). The aggregate costs to airlines will be substantially less than recent rises in fuel costs (Scheelhaase and Grimme, 2007). If changes in the consumption and operation of air transport are a policy objective then additional, non-market interventions will probably be required. Corresponding corrections, through preferential allocation or imposition of border tariffs to protect other industries, might also be applied to avoid displacement of energy-intensive activities from the EU. Such intersectoral analysis of the implications of emissions trading is developing but has yet to fully address the entry of the aviation industry in the medium to long term (Climate Strategies, 2006).

Issues raised by the inclusion of aviation the EU ETS are relevant to the voluntary consumption of credits, primarily those concerning the calculation of the warming effect of aviation. In the first instance, responsibility for a specific quantity of emissions must be assigned to the offset consumer. This is necessarily an estimate, as direct individual monitoring would be overly burdensome, even if means existed to isolate responsibility for warming into the future from participation in a collective activity such as purchasing an air fare and joining a scheduled flight. Offset credit retailers typically host emissions calculators on their websites to provide guidance on an appropriate quantity of credits to purchase to 'neutralize' the contribution to climate change of a given activity. The detail offered by the calculator varies between retailers, some categorizing flights into short, medium or long haul, others employing sophisticated models including multiple flight phases, typical load factors and known efficiency of aircraft employed on a given route. A survey of online calculators illustrated variations of more than a factor of three between retailers and substantial discrepancies even where stated per passenger km emissions factors and 'uplift' multipliers were the same (Gössling et al, 2007).

When compounded with an order of magnitude variation in the price per tCO_2-eq, the opportunity for consumer confusion in what is presented as a simple empirical exercise is substantial.

Further, uncertainties and inconsistencies remain within the understanding and representation of the multiple non-CO_2 climate impacts of aviation. As well as creating contrails and altering cloud formation, aircraft emit oxides of nitrogen (NO_x) that subsequently influence ozone and methane concentrations in the atmosphere. These warming and cooling effects vary over different timescales and their strength may be influenced by location, altitude, season and time of day (Peeters et al, 2007). From latest IPCC *Fourth Assessment Report* (AR4) figures it has been estimated that aviation causes a radiative forcing between 1.9 and 4.7 times as much as that due to CO_2 alone (Grassl and Brockhagen, 2007). This ratio refers to the radiative forcing of historic (long-lived) CO_2 emissions versus current (short-lived) non-CO_2 impacts, while for the purpose of offsetting, the future radiative forcing of 1t of GHG emitted would ideally be accounted for (Wit et al, 2005; Forster et al, 2006). Half the online calculators surveyed by Gössling et al (2007) used 'uplift factors' of between 1.9 and 3 and multiply the quantity of CO_2 emissions by this amount. While these are not strictly justified by the physics of the situation, there is undoubtedly a warming effect over and above CO_2 and for simplicity in the voluntary market inclusion may be warranted. Similar to ambiguities around the use of GWPs, the ultimate difficulty stems from the assumption of equivalence between emissions demanded by the conceptual framework of emissions trading. Entities must be 'framed' for commodity exchange in such a way that fundamentally different phenomena are made equivalent (Callon, 1998; Lohmann, 2005).

Problems with offsetting

Carbon offsetting is controversial on a number of scales, with criticisms levelled at individual projects, whole project types, the definition and operation of standards, protocols and audit procedures that endorse projects and generate credits, and the principles of emissions trading as a whole. The 'real' and 'verifiable' nature of the commodities is often used as a distinction between those with and those without formal verification procedures, through the CDM or otherwise. However, this serves to mask the fact that *all* baseline derived credits are the result of counterfactual constructions and social conventions within trading institutions. On this basis, 'Offsets are an imaginary commodity created by deducting what you hope happens from what you guess would have happened' (Welch, 2007). That is not to say that there is no differentiation in the likelihood of an individual project achieving emissions savings, nor that their governance structures are similarly transparent or equitable, as detailed earlier.

A case for additionality may be presented in different ways but ultimately a judgement decision must be made by a consumer, auditor or management board to accept a project. It is even possible to retrospectively apply for registration of an operational project under many standards if it can be argued that credit revenue was 'seriously considered in the decision to proceed with the project activity' (CDM: Guidelines for Completing the PDD Version 6.2, p11). The CDM outlines the following tests which are mirrored in voluntary standards as described above:

1   Regulatory Additionality: If a project is implemented to meet existing legal obligations then it is not additional. This is not sufficient alone to demonstrate additionality.
2   Investment Test: Revenue from the sale of credits is decisive in gaining investment in the project. These micro-economic considerations are subjective, especially where credit revenue is a small component of total project funding and may only make the difference between an 8 per cent and an 11 per cent internal rate of return. The test is vulnerable to manipulation because of information asymmetry between proponent and regulator (Haya, 2007).
3   Barriers Test: Are there any non-financial impediments to the project's go-ahead, for example lack of local skills or expertise? This may be controversial in cases where the project has positive medium- or long-term economic savings for the beneficiary.
4   Common Practice Test: The project must be shown to be dissimilar to other activities in its locality or industrial sector.

A recent review of Indian projects by a member of the CDM Registration and Issuance Team noted that one third of the 52 projects inspected failed to adequately demonstrate additionality (Michaelowa and Purohit, 2007; Davies, 2007). A similar case was found for hydroelectricity projects registered under the CDM in China. New projects registered with the CDM represent 5.1GW of capacity, a substantial proportion of total installation of 9GW in 2007, which should be considered against previous annual installations of around 7.7GW without CDM support (Haya, 2007). In this case, political and economic conditions are manifestly supportive, raising significant questions of any specific claims of additionality. These failings cannot be dismissed as unique to specific projects or auditors, nor do they invalidate the CDM as a whole. However, they point to inevitable, systemic weaknesses in crediting systems that can only ever be addressed to a limited degree. A separate mixed methods study by a member if the CDM Methodologies Panel identified competition between auditors as impacting on thoroughness of review and suggested that additionality was questionable for 40 per cent of registered projects representing 20 per cent of expected credits by 2012 (Schneider, 2007). The trade-off between 'flexibility' and climatological security is persistent and must be recognized by voluntary consumers of offsets and those who support the CDM as a central plank of international climate policy.

Issues with projects and project type

The majority of independent assessment of emissions markets and credit projects has been conducted on CDM projects because of its high profile, large volume and publicly accessible register of activities facilitating research. Text analysis of the 'pipeline' of registered projects has demonstrated that local social and ecological benefits are not presently realized by the compliance market (Cosbey et al, 2006; Olsen and Fenhann, 2008), possibly as a result of host nations' reluctance to reject any foreign investment. Indeed there are cases documented where CDM has been accused of politically legitimizing and financially supporting 'bad neighbour' industries such as sponge iron smelters or waste landfill sites (Lohmann, 2006) and in some cases projects have encountered popular resistance as a consequence of exacerbating environmental injustice (Smith, 2007). Although some failures are conspicuous, the withered mango trees funded by the pop group Coldplay for example (Dhillon and Harnden, 2006), the voluntary market's haphazard development makes it very difficult to generalize about the consequences of its growth for those involved in the projects.

Although land-use change is a substantial contributor to climate change, there has been warranted concern about its inclusion in a market-based climate policy. Carbon that is biologically sequestered in forestry or soils is problematic because of the potential for release at a later date, trees being vulnerable to fire, drought and pests, and soil to climate change or tillage. Industrial monoculture plantations have also drawn substantial and justifiable criticism from indigenous peoples, conservation and development organizations (Carrere and González, 2000; Bachram, 2004). Although there is support for small-scale, bundled community forestry from some quarters (Boyd et al, 2007), it is not clear how tensions between local welfare and self-determination are to be reconciled with international, institutional requirements for low cost, security and permanence. Moreover, forestry does nothing to move economies away from dependence upon fossil fuels or promote innovation into new technologies. Nevertheless, the co-benefits, real or presumed, of watershed protection, sustainable livelihoods, biodiversity conservation, easy comprehension and generic positive associations between trees and pro-environmental behaviour by Western consumers, mean that forestry projects will continue to be supported.

Criticisms of offsetting in principle

Voluntary and regulatory standards, such as the Gold Standard, that include project screening and environmental and social impact assessment prior to initiation may serve to mitigate many of the negative impacts and promote those projects with greater benefit to their host communities. However, fundamentally the governance of the voluntary market is such that the terms of exchange weigh in favour of the credit consumer who is by definition distant and isolated from its consequences.

There is a tension between the use of low-cost carbon projects in developing economies and efforts to develop and deploy new technologies in OECD countries. Offsetting acts as a disincentive to structural change in the consumption of energy, locking in highly emitting sociotechnical configurations (Unruh, 2002) and locking out alternatives that will be necessary given the profound and rapid reductions required to avoid dangerous climate change (Metz et al, 2007). The argument is made that market mechanisms may yet prove to be very successful at gathering 'low-hanging fruit' but in doing so are delaying inevitable changes and in the process misdirecting attention from existing arrangements that subsidize fossil-fuel extraction and consumption. Infrastructure lock-in through a prolonged period of low incentive to change, for example in the case of the tourism industry, the purchase of a new fleet of long-haul aircraft, and construction of new terminal facilities, could lead either to a write-off of resources or ultimately avoidance of change altogether. Credit regimes also have the potential to influence the offset host's policy development by creating a situation of moral hazard; actors may delay taking action to curb emissions in the short term for gain under a future regime (Hepburn, 2007).

A series of forceful ethical positions against offsetting have also come from proponents of social justice. Offsetting is predicated upon the profound difference in per capita emissions between industrialized and industrializing countries and it assumes that an equal price should be paid by all for the mitigation of climate change by 'outsourcing' reductions to economies where savings are, currently, low cost. 'Carbon colonialism' ignores historic responsibilities and in the case of voluntary retail offsets focuses attention on the individual not the society (Bachram, 2004), reducing what ought to be seen as a political problem to a financial transaction. The agenda for development and acceptable degrees of climate impact are set by technical, financial and political elites in the business as usual baselines of credits systems and not by those most at risk or through democratic means (Lohmann, 2001). Where there are opportunities for substantial wealth creation in the development of such markets the benefits accrue to the already wealthy (Bumpus and Liverman, 2008) and, as John O'Neill eloquently argues, to invoke a market solution to environmental disputes is to entrench the same social order that is responsible for production of those disputes in the first instance (O'Neill, 2007).

Conclusions

The anticipated growth in emissions from the aviation industry does not appear to be compatible with the objective of avoiding dangerous climate change, given the limited possibility for efficiency improvements through technological advance. The carbon offset industry provides services to corporations and individuals with ethical inclinations to voluntarily invest in projects that purport to compensate for the emissions that they are unable or unwilling to reduce. Similar to other neoliberal modes of governance, responsibility for action is devolved to the individual and governed by a system of non-state economic actors, in this case project developers, auditors and standards organizations (Bumpus and Liverman, 2008). Calculation and attribution, of both emissions from air travel and conversely reductions from offset projects, are problematic but are increasingly being formalized for better or worse.

Whether project-based institutions are effective in delivering emissions reductions is a far more important question for the compliance market, discharging major industrial and national commitments, than the retail voluntary market. Retail credit integrity is arguably first a matter of consumer protection as opposed to wider social welfare, as such voluntary initiatives are unlikely ever to effect sociotechnical change on the necessary scale. Initial optimism that the voluntary market would supply substantial new revenue streams for community-scale international development projects seems to be misplaced. The bulk of credits appear to come from projects similar to those in the compliance sector with low additional sustainable development benefits, the economizing action of the market mechanism meeting the demand for credits at least cost (Estrada et al, 2008; Hamilton et al, 2008). Eighty per cent of voluntary credit purchases are by private institutions citing corporate social responsibility and public relations as their primary motivation (Hamilton et al, 2008) and so there is clearly a public interest in these reduction claims being valid and not simply a hollow branding exercise or effort to delay formal regulation. In the case of the aviation industry, the detail of ICAO and IATA intention to develop a 'global emissions trading scheme that is fair, voluntary and effective' (IATA, 2008) must be thoroughly scrutinized and understood in relation to the wider compliance markets and ongoing growth in absolute emissions from air travel.

Setting aside questions of the integrity of credit projects, proponents of offsetting argue that familiarity with carbon footprints and acknowledgement of personal responsibility for emissions are positive outcomes of the voluntary retail market. Although these are plausible claims, there is very little empirical evidence to substantiate them (House of Commons, 2007). It is also worth noting that for the individual who is conscious of the climate change impact of their lifestyle there are a number of other financial transactions they could engage in. They may decide their money is better spent making a donation to a charity that implements low-carbon technologies in developing countries, but which does not pay a share dividend, employ auditors to quantify reductions or lawyers to claim property rights. Alternatively, they may choose to support an NGO that raises wider social awareness of the issue of climate change or lobbies for tougher government policy. They might even pay compensation for damages to an international development or climate adaptation charity at an estimated 'social cost of carbon'. All these options raise questions about an individual's responsibility to broader society, what it is to be an ecologically sensitive citizen and the implications of the penetration of financial norms into issues of environmental protection and social welfare. Communications from offsetting agencies often emphasize that they are only 'part of the solution' (Dembo and Davidson, 2007). As such, while they may offer some contribution they should not distract industry or policy makers from the long-term challenge of avoiding dangerous climate change.

References

Anderson, K., Bows, A. and Footitt, A. (2007) *Aviation in a Low Carbon EU*, Manchester: Tyndall Centre, September

Bachram, H. (2004) 'Climate fraud and carbon colonialism: The new trade in greenhouse gases', *Capitalism Nature Socialism* 15(4): 5–20

Boyd, E., Gutierrez, M. and Chang, M. Y. (2007) 'Small-scale forest carbon projects: Adapting CDM to low-income communities', *Global Environmental Change – Human And Policy Dimensions* 17(2): 250–259

Bumpus, A. and Liverman, D. (2008) 'Accumulation by decarbonisation and the governance of carbon offsets', *Economic Geography* 84(2): 127–155

Callon, M. (1998) *An Essay on Framing and Overflowing: Economic Externalities Revisited by Sociology*, Oxford: Blackwell, pp244–269

Cames, M., Anger, N., Böhringer, C., Harthan, R. O. and Schneider, L. (2007) *Long-Term Prospects of CDM and JI*. Dessau: Umweltbundesamt, available at www.umweltbundesamt.de

Capoor, K. and Ambroisi, P. (2008) *State and Trends of the Carbon Market 2008* Washington DC: World Bank, May

Carbon Finance (2008) 'Rejected Indian CDM projects head to CCX', *Carbon Finance*, 25 June, available at www.carbon-financeonline.com/index.cfm?section=lead&action=view&id=11339, accessed 12 August 2008

Carrere, R. and González, A. (eds) (2000) *Climate Change Convention: Sinks That Stink*, World Rainforest Movement, available at www.wrm.org.uy/actors/CCC/sinks.html

CD4CDM and EcoSecurities (2007) *Guidebook to Financing CDM Projects*, available at http://cd4cdm.org/Publications/FinanceCDMprojectsGuidebook.pdf

Chapman, M. (2006) 'Green government plan "a fiasco"', *BBC Radio Five Live*, 29 October, available at http://news.bbc.co.uk/1/hi/business/6092460.stm

Clarke, T. (2007) 'Great green smokescreen', *Channel 4: Dispatches*, 16 July, available at www.channel4.com/news/articles/dispatches/the+great+green+smokescreen/589267

Climate Strategies (2006) *Allocation and Competitiveness in the EU Emissions Trading Scheme: Options for Phase II and Beyond*, Technical report, Carbon Trust

Cosbey, A., Murphy, D., Drexhage, J. and Balint, J. (2006) *Making Development Work in the CDM Phase II of the Development Dividend Project*, Winnipeg: International Institute for Sustainable Development

Davies, N. (2007) 'Abuse and incompetence in fight against global warming', *The Guardian*, 2 June, available at http://business.guardian.co.uk/story/0,,2093836,00.html

Dembo, R. and Davidson, C. (2007) *Everything You Wanted to Know about Offsetting but Were Afraid to Ask*, Toronto: Zerofootprint, April, available at www.zerofootprint.net/item_images/16182/Everything_Zero_web.pdf

Dhillon, A. and Harnden, T. (2006) 'How Coldplay's green hopes died in the arid soil of India', *The Telegraph*, 29 April, available at www.telegraph.co.uk/news/main.jhtml?xml=/news/2006/04/30/ngreen30.xml&sSheet=/news/2006/04/30/ixhome.html

Elgin, B. (2007) 'Another inconvenient truth: Behind the feel-good hype of carbon offsets, some of the deals don't deliver', *Business Week*, 26 March, available at www.businessweek.com/magazine/content/07_13/b4027057.htm

Estrada, M., Corbera, E. and Brown, K. (2008) *How Do Regulated and Voluntary Carbon-Offset Schemes Compare?* Tyndall Working Paper No. 116, May, available at www.tyndall.ac.uk/publications/working_papers/twp116.pdf

Faris, S. (2007) 'The other side of carbon trading', *Fortune Magazine,* 30 August, available at http://money.cnn.com/2007/08/27/news/international/uganda_carbon_trading.fortune/index.htm?postversion=2007082911

Forster, P. M. D. F., Shine, K. P. and Stuber, N. (2006) 'It is premature to include non-CO_2 effects of aviation in emission trading schemes', *Atmospheric Environment* 40(6): 1117–1121

Gössling, S., Broderick, J., Upham, P., Ceron, J.-P., Dubois, G., Peeters, P. and Strasdas, W. (2007) 'Voluntary carbon offsetting schemes for aviation: efficiency, credibility and sustainable tourism', *Journal of Sustainable Tourism* 15(3): 223–248; doi: 10.2167/jost758.0

Grassl, H. and Brockhagen, D. (2007) *Climate Forcing of Aviation Emissions in High Altitudes and Comparison of Metrics: An Update According to the Fourth Assessment Report,* IPCC. Hamburg: Max Planck Institute of Meteorology, December, available at www.mpimet.mpg.de/wissenschaft/publikationen/papers/climate-forcing-of-aviation-emissions-in-high-altitudes-and-comparison-of-metrics.html

Grubb, M., Brack, D. and Vrolijk, C. (1999) *The Kyoto Protocol: A Guide and Assessment.* London: James & James/Earthscan

Hamilton, K., Sjardin, M., Marcello, T. and Xu, G. (2008) *Forging a Frontier: State of The Voluntary Carbon Markets.* Washington DC: Ecosystem Marketplace & New Carbon Finance, May

Harvey, F. (2007) 'Beware the carbon offsetting cowboys', *Financial Times,* 25 April, available at www.ft.com/cms/s/dcdefef6-f350–11db-9845–000b5df10621, dwp_uuid=3c093daa-edc1–11db-8584–000b5df10621.html

Harvey, F. and Fidler, S. (2007) 'Industry caught in "carbon credit" smokescreen', *Financial Times,* 26 April, available at www.ft.com/cms/s/6d52acc6-f392–11db-9845–000b5df10621.html

Haya, B. (2007) *Failed Mechanism: How the CDM is Subsidizing Hydro Developments and Harming the Kyoto Protocol.* Berkeley, CA: International Rivers, November

Hepburn, C. (2007) 'Carbon trading: A review of the Kyoto mechanisms', *Annual Review of Environment And Resources* 32: 375–393

House of Commons, Environmental Audit Committee (2007) *The Voluntary Carbon Offset Market,* Sixth Report of Session 2006–2007. London: The Stationery Office

IATA (2008) *Building a Greener Future,* Zurich: IATA, April, available at www.iata.org/NR/rdonlyres/22669B08–918C-4AB7–8D8F-8F9743BA8FE6/61062/BuildingaGreenerFutureApril2008.pdf

Johnston, I. (2007) 'A gift from Scotland to Brazil: Drought and despair', *The Scotsman,* 7 July, available at http://news.scotsman.com/index.cfm?id=1060072007

Kollmuss, A., Zink, H. and Polycarp, C. (2008) *Making Sense of the Voluntary Carbon Market: A Comparison of Carbon Offset Standards,* WWF Germany, Copyright 2008 by the Stockholm Environment Institute and Tricorona

Lohmann, L. (2001) 'The Dyson effect: Carbon "offset" forestry and the privatization of the atmosphere', *International Journal Of Environment And Pollution* 15(1): 51–78

Lohmann, L. (2005) 'Marketing and making carbon dumps: Commodification, calculation and counterfactuals in climate change mitigation', *Science as Culture* 14(3): 203–235

Lohmann, L. (2006) *Carbon Trading: A Critical Conversation on Climate Change, Privatisation and Power*, Uppsala: Dag Hammarskjöld Foundation

MacKenzie, D. (2008) 'Making things the same: Gases, emission rights and the politics of carbon markets', *Accounting, Organizations and Society* (in press), doi:10.1016/j.aos.2008.02.004

Metz, B., Davidson, O. R., Bosch, P. R., Dave, R. and Meyer, L. A. (eds) (2007) *Climate Change 2007: Mitigation*, Contribution of Working Group III to the Fourth Assessment Report of the Intergovernmental Panel on Climate Change, IPCC, Cambridge, UK: Cambridge University Press

Michaelowa, A. and Purohit, P. (2007) 'Additionality determination of Indian CDM projects: Can Indian CDM project developers outwit the CDM Executive Board?', *Climate Strategies*, Zurich, September, available at www.climatestrategies.org/uploads/additionality-cdm-india-cs-version9–07.pdf

Muir, H. (2004) 'Trees, the eco-investment of choice, but now campaigners question forests firm', *The Guardian*, 30 September, available at www.guardian.co.uk/waste/story/0,12188,1316050,00.html

Olsen, K. H. (2007) 'The clean development mechanism's contribution to sustainable development: A review of the literature', *Climatic Change* 84(1): 59–73

Olsen, K. H. and Fenhann, J. (2008) 'Sustainable development benefits of clean development mechanism projects: A new methodology for sustainability assessment based on text analysis of the project design documents submitted for validation', *Energy Policy* 36(8): 2819–2830

O'Neill, J. (2007) *Markets, Deliberation and Environment*, London: Routledge

Peeters, P., Williams, V. and Gössling, S. (2007) *Tourism and Climate Change Mitigation*, Breda: NHTV, pp29–50

Scheelhaase, J. D. and Grimme, W. G. (2007) 'Emissions trading for international aviation: An estimation of the economic impact on selected European airlines', *Journal of Air Transport Management* 13(5): 253–263, available at www.sciencedirect.com/science/article/B6VGP-4NY4RM4–1/2/a132cad5651272fff703251f92271c21

Schneider, L. (2007) *Is the CDM Fulfilling its Environmental and Sustainable Development Objectives? An Evaluation of the CDM and Options for Improvement*, Berlin: Öko-Institut

Shackley, S. and Wynne, B. (1997) 'Global warming potentials: Ambiguity or precision as an aid to policy?', *Climate Research* 8(2): 89–106

Smith, K. (2007) *The Carbon Neutral Myth: Offset Indulgences for Your Climate Sins*, London: Transnational Institute

Sustainable Aviation (2005) Technical report, AOA, BATA, SBAC, NATS, available at www.sustainableaviation.co.uk/

Unruh, G. C. (2002) 'Escaping carbon lock-in', *Energy Policy* 30(4): 317–325, available at www.sciencedirect.com/science/article/B6V2W-457VJ10–6/2/ac0d68f476e5ded60393ae05603bac92

Wara, M. (2007) 'Is the global carbon market working?', *Nature* 445(7128): 595–596. ISSN 0028–0836, available at http://dx.doi.org/10.1038/445595a

Welch, D. (2007) 'Enron environmentalism or bridge to the low carbon economy?', *Ethical Consumer* 106: 12–20

Wit, R. C. N., Boon, B. H., van Velzen, A., Cames, M., Deuber, O. and Lee, D. S. (2005) *Giving Wings to Emission Trading*. Delft: CE

16
Aviation and Climate Change: Assessment of Policy Options

Ben Daley and Holly Preston

Introduction

Mitigating the climate impacts of air transport represents a formidable challenge, especially given the projected rapid growth of demand for air travel, the strong links between air transport service provision and economic growth, the high abatement costs of the sector, and the limited potential for radical technological solutions to be found in the short to medium term (DfT, 2004). Success in meeting this challenge depends upon the formulation and development of effective policy; however, progress in developing appropriate policies to reduce the climate impacts of aviation has been limited (Pastowski, 2003, p180). In part, this slow progress is due to the complexity of bringing international aviation into the existing climate change mitigation regime without compromising the economic and social benefits that the industry delivers. In particular, improved access to international air transport markets is an important component of national and regional development strategies, and any attempts to constrain aviation growth for environmental reasons could have the unintended effect of blighting development – especially in countries that are highly dependent upon tourism and air travel. Hence policy makers face the critical challenge of mitigating the climate impacts of aviation while balancing a range of economic, social and other environmental considerations.

In that task, a range of instruments are available to policy makers, many of which have received scrutiny from a wide range of stakeholders. Proposals to cap aviation emissions, to impose taxes and emissions charges, to use or remove subsidies, to issue tradable permits for aviation emissions and to encourage the use of voluntary agreements have received critical attention from commentators (IPCC, 1999; Bishop and Grayling, 2003; Pastowski, 2003). While such proposals may have individual merit, they are also problematic for a variety of reasons. Regulatory policy instruments face the problem that varying obligations are placed on different countries under the Kyoto Protocol – and this principle of common but differentiated responsibility is likely to remain a feature of any post-2012 climate agreement. Market-based policy instruments must negotiate complex issues related to the varying competitiveness of air transport service providers, including the need to internalize differing costs of pollution while facilitating access to international air transport markets on an equitable basis between nations. Voluntary approaches – including carbon offsetting and a diverse range of other practices categorized as corporate responsibility initiatives – face the criticism that they are too weak to catalyse the profound behavioural change that is required to meet the challenge of climate change.

In this chapter, we consider the context of aviation and climate policy, summarizing broader climate policy frameworks and defining the current status of efforts to include aviation within those frameworks. We discuss various options for the future development of aviation and climate policy, focusing on three main types of approach: those based on regulatory, market-based and voluntary measures. We then explore some of the implications and issues related to aviation and climate policy. We argue that there are many reasons why the formulation and implementation of effective policy is a difficult, yet nonetheless vital, task; and we identify some underlying principles that are likely to characterize future policies. We suggest that any policy approach should be based on effective performance monitoring, involving the use of appropriate indicators, targets, reporting methods and auditing processes. Future aviation and climate policy is also likely to apply the precautionary and polluter pays principles more fully, and to be located within broader sustainable development frameworks. Finally, we argue that aviation and climate policy should be integrated with other policies – including transport, energy and broader environmental policies – to a much greater extent, in order to avoid creating confusion and contradictions.

The context of aviation and climate policy

Aviation and climate policy belongs within the context of broader climate policy frameworks. In the latter part of the 20th century, anthropogenic climate change emerged as a critical global environmental issue, largely due to the recognition that increasing human use of fossil fuels since the Industrial Revolution has raised atmospheric concentrations of greenhouse gases – particularly carbon dioxide (CO_2) – substantially above pre-industrial levels (IPCC, 2007). Subsequently, climate science has evolved rapidly and debates about climate change have progressed from a focus on acceptance of the issue and its scientific basis – on which there is now a broad consensus – to more detailed consideration of the impacts of climate change and the potential for mitigation and adaptation (IPCC, 2007). Hence attention is now focused on the formulation and implementation of effective climate policies, a task that has been difficult for a variety of reasons. Scientific uncertainty about the precise rate and impacts of climate change – especially at the regional scale – has been cited as a reason to postpone costly abatement initiatives. The complexity of the issue, due to the intricacy of global environmental systems as well as uncertainties about the operation and magnitude of feedback mechanisms, has also hindered decision making. Those difficulties are exacerbated by the high dependence of industrialized economies upon fossil fuels and the significant power of interest groups to influence negotiations about energy supplies and use. In addition, attempts to devise adequate responses to the challenge of climate change must address complex issues of equity: historically, the majority of anthropogenic climate forcing was caused by industrialized nations, yet future initiatives to curb greenhouse gas emissions – as well the now inevitable impacts of climate change itself – are likely disproportionately to affect developing nations.

Nevertheless, significant progress has been made internationally in developing a climate change policy framework. Following the establishment of the United Nations Framework Convention on Climate Change (UNFCCC) in 1992, and the adoption of the Kyoto Protocol in 1997, commitments to reduce greenhouse gas emissions have been made by most developed countries, and emissions monitoring and reporting have commenced, based on a system of national greenhouse gas inventories. The first commitment period under the Kyoto Protocol is due to expire in 2012, and negotiations are in progress to establish a successor global climate agreement. Given the likelihood that multiple forms of international cooperation will be required to mitigate greenhouse gas emissions, such a post-2012 agreement may include a range of agreements, including country-based agreements (among the top emitting countries, or between regional groups), sector-based agreements (for instance, for the energy and transport sectors), policy-based agreements (such as carbon taxes) and measures-based agreements (based on specific emission reduction strategies, such as energy efficiency strategies) (GLCA, 2007, p6).

At the regional level, some progress has been made within the EU in relation to the development of climate change policy. In March 2000, the European Commission (EC) launched the European Climate Change Programme (ECCP), which included a wide range of new policies and measures. The EC determined that stabilizing long-term greenhouse gas concentrations at 450ppmv CO_2-eq may avoid 'dangerous' climate change by providing a roughly 50 per cent chance that mean global temperature will remain within 2°C of pre-industrial levels (EC, 2008a). To achieve this goal, the EC set an ambitious target to reduce greenhouse gas emissions by 60–80 per cent by 2050 (compared with 1990 levels) by apportioning shares of global emissions to EU nations and by requiring commensurate emissions reductions of those nations. A major component of EU climate policy is the European Union Emissions Trading Scheme (EU ETS), launched on 1 January 2005, which requires all major emitters of CO_2 within the EU to monitor and report their emissions and to surrender a corresponding number of emissions allowances (EC, 2003a). The first trading period of the EU ETS ran from 2005 to 2007; the second trading period extends from 2008 to 2012, while the third is due to cover the period 2013–2020.

While these frameworks have started to establish a basis for long-term, effective climate policy, the position with respect to aviation is lagging behind (Pastowski, 2003). While domestic aviation emissions are reported in national greenhouse gas inventories and are counted towards Kyoto Protocol targets, emissions from international flights were not initially included in either the Kyoto Protocol or the EU ETS – partly because of difficulties in allocating international emissions to national inventories (IPCC, 1999, pp338–339; Lee et al, 2005; Owen and Lee, 2006; DfT, 2007, p14). Furthermore, aviation benefits from a range of economic incentives that have allowed the industry to avoid paying the full environmental costs of its activities. The aviation industry – including aircraft manufacturers, airlines and airports – is subsidized and receives major tax exemptions; jet fuel for international flights has historically been exempted from taxation; international air tickets are exempted from VAT; airlines and new regional airports receive direct aid; the industry receives investment grants, government loans, infrastructure improvement subsidies and launch aid; aircraft landing fees are cross-subsidized with parking and retail revenues at airports; and the production of aircraft is exempted from VAT (EC, 2006; Peeters et al, 2006, pp192–193; T&E, 2006, pp4, 12–13). Several countries levy ticket or fuel taxes on domestic flights, but those measures do not compensate for the general tax exemption of the sector (T&E, 2006, p12). Consequently, there have been calls for international aviation to be brought within international climate frameworks and to overcome the difficulties in allocating international aviation emissions to national inventories (Bishop and Grayling, 2003; Cairns and Newson, 2006; Peeters et al, 2006, p193).

The comparatively slow progress in formulating and implementing effective aviation and climate policy can partly be attributed to the position adopted by the International Civil Aviation Organization (ICAO), which has emphasized the need for international action – through ICAO – on the issue of aviation and climate change, but which is simultaneously opposed to the taxation of kerosene, unwilling to establish a dedicated aviation emissions trading system, and in favour of further analytical work and the use of voluntary measures (ICAO, 2004; Yamin and Depledge, 2004, p86; T&E, 2006, p16). Consequently, regional initiatives appear to offer greater potential in terms of stimulating effective policy responses. Efforts to mitigate the climate impacts of aviation emissions are already being made within Europe: the EC recently announced its decision to include commercial aviation within the EU ETS by 2012, although many questions remain about the details of how this will occur. Some commentators have suggested that, unless the scheme adopts both an early baseline year and an overall cap designed to be in keeping with a

450ppmv CO_2-eq cumulative emission pathway, the impact on aviation emissions could be minimal (*New Scientist*, 2007, p35). Diverse views have been expressed towards the inclusion of aviation in the EU ETS, ranging from those of environmentalists (who regard the proposed measures as an insufficient response to the scale of the challenge) to those of airline representatives (who claim that the proposed level of allocations is insufficient, given the projected increases in demand for air travel). The various policy approaches are discussed in greater detail in the following section.

Types of policy approach

Policy approaches fall into three main categories: regulatory, market-based and voluntary approaches (Roberts, 2004, pp156–161). Regulatory approaches involve the use of 'command-and-control' policy instruments – laws, regulations and standards – which are designed to set limits to human activities and which are enforced using sanctions. Market-based approaches provide economic incentives and disincentives in order to influence human behaviour, although compliance is not mandatory; those approaches involve the use of taxes, charges, subsidies and marketable permits. Voluntary approaches provide neither regulatory nor direct economic reasons for compliance, relying instead upon education and awareness-raising initiatives with organizations and individuals in order to influence their behaviour towards desired outcomes; such approaches rely upon collaborative practice, self-regulated codes of conduct, and the promotion of corporate responsibility. These three main types of policy approach are discussed in turn below.

Regulatory approaches

In general, regulatory approaches have been frequently used in environmental policy and management; they typically involve the definition and enforcement of standards. In setting standards, a regulatory body – usually a government department or agency – decides upon the level of the standard and then monitors and enforces performance in relation to that standard. Standards are often set for emissions into the environment and they may be applied to various targets, including ambient quality (such as air quality standards), emissions (such as emissions limits for any given operator, or the emissions standards imposed during aircraft engine certification), products, processes and inputs (such as fuel sulphur content standards). The use of standards is particularly appropriate in certain circumstances: (a) if a pollutant is damaging to human health in concentrations exceeding a certain level, in which case an upper limit is imposed; (b) if a pollutant is damaging to health at any concentration, in which case a complete ban may be imposed; (c) if a pollutant accumulates in the environment, in which case the standard is set at (or below) the critical level at which the rate of environmental assimilation of the pollution by environmental processes is equal to the rate at which the pollutant accumulates in the environment.

Standards are apparently straightforward policy instruments, and since they are quantity-based they may help to achieve an environmental goal of restricting emissions to a given level. However, several important issues are associated with their use. First, setting appropriate standards depends upon notions of the 'optimal' level of pollution – and such notions may be highly problematic. From an economic point of view, emissions standards should be set at the level where the marginal abatement cost (the cost of mitigating an additional unit of pollution) is equal to the marginal damage cost (the cost of the environmental damage caused by that unit of pollution). However, the position of the marginal environmental damage curve is rarely known with certainty, and in the case of climate impacts is highly contingent. Consequently, in the absence of unequivocal scientific or economic guidance, it can be difficult for authorities to know exactly where to set the standard. Second, standards may be cost-effective policy instruments if they are applied in a uniform manner across an economy, but if the costs of reducing emissions differ among polluters (as is likely) and varying standards are imposed, then they may become complex and costly to administer. Third, although standards appear to be fair as they do not discriminate between polluters, they may actually reinforce existing patterns of competitive advantage, since the cost of reducing emissions usually varies among polluters. Fourth, standards may provide polluters with an incentive to introduce cleaner processes, but only if polluters have sufficient confidence that the level of the standard will not change. Fifth, the ease of enforcing standards depends upon the ease of measuring and monitoring emissions and of applying sanctions such as fines; in the case of multiple-source, widespread, long-lived emissions (such as CO_2 emissions), monitoring and enforcement may present serious practical difficulties.

Regulatory measures in relation to climate change face a number of difficulties, not least the fact that different countries have varying obligations placed upon them under the Kyoto Protocol – and the principle of common but differentiated responsibility is likely to remain a feature of any post-2012 climate agreement. Nonetheless, regulatory measures are likely to form an important component of future aviation and climate policy. As far as the aviation sector is concerned, regulatory measures could take the form of fixed emissions limits (caps) or emissions reduction targets. Article 2.2 of the Kyoto Protocol states that Annex I nations should 'pursue limitation or reduction of emissions of greenhouse gases not controlled by the Montreal Protocol from aviation ... bunker fuels, working through the International Civil Aviation Organization...' (UN, 1998, p2; see also Yamin and Depledge, 2004, pp85–87). However, unlike most other sectors, international aviation was not subjected to any fixed limits or caps under the Kyoto Protocol, and as a result limited progress has been made in managing the greenhouse gas emissions of the sector since the Kyoto Protocol was signed (Faber et al, 2007, p13). Discussions are in progress to determine the potential for aviation to be subject to emissions limits in an international post-2012 climate agreement, although it is unclear whether such an approach will be politically acceptable given the importance of growing demand for international air transport for the economic development of nations (*The Economist*, 2006).

Debates about overall emissions limits for aviation raise the difficult issue of regulation methods: if emissions limits were to be implemented in the future, they could potentially be administered by ICAO, which already has an international governance role, is well positioned to ensure that emissions limits are compatible with existing policies, and could ensure that any detrimental impact on international transport is mitigated (Faber et al, 2007, p20). However, the regulation of any future overall emissions limits for aviation would be complex, for several reasons. First, the national emissions targets imposed by the Kyoto Protocol have been determined on a common but differentiated basis, and emissions limits applied to international aviation may need to be established on the same basis (for those countries that are parties to the Kyoto Protocol) – otherwise the principle of common but differentiated responsibility could be infringed. Second, countries that are not party to the Kyoto Protocol would presumably not be allocated aviation emissions limits; their international air carriers could therefore gain a competitive advantage (Faber et al, 2007, p77). Third, the specification of emissions limits by country may not prove to be feasible, and alternative allocation methods may be devised based on routes flown, nationalities of passengers, or ultimate destinations of cargo (Faber et al, 2007, pp77–78). Fourth, the scope of emissions limits would require careful consideration because aircraft have other climate impacts besides those of CO_2 emissions: the effects of oxides of nitrogen (NO_x) emissions on ozone and methane, the production of aerosols, and the formation of linear contrails and contrail-cirrus clouds. Given that the level of scientific understanding of some non-CO_2 climate effects of aviation is low, emissions limits or reduction targets may initially focus solely on CO_2 emissions, for which scientific understanding of the issue is more advanced (IPCC, 2007, p39).

Market-based approaches

Market-based approaches are founded on the idea of creating economic incentives and disincentives for particular activities. Under such approaches, polluters are not prohibited from causing environmental damage, but they incur financial penalties for doing so and hence are encouraged to bring environmental impacts within the scope of their decision making. Conversely, market-based approaches may be used to make environmentally desirable courses of action more advantageous to polluters. Therefore, to varying degrees, market-based approaches ascribe economic values to environmental goods and services, and they may encourage polluters to internalize the costs of their environmental degradation. Market-based policy instruments include a range of incentives and disincentives; the main types used in environmental management are taxes, charges, subsidies and tradable (or marketable) permits. All these types of policy instrument are either already in use or under consideration as a response to the climate impacts of aviation, and some will almost certainly form part of future policy frameworks. Yet implementing market-based mechanisms is not easy: complex issues must be negotiated such as the varying competitiveness of air transport service providers and the need to internalize varying costs of pollution while facilitating access to international air transport markets on an equitable basis between nations. One important point in any discussion of market-based policy instruments is that, in order for those instruments to function effectively, the legislative, executive and judicial organs of government should be independent – otherwise, economic and political distortions may occur (Bishop and Grayling, 2003; IPCC, 1999).

Environmental taxes

The principle of an environmental tax is to charge polluters in order to compensate for their environmental damage; hence it is consistent with the polluter pays principle. Environmental taxes were first proposed by Arthur Pigou, who argued that for emissions the tax should be set at the level where the marginal abatement cost is equal to the marginal damage cost; such an 'ideal' tax is known as a Pigouvian tax. Environmental taxes can be directed towards different targets, such as ambient quality, emissions, outputs and inputs, and they have already been applied to the management of air, water and noise pollution. However, in general, environmental taxes have been used less frequently than regulatory standards in environmental management – partly because industry interest groups often have significant power in decision-making processes and can often campaign effectively against the introduction of taxes.

A range of issues are associated with the use of environmental taxes, some of which are the same as the problems related to regulatory standards (see above). As with standards, the exact position of the marginal damage curve is unlikely to be known with certainty, so it is difficult to set Pigouvian taxes accurately. In contrast to standards, which are quantity-based instruments, taxes are price-based instruments. Since they involve no element of compulsion, taxes provide less certainty about the overall magnitude of environmental impacts: it is up to polluters how they respond to the tax, and the desired reductions in overall environmental impacts may not be achieved. Nevertheless, it is usually in the interest of polluters to attempt to achieve the optimal level of pollution, and hence taxes are relatively cost-effective. Yet taxes are not necessarily considered fair because polluters face a double burden: paying the tax and paying for abatement. However, taxes also raise revenue which could potentially be used to recompense polluters who adopt cleaner processes. Thus taxes can promote behavioural change by providing polluters with incentives to improve their environmental performance. Taxes are generally enforceable, although emissions still need to be monitored and regulators need to ensure that polluters are paying the correct amount of tax. Considerable debate has surrounded the potential of carbon taxes to stimulate CO_2 emissions reductions; some countries such as Norway have already introduced carbon taxes, but their value in prompting emissions reductions has been questioned – especially since the industrial sectors that are most reliant upon fossil fuels are exempted from the tax.

The issue of fuel taxation is critically important for aviation, given the sensitivity of the industry to kerosene prices. While the Chicago Convention does not specifically forbid the taxation of bunker fuel sold, it does legally preclude the taxation of fuel in transit (Wit et al, 2004). In 1996, ICAO adopted a resolution allowing individual countries to implement their own environmental fuel charges (Seidel and Rossell, 2001, pp28–29; Carlsson and Hammar, 2002, p366); nevertheless, only a few countries such as the US and Holland have introduced fuel taxes for domestic aviation, and the fuel used in international aviation remains untaxed (IPCC, 1999, p345; Cairns and Newson, 2006; Mendes and Santos, 2008). The EC has previously considered introducing an aviation fuel tax, but the idea was rejected on the basis that an international agreement on the matter would need to be secured (Pearce and Pearce, 2000, p3). The introduction of a tax on fuel used for international flights is potentially hindered by the complexities involved in creating the necessary legal framework – especially as fuel taxation is precluded by many existing bilateral air service agreements (ASAs) between nations, and extensive renegotiation of those agreements would be required (Mendes and Santos, 2008, p195). Further issues would also be likely to emerge if aviation fuel taxes were not implemented widely and consistently: if fuel taxes were not introduced globally, economic distortions could occur, creating an incentive for airlines to uplift cheaper fuel – by tankering – in countries where the tax did not apply, with the net effect that aviation emissions could increase – thereby negating the original purpose of the tax (Wit et al, 2004, p43).

In addition to fuel taxes, other forms of environmental tax represent policy options for the aviation industry. One possible means of restraining demand for air travel – and hence of curbing emissions – would be to impose Value Added Tax (VAT) on international air tickets, which are currently VAT-free, although this option is regarded as logistically complex (Cairns and Newson, 2006, pp78, 83). Another instrument that has attracted recent interest is the air passenger duty (APD), an excise duty applied in the UK and which is due to be extended to all countries in the Single European Sky. The APD is currently applied to the carriage of chargeable passengers on chargeable aircraft (those with authorized take-off weights of 10 tonnes or more, or 20 seats or more) departing from UK airports; it is payable by the operator of the aircraft. The UK Government doubled the APD on 1 February 2007 – a decision for which environmental reasons were cited. The UK Treasury predicted that increasing the APD would induce CO_2 emissions reductions of approximately 0.3 million tonnes per year by 2010–2011, and reductions of all greenhouse gas emissions of 0.75 million tonnes of CO_2-eq per year, although those claims have been challenged (Cairns and Newson, 2006, p83). Airline representatives generally regard the APD as a blunt instrument and argue that there is no guarantee that the tax is used for environmental purposes. On the other hand, increasing the

APD represented 'probably the quickest and simplest step that could be taken by a UK Government to increase the price of flying and thereby apply demand restraint' (Cairns and Newson, 2006, p83).

A range of practical and philosophical issues surrounds the use of environmental taxes. The level of the tax is critical: Cairns and Newson (2006, p53) acknowledged that 'very large increases in fares would be needed to make a difference to demand' and that such increases would be politically unacceptable. Without such large, behaviour-changing price signals, environmental taxes may simply generate additional revenue for governments. In addition, unlike charges (which raise funds for particular purposes; see below), taxes raise general revenue and may generate no measurable environmental benefit. Issues of sustainable development arise when taxes are potentially used for demand management, since they may have the unintended effect of blighting economic development and thereby transferring costs to other nations or to future generations. Taxes may be regarded as socially or geographically inequitable, as travellers living in the developed world – who are most likely be able to absorb additional costs – could make commensurate savings in other ways (for instance, by purchasing cheaper accommodation, if the flights form part of a holiday), while those who are less affluent could be proportionally more affected by the price increase. Furthermore, while environmental taxes apparently conform with the polluter pays principle (for instance, as airlines are required to pay the APD), those costs may be absorbed elsewhere in the business, reducing profitability, cash flow and retained earnings – and, in turn, affecting the ability of airlines to introduce cleaner aircraft to their fleets (IPCC, 1999, p346).

Emissions charges

The discussion presented above has highlighted the difficulties involved in introducing fuel taxes, owing to the complexity of ASAs and to the fact that taxes raise general revenue that may not necessarily be used for environmental protection (see Carlsson and Hammar, 2002, p366). In the case of aviation, such difficulties could potentially be circumvented by the use of emissions charges, which represent a straightforward means of increasing the cost of environmentally destructive practices (IPCC, 1999, p346). Mendes and Santos (2008, p195) have acknowledged that CO_2 emissions from aircraft are inextricably linked to fuel consumption, with the result that the imposition of emissions charges would inevitably be considered to be a form of fuel taxation. However, unlike fuel taxes, emissions charges would potentially face fewer legal obstacles as they are not explicitly precluded by legally binding agreements (Wit et al, 2004). Additionally, if emissions charges were introduced on an en route basis, there would be a smaller likelihood that tankering would occur in response (IPCC, 1999, p346; Wit et al, 2004).

Subsidies

Subsidies are another type of market-based policy instrument; in environmental management, they are used to provide direct incentives for environmental protection. Subsidies have been widely used in attempts to control pollution and to mitigate the financial impacts of regulations by helping polluters to meet the costs of compliance, and they may take the form of lump-sum grants, loans or tax allowances. In comparison with regulatory standards and taxes, subsidies are relatively straightforward instruments and are easier for authorities to administer. However, once a system of subsidies has been established, it may prove difficult politically for governments to remove them – as exemplified by the persistence of agricultural and energy sector subsidies in some developed economies. Subsidies can be targeted at production processes (with producers being paid to switch from a more polluting method of production to a cleaner one) or at emissions (with a subsidy per unit of emissions reduction being paid to polluters). As with other policy instruments, various issues are associated with the use of subsidies. Subsidies are cost-effective for individual polluters, but they may not be so for an industry as a whole, especially because they distort markets and – if poorly targeted – may hinder the efficiency and competitiveness of a sector. Inevitably, polluters are likely to welcome subsidies, but they contravene the polluter pays principle and other groups in society may regard them as unfair: subsidies require the community to pay the polluter rather than vice versa (Roberts, 2004, pp204–205). Yet, once subsidies have been introduced, they may provide polluters with incentives to introduce new, cleaner methods. While subsidies apparently do not need enforcing, regulators must ensure that polluters do not claim excessive payments – hence subsidies still require monitoring and enforcement.

In relation to aviation, subsidies could potentially be used to accelerate fleet replacement or to promote the development and use of alternative fuels (as well as other technologies) that could reduce the climate impacts of aircraft. Rising costs of kerosene – together with pressure to reduce the climate impacts of aviation – have resulted in extensive research and development activity focused on the potential of alternative aviation fuels (Lambert, 2008). The ICAO Committee on Aviation Environmental Protection (CAEP) has argued that the main driving force behind the development of alternative fuels is the high price of kerosene, and if that price were to fall then 'fiscal or other measures' would be needed for the prospect of alternative fuels to remain viable (CAEP, 2007, p4). Subsidies for the development and use of alternative fuels could potentially provide the economic support required to facilitate or accelerate their introduction (Lambert, 2008). At present, no provision for subsidies of alternative fuels exists within the UK aviation industry, although, in 2008, the UK Treasury acknowledged that alternative fuels – and particularly biofuels – could make a significant contribution towards reducing emissions in the transport sector (HM Treasury, 2008, pp97–98). The use of subsidies of alternative aviation fuels, however, is dependent upon proponents of those fuels overcoming multiple – and considerable – distributional, economic, ethical and technological hurdles (RCEP, 2002). In general, the trend in aviation and climate policy should ideally be towards the removal of current subsidies and privileges within the sector rather than the creation of new ones (Peeters et al, 2006, p195).

Tradable permits

Tradable (or marketable) permit schemes represent another market-based policy instrument, and one that has attracted scrutiny in relation to climate mitigation. Tradable permits constitute a quantity-based instrument that provides polluters with incentives to reduce pollution by creating a new market, with defined property rights (Gander and Helme, 1999; Seidel and Rossell, 2001, p29). Tradable permits have been used in environmental management for several decades, notably in the US Environmental Protection Agency's sulphur dioxide (SO_2) emissions trading programme, and to manage fish stocks in Iceland and New Zealand. Tradable permit schemes operate on a simple principle: (a) a total level of pollution is defined for a specific region; (b) permits equalling that level are subsequently distributed among polluters in the region; (c) those permits can then be traded, either among polluters or between the operational sites of individual polluters. Thus tradable property rights to pollute the environment are assigned to polluters. The overall level of emissions for the industry is fixed (as with a regulatory standard) but, once the market is operating, the distribution of permits – and hence of emissions – is determined by the polluters trading in the market. The trade in permits should in theory result in a concentration of emissions reductions at those sources where they can be achieved at least cost. On the other hand, polluters faced with high abatement costs can purchase permits from polluters who have achieved emissions reductions, as that course of action is cheaper than incurring abatement costs. For aviation, which would incur high abatement costs, the possibility of buying additional emissions permits from other sectors could offer a way of continuing to operate despite increasing constraints of greenhouse gas emissions at national or international levels (assuming that sufficient emissions reductions are achieved by other sectors; DfT, 2004).

Given that tradable permit systems rely upon emissions reductions occurring where they are cheapest to achieve, they are economically efficient instruments. Tradable permits provide polluters with an incentive to introduce cleaner processes, motivated by the prospect of having permits to sell if emissions reductions are achieved. In addition, as tradable permits are quantity-based, they may inspire greater confidence than other instruments (such as taxes) that the target level of pollution will not be exceeded. Polluters generally regard tradable permits as fairer than taxes, although this perception is heavily dependent on how the market is designed. However, some environmentalists regard tradable permits as being contrary to the polluter pays principle, and they may object to the notion of giving polluters 'rights' to cause environmental degradation. In practice, some environmentalist groups use tradable permit market schemes strategically, buying permits and then 'retiring' them from the market. Tradable permit markets may become highly complex, and experience suggests that administration, monitoring and transaction costs may be higher than expected. Regulatory authorities are required to monitor and verify both emissions and the transactions by which permits are exchanged; if strict trading rules are not enforced, then incentives could be created for polluters to exceed permitted emissions levels.

Under the Kyoto Protocol, the use of tradable permits within emissions trading schemes is evolving as an important element of international climate policy, and tradable permits are also in use at the sub-national level: for example, in the Chicago Climate Exchange. The largest scheme in the world is the EU Emissions Trading Scheme (EU ETS), now in its second trading period. Aviation was not included in the first round of the EU ETS, but a resolution adopted by the European Parliament in July 2006 recognized that emissions trading could play a significant part in addressing the climate impacts of aviation; subsequently in December 2006 the EC adopted a proposal to include aviation within the EU ETS (CEC, 2006). The proposal aims to bring aviation into the trading scheme in two stages, commencing in 2011 with intra-EU flights (domestic and international flights between EU airports), and then expanding in 2012 to include all international flights arriving or departing from EU airports (CEC, 2006). The proposal is ambitious and will face significant obstacles. The first stage, covering flights between EU airports, falls entirely within EU jurisdiction and could potentially be monitored by EUROCONTROL (Wit et al, 2005). However, when all international flights are due to be brought within the scheme in 2012, the scheme is likely to face resistance from non-EU countries as well as generating vastly increased complexity in implementation and monitoring. A range of issues remains to be resolved, particularly in relation to trade rights, the initial allocation of permits, the avoidance of 'windfall' benefits due to the over-allocation of permits, the possible use of a factor to account for the non-CO_2 climate effects of aviation, and the geographical coverage of the scheme (IPCC, 1999, pp346–347; Lee and Sausen, 2000; DfT, 2004; Karmali and Harris, 2004; Lee, 2004; Wit et al, 2005, p60; Forster et al, 2006; Mendes and Santos, 2008).

Voluntary measures

Policy approaches based on voluntary measures rely upon organizations and individuals making decisions that take account of environmental concerns even in the absence of direct regulatory requirements or economic incentives. Such policy approaches may be apparently 'toothless'; yet decisions to improve environmental performance on a voluntary basis may be motivated by a variety of concerns. Polluters may believe that working cooperatively with regulators is more likely to lead to sympathetic, 'light touch' regulation of their processes, and indeed the establishment of such cooperative relationships is frequently sought by regulatory authorities. In addition, polluters may perceive greater opportunities to influence the regulatory process if they can demonstrate substantial voluntary efforts to improve their environmental performance. Polluters may adopt voluntary measures in anticipation of stricter regulation in the future, especially if early adoption offers them a competitive advantage.

Multinational companies may voluntarily adopt cleaner processes across their entire operations so as to standardize their processes across countries or regions, and they may seek to maximize their access to worldwide markets by adopting processes that would comply with the environmental regulations of the strictest country. Even in the absence of direct economic incentives to improve environmental performance, organizations may do so voluntarily if they believe that consumer expectations require such action. Hence companies can improve their consumer relations and brand images by demonstrating corporate responsibility, either environmentally or socially. A further reason for organizations or individuals to adopt voluntary measures may be the influence of individual entrepreneurs with environmentalist attitudes and motivations.

In relation to aviation and climate policy, voluntary measures currently focus on the use of carbon offsetting, on commitments to achieve carbon neutrality, and on the adoption of a range of broader corporate responsibility initiatives; those measures are discussed below. However, several general issues relate to the use of voluntary measures and they require brief mention. First, the effectiveness of voluntary agreements for environmental protection has received critical scrutiny. Voluntary agreements vary widely in their quality, from vague declarations of corporate good intentions to specific statements about environmental targets, strategies, indicators and performance. While high-level, aspirational statements may play a role in establishing environmentalist concerns within corporate cultures, in general voluntary measures require specific, measurable, time-bound targets to be set, and progress against those targets to be monitored and reported, if they are to prompt improvements in environmental performance. Second, voluntary agreements may be limited in their effectiveness if they rely upon self-regulation. Instead, organizations claiming to improve their environmental performance on a voluntary basis would ideally subject those claims to external, independent verification. Third, a wide gap may exist between actual corporate environmental performance and consumer expectations of that performance – even for 'leading edge' organizations. Voluntary measures may therefore expose the most progressive organizations to serious reputational risk. In this case, voluntary measures can potentially penalize the very organizations that are demonstrating progress in addressing environmental concerns. Hence voluntary measures are ideally used in conjunction with environmental education and awareness-raising programmes to ensure that consumers understand the environmental issues, the options for their mitigation, and the cost implications for organizations.

Carbon offsetting has become a popular response to the challenge of climate change; in 2006 an estimated 1.5 million people in the UK paid to offset the emissions of a flight (*New Scientist*, 2007, p35). The subject of carbon offsetting has received attention from several authors (see Jardine, 2005; Bayon et al, 2007; Gössling et al, 2007; Rousse, 2008). Here, we simply summarize some of the main issues associated with this voluntary activity, especially in relation to aviation. Those issues relate mainly to the measurement of emissions and to the permanence and credibility of offsets. The main areas of concern are:

- Offsetting is not a sufficient measure to address climate change.
- It does not address all the climate impacts of aviation.
- It requires an accurate measure of the emissions generated.
- It requires an accurate measure of the emissions saved elsewhere.
- It requires an appropriate price to be put on 1 tonne of CO_2-eq.
- It requires demonstrating additionality, which may represent a considerable challenge.
- Offsetting schemes are unregulated, may be overpriced and are vulnerable to fraud.
- Schemes can be inefficient.
- Offsets may not be permanent.
- Schemes may create problems of leakage.
- Projects may have mixed sustainable development co-benefits.
- Schemes may be a distraction from the real challenge of reducing emissions, and hence could delay the transition to a low-carbon economy.

Given the range of issues listed above, offsetting is now acknowledged to be a highly problematic response to the challenge of climate change. Most significantly, in offsetting schemes, commercial and environmental benefits have become entangled to the extent that a crisis of legitimacy has occurred in the voluntary carbon market. This lack of credibility has been acknowledged by Brouwer et al (2007, p7), who stated: 'The most important reason for travellers to protest against paying [for carbon offsetting] is passenger disbelief that the carbon travel tax and the proposed trees for travel program will have any real impact.' Offsetting schemes are conceptually problematic: they have emerged not from attempts by environmentalists and climate scientists to design an appropriate response but from politicians and business executives trying to meet the demands for action while preserving the commercial status quo (*The Guardian*, 2007, p15). However, such criticisms could simply indicate that offsetting schemes require careful design and rigorous monitoring. Appropriate forms of offsetting may nevertheless play an important role within an overall response to climate change, as acknowledged by Friends of the Earth, Greenpeace and WWF-UK (Friends of the Earth, 2006). However, carbon offsetting should be regarded as a last resort rather than a preferred course of action. Where offsetting projects form part of a broader climate change strategy, the selection of projects should be considered carefully to ensure that the expected benefits are achieved – although this task is currently hindered by the lack of legal standards for offsetting schemes. Efforts are being made to develop such a standard for offsetting schemes (DEFRA, 2007).

The voluntary carbon market is relatively new and rapidly expanding, and carbon offsetting has only recently been considered in relation to the climate impacts of air transport. One recent study of offsetting, which focused on the willingness of air travellers to pay to offset their CO_2 emissions, suggested that 'a substantial demand for climate change mitigation action' exists among travellers from Europe, North America, Asia and the rest of the world, although some differences were found between those groups (Brouwer et al, 2007, p1). The study indicated that the substantial willingness of air travellers to pay for offsetting represents a 'convenient truth': the market potential for carbon offsets could account for more than €23 billion in climate change mitigation activities annually (Brouwer et al, 2007, pp12–13). In another study, Gössling et al (2007) investigated the efficiency and credibility of voluntary carbon offsetting schemes for aviation. Those authors acknowledged the possibility that air travel might become more expensive or even restricted in the future for environmental reasons. Gössling et al (2007) considered the significant differences between the approaches used by offsetting providers in relation to emissions from air travel; those differences centred on the calculation of emissions, compensation measures chosen, price levels, company structures and evaluation processes (Gössling et al, 2007, p223). As a result of their analysis, the authors concluded that the subject of voluntary offsets for aviation is an increasingly contested issue, and that increased regulation of offsetting schemes for air travel is required.

Carbon offsetting has received considerable attention within the air transport industry as a strategy to assure stakeholders that the industry is taking action to mitigate its climate impacts. Offsetting schemes now form an increasing part of the air transport industry's response to concerns about climate change, but those schemes are still not mature and their effectiveness is disputed. Overall, carbon offsetting is not a panacea for climate change, although it may have a role in an integrated climate change response, especially in the short term, particularly because it allows for immediate action on the part of environmentally motivated individuals and organizations. However, offsetting schemes should form part of an overall, integrated aviation and climate policy that is focused primarily on reducing greenhouse gas emissions and that contributes to the overall transition to a low-carbon economy, rather than being simply mechanisms for raising revenue. Carbon reduction schemes should be robust, verified and trustworthy; they should include reasonable and transparent carbon calculations and accountancy frameworks, and they should be rigorously monitored and audited at all levels. In terms of the projects funded, carbon sequestration projects have attracted particular criticism for their lack of permanence and for the difficulties in accounting their costs and benefits, and emissions reductions schemes are far preferable. Offset providers should ideally seek accreditation by an internationally recognized organization (such as the Gold Standard Foundation). Critically, offsetting requires the demonstration of additionality, which represents a considerable challenge for aviation because CO_2 reductions are associated with improved fuel efficiency – for which a strong commercial incentive already exists. Given these caveats, offsetting represents an opportunity to achieve environmental gains in a manner that is practical and easily understood by businesses. Bayon et al (2007, p107) have argued that offsetting has 'helped breathe new life into a global market in voluntary carbon emissions reductions that, one way or another, will play an important role in our efforts to stem climate change for years to come'.

The use of carbon offsetting may form a component of corporate commitments to achieve carbon neutrality. Within the aviation industry, such commitments are now being made by some airport operators; however, those commitments involve important issues of definition and coverage. Airport operators define their spheres of responsibility and influence in various ways, and in particular they may differ in their 'ownership' of aircraft emissions operating in the vicinity of the airport. Some airport operators accept responsibility for aviation emissions produced throughout the aircraft landing and take-off (LTO) cycle, while others restrict their responsibility to those emissions generated while aircraft are parked at the gate or are manoeuvring on the apron and taxiways. Such differences in coverage have potentially large implications for the magnitude of the carbon burden to be mitigated, and for the possibility that some emissions may not be apportioned to any particular polluter. However an airport's sphere of responsibility is defined, airport operators have a much larger sphere of influence over airlines and, in addition to achieving carbon neutrality for their own operations, could focus greater efforts on encouraging airlines to operate fleets of cleaner aircraft.

Both the use of carbon offsetting and the declaration of commitments to achieve carbon neutrality belong within the context of corporate responsibility approaches. The idea of corporate responsibility requires organizations to make high-level policy commitments to environmental protection, which are then ideally developed in a suite of more specific plans, programmes and initiatives. Corporate responsibility initiatives require organizations to assess their environment performance, to set targets for improvement, to develop appropriate strategies, to allocate adequate resources to the task, and to monitor and report their progress. Within the aviation industry, many manufacturers, airlines and airport operators have adopted corporate responsibility initiatives, many of which are based upon the implementation of an environmental management system (EMS) and on the publication of regular corporate environmental reports. Critically, both the implementation of an EMS and the corporate environmental reporting process should conform to agreed standards for the industry – if not more widely. In particular, corporate environmental reporting should be externally, independently verified in order to ensure that the environmental benefits claimed have in fact occurred. Such verification can be promoted by the adoption of internationally recognized standards for environmental reporting. Approaches to corporate responsibility being developed by leading edge organizations involve detailed reporting of their environmental performance with reference to independent standards of this type, such as those developed by the Global Reporting Initiative (GRI). Overall, the value of voluntary measures is highly dependent upon the institution and maintenance of such industry standards, including the negotiation and acceptance of appropriate codes of conduct.

Evaluation of policy options

In the previous section, a range of policy instruments was discussed and a variety of issues in their use considered. Here we provide an overall evaluation of the policy options and highlight some overarching themes. We emphasize that policy approaches should be based on effective performance monitoring and reporting, involving the appropriate use of targets, indicators, metrics, reporting methods and auditing procedures. Policy approaches should be transparent and any areas of uncertainty should be clearly identified in order to build consumer confidence. We also emphasize that policy approaches involving regulatory instruments are likely to be ineffective without adequate enforcement, that market-based approaches require careful accounting and auditing, and that even voluntary measures require external verification if they are to inspire confidence. In addition, in this section, we reiterate the importance of the precautionary and polluter pays principles, both of which are central to sustainable development frameworks; failure to incorporate those principles fully in aviation and climate policy is likely to reinforce inconsistencies and contradictions between policies. Policy integration remains an important goal, especially with respect to energy, transport and other environment policies, and a significant challenge for policy makers.

It is futile to implement policies if they cannot be enforced. Policy enforcement, in turn, depends upon effective monitoring mechanisms; hence the monitoring of environmental impacts, and of the effectiveness of policy responses, is of vital importance. Yet monitoring presents serious issues for governments as monitoring can be technically complex: it requires ongoing investment, and the costs can be high. Such difficulties are compounded for aviation, which operates across national boundaries and spans many jurisdictions. While responsibility for monitoring the climate impacts of domestic aviation could be attributed to national governments, monitoring international aviation would require coordination by an independent, international organization (see Purvis, 2004; Müller, 2005). Even with such a monitoring framework in place, various issues would be involved in monitoring the effectiveness of a policy. Polluters and regulators have unequal information: polluters generally know their emissions levels better than regulators do, which may create an incentive for non-compliance. Polluters can, in principle, evaluate the potential benefits of non-compliance (such as avoiding abatement costs), the magnitude of any penalty, and the likelihood of being caught. This may present a particular difficulty for the monitoring of aviation emissions, since fuel consumption data (from which CO_2 emissions are calculated) are sensitive, proprietary information that is carefully guarded by airlines. Added to these issues are the potential difficulties in apportioning blame for emissions (as it may not be obvious who is responsible for any increase) and difficulties in finding credible sanctions (as fines imposed for causing environmental damage have been historically very low and in some cases not imposed at all).

The selection of appropriate targets is another essential part of any policy approach. Targets provide actors with clear goals and they may assist with monitoring as they can inform benchmarking. However, setting appropriate and equitable targets can be a difficult task: different performance may be expected of different polluters; there may be questions about the legitimacy and impartiality of the target-setting process; and there may be disagreements about what precisely needs to be done for targets to be considered met. Similar issues relate to the selection and use of indicators and metrics: their selection is an inherently political process; they may be technically complex; and they may exclude environmental impacts of considerable concern. Given such difficulties, it is vital that the reporting of environmental performance is as transparent as possible in order to establish and build consumer confidence. Reporting the outcomes of any policy should also be consistent and regular so as to inform stakeholders about progress, to enable the identification of trends, and to reveal any requirements for further policy interventions. Auditing is a further, essential part of the policy framework: it should be undertaken externally, independently, and as transparently as possible.

Any policy approach to the impacts of aviation on climate should be based on the precautionary principle, that is the concept that, where there are threats of serious or irreversible damage to human health or to the environment, lack of full scientific certainty should not be used as a reason for postponing action (Mintzer et al, 1994). The precautionary principle is especially relevant in the case of atmospheric impacts, since those impacts may be difficult to detect and may involve feedback mechanisms that are poorly understood. The precautionary principle was articulated in the 1992 Rio Declaration on Environment and Development (Principle 15) (UNCED, 1992) and now forms a central element of sustainable development frameworks. In relation to the impacts of aviation on climate, the precautionary principle could be invoked in several ways: (a) to make allowance for uncertainties in general climate change science, particularly with respect to the regional impacts of climate change; (b) to take account of the non-CO_2 climate impacts of aircraft; (c) to account for uncertainties in the projected demand for air travel; and (d) in consideration of the fact that the likely impacts and costs of climate change are not yet fully known, especially at the regional level. Under the precautionary principle, such areas of uncertainty should not preclude the development and implementation of policy approaches that take account of the full range of potential impacts of aviation on climate, and the full costs that may consequently be borne by societies.

Aviation and climate policy should also incorporate the polluter pays principle, which states that any party causing environmental degradation should bear the full cost of that degradation: either the cost of environmental remediation or the cost in terms of lost environmental goods and services. Currently, the polluter pays principle is not sufficiently applied to international (or even domestic) aviation, as the external costs of emissions – as well as of other environmental impacts – are not fully borne by the industry. While some aviation industry representatives argue that such external costs are outweighed by the strong contribution of the industry to economic growth, this situation can nevertheless be regarded as inequitable across economic sectors (EC, 2007a, p8; 2007b, p8). Efforts have been made in Europe to embed the polluter pays principle more fully in policy development; in 2007 the EC undertook a consultation on the 'Preparation of an Impact Assessment on the Internalisation of External Costs', which proposed developing a method to institutionalize the polluter pays principle and to ensure that prices reflect social costs, although the proposal was challenged on the basis that it could impact comparatively heavily upon the transport sector (EC, 2007a, 2007b, 2008b). With respect to aviation, care would be required in order to apply the polluter pays principle equitably, ensuring that responsibility for environmental degradation is apportioned appropriately between manufacturers, airlines, airport operators, passengers and freight distributors. The costs of aviation emissions would need to be apportioned equitably between the aviation industries of different countries.

The foremost challenge facing policy makers in the task of developing and implementing aviation and climate policy is that of policy integration. Aviation and climate policies should ideally be integrated fully with other policy frameworks, particularly with sustainable development frameworks, energy policies, transport policies and other environmental policies. Sustainable development frameworks generally incorporate the idea that actions today should not compromise the ability of future generations to meet their own needs (the principle of inter-generational equity), nor should it hinder the ability of people today to meet their basic needs (the principle of intra-generational equity) (WCED, 1987; Upham, 2001; Baker, 2006). Thus the economic, social and environmental dimensions of development should be considered together in formulating policy – a balance that is difficult, yet vital, to achieve. Above all, sustainable development frameworks suggest that progress towards limiting the climate impacts of aviation through policy should not lead to unacceptable social impacts, especially upon the poorest communities of the world. This insight must also be balanced against the fact that failing to act to mitigate climate impacts will also lead to disproportionate impacts upon those same communities.

In the UK, this challenge of policy integration has been revealed dramatically in recent scholarship that has emphasized the large disparity between aviation policy and climate policy, given the UK Government's commitment to achieve ambitious CO_2 reduction targets (Bows et al, 2006). Without prompt action to curtail the growth of demand for air travel, forecasts indicate that all other UK sectors would have to almost completely decarbonize by 2050 in order to compensate for aviation emissions (Bows et al, 2006, p3). The authors argue that the use of a 'contraction and convergence' policy regime is required in order to achieve the required emissions reductions; aviation policy should therefore be compatible with – rather than contrary to – such a regime. With respect to broader transport policies, aviation and climate policies should be situated within wider strategic approaches to integrated transport planning, which would ideally focus on the potential for environmental efficiencies to be achieved through the use of intermodality where possible (Andersson and Hasson, 1998; EC, 2001, p116; 2003b, pp4, 14; EEA, 2006). Another major area where greater policy integration and consistency is required is within aviation policy itself. In particular, the interactions between the climate impacts and other environmental effects of aviation (including local air pollution and aircraft noise) result in the necessity for trade-offs to be made. Consequently, the climate impacts of aircraft are greater than they potentially might be, due to design requirements to limit NO_x emissions and noise. Such trade-offs illustrate the need for an integrated approach to policy development and implementation, in order to avoid reinforcing confusion and contradictions.

Given the scale and complexity of the challenge of mitigating the climate impacts of aviation – and the fact that different policy instruments have different strengths and weaknesses – it is likely that future aviation and climate policy will involve a combination of many of the types of policy instrument reviewed above. Such a 'patchwork' policy approach has been identified by Pastowski (2003) as the most likely scenario for aviation, based on his assessment of the effectiveness, timing and political level of a wide range of policy instruments. Hence regulatory, market-based and voluntary measures will probably all play a part in aviation and climate policy, although the indications are that some policy instruments (such as tradable permits) are far more politically acceptable than others (such as fuel taxes) – and are likely to remain so, at least until the existing system of bilateral air service agreements (ASAs) is superseded. It also appears increasingly likely that international aviation will be brought within the scope of a post-2012 international climate agreement, although the precise form of such a development remains unclear. Considering the recent evolution of broader climate policy, the development and increasing significance of the EU ETS, and the lack of strong leadership by ICAO on this issue, regional initiatives are likely to determine the course of international aviation and climate policy.

Conclusion

Aviation and climate policy has received considerable attention recently, for several reasons: deepening concerns that aviation does not pay its external costs; more profound awareness that climate change requires a substantial, urgent response; and acknowledgement that, by 2050, the growth of demand for air travel could potentially consume almost all the emissions savings achieved by other sectors of the economy. Consequently, policy makers are under increasing pressure to develop and implement appropriate responses to mitigate the impacts of aviation on climate. In this chapter, we have reviewed and evaluated a range of policy options available to policy makers in that task; those options include regulatory measures (standards), market-based measures (taxes, emissions charges, subsidies and tradable permits) and voluntary approaches (carbon offsetting, commitments to achieve carbon neutrality, and other corporate responsibility initiatives). We have suggested that any policy approach will most likely involve many of those instruments; that it should ideally be consistent with the precautionary and polluter pays principles; and that it should be integrated with other policies, including sustainable development frameworks and energy, transport and other environmental policies. The last of these challenges – that of policy integration – is a formidable one and it will require detailed, extensive work to negotiate an approach that does not reinforce existing confusion and policy contradictions nor blight the economies and societies of developing nations.

Despite the scale of the challenge, some elements of a future aviation and climate policy framework are already emerging. Some of the instruments reviewed in this chapter are clearly more acceptable politically than others, and policy approaches will crystallize around those preferred instruments insofar as they are successful in achieving emissions reductions at reasonable cost. Emissions trading schemes have been hitherto more acceptable to industry representatives than fuel taxation, for instance, and the EU has demonstrated international leadership in establishing the EU ETS and in resolving to bring international aviation within its scope by 2012. As Bishop and Grayling (2003, p7) have acknowledged, 'The most economically efficient and environmentally sure way of controlling aviation emissions would be to include them in an open, international emissions-trading regime, with global emissions capped at a level that reflects environmental capacity.' The work of Bows et al (2006) indicates that for aviation that level (reflecting environmental capacity) should be defined within a broader 'contraction and convergence' policy regime. Alongside the use of emissions trading, policy makers are also likely to employ a range of other instruments of which the option of most immediate value may be the removal of the existing subsidies and privileges that cause environmental inefficiencies to persist in the aviation industry (Peeters et al, 2006, p195). Prompt adoption of such policy options could substantially reduce the impacts of aviation on climate, but they will require resolve on the part of policy makers, cooperation on the part of industry representatives, and carefully targeted research and monitoring.

References

Andersson, T. and Hasson, P. (1998) 'Why integrated transport systems?', *OECD Observer* 211, pp27–31

Baker, S. (2006) *Sustainable Development*, Routledge Introductions to Environment Series, London: Routledge

Bayon, R., Hawn, A. and Hamilton, K. (2007) *Voluntary Carbon Markets: An International Business Guide to What They Are and How They Work*, London: Earthscan

Bishop, S. and Grayling, T. (2003) *The Sky's the Limit: Policies for Sustainable Aviation*, London: Institute for Public Policy Research

Bows, A., Anderson, K. and Upham, P. (2006) *Contraction and Convergence: UK Carbon Emissions and the Implications for UK Air Traffic*, Technical Report No. 40, February, Manchester: Tyndall Centre for Climate Change Research

Brouwer, R., Brander, L. and van Beukering, P. (2007) *'A Convenient Truth': Air Travel Passengers' Willingness to Pay to Offset their CO$_2$ Emissions,* Amsterdam: Institute for Environmental Studies: Vrije Universiteit

CAEP (Committee on Aviation Environmental Protection) (2007) The Potential Use of Alternative Fuels for Aviation, CAEP Seventh Meeting, Montreal, Canada, 5–16 February

Cairns, S. and Newson, C. (2006) *Predict and Decide: Aviation, Climate Change and UK Policy,* Oxford: Environmental Change Institute

Carlsson, F. and Hammar, H. (2002) 'Incentive based regulation of CO$_2$ emissions from international aviation', *Journal of Air Transport Management* 8: 365–372

CEC (Commission of the European Communities) (2006) *Proposal for a Directive of the European Parliament and of the Council amending Directive 2003/87/EC so as to include Aviation Activities in the Scheme for Greenhouse Gas Emission Allowance Trading within the Community,* available at http://europa.eu/scadplus/leg/en/lvb/l28012.htm, accessed 12 June 2008

DEFRA (Department for Environment, Food and Rural Affairs) (2007) *Climate Change: Carbon Offsetting – Code of Best Practice,* available at www.defra.gov.uk/environment/climatechange/uk/carbonoffset/codeofpractice.htm, accessed 12 July 2007

DfT (Department for Transport) (2004) *Aviation and Global Warming,* London: DfT

DfT (2007) *Consultation on the Emissions Cost Assessment,* August, London: DfT

EC (European Commission) (2001) *European Transport Policy for 2010: Time to Decide,* White Paper, Luxembourg: Office for Official Publications of the European Communities

EC (2003a) *Directive 2003/87/EC of the European Parliament and of the Council of 13 October 2003: Establishing a Scheme for Greenhouse Gas Emission Allowance Trading within the Community and Amending Council Directive 96/61/EC,* Brussels: EC

EC (2003b) *Europe at a Crossroads: The Need for Sustainable Transport,* Brussels: EC

EC (2006) *Climate Change: Commission Proposes Bringing Air Transport into EU Emissions Trading Scheme,* Press Release, IP/06/1862, 20 December, Brussels: EC

EC (2007a) *Preparation of an Impact Assessment on the Internalisation of External Costs Consultation Document,* available at http://ec.europa.eu/transport/white_paper/consultations/doc/2007_consultation_paper_en.pdf, accessed 16 June 2008

EC (2007b) *Results of the Consultation on the Internalisation of External Costs,* available at http://ec.europa.eu/transport/costs/consultations/index_en.htm, accessed 16 June 2008

EC (2008a) *Climate Change,* available at http://ec.europa.eu/environment/climat/home_en.htm, accessed 9 June 2008

EC (2008b) *Joint Statement on the EC Consultation on the 'Preparation of an Impact Assessment on the Internalisation of External Costs',* available at http://ec.europa.eu/transport/costs/consultations/index_en.htm, accessed 29 May 2008

The Economist (2006), 'The dirty sky', 10 June, p10

EEA (European Environment Agency) (2006) *Transport and Environment: Facing a Dilemma – TERM 2005,* EEA Report No. 3/2006, Copenhagen: EEA

Faber, J., Boon, B., Berk, M., den Elzen, M., Olivier, J. and Lee, D. (2007) *Climate Change Scientific Assessment and Policy Analysis: Aviation and Maritime Transport in a Post 2012 Climate Policy Regime,* Delft: CE

Forster, P. M. de F., Shine, K. P and Stuber, N. (2006) 'It is premature to include non-CO_2 effects of aviation in emissions trading schemes', *Atmospheric Environment* 40: 1117–1121

Friends of the Earth (2006) *Joint Statement on Offsetting Carbon Emissions*, London: Friends of the Earth, Greenpeace and WWF-UK

Gander, S. and Helme, N. (1999) 'Emissions trading is an effective, proven policy tool for solving air pollution problems', *ICAO Journal* 54(7): 12–14, 28–29

GLCA (Global Leadership for Climate Action) (2007) *Framework for a Post-2012 Agreement on Climate Change: A Proposal of the Global Leadership for Climate Action*, available at www.unfoundation.org/files/pdf/2007/GLCA_Framework2007.pdf, accessed 9 June 2008

Gössling, S., Broderick, J., Upham, P., Ceron, J.-P., Dubois, G., Peeters, P. and Strasdas, W. (2007) 'Voluntary carbon offsetting schemes for aviation: Efficiency, credibility and sustainable tourism', *Journal of Sustainable Tourism* 15(3): 223–248

The Guardian (2007) 'The inconvenient truth about the carbon offset industry', 16 June, 14–15

HM Treasury (2008) *Budget 2008: Stability and Opportunity: Building a Strong, Sustainable Future*, Economic and Fiscal Strategy Report and Financial Statement and Budget Report, March, London: The Stationery Office

ICAO (International Civil Aviation Organization) (2004) *Updating of Resolution A33–7: Consolidated Statement of Continuing ICAO Policies and Practices Related to Environmental Protection*, Agenda Item 15 adopted at the 35th ICAO Assembly, Montreal, October

IPCC (Intergovernmental Panel on Climate Change) (1999) *Aviation and the Global Atmosphere*, A Special Report of IPCC Working Groups I and III, in Penner, J. E., Lister, D. H., Griggs, D. J., Dokken, D. J. and McFarland, M. (eds) *Special Report of the Intergovernmental Panel on Climate Change*, Cambridge: Cambridge University Press

IPCC (2007) *Climate Change 2007: Synthesis Report*, Contribution of Working Groups I, II and III to the Fourth Assessment Report of the Intergovernmental Panel on Climate Change, Core Writing Team Pachauri, R. K. and Reisinger, A. (eds) Geneva: IPCC

Jardine, C. (2005) *Calculating the Environmental Impact of Aviation Emissions*, Report commissioned for Climate Care, June, Oxford: Environmental Change Institute

Karmali, A. and Harris, M. (2004) 'ICAO exploring development of a trading scheme for emissions from aviation', *ICAO Journal* 59(5): 11–13, 25

Lambert, C. (2008) 'Alternative aviation fuels', SBAC Aviation and Environment Briefing Papers No. 4, available at www.sbac.co.uk/pages/92567080.asp, accessed 12 June 2008

Lee, D. S. (2004) 'The impact of aviation on climate', in Hester, R. E. and Harrison, R. M. (eds) *Transport and the Environment*, Issues in Environmental Science and Technology No. 20, Cambridge: The Royal Society of Chemistry, 1–23

Lee, D. S. and Sausen, R. (2000) 'New directions: Assessing the real impact of CO_2 emissions trading by the aviation industry', *Atmospheric Environment* 34: 5337–5338

Lee, D. S., Owen, B., Graham, A., Fichter, C., Lim, L. L. and Dimitriu, D. (2005) *Allocation of International Aviation Emissions from Scheduled Air Traffic – Present Day and Historical*, Final Report to DEFRA Global Atmosphere Division, Manchester: Manchester Metropolitan University

Mendes, L. M. Z and Santos, G. (2008) 'Using economic instruments to address emissions from air transport in the European Union', *Environment and Planning* 40: 189–209

Mintzer, I. M., Leonard, J. A. and Chadwick, M. J. (1994) *Negotiating Climate Change: The Inside Story of the Rio Convention*, Cambridge: Cambridge University Press and Stockholm Environment Institute

Müller, B. (2005) 'Climate change post-2012: Transatlantic consensus and disagreements', *Journal for Energy Literature* 11(1): 1–10

New Scientist (2007) 'Green sky thinking', 24 February, 32–38

Owen, B. and Lee, D. S. (2006) *Study on the Allocation of Emissions from International Aviation to the UK Inventory – CPEG7*, Final Report to DEFRA Global Atmosphere Division, Manchester: Manchester Metropolitan University

Pastowski, A. (2003) 'Climate policy for civil aviation: Actors, policy instruments and the potential for emissions reductions', in Upham, P., Maughan, J., Raper, D. and Thomas, C. (eds) *Towards Sustainable Aviation*, London: Earthscan, 179–195

Pearce, B. and Pearce, D. (2000) *Setting Environmental Taxes for Aircraft: A Case Study of the UK*, CSERGE Working Paper GEC 2000–26, available at www.uea.ac.uk/env/cserge/pub/wp/gec/gec_2000_26.htm, accessed 11 June 2008

Peeters, P., Gössling, S. and Becken, S. (2006) 'Innovation towards tourism sustainability: Climate change and aviation', *International Journal of Innovation and Sustainable Development,* 1 (3): 184–200

Purvis, N. (2004) 'The perspective of the United States on climate change and the Kyoto Protocol', *International Review for Environmental Strategies* 5(1): 169–178

RCEP (Royal Commission on Environmental Pollution) (2002) *The Environmental Effects of Civil Aircraft in Flight*, Special Report, London: RCEP

Roberts, J. (2004) *Environmental Policy*, Routledge Introductions to Environment Series, London: Routledge

Rousse, O. (2008) 'Environmental and economic benefits resulting from citizens' participation in CO_2 emissions trading: An efficient alternative solution to the voluntary compensation of CO_2 emissions', *Energy Policy* 35: 388–397

Seidel, S. and Rossell, M. (2001) 'Potential policy tools for reducing emissions shift emphasis to economic incentives', *ICAO Journal* 56(4): 27–29, 34

T&E (European Federation for Transport and Environment) (2006) *Clearing the Air: The Myth and Reality of Aviation and Climate Change*, Brussels: T&E and CAN-Europe (Climate Action Network Europe)

UN (United Nations) (1998) *Kyoto Protocol to the United Nations Framework Convention on Climate Change*, available at http://unfccc.int/resource/docs/convkp/kpeng.pdf, accessed 11 June 2008

UNCED (United Nations Commission on Environment and Development) (1992) *The Rio Declaration on Environment and Development*, available at www.unep.org/Law/PDF/Rio_Declaration.pdf, accessed 25 July 2008

Upham, P. (2001) 'A comparison of sustainability theory with UK and European airports policy and practice', *Journal of Environmental Management* 63: 237–248

WCED (World Commission on Environment and Development) (1987) *Our Common Future*, Brundtland, H. (ed) Oxford: Oxford University Press for the WCED

Wit, R. C. N, Kampman, B. and Boon, B. H. (2004) *Climate Impacts from International Aviation and Shipping: State-of-the-Art on Climatic Impacts, Allocation and Mitigation Policies*, Report for the Netherlands Research Programme on Climate Change, Scientific Assessments and Policy Analysis (NRP-CC), Delft: CE

Wit, R. C. N., Boon, B. H., van Velzen, A., Cames, M., Deuber, O. and Lee, D. S. (2005) *Giving Wings to Emissions Trading: Inclusion of Aviation Under the European Emission Trading System (ETS): Design and Impacts,* Report for the European Commission, DG Environment, Delft: CE

Yamin, F. and Depledge, J. (2004) *The International Climate Change Regime: A Guide to Rules, Institutions and Procedures,* Cambridge: Cambridge University Press

17
Conclusion

Paul Upham and Stefan Gössling

It is tempting to subtitle this conclusion: *where do we go from here?* As the chapters in this book have shown that absolute reductions in greenhouse gas emissions will only be possible if growth in aviation is reduced, the answers to this question will tend to vary according to how an actor or stakeholder expects their economic interests to be affected by such a scenario. Those supportive of the technologically improved status quo tend, not surprisingly, to represent industry positions. These stakeholders perceive that they have much to lose from any reduction in growth. They tend to have national government support and generally point to the ambitious technological targets that the industry has set for itself. A notable example is the *Sustainable Aviation* initiative (www.sustainableaviation.co.uk/), which represents over 90 per cent of UK airlines, airports and air navigation service providers, as well as all major UK aerospace manufacturers (Sustainable Aviation, 2006). This grouping sees the inclusion of aviation in EU ETS as 'an important step towards a broader international agreement to address aviation emissions', and states that the industry is on track to meet the ACARE (Advisory Council for Aeronautics Research in Europe) improvement targets for fuel burn, noise, and nitrogen oxides (NO_x) of 50, 50 and 80 per cent respectively, for new aircraft in 2020 compared with their equivalents in 2000. They also note that alternatives to aviation kerosene, such as biofuels, continue to be assessed (Sustainable Avaiation, 2006). Those without a direct economic interest in the aviation industry may still perceive a substantial indirect interest in aviation growth – for example, local and regional authorities with airports in their locality.

For the above stakeholders, open system emissions trading has been the preferred solution (of those on offer) for several years – it was 2001 when the consultancy Arthur Andersen told IATA that a closed system would lead to emissions permit costs perhaps 10–20 times higher than those of an open system (Arthur Andersen, 2001). Yet preference for an open system is premised on the belief that other economic sectors have cheaper and more readily available options for emissions mitigation, so that their surplus emissions allowances or credits will enable aviation growth to continue while the emissions trading system as a whole regulates an aggregate, climate-friendly cap. Would that this were so! Bows et al (from 2005 – see Chapter 4 this volume for updates) have been prominent among those who have for several years drawn attention to the startling implications of projected aviation emissions for our ability to avoid an equitable breach of a global 2°C temperature increase. There is no scope for a sustained increase in greenhouse gas emissions by industrially developed economies. Without substantial reductions very soon, we will simply not be able to meet the +2°C threshold and we will incur the greater costs of higher temperatures.

It is worth referring at this point to the interim results of the EC-funded ADAM project on European climate adaptation and mitigation policy options, which at the time of writing have just been issued (ADAM, 2008). To achieve the EU climate policy objective, atmospheric concentrations of greenhouse gases will have to be stabilized below 450ppm CO_2-equivalent, and this implies that global emissions will need to be reduced by about 50 per cent below 1990 levels by 2050. The first model runs conducted for ADAM suggest that known technical measures would have sufficient potential to deliver such an ambitious reduction (ADAM, 2008). This is reassuring, if not too surprising, but it needs to be seen in the light of other results obtained under the same project. Again confirming what we would deduce intuitively, the project is finding that it is mainly those climate policies that deliver co-benefits, such as energy security or technological innovation, that have been adopted across Europe to date. That is, climate policies are only being implemented where there are co-benefits (and, we might add, where these benefits are to influential stakeholders). The project team argue that, over the longer term, if more ambitious emissions reduction targets are to be met, this approach to climate policy may need to become a 'more radical one, with a greater degree of demand management and willingness to address established sectoral priorities'. In other words, economic actors are going to have to change the way they view their industries – perhaps some more than others.

Should the aviation sector be among those to face up to the need for substantial changes? Are there any reasons why aviation should be a special case? We would say not, and probably the industry would agree, but perhaps only because current climate policies globally are far weaker than required, such that emissions rates are outstripping environmental efficiency gains. A global carbon emissions trading system with both the overall cap and national allocations commensurate with an upper limit of +2°C would (or should) go a long way to managing aviation and other emissions in a downward direction, but politically this still seems many years away. By the time that it becomes politically feasible (assuming a rational response to evident warming), +3°C will be much more likely, with its correspondingly higher damage. The same can be said for emissions limits at the personal level, that is mandatory individual carbon budgets: however this problem is approached, whether globally or individually, the need for limits is clear but the will to accept them is lacking, the trends to higher personal and national mobility are upwards and technological solutions are unable to deliver the rates of reduction required to compensate for the additional growth.

Since the first Earthscan book on this topic *Towards Sustainable Aviation* (Upham et al, 2003), recognition and acceptance of climate change has increased, particularly in Europe and the UK, but also, if to a lesser extent, elsewhere. The willingness to take action has also increased at national, transnational and individual levels, and the physical changes in climate and weather systems are also more evident. What has yet to change is the willingness to take genuinely effective and substantive action in a coordinated way, at a global level, such that no government perceives its national economic interests to be threatened. The mindset for this does not yet exist, but it must come. For us it can't come soon enough.

References

ADAM (2008) *Adaptation and Mitigation Strategies. ADAM Interim Results*, Norwich: Tyndall Centre for Climate Change Research, University of East Anglia, available at http:adamproject.info/index.php/Download-document/314-ADAM-Interim-Results-June-2008-Web.html, accessed 6 November 2008

Arthur Andersen (2001) *International Air Transport Association. Emissions Trading for Aviation. Workstream 3: Key Findings and Conclusions,* IATA, available at www.iata.org/NR/ContentConnector/CS2000/Siteinterface/sites/mgr/file/final_report.pdf, accessed 29 July 2008

Bows, A., Upham, P. and Anderson, K. (2005) *Growth Scenarios for EU and UK Aviation: Contradictions with Climate Policy,* Tyndall Centre, report for Friends of the Earth, The University of Manchester, available at www.foe.co.uk/resource/reports/aviation_tyndall_summary.pdf and www.foe.co.uk/resource/reports/aviation_tyndall_research.pdf, accessed 29 July 2008

Sustainable Aviation (2006) *Sustainable Aviation Progress Report 2006,* available at www.sustainableaviation.co.uk/images/stories/key%20documents/report06final.pdf, accessed 29 July 2008

Upham, P., Maughan, J., Raper, D. and Thomas, C. (eds) (2003) *Towards Sustainable Aviation: Trends and Issues,* London: Earthscan

Index